Religion, Modernity and Postmodernity

Religion and Modernity

There is now, more than ever, a need to reassess and redefine the position of religion in the modern world.

Religion and Modernity is a major new series which aims to make accessible to a wide audience some of the most important work in the study of religion today. The series invites leading scholars to present clear and non-technical contributions to contemporary thinking about religion around the globe.

Using modernity as a touchstone, volumes in the series aim to summarise, evaluate and advance reflection on a broad range of topics and transformations of religion. Matters addressed include: the encounter of traditions of all kinds with the complexities of modernity and post-modernity; accounts of religious dynamics bearing on religions' decline or growth; the ways in which the religious is used in the spheres of culture and society; and the relationships between the secular world and the theological domain.

The series is geared primarily to the needs of college and university students doing theology and religious studies courses, but is also relevant to cultural studies, history, philosophy and sociology students. The series also aims to engage a wider audience: all those interested in how religion is facing up to modernity and how it is faring in connection with the power struggles of nationalists, the indulgences of consumers and the quest for the absolute at a time of some turmoil.

Published Works

Don Cupitt	Mysticism After Modernity
Paul Heelas, with the assistance of David Martin and Paul Morris	Religion, Modernity and Postmodernity

Forthcoming

Nancy McCagney	Religion and Ecology
Juan Campo	Pilgrimage and Modernity
David Smith	Hinduism and Modernity

Religion, Modernity and Postmodernity

Edited by
Paul Heelas,

with the assistance of
David Martin and Paul Morris

BLACKWELL *Publishers*

Copyright © Blackwell Publishers Ltd, 1998

First published 1998

2 4 6 8 10 9 7 5 3 1

Blackwell Publishers Ltd
108 Cowley Road
Oxford OX4 1JF
UK

Blackwell Publishers Inc.
350 Main Street
Malden, Massachusetts 02148
USA

British Library Cataloguing in Publication Data

A CIP catalogue record for this book is available from the British Library.

Library of Congress Cataloging-in-Publication Data

Religion, modernity and postmodernity / edited by Paul Heelas and
David Martin.
    p.   cm. — (Religion and modernity)
Includes bibliographical references and index.
    ISBN 0–631–19847–4 (alk. paper). — ISBN 0–631–19848–2 (pbk. :
alk. paper)
    1. Religion and culture. 2. Postmodernism—Religious
aspects—20th century. 3. Religion—History—20th century.
I. Heelas, Paul. II. Martin, David. III. Series.
BL65.C8R454 1998
200—dc21   97–29586
                                              CIP

Typeset in 10 on 12½ pt Meridien
by Graphicraft Typesetters Ltd., Hong Kong
Printed in Great Britain by
T.J. International Padstow, Cornwall

This book is printed on acid-free paper

contents

List of Contributors   vii

1   Introduction: on differentiation and dedifferentiation   1
   Paul Heelas

2   Cathedrals to cults: the evolving forms of the religious life   19
   Steve Bruce

3   Terminal faith   36
   Mark C. Taylor

4   Postmodern religion?   55
   Zygmunt Bauman

5   Tradition, retrospective perception, nationalism and modernism   79
   Ninian Smart

6   From fundamentalism to fundamentalisms: a religious ideology in multiple forms   88
   Bruce B. Lawrence

7   From pre- to postmodernity in Latin America: the case of Pentecostalism   102
   Bernice Martin

8   Secularization and citizenship in Muslim Indonesia   147
   Robert W. Hefner

9   Religion and national identity in modern and postmodern Japan   169
   Winston Davis

10   The construals of 'Europe': religion, theology and the problematics of modernity   186
   Richard H. Roberts

11   Post-Christianity   218
   Don Cupitt

12   Kenosis and naming: beyond analogy and towards *allegoria amoris*   233
   Graham Ward

13 Sublimity: the modern transcendent   258
    John Milbank

14 The primacy of theology and the question of perception   285
    Phillip Blond

15 The Impossible   314
    Kevin Hart

Index   332

contributors

Zygmunt Bauman, Department of Social Policy and Sociology, University of Leeds, UK.

Phillip Blond, Faculty of Divinity, University of Cambridge, UK.

Steve Bruce, Department of Sociology, University of Aberdeen, UK.

Don Cupitt, Faculty of Divinity, University of Cambridge, UK.

Winston Davis, Department of Religion, Washington and Lee University, USA.

Kevin Hart, Department of English and Centre for Studies in Religion and Theology, Monash University, Australia.

Paul Heelas, Department of Religious Studies and the Institute for Cultural Research, Lancaster University, UK.

Robert W. Hefner, Department of Anthropology and the Institute for the Study of Economic Culture, Boston University, USA.

Bruce B. Lawrence, Department of Religion, Duke University, USA.

Bernice Martin, Department of Social Policy and Social Science, Royal Holloway, UK.

David Martin, Department of Religious Studies, Lancaster University, UK.

John Milbank, Faculty of Divinity, University of Cambridge, UK.

Paul Morris, Department of Religious Studies, Victoria University of Wellington, New Zealand.

Richard H. Roberts, Department of Religious Studies, Lancaster University, UK.

Ninian Smart, Department of Religious Studies, University of California Santa Barbara, USA.

Mark C. Taylor, Williams College, USA.

Graham Ward, Faculty of Divinity, University of Cambridge, UK.

CHAPTER ONE

introduction:
on differentiation and
dedifferentiation

Paul Heelas

> ... a religion handed down by tradition, formulated for a whole group and which
> it is obligatory to practise [then] a free, private, optional religion, fashioned accord-
> ing to one's own needs and understanding.
>
> (Emile Durkheim, in Pickering, 1975, p. 96)

Postmodernity, together with postmodern religion, has been variously
conceived. For some, the disintegration of the certainties of modernity
has left a situation in which postmodern religion – Gnostic or New Age
spirituality – can develop. For others, the distressing certainties of modernity have resulted in the valorization of a premodern past. For yet others,
postmodern religion belongs to that great counter-current of modernity,
namely the Romantic movement. And then there are those who associate
postmodern religion with changes taking place within the mainstream of
capitalistic modernity.[1]

Rather than dwelling on these and the many other – and often contradictory – ways in which the term 'postmodern' has been applied to
religion, the primary aim is to develop an analytical (and thus 'modern')
way of looking at things: a scheme which serves to pull together much
of the literature – including much of what appears in this volume – as
well as raising questions which demand further inquiry.[2]

Modernity

One of the great marks of modernity, it has frequently been claimed,
is that it is characterized by a number of *differentiations*. Accordingly, it
comes as no surprise to find theorists such a Scott Lash (1990) claiming
that the great mark of the postmodern is *dedifferentiation*. The situation,

however, is considerably more complicated than this in that *both* differentiating and dedifferentiating processes are taking place within *both* modernity and postmodernity.

Differentiation

To begin to untangle this, let us start with modernity. There is absolutely no doubting the fact that differentiation has taken place. Whether it be the intensification of premodern, Medieval differences, or the development of new ones, modernity has emphasized a whole range of contrasts: to do with the division of labour; the division between work (belonging to public life) and the home (the private realm); the construction of national or 'tribal' identities. Or one might think of contrasts which have developed within the ethical culture, the turn to the self existing in tension with traditionalist collectivism, expressivism with utilitarian individualism. To use Daniel Bell's (1976) phrase, modernity is riddled with 'cultural contradictions'. And from a more abstract point of view, modernity is characterized by the attempt to 'pin down': to establish the determinate; to find order by way of classification; to explain how things work by distinguishing between essences and finding relevant mechanisms of operation.

As for religion, the evidence might well begin with the Reformation. The gulf between God and the person became more radically articulated, as did the gulf between God and nature. Exclusivistic sects rapidly proliferated. Then there was that early fracture line, between Protestantism and Roman Catholicism, which resulted in the Thirty Years War. As for later fracture lines, we can think of that functional differentiation which occurred with regard to religion and politics (or the secular state); or that which has taken place as science separated itself off from the religious life. Then there is the consideration that religion has become more internally differentiated, very considerable contrasts now existing between traditional, authoritative religions of the text, liberal teachings with a strong dose of humanism, prosperity teachings stamped with the mark of utilitarian individualism, and all those alternative spiritualities or New Age teachings with their emphasis on the expressive.

Dedifferentiation

Despite the importance of differentiating processes, however, there is also no doubting the fact that modernity has witnessed powerful countervailing tendencies – now in favour of dedifferentiation. The search has been for the unifying or the unitary; for the same; for the transcendental, in the Kantian sense of the necessary and the universal. With regard to morality, Kantians have sought unconditional or categorical imperatives, serving as laws for everyone; and on the ground, human rights legislation has spread throughout the world. With regard to what it is to be human, modernity has seen the construction of 'humanity' – the acknowledgement that, in a fundamental sense, all people are the same and that cultural (etc.) differences are (relatively) unimportant. And with regard to nature, Romantics – and their successors – have thought in terms of a unifying soul of the world.[3]

Indeed, the Romantics and their (expressivist) successors serve to highlight the process of dedifferentiation. In the words of Abrams (1973), 'what was most distinctive in Romantic thought was the normative emphasis on . . . an organized unity in which all individuation and diversity survive . . . as distinctions without division' (p. 185). The quest was for the unitary which lies 'within' or 'behind' (relatively) insignificant differences. The quest was to articulate the whole, namely that which runs through the human, the natural and the divine.

Looking more generally at dedifferentiation with regard to religion, just as modernity has seen the development of the ethic of humanity, so has it witnessed the – interplaying – development of the spirituality of the perennial. Religious exclusivism has, in measure, given way to religious inclusivism. Denominations – by definition less exclusivistic than sects – have come to dominate mainstream religious life. Increasing numbers of people are prepared to move from denomination to denomination, finding much the same truth behind differences. The ecumenical movement has waxed. Prince Charles speaks of becoming 'Defender of Faith', reflecting the views of all those inclined to find much the same spirituality at the heart of all religious traditions. And on a somewhat different note, it might be added, it is arguably the case that dedifferentiation has also taken place with regard to the secular–sacred boundary. In measure, the religious has become less obviously religious, the secular less obviously secular. This can be considered, for example, in connection with expressive individualism. An estimated 10 per cent or more of Western populations now speak the language of 'authenticity', of 'being true to oneself': and this is to operate in some sort of indeterminate zone, the language being humanistic, the ontology smacking of the Immanent. Rain forests are treated *as if* they were sacred; the boundary between the sacred and the secular loses its hold in many alternative therapies and healing provisions.

Modernity, we have seen, can be thought of as an amalgam of various differentiations and dedifferentiations. Furthermore, differentiation can never be total: boundaries, if they were to become too strong, would make social life impossible. Equally, dedifferentiation can never be comprehensive: for the same or the whole to exist there must be something different. And each process elicits the other. Stephen Toulmin, in *Cosmopolis:*

The Hidden Agenda of Modernity (1990), claims that the Enlightenment search for the universal was elicited by the Thirty Years War – an event which served to highlight the dangers of difference. Conversely, it might be argued, the weight of uniformity can encourage the proliferation of particular individual and cultural identities.

Postmodernity

I think that most readers will agree that most if not all of the developments discussed above belong to 'modernity'. Let us now turn to more controversial claims about the sociocultural, claims which see the religious (or aspects of the religious) having become postmodern.

Dedifferentiation

James Beckford (1992), in a succinct characterization of postmodernity which deserves full citation, notes the following features:

1 A refusal to regard positivistic, rationalistic, instrumental criteria as the sole or exclusive standard of worthwhile knowledge.
2 A willingness to combine symbols from disparate codes or frameworks of meaning, even at the cost of disjunctions and eclecticism.
3 A celebration of spontaneity, fragmentation, superficiality, irony and playfulness.
4 A willingness to abandon the search for over-arching or triumphalist myths, narratives or frameworks of knowledge. (1992, p. 19)

Combining the first and the last of his four points, the claim is that truth provided by the exercise of reason and the transmission of tradition is – at least in measure – weakened, even abandoned. Differences, we can go on to add, become *deregulated* or unpoliced. The different becomes 'simply' the different, this in the sense that this mode of distinction has become liberated from 'strong' distinguishing features. That is to say, detraditionalization, as well as the (relative) abandonment of what reason can ascertain, serves to ensure that people no longer know what – in some cultural or absolute sense – is true or what is false; is legitimate or not; is to be valued or not. Or so it is claimed.

The cultural becomes disorganized; less black and white. The distinction between the high and the low fades away. The claim that one tradition should be adhered to because it, and it alone is valid, is rendered invalid. And rather than authority and legitimacy resting with established orders of knowledge, authority comes to rest with the person (assuming, of course, that the subject remains cohesive enough, intact enough, to exercise authority). The process is of individualization. It involves, among other things, the decline of the institutional determination of life choices and instead the reflexive reconstruction of identity. What the traditional used to demand has transformed into lifestyle options.

Thinking of the significance of this for religion, postmodern religion – as a number of scholars have called the development – is very much in the hands of the 'free' subject (again, assuming that the subject has not disintegrated into a series of discourses or cultural processes). The deregulation of the religious realm, combined with the cultural emphasis on freedom and choice, results in intermingled, interfused, forms of religious – or 'religious'-cum-'secular' – life which exist beyond the tradition-regulated church and chapel. People no longer feel obliged to heed the boundaries of the religions of modernity. Instead, they are positively encouraged to exercise their 'autonomy' to draw on what has diffused through the culture. Somewhat revising James Beckford's second point, they show a 'willingness to combine symbols from (previously) disparate codes or frameworks of meaning'. They – so to speak – raid the world, drawing on whatever is felt desirable: the religious (perhaps shamanism and Christianity); the religious and the non-religious (perhaps yoga and champagne). Sometimes this is done sequentially, in the case of Prince Charles, moving from hunting foxes (traditionalism) to talking to trees (New Age) to hunting foxes again. And sometimes this is done by fusing the previously marked off: and hence the popularity of the term 'hybridity' among postmodern theorists. (My favourite example is Zennis, a fusion of Zen and tennis.)

A related way in which it can be argued that this kind of religion is postmodern is by pointing to the fact that it would often appear to be associated with forms of pragmatism and relativism: ethics associated with postmodernity through the work, for example, of Richard Rorty (1980) and Ernest Gellner (1992). Instead of authoritative narratives or other forms of knowledge providing truth, 'truth' is seen in terms of 'what works for me'. People have what they *take* to be 'spiritual' experiences without having to hold religious *beliefs*. (Indeed, it is precisely because of this outlook that those concerned can draw on beliefs or rituals which the modernist would keep apart.) And this results in a form of relativism: religion beyond belief is religion where 'truth' is relative to what one takes to be involved in satisfying one's requirements.

A final consideration to be borne in mind when claiming that individualized, deregulated religion is postmodern is that it belongs to postmodern consumer culture. This culture, writes Zygmunt Bauman (1991) is 'dominated by the postmodern values of novelty, of rapid (preferably inconsequential and episodic) change, of individual enjoyment and consumer choice' (p. 278). And, as Mike Featherstone (1991) puts it, the culture is one with 'a strong emphasis . . . upon the sensory overload, the aesthetic immersion, the dreamlike perceptions of de-centred subjects, in which people open themselves up to a wider range of sensations and emotional experiences' (p. 24). The argument can then run that dedifferentiated religion – precisely because it is deregulated, operating apart from the disciplines of the church and the chapel as a cultural resource – can serve as a vehicle for acts of consumption. The products on offer are powerful experiences; the venues are spiritual Disneylands (see Heelas, 1994).[4]

Differentiation

Difference is not absent in dedifferentiated religion. There is variety: shamanic experiences – presumably – are not exactly the same as fire-walking; encountering 'cyberia' at a rave is not identical to practising yoga. But differences are 'simply' differences – perhaps not at the experiential level, but certainly in the sense that they are not sustained by judgements, evaluations, legitimizations and other forms of 'hard' knowledge.

We now turn to a rendering of postmodernity where difference is of considerably greater significance. We also turn to a rendering which might well not have the same on-the-ground plausibility as dedifferentiated religion. For it often appears to be informed by what philosophers, and others, argue for or would like to happen.

Postmodernity is now conceived of as a (relatively 'empty') form of liberalism, valuing equality, respect for the other, and the freedom to be different. Thus as Seyla Benhabib (1992) notes, 'postmodernism presupposes a super-liberalism, more pluralistic, more tolerant, more open to the right of difference and otherness . . .' (p. 16). And more specifically, as Steven Connor (1997) observes in his discussion of Lyotard,

> What is representative about postmodern science is its abandonment of centralizing narratives. Lyotard embraces fondly a vision of a world in which multiple, incompatible language-games flourish alongside each other, believing that it is not worth attempting to create a conversation or consensus between them, since 'such consensus does violence to the heterogeneity of language games' . . . (1997, p. 29)

Postmodernists who attach importance to this kind of difference are critical of what they take to be the authoritarian and imperialistic operations of the grand narratives of modernity, especially those which are taken to impose uniformity rather than allow diversity. These narratives – often identified as such, one suspects, precisely because of this (discerned) function – are held to drown out the voices and experiences of the marginal, the weak, the particularities of the Nietzschian 'the little things', those who do not conform to the Enlightenment project. The essentialized ethic of humanity, for example, is held to obliterate the right of women to be different; or the rights of other cultures to exist beyond the confines of (UN) human rights. But as well as being critical of the grand narratives of modernity, postmodernists of the kind under consideration are typically convinced that this kind of knowledge is in any case being eroded. In the words of Connor, again discussing Lyotard, there is 'a shift from the muffled majesty of grand narratives to the splintering autonomy of micronarratives' (p. 28).

Difference is important. For Lyotard, and others, it is significant or solid enough to generate the incommensurable or the incompatible. But this is not held to be the difference of the essentialist, of the modernist classifier or discriminator; it is not the structural differentiation of the grand narrative, the tradition-maintained. So the challenge, whether in philosophical thought or in – say – new social or religious movements, is to find ways of *being* different – and thus being liberated – without being essentialistic; without having that core on which to ground one's case.[5]

Without going into this challenging matter any more deeply, let us take stock. Simplifying matters a great deal, what might be thought of as the *cultural extremity* reached – or approximated – by postmodern dedifferentiation is the 'freedom' of the self to draw on all that is available to satisfy itself. In contrast, the *cultural extremity* of postmodern differentiation is the 'freedom' of the self to express or live itself rather than being dominated by others. The dedifferentiating and differentiating processes are also bound up with one another in that each can generate the other. On the one hand, dedifferentiation – associated as it is with the process of individualization – can generate difference. Quite simply, those freedom-loving people engaged in constructing their own ways of life are quite likely to differ in how they set about doing this. And on the other hand, it has been claimed that differentiating processes result in the dedifferentiated. In the words of Stephen Crook et al. (1992), a differentiated culture 'reaches its limit when "hyperdifferentiation" leads to a proliferation of divisions which effectively erodes the significance of distinctions between autonomous [cultural] spheres' (p. 221).

Reflection

Postmodern dedifferentiation is associated with the deregulation and disorganization of traditions, fragments merging with a plethora of other cultural phenomena to create a series of complex and often ephemeral hybrids; modern dedifferentiation is associated with the construction of the whole, the unitary. Postmodern differentiation is associated with the encouragement of microdiscourses, if only by default being of equal standing; modern differentiation is bound up with the construction of essential differences and hierarchies of value and discrimination.

Postmodernity, as it has been discussed thus far, can be thought of as a transformation of the liberal ethic of modernity. That ethic has traditionally served to cater both for difference (respect for others, pluralism) and for the same (equality, the human). In its transformed version, differentiating processes (allowing equality-cum-diversity) are seen as pitted against the dedifferentiating processes of modernity (associated with trends towards totalizing universals), whereas postmodern dedifferentiating processes (encouraging the view that cultural products are of equal potential value) are seen as pitted against the differentiating processes of modernity (establishing value and truth boundaries).

So, to the straightforward – but highly controversial – key to the matter. At the very heart of the transformation under consideration is the claim that postmodern differentiation and dedifferentiation operate in a new way. They are not regulated by grand narratives, whether these are narratives of religion, humanity, science, emancipation, growth, human self-realization, Marxism, liberal economic theory or high art. Whereas the differentiations of modernity are associated with legitimating and authenticating cultural formations (for example, the role played by religion in the construction of national identities), the differentiations of postmodernity operate in terms of freedom and micronarratives. And whereas the dedifferentiations of modernity take the form of totalizing formations (for example, the ethic of humanity), the dedifferentiations of the postmodern primarily operate in terms of individual choice.[6]

Judith Squires (1993) writes:

> The postmodern condition may be characterized . . . as involving three key features: the death of Man, History and Metaphysics. This involves the rejection of all essentialist and transcendental conceptions of human nature; the rejection of unity, homogeneity, totality, closure and identity; the rejection of the pursuit of the real and the true. In the place of these illusory ideals we find the assertion that man is a social, historical or linguistic artifact; the celebration of fragmentation, particularity and difference; the acceptance of the contingent and apparent.   (p. 2)

Many other statements could be provided spelling out the 'loss' thesis. Of radical detraditionalization; of the death of the author; of the death of God as the author; of the ways in which Enlightenment reason has turned its critical knowledge of the social construction of knowledge on its own truth claims.

Should religion today be theorized in terms of modernity or postmodernity? Ignoring, for present purposes, the possibility that we should apply postmodern 'thinking' to the study of religion, the crucial thing to explore is whether or not religions are operating beyond traditions.

Have religions, that is to say, become liberated from the differentiations and dedifferentiations – together with their respective values, truths, ontologies, meanings and rituals – of the grand narrative? We must be careful. Perhaps some postmodernists have translated their postmodernity into religious practice, a religion of the micronarrative, or micronarratives, with no real author; dedifferentiated (deregulated) religion of choice certainly exists; and there might well be religions of pragmatism and performativity rather than of transcendental truth. However, against those who emphasize the massive loss of tradition, or of grand narratives, the argument is that traditions are in fact by no means as close to death as is often made out, and indeed in many contexts show signs of considerable vitality.

This leads on to another (related) question. Could it be the case that modernity is too complex and variagated, with too many *strands* or cultural trajectories, for religion to become 'post'? The argument, in this regard, is that virtually everything discussed in the present context under the heading 'postmodernity' can be found within the setting of modernity. Grand (religious) narratives have for long been under threat. Detraditionalization is nothing new. As indicated by Durkheim, in the quotation with which we began deregulated religion has been around for a long time, as has religion detraditionalized to 'beyond belief'. I certainly do not think that the New Age Movement – a favoured candidate for those who want to link religion with the postmodern – is original enough to be treated in this way (compare Lyon, 1993, with Heelas, 1996). And postmodern differentiated religion – if indeed it actually exists on the ground today – could also have been around for a long time in theological quarters.

I must admit that I am not all that happy with 'periods' or 'conditions'. Cultural history is surely the history of the interplay of processes of detraditionalization and traditionalization, in turn interplaying in various ways with processes to do with dedifferentiation and differentiation. Perhaps the 'post' will only appear, in any significant sense, when technological advance takes us into the brave new world of technoexperience, even the mingling of nerve and optic fibres. Or is this a figment of cyberbabble?[7]

The Contributions

Essays have been organized so that the volume progresses from the more general (historical or social scientific), through the international (social and cultural), the essays by Richard Roberts and Don Cupitt then making the transition to the theological. They have also been organized so as to reveal interesting similarities and points of difference. Having been provided with the general theme of the volume, contributors have, of course, had an absolutely free rein in deciding whether to portray, conceive, construct or theorize religion in terms of 'modernity' or in terms of 'postmodernity'. It might be noted – and it might be of significance – that the majority have opted for the former. The editor would also like to note how pleased he is to have been able to draw on a number of scholars studying religion beyond the confines of North America and the European Union.

Introducing the contributions, Steve Bruce (chapter 2) comes to an uncompromising conclusion: '"postmodernity" . . . is unnecessary' when it comes to the study of religious change, 'and, given the tendentious theoretical baggage associated with the term, best avoided'. Bruce shows that 'the church form of religion is challenged first by sects and why both forms then evolve into the denomination'. He also draws attention to 'the large number of alternative religions, organized, if that is not too strong a word, in a "cultic milieu"' which exist today. The shift in emphasis, as he sees it, is from the exclusivistic to forms of religion which are much more tolerant of apparent differences between religious teachings and practices; which, indeed, are frequently advocates of perennialism. The shift is also theorized, one claim being that modernization has produced a basic cultural egalitarianism: an egalitarianism which has then encouraged the (relative) dedifferentiation of the religious realm.

Mark Taylor (chapter 3) provides us with a very different history in that the language is of mining, alchemy, electricity, the hallucinogenic, the generative matrix. Broadly corresponding to Bruce's 'cultic milieu', this is a history which leads up to the 'New Age'. 'The vision of the alchemist's creative power', we read, 'emerges in the recurrent fantasy of creating an homunculus'; and 'the aspiration to create an homunculus expresses the desire to become God'. The homunculus of the ancient alchemists, it is argued, 'is the distant ancestor of contemporary alchemists, replicants, androids, terminators, and cyborgs'. Today, in our 'post-industrial' world, for 'those who have terminal faith, to become one with the matrix is to attain immortality by being transformed into the divine'. The history, then, is one of breaking through barriers: the 'ecstasy of all-at-onceness and all-at-oneness'; the search for that primal *Indifferenzpunkt* (Schelling) which 'collapses differences in an identity that can bear nothing other than itself'; that 'New Age in which all are one and one is all'; the 'gradual removal of the barriers separating the human and nonhuman as well as interiority and exteriority'; in short, it is a history of 'the collapse of differences'.

'Postmodern men and women', writes Zygmunt Bauman (chapter 4), 'do need the alchemist able, or claiming to be able, to transmogrify base uncertainty into precious self-assurance, and the authority of approval (in the name of superior knowledge, or access to wisdom closed to the others) is the philosophical stone these alchemists boast of possessing.' We are in a land of experts in identity problems: the counsellors, the personality healers, the self-help literature, all those tackling the uncertainties of the postmodern condition. In addition, numerous 'self-improvement' movements (for example) cater for 'this-worldly transcendence'. Postmodern consumer culture is the world of 'sensation-gathering and sensation enhancement'. The 'aristocracy of consumerism' seeks out those who provide 'peak experiences', the ecstatic. 'Breaking the boundaries of the self' – once reserved for mystics – 'has been put by postmodern culture in every individual's reach.' For Bauman – and this in contrast to Taylor's handling of somewhat similar material – none of this is really 'religion'. Religion only comes into the picture when attention is turned to fundamentalism: 'There is, though, a specifically postmodern form of religion, born of internal contradictions of postmodern life . . .'. And fundamentalism is the religion of 'the poor of today', namely 'flawed consumers'.

The next two essays tell a very different story. Whilst Ninian Smart (chapter 5) accepts that detraditionalization has taken place – like Bruce, linking it to the evolution of modern individualism – his main thrust is to emphasize the importance of traditions today. More exactly, his concern is to show that our era, like others, 'is one of the invention and reinvention of traditions, not one of detraditionalization *per se*'; and that most traditions 'are young'. We find the 're-traditionalization' of religion, in particular associated with the construction of those other great new(ish) traditions of modernity, nation-states. Rather than there being any scope for postmodern processes here, there is plenty of scope for the operation of the differentiating processes of modernity.

Bruce Lawrence (chapter 6) suggests that 'There are multiple relationships – more oppositional than complementary, but necessarily both – which characterize fundamentalism and nationalism.' Analysis of such relationships must take into account the fact that 'There is not a single brand of global fundamentalism but three major brands and countless hybrid forms of each brand.' The brands are exemplified by the 'Christian literalist', the (supposed) 'Muslim terrorist' and the 'Jewish political activist'. Unlike Bauman, Lawrence then theorizes fundamentalism in terms of 'the contradictions of late capitalism'. The basic message, it is argued, is that 'the symbolic and emotive power of fundamentalism is as authentically modern as it is persistently disruptive'.

Bernice Martin (chapter 7), in the most substantial essay of this volume, concentrates on a somewhat different kind of traditionality, that of the Pentecostalism of Latin America. Martin grounds her analysis in the work of those postmodern 'realists' who explore various processes – fragmentation, contradiction, the symbiosis of the local and the global, the contraction of space and time, the fusion of high and low culture, the prevalence of spectacle and so on – by relating them to 'new structures of global capitalism, the communicative logic of the technologically new systems of information and communication and the pivotal role of cultural as well as other kinds of technical experts within postindustrial capitalism'. With this frame of reference, Martin is able to construct a very different portrayal of 'traditional' religion than that provided by Smart and Lawrence (and, it might be added, Bauman, on the grounds that the analysis is of the empirical reality of Pentecostal everyday life rather than of the abstract level of belief systems). As she summarizes the argument, 'I shall first outline the structural changes in Latin America which herald postmodernity; then examine the role of the new Protestant movement in this transformation; and finally point to some recent developments within Brazilian Protestantism which display exuberantly postmodern cultural features.' Martin argues that Pentecostalism acts as a bridge from the traditional to the postmodern by introducing postmodern adoptions within an apparently traditional frame. As for the nature of this postmodernity, it might well be suggested that we are looking at postmodern differentiation. Pentecostals are Pentecostals, but the difference which they embrace – it could well be the case – is not the difference of the traditionalist of modernity. As Martin puts it, this is 'a boundary-breaking movement'.

Robert Hefner (chapter 8) takes us to another part of the world, another religion, and another rendering of the encounter between tradition and the contemporary world. Hefner distinguishes between two camps in the construction of the modern Indonesian nation: 'Some rivals in this contest reject religious disestablishment and insist on a direct and literal application of Islamic law to all aspects of government and social life. Others insist that such a view distorts the true meaning of Islam, attributing a fixed and closed quality to what is supposed to be a universal and thus open ethical system.' The contrast is between the more exclusivistic and the more inclusivistic. And, it is argued, the latter are doing well: 'what is remarkable about Indonesia is that, at the moment, so many Muslim leaders endorse this civil-pluralist understanding of religion rather than the establishmentarian view'. Many, that is to say, support secularization, in the specific sense of desacralizing that which is wrongly sacralized – namely that which is divisive. Hefner then moves on to make the general point that 'there are commonalities to religious change in the modern age'. Among other factors, the (relative) detraditionalization-cum-dedifferentiation of religion found in Indonesia is attributed to 'the thoroughly modern conundrum of how to balance pluralism with the ethicopolitical need to devise culturally viable terms for national citizenship'. The search for religious renderings of unity within diversity, then, is a feature of modernity.

Winston Davis (chapter 9) discusses national identity, a recurrent theme of the present volume. His particular concern is with Japan, more specifically the 'Theory of Japanese Culture' (*Nihon-bunka-ron*). This 'Theory' is sustained by 'a barrage of popular books, newspapers and magazine articles, and even scholarly works'. Announcing national identity, the Theory is characterized in terms of its 'essentialism, the overemphasis placed on uniqueness, the implict nationalism and the occasionally outrageous instances of racism' (although Davis does note exceptions, as when MARUYAMA Masao portrayed modernity in liberal terms). The Theory clearly serves as a strong identity differentiator. What is especially interesting is that the modernist culture Theory has appropriated the postmodern for its own ends. 'Indifference to logic (even in critical thought), the ahistoric orientation of Buddhism and Shinto, fascination with futurology, and the recent truimph of "technopunk" in science fiction and TV commercials are all cited as "proof" that Japan has become the world's first postmodern culture.' In Japan's 'largely secular culture', advocates of Japan Theory 'play the role priests and theologians used to play in religiously based civilizations'. And the identity they announce, by way of postmodernity, is highly ethnocentric, and elitist differentiating: 'West: modern; Japan postmodern'; 'West loses; Japan wins'.

Richard Roberts (chapter 10) brings us back to Europe, and shifts the gear – for the volume as a whole – from the sociocultural to the theological. The investigation is informed by 'the historic emergence of the "souls" or cultural identities of "Europe"', this being envisaged 'as a way of construing in a contextualized way the problematic interactions of premodernity (Christendom, tradition and the *ancien régime*), modernity (the dialetic of Enlightenment, Communism, instrumental reason and European integration) and postmodernity (inaugurated by the progressive triumph of the market, fluidity of identities, the collapse of Communism and the "End of History"'. The addition of the postmodern to the premodern and the modern itself, argues Roberts, means that the remit and tasks of 'Divinity' must change. 'The theologian', the argument continues, 'must strive to enunciate, symbolize and enact principles of human cohabitation in a pluralist and particularist environment'; must exemplify 'a concern with the binding together of humankind on the level of the claim that ultimate cultural universals manifest themselves, paradoxically, in the particularities of the extraordinary diversity of socially-embedded cultural practices of religion'; and must deal with 'a transcendent reference point in relation to which all human activity is experienced as relative'.

Don Cupitt (chapter 11), akin to Roberts, argues that our world is such that 'philosophy, religion and ethics need all to be drastically rethought'. One reason is that 'orthodoxy, essences and authority are dead'. Another is that orthodoxy, essences and dogmatic authority *should* be dead. 'Dogmatic religion', writes Cupitt, 'works by the "logic of difference": it includes by excluding, encourages hostility and (to an astonishing degree) inhibits thought.' In addition, Cupitt suggests that the 'context' for a new theology is provided by the fact that we live in terms of 'a pyrotechnic world-view, a world of broadcast physical energies and cultural signs, pouring out'; a 'mediascape'; 'an aestheticized designer-world'. With these considerations informing the argument, the proposal – with the future very much in mind – is for a 'philosophy' which combines an 'energetic Spinozism', a 'poetical theology' and a 'solar ethics'. As for the nature of this radically detraditionalized theology or world-view, Cupitt's primary – anti-realist – contention is that 'the world is an outsideless and continuously outpouring stream of language events'. With language or language-dependent experience leading the way, the theology is beyond (dogmatic) belief. It is one of practice, Cupitt citing Nietzsche's 'A new way of living, not a new belief. . . evangelic practice alone leads to God, it is God!' to write of 'living, affirming life's value just by the way we plunge into it'. It is one of 'ecstatic immanence'; of the 'poetical'; of 'cosmic humanism'; 'of our utter immersion in and unity with the whole flux of existence'. Cupitt thus provides a theological rendering of what – in this volume – is given a more cultural historical portrayal by Taylor.

Graham Ward (chapter 12) begins with the point that 'At the end of modernity the doctrine of kenosis is having a revival both theologically and philosophically.' His essay is situated by way of reference to two forms of theology: a radicalized form of theological liberalism which – as in the work of Mark C. Taylor – attends to the immanent and envisages kenosis in terms of 'endless circulations of significance and desire in intratextual reality'; and the work of French conservative Catholics where 'the Kenotic economy is inseparable from a trinitarian "philanthropy"'. It is also situated by way of reference to 'the philosophical use of the metaphor of "pouring oneself out"', as found in the later work of Jacques Derrida (for example), where Kenosis 'is language in crisis'. For Ward, 'theology is a form of discourse'; citing Julia Kristeva, it is 'a discourse of love directed to an impossible other'. The argument is 'for a realism of theological discourse founded upon the notion of *allegoria amoris* – a kenotic discourse of love whose *dunamis* is the co-operation of an intratrinitarian and an anthropological eros and whose domain is creation itself'. The distinctive shift is from 'analogy' (associated with traditional epistemology and ontology) to 'allegory'. 'The kenotic economy . . . narrates a story of coming to know through coming to love – love given, love endured. Hence, the category employed as a vehicle for this dwelling within and performance of the knowledge of God as it emerges through the doctrine of kenosis, is an allegory (rather than an analogy).'

John Milbank (chapter 13) explores the relationship between 'the sublime' and 'the beautiful'. His question is 'whether the modern and postmodern sundering of the sublime from the beautiful and consequent substitution of sublimity for transcendence is an authentic critical gesture'.

His answer is unequivocal: 'the substitution of the sublime for transcendence is but an arbitrary gesture, rendering the subject unnecessarily empty and unmediated by objectivity'. In somewhat greater detail, 'the distinction and hierarchical elevation of the sublime [to the putatively transcendent] discloses its secret truth to be absolute self-sacrifice without return'. But to 're-integrate' the sublime and the beautiful 'returns us from the sublime to the genuine transcendent, and then, in consequence, allows us to rethink the sacrificial'. As for why modernity and postmodernity have encouraged the construction of the sumblime – that 'mere subjective gesture' – Milbank argues that it has been 'derived from a "Protestant" genealogy, together with an unacknowledged resignation to a capitalist duality of public indifferent value mediating private and meaningless preference'. The subjectivity of the sublime is seen as being bound up with 'the turn to the subject'.

Like Milbank, Phillip Blond (chapter 14) sees modernity as having had negative consequences for theology. 'Theology', writes Blond, 'has lost its object. It can no longer point to anything with ostensive certainty and say the word "God".' Indeed, God 'has become pluralized into a general spirituality and identified with virtually anything whatsoever'. Of particular note, modernity – in the form of Protestant thinking – 'focuses on the interior event of revelation between the sinner and God', Blond continuing that he 'would suggest that the price of this theological evacuation from the external world is the rise of immanentist subjectivity and its denial of any external relation whatsoever'. 'To speak very simply', Blond argues, 'immanence produces idols that stand in front of transcendence and conceal a higher phenomenology'. As for Blond's theological response, 'Against this interiorization of faith . . . we would need to suggest that faith has an exterior correlate.' And as he puts it towards the end of his essay, 'We have pursued the possibilities of perception, down through all the conceptual architectonics, all the transcendental conditioning, to the origin of our cognitions – our contact with the external world'.

Kevin Hart (chapter 15) brings the volume to a close. His topic – 'the impossible' – does not lend itself to an easy introduction. Essentially, though, it is formulated in terms of a debate, which took place in the later 1950s, between Yves Bonnefoy and Maurice Blanchot. It concerns the nature of, and the relationship between, poetry and the sacred. Bonnefoy, we read, condemns 'a divine poetry that detaches itself from the material world and endorses a moral poetry that is earthed in the here and now, a poetry that nonetheless affirms the sacred nature of what is'. Blanchot, on the other hand, 'asks us to consider that those eminent human possibilities, art and religion, both respond to an obscure dimension that tolerates no God or gods, is impossible to name since it is neither phenomenon nor nounenon, and is therefore to be called "the impossible"'. Blanchot, in particular, presages Derridaian postmodern thinking, with his claim that 'The essence of literature is not to be found in what it explicitly asserts but in its continual annihilation of the meanings which language forces it to compound with, in its flight toward its goal of silence.'

Religion Without an Ultimate 'Author'?

I would like to close this introductory chapter by returning to the cultural realm to raise a question which pertains to the future of religion. The question can be couched in terms of a passage in David Harvey's *The Condition of Postmodernity* (1989). Discussing Derrida, Harvey writes,

> the cultural producer merely creates raw materials (fragments and elements), leaving it open to consumers to recombine those elements in any way they wish. The effect is to break (deconstruct) the power of the author to impose meanings or offer a continuous narrative. (1989, p. 51)

There is little doubt that there has been a shift of emphasis in favour of dedifferentiated religion. Even though God *might* remain the ultimate author, when religion is functioning beyond the church and chapel the authority of God – as exercised through the institutionalized – is obviously diminished. Religion can only too readily become swallowed up by individual desire. The X file culture which appears to surround us might benefit by way of detraditionalization; might be (relatively) popular precisely because it is not (obviously) policed. But the more that people come to treat religion as a consumer item, the less likely they are to be attracted to the 'real' thing. It might well be claimed that the omens for *religion* – as something requiring discipline, obedience, the exercise of the supra-individual, authorial – are not too good.

Acknowledgement

I would like to thank Linda Woodhead, of the Department of Religious Studies at Lancaster University, for the long discussions we have had about issues pertaining to this introductory essay and related matters.

Notes

1   Concerning the first of these four options, Houston Smith (1982) claims that the genuine 'postmodernist' seeks the 'sacred unconscious'; is on the path to Enlightenment; is one who 'lives in the unvarying presence of the numinous' (p. 182); see also David Griffin (ed.) (1988). Concerning the second, one can think of Akbar Ahmed (1993) and his suggestion, 'If modern meant the pursuit of Western education, technology and industrialization in the flush of the post-colonial period, postmodern would mean a reversion to traditional

Muslim values and a rejection of modernism' (p. 32). Thinking of the third, consider Bryan Turner's (1991) argument that 'the recent critique of modernity by postmodern theorists may be regarded as a contemporary manifestation of a much longer set of oppositional movements [including the Romantic Movement] against the rationalising tendency of the modern project' (p. xviii). The last option is argued, in this volume, by Bernice Martin.

2   Like much of the literature about postmodernity, this introductory chapter is written in terms of academic procedures which have a long history, and which certainly belong to modernity.

3   An interesting claim concerning dedifferentiation, made recently by Paul du Gay (1996), has to do with the collapse of the distinction between the realms of consumption and of production.

4   Of the very considerable literature conceiving postmodernity in terms of dedifferentiation, attention might be paid to Alex Seago's *Burning the Box of Beautiful Things: The Development of a Postmodern Sensibility* (1995), on the desire to transgress the boundary of high art and mass culture; Mike Featherstone's edited volume, *Postmodernism* (1988), on the dissolution of established categories and identities; and an article by Kenneth Thompson (1992) – 'Social Pluralism and Post-Modernity' – which includes discussion of how 'constructive post-modernism . . . combines elements of religion, psychology and business' (p. 249).

5   How difference is conceived by postmodernists varies considerably, ranging from incommensurability claims to the use of terms like 'diversity'. To provide some additional illustrations, consider Zygmunt Bauman (1992) and his claim that 'institutionalized pluralism' and 'variety' are two of the 'most conspicuous features of the postmodern condition' (p. 187); Charles Jencks (1992), who refers to 'an intense concern for pluralism' and 'an acknowledgment of difference and otherness' (p. 7); or the work of Foucault, who sees a proliferation of micronarratives and foci of power in a centreless universe. See also Vattimo (1991).

6   A good discussion of grand narratives is provided by Connor in the second chapter of his *Postmodernist Culture* (1997).

7   For readers wishing to pursue additional ways of envisaging modernity, postmodernity and religion, useful collections are provided by Philippa Berry and Andrew Wernick (1992) and Kieran Flanagan and Peter Jupp (1996). Steven Connor (1997) includes a useful bibliography, 'Postmodernism and Religion' (pp. 317–18). On detraditionalization, see Heelas, Lash and Morris (1996).

References

Abrams, M. H. 1973: *Natural Supernaturalism: Tradition and Revolution in Romantic Literature*. London: W. H. Norton & Company.

Ahmed, Akbar 1993: *Postmodernism and Islam: Predicament and Promise*. New Delhi: Penguin Books India.

Bauman, Zygmunt 1991: *Modernity and Ambivalence*. Cambridge: Polity.

—— 1992: *Intimations of Postmodernity*. London: Routledge.

Beckford, James 1992: Religion, Modernity and Post-Modernity. In B. R. Wilson (ed.), *Religion: Contemporary Issues*. London: Bellew, pp. 11–27.

Bell, Daniel 1976: *The Cultural Contradictions of Capitalism*. London: Heinemann.

Benhabib, Seyla 1992: *Situating the Self: Gender, Community and Postmodernism in Contemporary Ethics*. Cambridge: Polity.

Berry, Philippa and Andrew Wernick (eds) 1992: *Shadow of Spirit: Postmodernism and Religion* London: Routledge.

Connor, Steven 1997: *Postmodernist Culture: An Introduction to Theories of the Contemporary*. Oxford: Blackwell.

Crook, Stephen, Jan Pakulski and Malcolm Waters 1992: *Postmodernization: Change in Advanced Society*. London: Sage.

Featherstone, Mike 1988: *Postmodernism*. London: Sage.

—— 1991: *Consumer Culture and Postmodernism*. London: Sage.

Flanagan, Kieran and Peter Jupp (eds) 1996: *Postmodernity, Sociology and Religion*. Basingstoke: Macmillan.

du Gay, Paul 1996: *Consumption and Identity at Work*. London: Sage.

Gellner, Ernest 1992: *Postmodernism, Reason and Religion*. London: Routledge.

Griffin, David Ray (ed.) 1988: *Spirituality and Society*. Albany: State University of New York Press.

Harvey, David 1989: *The Condition of Postmodernity*. Oxford: Blackwell.

Heelas, Paul 1994: The Limits of Consumption and the Postmodern 'Religion' of the New Age. In Russell Keat, Nigel Whiteley and Nicholas Abercrombie (eds), *The Authority of the Consumer*. London: Routledge, pp. 102–15.

—— 1996: *The New Age Movement: The Celebration of the Self and the Sacralization of Modernity*. Oxford: Blackwell.

——, Scott Lash and Paul Morris 1996: *Detraditionalization: Critical Reflections on Authority and Identity*. Oxford: Blackwell.

Jencks, Charles 1992: *The Post-Modern Reader*. London: Academy Editions.

Lash, Scott 1990: *Sociology of Postmodernism*. London: Routledge.

Lyon, David 1993: A Bit of a Circus: Notes on Postmodernity and New Age. *Religion*, 23 (2), pp. 117–26.

Pickering, W. S. F. 1975: *Durkheim on Religion*. London: Routledge & Kegan Paul.

Rorty, Richard 1980: *Philosophy and the Mirror of Nature*. Princeton: Princeton University Press.

Seago, Alex 1995: *Burning the Box of Beautiful Things: The Development of a Postmodern Sensibility*. Oxford: Oxford University Press.

Smith, Houston 1982: *Beyond the Postmodern Mind*. New York: Crossroad Publishing.

Squires, Judith 1993: Introduction. In Judith Squires (ed.), *Principled Positions. Postmodernism and the Rediscovery of Value*. London: Lawrence & Wishart, pp. 1–13.

Thompson, Kenneth 1992: Social Pluralism and Post-Modernity. In Stuart Hall, David Held and Tony McGrew (eds), *Modernity and its Futures*. Cambridge: Polity, pp. 221–71.

Toulmin, Stephen 1990: *Cosmopolis: The Hidden Agenda of Modernity*. Chicago: University of Chicago Press.

Turner, Bryan 1991: *Religion and Social Theory*. London: Sage.

Vattimo, Gianni 1991: *The End of Modernity*. Cambridge: Polity.

CHAPTER TWO

cathedrals to cults: the evolving forms of the religious life

Steve Bruce

Introduction

The purpose of this essay is to identify what strikes me as the prevailing ethos of religious belief and behaviour in modern societies (by which I mean specifically the industrial democracies of western and northern Europe, North America, and Australia and New Zealand), and consider to what extent that ethos offers warrant for talking about 'postmodern' as distinct from 'modern' religion. A more fulsomely argued and illustrated version of this account can be found in my *Religion in the Modern World: From Cathedrals to Cults* (Bruce, 1996).

It is not false humility to note that there is little new in what follows. Most of the specific propositions are so well known that they have names (the Niebuhr thesis, for example). In so for far as there is novelty in this account, it is in claiming that the well-known organization typology of church, sect, denomination and cult can be applied to describe economically a process of social evolution.

I will begin with some quotations which exemplify the start and finish of the process I want to understand. They concern the nature of truth and authority and the social relationships that are associated with divergent attitudes to the status of the truth. The first is from Bishop Augustine of Hippo, by no means the most intolerant of the Church Fathers

There is an unjust persecution which the ungodly operate against the Church of Christ; and a just persecution which the Churches of Christ make use of towards the ungodly. . . . The Church persecutes out of love, the ungodly out of cruelty. (Kamen, 1967, p. 14)

As a dissenter from the orthodoxy of his time one might have expected Martin Luther to take a more charitable view of diversity, but he heavily constrained his claims for freedom of conscience which, he argued: 'cannot be absolute freedom because no one can be free from the obligations of truth' (Kamen, 1967, p. 30).

My third quotation is from a statement written by Tissington Tatlow for the British Student Christian Movement (SCM) in 1910. Since the SCM's foundation at the end of the previous century, Tatlow, a young Church of Ireland evangelical, had been intimately involved in trying to make it acceptable to the British churches beyond its evangelical base. He and other activists had frequently been put on the spot by suspicious bishops asking what the movement stood for. The following statement of the 'interdenominational' position (consciously contrasted with an 'undenominational position) became the foundation of the 1910 World Missionary Conference (WMC) in Edinburgh and was the credo on which the entire ecumenical movement was to develop. Tatlow described the SCM as follows:

> The Student Christian Movement is interdenominational in that while it unites persons of different religious denominations in a single organization for certain definite aims and activities, it recognises their allegiance to any of the various Christian Bodies into which the Body of Christ is divided. It believes that loyalty to their own denomination is the first duty of Christian students and welcomes them into the fellowship of the Movement as those whose privilege it is to bring into it, as their contribution, all that they as members of their own religious body have discovered or will discover of Christian truth.   (Tatlow, 1933, p. 400)

It is worth noting a few things about this statement. First, it is pragmatic. It was produced, not out of idle philosophizing, but out of the need to find ways in which organizations which had previously competed with or avoided each other could co-operate in their common interests in evangelizing in universities and in the world at large. Secondly, it was produced by people who were keenly aware of religious diversity. Tatlow and his fellow SCM activists and the promoters of the 1910 WMC were people who were involved in foreign missions and hence who were keenly aware of the minority status of their own beliefs and of the great plurality of religions. Thirdly, by not defining the limits to the Body of Christ or specifying 'Christian truth', the statement implicitly opens the way to its supporters accepting an ever greater range of beliefs as all being in some sense valid. Fourthly, and most importantly, implicit in it is what was later to become explicit: *relativism and perennialism*.[1] At the heart of Tatlow's draft was the notion that in the dark cloud of apparent contradiction could be found the silver lining of fundamental unity. Where previously, in what was known as 'non-denominational' work, co-operation required that differences be tactfully overlooked, now they were to be celebrated while the law of non-contradiction was suspended. Where the Bishop of Hippo would, out of love, of course, persecute those who differed with him, the Bishops of the major Christian churches that formed the ecumenical movement would endorse everything from high Catholicism through the evangelicalism of the Salvation Army to the pantheism of American native religion.

My fourth quotation comes from Sir George Trevelyan, doyen of British New Age spirituality, who concluded one account of his beliefs with the words: 'This is what things look like to me. If it doesn't seem like that to you, you don't have to accept what I say. Only accept what rings true to your own Inner Self' (in Greer, 1995, p. 159).

A Vocabulary

With concerns as broad as those of this essay, there is an ever-present danger of unsupported generalization masking insupportable interpretations of the historical record. To somewhat reduce this danger, I want to introduce a vocabulary which allows me to specify briefly but clearly and consistently my concerns. Roy Wallis built on the previous work of Ernst Troeltsch, Howard Becker, Bryan Wilson, Benton Johnson and Roland Robertson in clarifying the distinctions between the four most commonly used terms for religious organizations – church and sect, cult and denomination – to offer a simple but useful analytical device, as shown in figure 2.1. Wallis notes that most of the important differences in how people organize their religious lives can be identified if we look at just two issues: (a) Does the religion see itself as having a unique grasp of salvational knowledge? and (b) Is the religion seen by others as respectable or deviant?

Figure 2.1   A typology of ideological organizations

		External Conception	
		Respectable	Deviant
Internal Conception	Uniquely Legitimate	CHURCH	SECT
	Pluralistically Legitimate	DENOMINATION	CULT

Source: Wallis, 1976, p. 13.

Many Mormons believe that their organization offers the only way to God. Hence they try to persuade people to become Mormons. For Mormons, the Church of Jesus Christ of Latter-Day Saints is *uniquely legitimate*. The Roman Catholic Church has historically taken a similar view (though, like the Mormon Church, it is now moderating its claims in certain contexts). Members of the Exclusive or 'Closed' Brethren also take the view that they and they alone have the Way. But there is considerable difference in the popularity, acceptability and prestige of the Catholic Church, the Mormons and the Exclusive Brethren. One can clearly see the difference in the way the media treat them. It is common for radio and television documentaries to be highly critical of the tight way in which the Brethren socialize their children to become the next generation of the Brethren. It is rare to see similar arguments being made about Catholic schooling or about the Catholic Church's insistence that the children of mixed marriages be raised as Catholics. Hence we would say the Catholics are a 'church' but the Brethren are a 'sect'. The position of the Mormons allows me to stress one aspect of the Wallis model which, although not central to this essay, is interesting: its social relativity. He is not looking for the unchanging essence of any phenomenon but the reality of its life in this or that place. The Mormons began as a highly deviant (and much persecuted) sect. In many parts of the world, they remain a deviant sect. But in Utah, they have achieved such numerical superiority as to be able to act as if they formed a 'church'.

Consider the bottom half of the table. What the denomination – the Methodists would be an example – and the cult have in common is that they do not claim a unique possession of the truth. They think they have something to offer, that you might be better off being a Methodist than a Baptist, but they recognize other organizations as being every bit as valid as themselves. They think of themselves in the terms of Tatlow's interdenominational basis for the ecumenical movement. Similarly, the vast majority of purveyors of cultic wisdom and esoteric practice do not expect or seek the monogamous commitment of their followers. Indeed the relationship between purveyor and consumer is so loose that terms such as member, adherent and follower are usually inappropriate in the cultic milieu. Cults see themselves as simply one of many guides on the single but very broad road to enlightenment.

Again what separates them is the top line: the extent to which they have succeeded in establishing themselves in their society. The Methodists are a respectable part of our social and cultural landscape; cults are not.

It is worth adding here that not only will specific religious organizations vary in their form with time and place but in any one setting they may offer different presentations to different audiences, both as a recruiting tactic and as a necessary accommodation to the responses of followers. For example, the leadership and core members of the Church of Scientology tend to see their religion as uniquely legitimate, but this is down-played in initial contacts with the public. During the recruitment process, the sectarian qualities become clearer but none the less many consumers persist in 'taking away' some Scientology expertise and incorporating it in their own ideological packages rather than becoming committed members of the Church of Scientology.

Secularization

The point of introducing these distinctions is to offer a very simple way of describing the major changes in the religious climate of the Western world. We can observe the possibility and popularity of the four forms of religion in different sorts of society. I am not suggesting that sects were unknown prior to the Reformation, and that denominations and cults were unknown prior to the last quarter of the nineteenth century; would that history were so simple! Even within the massive consensus of the Holy Roman Empire one had Christian humanists (of whom the young Erasmus would be a good example) who searched for some common values to unite the range of religious expression they confronted. However, I am suggesting that there is a crucial difference in the number, size and popularity of the exemplars of the various forms. Further, I am suggesting that close inspection of what may at first sight appear to be cases out of time and place will often reinforce the point.

The key to the shift between these four forms is *modernization*. With no suggestion of claiming the intellectual status of Max Weber, I want to be clear that I am using the term in the manner of the sadly often misunderstood Protestant ethic thesis (Weber, 1976). By modernization, I refer to a *historically and geographically specific* package of major social, political and economic changes that came with urbanization and industrialization in western Europe, and to the form of consciousness associated with those changes (see Berger, Berger and Kellner, 1974). I am not at this point making any universal claims or offering observations about societies that have more recently been affected by some of those changes. The extent to which the patterns may be repeated will depend on the extent to which new circumstances match the old.

Modernization makes the church form of religion impossible. The church requires either cultural homogeneity or an elite sufficiently powerful to enforce conformity. Societies expand to encompass ever larger numbers of religious, ethnic and linguistic groups and improved communication brings increased knowledge of that diversity. Modernization also undermines the hierarchical and rigid social structures which permit the maintenance of monocultures. What at first sight might appear to be paradoxical changes combine to encourage and legitimate diversity.

First, as Durkheim notes in his distinction between mechanical and organic solidarity, the increased division of labour and growth of economies creates ever greater social diversity and social distance (Durkheim, 1964). The feudal estate and closed village become the town and the city. The medieval old town of Edinburgh, where people of very different 'stations' lived on different floors of the same tenement and threw their excrement into the same street, was replaced with the New Town, inhabited by the bourgeoisie and their servants, separated from the trades and the factories. Increasingly, different social circumstances created increasingly different cultures, and that expressed itself in religious diversity as different social groups reworked the dominant religious tradition in ways that made sense from their position in the world.

At the same time, as Gellner (1983) in his theory of nationalism persuasively argues, modernization produced a basic egalitarianism. A division of labour need not undermine a hierarchical society (the caste system of India is profoundly hierarchical and the castes are defined by their occupations) but economic development also brought change and the expectation of further change. And it brought occupational mobility. People no longer did the job they always did because their family always did that job. Occupational mobility made it hard for people to internalize visions of themselves that suppose permanent inferiority. One cannot have people improving themselves and their class position while thinking of themselves as fixed in a station or a degree or a caste in an unchanging hierarchical world. Modern societies are thus inherently egalitarian.

Economic expansion increased contact with strangers. Profound inequalities of status are tolerable and can work well when the ranking system is well known and widely accepted as legitimate. Soldiers can move from one regiment to another and still know their place because there is a uniform ranking system and one's rank is displayed on one's uniform. Economic innovation and expansion means constant change in the nature of occupations, and increased mobility, both of which in their different ways mean that we have trouble placing people. There is no way of ensuring that we know whether we are superior or subordinate to this or that new person.

The separation of work and home, of the public and the private, further makes for equality. 'Serf' and 'peasant' were not job descriptions; they were enveloping social, legal and political statuses. One cannot be a serf during working hours and an autonomous individual for the evenings and at weekends. A temporary work-role is not a full identity and though work-roles may be ranked in a hierarchy, they can no longer structure the whole worldview. In the absence of a shared belief system which would sanction inequality and subjection (and the decline of religion usually removes that), egalitarianism becomes the default position.

The precondition of employability, dignity, full moral citizenship and an acceptable social identity is a certain level of education, which must include literacy – and literacy in a single language common throughout the economy. Once this was recognized, socialization became standardized and placed in the hands of a central agency; not a family, clan or guild but a society-wide education system. It required a single cultural and linguistic medium through which people could be instructed.

Gellner is not, of course, saying that in modern societies everyone is equal. His point is that the profound and fixed division of rights one finds in traditional and feudal societies is incompatible with economic development. Modernization and the development of the capitalist economy require the end of the old world.

The fundamental egalitarianism that came with modernization meant that, at the political level, the costs of coercing religious conformity were no longer acceptable: the state was no longer willing to accept the price in social conflict and adopted a position of neutrality on the competing claims of various religious bodies. In some settings, the neutrality was explicit (as in the Constitution of the United States); in others, it was implicit (as in the fudge which left the Established Churches of England and Scotland with notional advantages over their competitors but removed their real privileges). At the level of individual consciousness, it made it ever more difficult (though, of course, still possible) to dismiss religious views at odds with one's own as being of entirely no account.

Let us go back and pick up another thread of change to follow. In some countries, where the Lutheran influence predominated, the religious upheavals of the Reformation were largely contained within the church form. In others, religious dissent, accelerated by the social changes of the early modern period, created a profusion of 'sects', most of which initially tried to establish themselves as the church. It was only after failing to achieve power, either through becoming the majority religion or by effecting a minority coup, that many of them discovered the principle of toleration and evolved into denominations (Bruce and Wright, 1995).

At the same time as external relations with other religious organizations and with the state were giving the sect good reason to moderate its claims, there were a variety of internal pressures in the same direction. This is the well-known Niebuhr thesis (1962). For millenarian sects, the failure of the world to end is one problem that must be faced. For almost all sects the position of the children of the sectarians calls into question the initial hard demarcation between the saved and the unregenerate. It is natural for sectarians to suppose that their children, who have been raised in the faith, are not quite the same as the children of outsiders.

Gradually the strict membership tests are relaxed. Survival for any length of time brings assets (buildings, publishing houses, and capital) which require to be managed. The creation of a bureaucratic structure in turn brings officials whose interests are to a degree at odds with the original radical impetus of the sect. The asceticism of the sect may well result in upward social mobility. Even if there is no independent 'Protestant ethic' effect, most sects have endured in circumstances of general economic growth. Increasing prosperity means that the sacrifices inherent in asceticism are proportionately ever larger. When coupled with the lower levels of commitment found among those generations which have inherited their sectarianism rather than acquired it through choice, the result is a gradual relaxation of Puritanism and a gradual accommodation to the ways of the world.

Of course there is nothing inevitable about this general trend. Wilson (1990, 1993) explores a variety of ways in which certain sects have avoided the erosion of their initial radical sectarianism. To give just one example, the moderating effects of increased prosperity can be blunted if, as is the case with the Seventh Day Adventists, that prosperity is channelled and controlled by the sect itself, and can thus serve as a device for maintaining commitment (Bull and Lockhart, 1989). However, we cannot look at the sect's deployment of commitment mechanisms in isolation from the sect's surrounding environment. The sectarian form of religion is demanding and it is potentially disruptive because it challenges other belief systems and modes of behaviour (religious and secular). To the extent that a nation-state or a society is prepared to allow its people social space in which to create their own subcultures, the sect form can prosper (as one sees with fundamentalism in America). However, the distance between its beliefs and those of most people in the modern world is so great that few outsiders will be attracted and its success will depend on socializing its children in the faith. The sect's potential for conflict ensures that it is marginalized in modern democracies.

Those such as Jeffrey Hadden (1987) who point to the recent new Christian right in the United States as refutation might note the movement's record. On what John Garvey calls its defensive agenda – the assertion of the right to be treated as other minorities – it has had some very limited successes (Garvey, 1993). For example, the Courts have decided that the separation of church and state does not prevent evangelical students using school classrooms for private after-hours meetings. But it has signally failed on its offensive agenda. The Supreme Court has maintained the 'no nothing' line on state endorsement of particular religious beliefs and practices and has rejected decisively the claim that the Biblical creation account of the origins of the world should be taught wherever a secular evolutionary account is given in schools.

That the sectarian form of religion is demanding of its members and requires a social structure loose enough to allow effective subcultures, means that its influence in the modern world is limited. That the mass media frequently print or broadcast 'scare stories' about the growth of fundamentalism (often inspired by a failure to appreciate that Iran is very unlike Britain or America) is not evidence to the contrary. It is evidence of the failure of commentators to appreciate that the numerical decline of the denominational form of religion leaves the sectarians as an ever greater part of the ever smaller number of believers.

Thus far in what must be a massively simplified view of the history of religion in the West, we have seen first the church form faced with competition from the sect and then both churches and sects tending to become denominations. Where does the cult come into this account? First with the new religious movements of the 1960s and 1970s and then with the New Age religion of the 1980s, we have seen a flowering of alternative religions, some re-workings for the Western mind of traditional Eastern religions, others spiritualized versions of lay psychotherapies that are the bastard children of Freud and Jung. In terms of numbers, new religious movements and New Age religiosity are insignificant. Field sports are more popular than alternative religions. There are more train spotters than white witches, magicians, and pagans. However, the cult form of religion is, I would argue, emblematic.

First, there is the point that the decline in the main religious traditions leaves every larger numbers of people free to experiment; free because they are not personally tied to an older form and free because the decline of that older form reduces its ability to stigmatize cultic alternatives as 'deviant'. Secondly, there is the core belief of New Age religion in the divinity of the self. Grounded in some variant of the Hindu and Buddhist view that the apparent diversity of matter disguises a fundamental unity and hence that 'all is one', it argues that we should no longer seek God outside ourselves but within. For we are both all God's children and all God. I want to suggest that this substantive proposition is, like the interdenominational position of the liberal denominations and the ecumenical movement, both an article of faith and a necessary adjustment to the fact of minority status. Just as most conservative schismatic sects came to love the principle of toleration once they had failed to achieve a position of power in which they could enforce conformity to their own beliefs, so the purveyors of the cultic world have found a happy match of principle and expedience in eclecticism and relativism.

Finally, the cultic milieu is emblematic of modern religion in openly laying claim to what for the last half-century has been an implicit principle of much involvement in traditional religion: the right of the sovereign individual to determine what is truth and what is falsity.

Individualism used to mean the freedom to dissent; now it means the right to determine, not simply what one likes to do, but what is the case. It has grown from being a political and behavioural principle to being an ontological device.

Just to clarify the argument, I will briefly deal with two common objections to this sociological gloss of history. It is certainly true that something like the profusion of religious beliefs we now see in the New Age milieu could also be found during the English Civil War and Commonwealth periods. However, the range of beliefs was considerably narrower; they were all Protestant Christian. But more important for the sociologist is the fact that most of the alternatives available during the Commonwealth were *competing sects*, each certain of its unique grasp of the truth and of the falsity of the positions of the Church of England. In the New Age we see a cultic milieu, a world in which individuals select from a diverse range of beliefs and supernaturalisms, very few of the purveyors of which claim to be uniquely legitimate. Even if the promoting organization is supported by an inner circle of full-time officials who claim a unique grasp of the truth, such claims are routinely rejected by the consumers of their product and the awareness that such a fate can hardly be avoided is daily reflected in them moderating their claims for public consumption. Whatever those in the inner circle of Transcendental Meditators privately think, their newspaper advertisements stress that 'no change of belief is required'. To put it simply, we have previously had alternatives but they have been competing sects, not co-operating and complementary cults.

Similarly, early premodern spokesmen for toleration will usually turn out on close inspection to have in mind a considerably narrower range of what is permissible than the average liberal Christian. Those Congregationalists and Presbyterians of the English Civil War period who argued for toleration (and there were many who opposed it) wished it to include themselves and the state church but did not allow Roman Catholics or Quakers the privilege.

Is this Postmodern?

At first sight, these basic patterns seem to offer confirmation of certain versions of a 'postmodernity' story in that we see a decline in the strength of tradition and an increase in the extent to which individuals select their own idiosyncratic versions of available religious traditions. Those people who remain in denominations are increasingly selective about what parts of their organization's teachings they will accept (as one sees with the contraceptive practice of most Roman Catholics[2]), and feel free to add their own even heretical innovations (for example, surveys have shown an increasing number of Christians believing in reincarnation).

Against this one can place the endurance of sectarian forms of religion. Indeed, in most Western societies, what is often described loosely as the decline of the churches is more accurately the decline of the mainstream churches. If one is looking for stability and even slight growth, one finds it in the forms of religion that are least 'postmodern'.

But the relative growth of sectarian forms of religion could be reconciled to a vision of postmodernity if one noted the considerable movement *between* conservative Protestant sects. The recent growth of independent Christian fellowships (the so-called 'house church movement') has depended a great deal on defections from older forms of Protestant dissent (in particular, the Baptist churches). In my research on religious behaviour in Belfast, I found many couples who practised a form of the 'seekership' that was much described in the literature on the new religious movements of the 1970s. One might be raised in the Baptist Church, but then move to an Independent Methodist congregation, and later to a gospel hall before settling on the Pentecostal Church of God.

This looks like an example of the consumerist orientation to religious belief noted by those keen on interpreting the world through the lenses of 'postmodernity' but it is possible to distinguish this behaviour from the apparently similar sampling of revelations and therapies that characterizes the cultic milieu. We need to distinguish between aggregate behaviour and individual motivation and consciousness. The sectarian seeker remains within the classic sectarian mode of supposing, at each stopping place, that this is the one unique, divinely ordained truth. The sectarian seeker is not a relativist nor a radical Unitarian who insists that the diversity of matter is fundamentally united in cosmic consciousness. Though the seeking career of many sectarians shows that they exercise choice, they see their choosing as being guided by an external authority (the will of God) and deny their own part in the process.

We might suppose that, like the serial monogamist, the serial sectarian will remember the number of times that he has thought he has found the true church of God, gradually become aware of his own role in selection, and move towards the relativism of the denomination and cult. This is an empirical issue. What I would say is that denying the authorship of one's actions and playing down the extent of change have very different consequences from asserting the divine self, celebrating change, and asserting either relativism or perennialism.

The Origins of Individualism

Many accounts of secularization, especially those of critics who wish to pastiche the approach, concentrate on the supposed clash of ideas between science and religion. As the above brief summary will indicate, I believe the competing ideas of science to be far less of a threat to religion than cultural diversity, which in turn makes me interested in the patterns of social relations which determine how competing ideas are handled. The irony is that Christianity dug its own grave. Innovations pressed to rejuvenate the Church undermined it. David Martin in his usual elegant but elliptical style has written that: 'The logic of Protestantism is clearly in favour of the voluntary principle, to a degree that eventually makes it sociologically unrealistic' (1978, p. 1). The religion created by the Reformation was extremely vulnerable to fragmentation because it removed the institution of the church as a source of authority between God and man. If by reading the scriptures everyone was able to discern God's will, how would subsequent disputes be resolved? Being a theist who believed in one God, one Holy Spirit which dwelt in all of God's creation, and one Bible, the Protestant could hope that the righteous would come to agree, but history proved that hope false.

The Reformation did not arise out of nothing and I could have started this account at an earlier point to show the social, political and economic changes that encouraged the Reformation. But if we take it as our starting point we can see the tremendous effects it had in laying the foundations for 'modernity'. To repeat the point of the last paragraph, it inadvertently fragmented the dominant religious culture and created the competition which, in tolerant and egalitarian societies, would lead to relativism and perennialism. By insisting that all people had a responsibility for their own spiritual state, the Reformation also contributed directly to the growth of individualism. It required ordinary people to become better informed about their religion, and in producing the means to service that need (printing, the spread of literacy, and the use of the vernacular), it further encouraged the trend. It also contributed to the rationalization of the world, hence to the growth of modern science and technology, and thus inadvertently contributed to the erosion of religion.

But asserting the centrality of the Reformation in this way leaves us with something of a problem. A historian of ideological innovation (Kamen (1967) would be a fine example) might well look at what the post-modernists claim to be a novel condition and point out that the origins of the phenomenon are located four hundred years earlier. The sociologist and social historian would note that, incipient though individualism (and the relativism it requires) might have been, it did not flower until the end of the nineteenth century and bloom until after the 1939–45 war. Why not?

Although the details are complex, an underlying explanation for this lag can be found in inertia, lack of democracy, social homogeneity, and the authority of rationality. First, we should note the inertia given in the fact that each generation was socialized into the beliefs of the previous, not the next. Luther, Calvin and Zwingli were raised in a 'Catholic' world and only moved so far from its thinking. Zwingli showed his continuity with the previous order when he said:

> Why should the Christian magistrate not destroy statues and abolish the mass? . . . This does not mean that he has to cut the priests' throats if it is possible to avoid such a cruel action. But if not we would not hesitate to imitate the harshest examples. (Kamen, 1967, p. 46)

The history of eighteenth-century Scottish dissenting Presbyterianism, as it reluctantly shifted from a principled commitment to a state-established and enforced church to the principle of voluntarism, was decorated with heresy trials as those individuals who moved too fast were expelled, only to see their damnable heresy become first the practice and then the principle of the next generation. But the broadening of possibilities seems logarithmic rather than linear.

Secondly, the lack of democracy and egalitarianism was a key inhibitor. As long as people were not free to make many choices about this world, they were unlikely to feel free to make many about the next.

Thirdly, although not asserting any simple connection between social conditions and ideology, I am supposing that there is some sort of relationship between diversity of experiences of the mundane world and diversity of visions of the supernatural. A straightforward linear relationship is unlikely because of the ability of particular social groups to recruit others to their vision. The Victorian British bourgeoisie worked hard to socialize the rough urban working class into respectability via evangelical Protestantism but even so far as they succeeded they did not prevent 'Nonconformity' being divided into competing sects (nor, interestingly, did they prevent it spawning radical political movements and alternative institutions). To take the very long view, I would argue that the general and accelerating increase in the division of labour produced an ever greater variety of life circumstances. While initially this was expressed through 'classes', it eventually made the quite narrow visions of those groupings precarious. To reverse the point, the relative lack of economic and social diversity in previous centuries was a major inhibition on the individualism implicit in Protestantism.

To stress the social bases of belief is neither to ignore nor to neglect the influence of ideas and culture in their own right. While the rationality of science and technology is rightly offered as a general threat to the plausibility of supernatural belief systems, there is one way in which the enormous success of rationality inhibited the fragmentation of religious tradition into solipsism, and that is by maintaining the idea that there could be authoritative knowledge. For the scientists of the nineteenth and early twentieth centuries there was just one world, accessible by one approach. If two sets of research findings were in contradiction, then at least one set was wrong. In so far as the findings of natural science contradicted the beliefs of the churches, technological consciousness reduced a sense of mystery and uniqueness, and technology provided solutions for problems for which people had previously sought religious recourse, rationality was indeed a threat to religion, but until recently the authority of science did provide a bulwark against an individualistic ontology.

In terms of social relations, one sees the authority of rationality in the rise of professions which used their knowledge as the basis for power. I can only allude to the argument here but it seems clear that there has recently been an erosion in the authority of science and of the professions. Most of us still go to properly accredited medical professions for cures for our ailments but there is no longer the widespread certainty that 'the doctor knows best'. Our current scepticism about science is no better founded than our previous credulity but it is widespread.

One does not want to exaggerate the importance of one's own discipline but it does seem that sociology has been implicated in this weakening of faith in the possibility of authoritative knowledge. Part cause and part symptom, one element of sociological thought has now passed into the taken-for-granted knowledge of Westerners. We all practise a debunking sociology of knowledge that imputes interests to those who claim to be disinterested. The English prostitute Mandy Rice-Davies's famous response to a client's denial of her claims – 'Well, he would say that, wouldn't he?' – has become firmly embedded in the way we respond to any assertion or claim. Though the term 'hermeneutic' is still foreign to most people, the general notion that different sorts of people will see the world in different ways has become deeply embedded in our culture.

As a sign of just how far we have moved from the confidence in our ability, by rational inspection, to discover the truth, let me quote from the essay of a good final-year sociology student who concluded a discussion of the problems of source bias by saying: 'In an ideal world there would always be a balance of sources to present everyone's view.' She did not write: 'In an ideal world we would research our way past bias to the truth.' No, the best we can hope for now is equality of opportunity to assert our prejudices.

Conclusion

In this extremely broad sociological interpretation of the religious history of modern societies, I have tried to express the major changes with some conceptual consistency by using the reformulation of 'church', 'sect', 'denomination' and 'cult' proposed by the late Roy Wallis. I have tried to show why the church form of religion is challenged first by sects and why both forms then evolve into the denomination. The church form may survive where ethnic or national conflict places a premium on ethnic solidarity and thus retards fragmentation. The sect form may endure where the social circumstances allow the creation and mainten-ance of a cultural hegemonic sub-society. The social space left by the decline in the popularity of the major tradition allows entry to large numbers of alternative religions, organized, if that is not too strong a word, in a 'cultic milieu'. That is the European pattern; the North American and Australasian is slightly different. There, because the countries have been formed by waves of immigration there is less of a hegemonic culture and much greater space for experimentation with culture and lifestyles, even while the Christian tradition remains strong. Either way, the denomination and the cult share in common their pluralistic legitim-acy and their relativism (implicit in one, explicit in the other). Indeed, as the previously dominant Christian culture weakens it becomes ever harder to distinguish denominations and cults sociologically (though one may do so by the source of their ideas: Christian for the former; Hindu/Buddhist or secular psychotherapy for the latter) because cults are no longer terribly deviant.

As much misplaced argument about the secularization approach to religious change shows, the above argument is readily misunderstood and it should be stressed that this is a context-specific model. As I have noted, there are circumstances in which religion retains its church form and in which sects survive and prosper, and I have delineated these in detail elsewhere (Bruce, 1996). In this account I am making no uni-versal causal claims. I am not suggesting, for example, that an increased division of labour always brings cultural diversity. It does so only in democracies or where the oligarchy is prepared to tolerate it (the posi-tion of Stalin's USSR with regard to those aspects of the culture of ethnic minorities that did not threaten the power of the Communist Party, for example). Social diversity is far more likely to produce religious frag-mentation in Protestant cultures than in Roman Catholic ones, where the result is rather the division of the population into an enduringly Catholic bloc (though with class differences over exactly what it means to be a Catholic) and a secular bloc. What I am saying, as Weber said, is that in the circumstances of the countries of Protestant western Europe and those new worlds most influenced by the old, the individualism inherent in the Reformation produced a series of changes which culmin-ated in our present religious culture: a culture in which, as Peter Berger put it, individuals create their God rather than the other way round (Berger, 1980).

Given the vastly different things that can be meant when people use the notion of 'postmodernity' there seems little point in arguing about whether orientations to religion that range from selective attention to a denomination's teaching to an explicitly individualistic ontology offer support for the claim that we are now in a 'postmodern' era. In so far as my observations about religious change lead me to a view on that debate, my conclusion is that 'postmodernity' in this context is unnecessary and, given the tendentious theoretical baggage associated with the term, best avoided. What I have sought to do is demonstrate that the major patterns of change can be explained by the operation of those characteristics which Weber, Gellner and Berger regarded as the essence of modernity.

Notes

1 Precisely because the innovation was implicit there was no open discussion of whether what was meant was that divergent positions were equally valuable because no system existed for adjudicating which was true (relativism), or that divergence was merely a surface appearance which masked an underlying unity (perennialism). Only the most radical Unitarian universalists would have argued for the latter. Perhaps the best way of describing it is to say that an under-stated relativism was adopted as an interactional device and it gradually became a rarely stated perennialism through the course of the twentieth century.

2 The description of the Roman Catholic Church as a denomination might seem surprising but it follows from the distinctions made above concerning (a) area variations and (b) tensions between officials and laity. In parts of the world where it continues to enjoy hegemony the Catholic Church acts like a 'church' in the sociological sense. In places where it is a minority faith (the US is a clear case) it acts like a denomination. Furthermore (in parallel with the point about Scientology being a sect in the eyes of its professional officials but a cult in the eyes of most consumers of its product), most Roman Catholics in industrial societies act as though their religion was of the denominational, rather than the churchly, type.

References

Berger, Peter L. 1980: *The Heretical Imperative: Contemporary Possibilities of Religious Affirmation.* London: Collins.

——, Berger, Brigitte and Kellner, Hansfried 1974: *The Homeless Mind.* Harmondsworth: Penguin.

Bruce, Steve 1996: *Religion in the Modern World: From Cathedrals to Cults.* Oxford: Oxford University Press.

—— and Wright, C. 1995: Law, religious toleration and social change. *Journal of Church and State* 37: 103–20.

Bull, Malcolm and Lockhart, Keith 1989: *Seeking a Sanctuary: Seventh Day Adventism and the American Dream.* New York: Harper and Row.

Durkheim, Emile 1964: *The Division of Labor in Society.* New York: Free Press.

Garvey, John H. 1993: Fundamentalism and American law. In Martin Marty and R. Scott Appleby (eds), *Fundamentalisms and the State: Remaking Politics, Economics and Militance,* Chicago: University of Chicago Press, pp. 28–49.

Gellner, Ernest 1983: *Nations and Nationalism.* Oxford: Blackwell.

Greer, Paul 1995: The Aquarian confusion: conflicting theologies of the New Age. *Journal of Contemporary Religion* 10: 151–66.

Hadden, Jeffrey K. 1987: Towards desacralizing secularization theory. *Social Forces* 65: 587–611.

Kamen, Henry 1967: *The Rise of Toleration.* London: Weidenfeld and Nicolson.

Martin, David 1978: *The Dilemmas of Contemporary Religion.* Oxford: Blackwell.

Niebuhr, H. Richard 1962: *Social Sources of Denominationalism.* New York: Meridian.

Tatlow, Tissington 1933: *The Story of the Student Christian Movement.* London: SCM Press.

Wallis, Roy 1976: *The Road to Total Freedom: A Sociological Analysis of Scientology.* London: Heinemann.

Weber, Max 1976: *The Protestant Ethic and the Spirit of Capitalism.* London: George Allen and Unwin.

Wilson, Bryan 1990: How sects evolve: issues and inferences. In Bryan Wilson, *The Social Dimensions of Sectarianism: Sects and New Religious Movements in Contemporary Society,* Oxford: Oxford University Press, pp. 105–27.

—— 1993: The persistence of sects. *Diskus* 1: 1–12.

CHAPTER THREE

terminal faith

Mark C. Taylor

Cyberspace. A consensual hallucination experienced daily by billions of legitimate operations, in every nation, by children being taught mathematical concepts . . . Lines of light ranged in the nonspace of the mind, clusters of data.

(William Gibson, 1984, p. 51)

Much more than the philosophic theory of the unity of matter, it was probably the old conception of the Earth-Mother, bearer of embryo-ores, which crystallized faith in artificial transmutation (that is, operated in a laboratory). It was the encounter with the symbolisms, myths and techniques of the miners, smelters and smiths which probably gave rise to the first alchemical operations.

(Mircea Eliade, 1978, p. 148)

The end is approaching . . . approaching without arriving from the ever-not-so-distant future. We are counting down or up to the end and the beginning of the millennium. As in the past, the transition from one to another millennium appears to be a time of endings as well as beginnings, deaths as well as rebirths. The darker the old era seems, the brighter the New Age appears. Always inscribed within an economy of redemption, millenarianism promises a new world in which all things are transformed. When interpreted religiously, and it is difficult to imagine a millenarianism that is not implicitly or explicitly religious, the New Age appears to be the end of time and the dawn of eternity. As such, the end of time is, in effect, the collapse of space. In the strange space of endtime, many believe that the dreams of ontotheology and theoesthetics come true. Presence becomes totally present in a kingdom that is completely realized here and now. This is an old, old story – a story that is as old as history itself. But it is also new – as new as today's New Age.

This century, which is ending with the return of millenarianism in the guise of technophilia, began with apocalyptic dreams that have repeatedly run wild. Throughout modernity, diverse representatives of the avant-garde have been united by a certain millenarianism that usually borders on the apocalyptic. Though the vision of the New Age varies, the expectation of a cataclysmic reversal or radically transformative revolution remains remarkably constant. Whether change is understood as outward or inward, sociopolitical or psycho-mystical, the birth of the new always seems to require the death of the old. No redemption without sacrifice; no resurrection without crucifixion. The sacrificial fires whose light marks the dawn of the New Age purge the old epoch of its impurities. With the eclipse of God, the high priest of salvation becomes the artist who is the architect of the New Jerusalem.

Nowhere are the far-reaching implications of the transfer of authority from priest to artist–architect more apparent than in Italian Futurism, which emerged in the years immediately prior to the outbreak of the First World War. Fully committed to the modernist project of industrialization, Filippo Marinetti calls for a break with the pastoral past and a rush into the urban future. The machine, steam, and electricity – above all electricity – are the vehicles that will transport the futurist into the New Age. Electricity creates the possibility of *speed*, which promises to break the chains that bind humankind to time and space. In the famous manifesto, published in *Le Figaro* on 20 February 1909, Marinetti declares:

> We stand on the last promontory of the centuries! . . . Why should we look back, when what we want is to break down the mysterious doors of the Impossible. Time and Space died yesterday. We already live in the absolute, because we have created eternal, omnipresent speed.   (In R. W. Flint (ed.), 1972, p. 41)

The hallucinogenetic effect of speed translates one from the world of time and space into the omnipresence of the absolute.

It is important to note that Marinetti was not alone in his search for an aesthetic of speed. Cubism's experiments with simultaneity, and suprematism's probing of the fourth dimension, can also be understood as a quest for the experience of an all-at-onceness that is an all-at-oneness. As Einstein had argued only a few years before these artistic innovations, when we reach the speed of light, time itself is reversed. Nor was Marinetti the only one to believe that his dream of omnipresence could be realized through electricity. For many early twentieth-century artists and non-artists, the Eiffel Tower, completed in 1889 for the Paris World's Fair commemorating the centenary of the French Revolution, became the symbol of the New Age. At the end of the first decade of the twentieth century, however, the Eiffel Tower and its image underwent an important change that both recalls the shift from the eighteenth to the nineteenth century and anticipates the transition from the mechanical age of industrial capitalism to the electronic age of postindustrial capitalism. In 1909, the year in which Marinetti published his Futurist Manifesto, the first regular broadcast system was installed on the Eiffel Tower. Though

Robert Delaunay's paintings from this period present the Tower as a synecdoche for modernity, the significance of its electrification only becomes evident in Vincente Huidobro's 1917 work entitled *Eiffel Tower*, which was dedicated to Delaunay:

> Eiffel Tower
>   Guitar of the sky
>
> Your wireless telegraphy
> Draws words to you
> As a rose-arbour draws bees
>
> In the night the Seine
> No longer flows
>
> Telescope or bugle
> Eiffel Tower
>
> And a beehive of words
> Or the night's inkwell
> At the dawn's base
> A spider with wire feet
> Spins its web with clouds . . .
>   A bird calls
>   In the antennae
> Of the wireless
>
> It is the wind
> The wind from Europe
> The electric wind.
> (In R. W. Flint (ed.), 1972, pp. 37–8)

The wire web at the feet of the Tower grounds the wireless net created by the signal beamed around the world. For visionaries, the electric wind from Europe promised to unify the planet.

There is, however, a dark side to such futuristic visions. While there is no necessary relation between modernism and totalitarianism, a disturbing number of modernists were drawn to fascism. Speed not only creates 'a new aesthetic', but, as Paul Virilio (1986) argues, is 'the essence of war'. For Marinetti, war is the purifying ritual through which we must pass if we are to enter the New Age. In his incendiary Manifesto, he defiantly proclaims:

> We will glorify war – the world's only hygiene – militarism, patriotism, the destructive gesture of freedom-bringers, beautiful ideas worth dying for, and scorn for women.   (In R. W. Flint (ed.), 1972, p. 42)

Marinetti's longing for war was soon satisfied. What started as faint sparks spread with electrifying speed to ignite a holocaust that quickly became all-consuming. According to those who fanned the flames of war, the heat generated in furnaces and ovens on and off the battlefield was supposed to burn away darkness, dirt, and disease and leave only light, cleanliness, and health. The colour of this apocalyptic light was gold – gold as pure as Margarete's flaxen locks.

It is a surprisingly short step from the futurists' apocalypticism to the cybertopia many project for the next century. Some of the most imaginative, compelling, and disturbing visions of possible futures opened by the current telecommunications revolution grow out of a curious mixture of vestiges of the 1960s drug counter-culture, New Age religion, and technophilia. Before fast-forwarding to the end of the century and beyond, it will be helpful to rewind from the beginning of this century, through the nineteenth century, to the ancient sources of modernism.

In a 1969 *Playboy* interview, Marshall McLuhan, whose reading of the mediascape remains surprisingly relevant despite its shortcomings, suggested a startling series of relays whose connection is far from obvious:

> LSD is a way of mining the invisible electronic world; it releases a person from acquired verbal and visual reactions, and gives the potential of instant and total involvement, both all-at-onceness and all-at-oneness, which are the basic needs of people translated by electric extensions of their central nervous systems out of the old rational, sequential value system. The attraction of hallucinogenic drugs is a means of achieving empathy with our penetrating electric environment, an environment that in itself is a drugless inner trip. (In Howard Rheingold, 1991, p. 323)

Mining . . . hallucinogenic drugs . . . electronics . . . all-at-onceness . . . all-at-oneness. The hidden fibre that links these disparate points is forged in the crucible of alchemy.

Alchemy is, of course, the magico-religious practice intended to transform base metals into gold. Closely related to different strands of medieval Jewish and Christian mysticism and extremely important for the rise of modern science, alchemy originates in ancient rituals associated with mining and metallurgy.[1] Mircea Eliade argues that throughout history, in many cultures, the activities of mining are closely related to religions devoted to the earth goddess. Within this framework, the earth is the generative matrix from which all arises and to which everything longs to return. Minerals are believed to be embryos that grow within the womb of Mother Earth. Gestation is a process of purification in which all minerals, given enough time, will eventually turn into gold. 'It is indeed remarkable', Eliade observes, that 'traditions, as numerous as they are widespread, should bear witness to this belief in the finality of nature', Eliade continuing,

If nothing impedes the process of gestation, all ores will, in time, become gold. 'If there were no exterior obstacles to the execution of her designs,' wrote a Western alchemist, 'Nature would always complete what she wished to produce . . . That is why we have to look upon the births of imperfect metals as we would on abortions and freaks that come about only because Nature has been, as it were, misdirected, or because she has encountered some fettering resistance or certain obstacles that prevent her from behaving in her accustomed way . . . Hence although she wishes to produce only one metal, she finds herself constrained to create several. Gold and only gold is the child of her desires. Gold is her legitimate son because only gold is a genuine production of her efforts.'   (Eliade, 1978, p. 50)

The labour of the miner assists the labour of the Mother. The miner serves as something like a gynaecologist and obstetrician who attempts to prevent abortions, freaks, and bastards and tries to facilitate the birth of a legitimate son. For the miner, the son is the gold that glimmers with the colour of the sun. While probing the darkest depths of the Mother, the miner remains committed to a solar religion.

The role of the miner–gynaecologist–obstetrician is to accelerate the labour process. In other words, the miner's contribution to nature is *speed*. The agents of speed are heat and fire. Within the religious economy of mining, it is not sufficient simply to extract the embryo or foetus from the womb. The birth process must be completed by polishing and refining the son through cleansing and purification procedures. The need for purity and refinement gave rise to the techniques and rituals of metallurgy. The metallurgist is the 'master of fire' who generates the heat necessary to speed up the transformation of the base into the pure. The process in which dark and dirty traces of the base underground are purified to form rarefied products that are light and clean is called *sublimation*. It is the metallurgist and not the psychoanalyst who first develops the techniques of sublimation. Sublimation takes place in ovens or furnaces that serve as a substitute womb or artificial uterus. Since the womb/uterus and furnace/oven are closely associated, the site of metallurgical practice had to be sanctified by either animal or human sacrifices. Lingering traces of the ancient human sacrifice can be found in the ashes that remain in twentieth-century ovens constructed for no less sinister rituals of purification.

The smelting required for purification involves a dissolution of formed substance into *prima materia*. The process of transformation that the metallurgist seeks to speed up presupposes that all substances are variations of an original Ur-substance. Fire burns away polluting differences and returns the many to the one in which they all originate. In this way, birth presupposes death. The ritual sacrifice that sanctifies the womb–oven prefigures the sacrifice enacted in the heat of the furnace. Furthermore, smelting entails something like a *regressus ad uterum* that returns matter to its original matrix. Mother, material, and matter meet in *mater*, which is their common origin.

These remarks suggest that the sublimation enacted by the metallurgist can be interpreted in many ways. The sublimation of base material into gold actually sublimates the primordial desire for the mother. The subtext of mining and metallurgy is, in effect, incest. If earth is Mother Earth, then entering the earth is penetrating the mother. The famous sixteenth-century alchemist Paracelsus writes:

> And yet it seems to me, the door of the Promised Land still stands
>   open for me,
> And that we must come remoulded from the mother's body.
> For I cannot otherwise reach the Kingdom of Heaven
> Unless I am born a second time.
> Therefore my desire is to return to the mother's womb
> That I may be regenerated, and this I will do right soon.
>   (In Robert Gray, 1952, p. 32)

Eros and thanatos meet in the desire for incest, which holds the promise of returning to a time, 'before' culture, when everything was one. If read in this way, the rituals associated with mining point to a variation of Freud's myth of origins. Technology, which is one technique for sublimating our most profound desire, originates at the mouth of the mine. Prohibiting what it allows and allowing what it prohibits, technology forms a supplementary matrix that simultaneously opens and closes the original matrix for which we long. The fibre of this matrix must, for the moment, be left dangling, but it will return later in and with a new light.

Alchemy extends and refines the techniques of metallurgy. No longer satisfied with speeding up nature by merely generating heat, the alchemist seeks a supplement to the supplement of fire. In alchemy, the religious prosthesis gives way to the chemical prosthesis. The philosophers' stone is the magical substance that is supposed to transform base metals into gold. One of the most common forms of this 'stone' was a fine white powder, which, in some rituals, served as an elixir. The alchemical elixir is the descendant of yet more ancient hallucinogenic drugs that were not only thought to have restorative and curative powers but were also believed to be 'chemical' agents of religious ecstasy. The association of the philosophers' stone and elixirs with religious rituals points to the underlying motivation for alchemical practice. Far from being driven by so-called materialistic concerns, alchemy is, as Eliade insists, 'a spiritual technique and a soteriology'. The soteriological technique employed by the alchemist presupposes the isomorphism of the macrocosm and the microcosm. Since the outer and the inner are of a piece, to change one is to transform the other. By refining base metals into gold, the alchemist seeks to purify himself. The goal of alchemy is to become as good as gold – pure gold. Gold is not just any substance but is the most rarefied form of the *prima materia* that is the true substance of all things. In other words, gold is, in effect, God. To become as good as gold is to become God. In his *Opus Mago-Cabbalisticum et Theosophicum*, Georg von Welling writes:

> our intention is not directed towards teaching anyone how to make gold but towards something much higher, namely how Nature may be seen and recognized as coming from God and God from Nature. . . . We wish with all our hearts that all men might seek and find not gold but God. (In Robert Gray, 1952, p. 19)

If gold is the purest form of nature and the divine is immanent in the natural, then the alchemist's true goal is to become God. In other words, alchemy's magical elixir is supposed to bestow immortality. Over the years, the white powder of the philosophers' stone has taken many forms, whose traces can be detected in Acid, Angel Dust, Ecstasy, and especially Speed. When the dose is right or the charge great enough, speed breaks the chains of space and time. 'Like the good "philosopher" or mystic that he was', Eliade concludes, the alchemist 'was afraid of time':

> He does not admit himself to be an essentially temporal being, he longed for the beatitude of paradise, aspired to eternity and pursued immortality, the *elixir vitae*. . . . Above all we must bear in mind that the alchemist became the master of Time, when, with his various apparatus, he symbolically reiterated the primordial chaos and the cosmogony or when he underwent initiatory 'death and resurrection'. Every initiation was a victory over death, i.e., temporality; the initiated proclaimed himself 'immortal'; he had forged for himself a post-mortem existence that he claimed to be indestructible. (Eliade, 1978, pp. 174–5)

In this way, the alchemist anticipates the futurist's quest for 'eternal, omnipresent speed'.

Though alchemy starts with the effort to assist mother nature by speeding up her labour, the metallurgist ends by becoming something like a god. The vision of the alchemist's creative power emerges in the recurrent fantasy of creating an homunculus.[2] The homunculus, as we shall see, is the distant ancestor of contemporary alchemists' replicants, androids, terminators, and cyborgs. Since divine power is nowhere more evident than in the capacity to make something like a human being, the aspiration to create an homunculus expresses the desire to become God.

As humankind's Faustian strivings demonstrate, the creator is always in danger of losing control of his creation.[3] From the homunculus and the golem to Frankenstein and the Terminator, the cyborg not only promises immortality but also threatens destruction. Though not immediately evident, the genealogy of the cyborg uncovers the fibre that links the final point in McLuhan's scattered circuit: mining . . . hallucinogenic drugs . . . electronics. When the golem is electrified, the matrix, which was first the mine and then the furnace or oven, becomes the net, which is also known as 'the matrix'. The transition from the religious, to the chemical, to the electronic prosthesis extends the process of sublimation in which matter becomes increasingly rarefied and idealized, and thus appears ever lighter until it is nothing other than light itself. At this point, the thread we have been tracing becomes a fibre optic stitched to form other nets. The way from the matrix to the Net passes through the grid of nineteenth-century speculative philosophy.

The importance of alchemy and the so-called occult sciences for nineteenth-century romanticism and idealism has not been sufficiently acknowledged.[4] In view of the religious dimensions of alchemy, it is hardly accidental that 'mining and disciplines like geology and mineralogy exerted on the Romantic scientists an almost magical attraction; many of the Romantics (e.g., Novalis, Setffens, von Humboldt, Baader, and Schubert) studied at the famous Mining School at Freiberg' (H. Snelders, 1970, p. 194). The romantics, like their alchemical precursors, were searching for the philosophers' stone that would allow them to enjoy the ecstasy of all-at-onceness and all-at-oneness. While for some, like Coleridge, Baudelaire and de Quincey, the agent was chemical, for others, like Schelling and Hegel, the drug was philosophical. Hegel, for example, freely admits his interest in mysticism and occultism. Like the mystics, the goal of his system is the unitive ecstasy in which eros and thanatos become One in the generative matrix, whose earlier guise is the Earth Mother. The relay that permits this translation is electricity.

Within Hegel's speculative vision, the absolute is initially an occult force that gradually reveals itself in nature and history. Though the macrocosm and microcosm perfectly mirror each other, the logos that constitutes the identity of differences is more clearly manifested in some things and events than in others. Once recognized, the absolute appears in all times and all places. In the natural realm, the absolute is nowhere more apparent than in the inextricably interrelated phenomena of light and electricity.

Hegel's entire philosophical system represents a subtle revision and refinement of Schelling's philosophy of nature. Two years after leaving the Tübingen theological seminary, where he had shared a room with Hegel and Hölderlin, and one year before assuming a professorship in

Jena, which was the centre of German romanticism, the young Schelling published *Ideas for a Philosophy of Nature* (1988). In many ways, this remarkable work set the course for subsequent German idealism and, by extension, established the direction for much twentieth-century philosophy and art. Schelling devotes an entire chapter of his study of nature to the problem of electricity. The reason for his fascination with electricity is clear: in this elusive phenomenon, he discerns the ideal expression of the absolute in the domain of nature. The absolute, according to Schelling, is 'the point of indifference', from which everything emerges and to which all returns. The 'one originally quiescent force' suffers division into contrasting positive and negative charges. These opposites proceed to draw together in an effort to reconstitute the unity that has been lost. When extrapolated from the particular phenomenon of electricity to reality as a whole, the cosmos appears to be an infinite play of opposites whose goal is the recovery of an original oneness.

Hegel's trenchant criticism of Schelling tends to obscure the abiding debt he owes to his erstwhile friend and room-mate. From Hegel's perspective, Schelling's version of absolute idealism is, in every sense of the word, regressive. The primal *Indifferenzpunkt* for which Schelling searches collapses differences in an identity that can bear nothing other than itself. Though sharing Schelling's desire for unity, Hegel maintains that any return to an original oneness is impossible. For the division and fragmentation plaguing modern experience to be overcome, there must be a progressive dialectical process in which differences are preserved but opposition is negated. In his reworking of Schelling's account of electricity, Hegel discloses the genealogy of his own notion of the absolute.

Electricity, Hegel (1970) acknowledges, 'appears as an occult agent, and resembles the occult qualities assumed by the scholastics' (p. 170). The task of the philosopher is to render this occult agent perfectly transparent. In his most concise formulation of the philosophico-ontological significance of electricity, Hegel writes:

> Electricity is infinite form differentiated within itself, and is the unity of these differentials; consequently the two bodies are inseparably bound together, like the north and south poles of a magnet. Magnetism is mere mechanical activity, however, and is therefore merely an opposition in the activity of movement. . . . In electricity, however, these fluctuating differentials are physical, for they are in the light. . . . Negative electricity is attracted by positive electricity, but repulsed by negative. In that the differentials unite themselves, they communicate themselves to each other; as soon as they have posited a unity, they fly apart again, and vice versa. . . . In the electrical process, each of the two distinct bodies has a differentiated determination that is only posited through the other, but in the face of which the further individuality remains free and distinct. (1970, p. 174)

While remaining thoroughly committed to the unitive metaphysics of light that runs throughout the ontotheological tradition, Hegel insists that light does not simply destroy differences but is 'the sublation of diremption'. The notion of sublation [*Aufheben*] is Hegel's translation of alchemical sublimation. Through the process of sublation, opposition is negated by establishing the unity of differences. The difference between Hegel's unity *in the midst* of differences and Schelling's *Indifferenzpunkt* is reflected in their alternative interpretations of electricity.

According to Hegel, the differential structure of electricity does not emerge from an initially undifferentiated identity. To the contrary, electricity is originally a unity of differences. Apart from the difference between positive and negative charges, there can be no electricity. Within the electrical process, differences are constituted in and through each other. In this way, electricity displays the infinite form, which is differentiated within itself and, as such, is the unity of differentials. When philosophically comprehended, this form, which is the substance of all things, appears as spirit. For Hegel, the philosophers' stone is nothing other than philosophical knowledge. Like the white powder that establishes the unity of differences, this knowledge is the golden light of the world. Speculative reason reveals the individual to be a particular incarnation of the divine logos, which is the generative matrix where all things arise and pass away. To apprehend oneself as a moment in the life of the absolute is to overcome time and space by grasping their eternal essence.

The Hegelian logos is the blueprint for wiring the twenty-first century. Alchemy's occult forces and Hegel's electric spirit are actualized in the electronic telecommunications network that is transforming the globe into a single complex net or web. The matrix is the electronic embodiment of the Hegelian logos, which, rumours to the contrary notwithstanding, is the mother of us all. Jack in . . . Jack out . . . Jack off. Matter . . . Material . . . Mother . . . Matrix . . . Sublation . . . Sublimation. Within the net, everything speeds up until we make the quantum leap into cyberspace. Though cyberspace is a sci-fi projection of what our near-future seems to hold, it effectively captures many of the most important features of present-day experience. Three decades ago, Marshall McLuhan (1964) argued that,

in the mechanical age now receding, many actions could be taken without too much concern. Slow movement insured that the reactions were delayed for considerable periods of time. Today the action and the reaction occur almost at the same time. We actually live mythically and integrally, as it were, but we continue to think in the old, fragmented space and time patterns of the pre-electric age. (1964, p. 4)

As the subtitle of his book *Understanding Media: The Extensions of Man* (1964) indicates, McLuhan saw electronic media as prosthetic extensions of the human organism. Computers become the brains, engines the legs, video cameras the eyes, telephones the ears, and wires the veins and arteries of the world organism. The lifeblood of this corporate body is, of course, electricity. The movement from the industrial to the electronic age repeats the shift from mechanical to organic metaphors for envisioning reality, which marked the transition from the eighteenth to the nineteenth century. In McLuhan's neo-romanticism and neo-idealism, organicism displaces mechanism to form a vision of a harmonious New Age in which all are one and one is all. Anticipating many insights usually attributed to Jean Baudrillard, McLuhan maintains that the implosion characteristic of experience in the electronic age is created by speed. When speed reaches a certain point, time and space collapse and distance seems to disappear.

It is easy to dismiss McLuhan's musings as a curious variation of the nostalgia that characterized so much of the 1960s counter-culture. But what makes the association between McLuhan's global village with Haight Ashbury and Woodstock so intriguing is that the 1960s counter-culture is usually depicted as technophobic. In rituals re-enacting so-called primitive rites, many people in the sixties sought to flee the strictures of culture and return to 'mother' nature. The return to the womb of the mother was often brought about with the help of a pharmacological supplement. For the members of the counter-culture, the white powder of the alchemist took the form of the white powder of psychedelics. The stone of the philosopher became the stoned of the tripper.

Though the 1980s and 1990s seem far from the 1960, the distance between Haight Ashbury and Silicon Valley is not as great as it initially appears. The counter-culture's technophobia always harboured a technophilia that promised to transform the chemico-religious prosthesis into the electronic prosthesis. Many of the vibrations that created the feelings of cosmic harmony were electronically generated. When John Perry Barlow, who is the lyricist for the Grateful Dead, publishes his Internet address in the pages of the slickest publication – *Mondo 2000* – promoting electronic telecommunications technology as the mind-altering agent that will bring the New Age, the circuit joining sixties drug culture with 1980s–90s technoculture is complete. Stuart Brand, one-time member of Ken Kesey's Merry Pranksters, founder of the *Whole Earth Catalogue* and author of *The Medial Lab: Inventing the Future at M.I.T.*, makes the telling point clearly and concisely: 'This generation swallowed computers whole, just like dope.'[5]

As its name suggests, the Berkeley-based *Mondo 2000* is an explicitly millenarian magazine. Mixing the most advanced telecommunications technology and imaginative software with designer drugs and mystico-eroticism, the contributors to *Mondo* create a blueprint for a cybertopia in which all desires will be immediately fulfilled. Transferring his hopes from a psychedelic to a technological revolution, contributing editor Timothy Leary preaches: 'Turn On. Boot Up. Download.' Elaborating Leary's technofantasies, editors Queen Mu and R. U. Sirius explain the broader vision of the future that unfolds in the pages of *Mondo 2000*:

> We're talking Cyber-Chatauqua; bringing cyberculture to the people! Artificial awareness modules. Visual music. Vidscan magazines. Brain-boosting technologies. William Gibson's Cyberspace Matrix – fully realized!
> Our scouts are out there on the frontier sniffing the breeze and guess what? All the old war horses are dead. Eco-fundamentalism is out, conspiracy theory is démodé, drugs are obsolete. There's a new whiff of apocalypticism across the land. A general sense that we are living at a very special juncture in the evolution of the species . . .

Yet the pagan innocence and idealism that was the sixties remains, and continues to exert its fascination on today's kids. Look at old footage of *Woodstock* and you wonder: where have all those wide-eyed, ecstatic, organism-slurping kids gone? They're all across the land, dormant like deeply buried perennials. But their mutated nucleotides have given us a whole new generation of sharpies, mutants, and superbrights, and in them we must put our faith – and power.

> The cybernet is in place. If fusion *is* real, we'll find out about it fast. The kids are at the controls. . . . We're talking about Total Possibilities. Radical assaults on the limits of biology, gravity and time. The end of Artificial Scarcity. The dawn of a new humanism. High-jacking technology for personal empowerment, fun and games. Flexing those synapses! Stoking those neuropeptides! Making Bliss States our normal waking consciousness. *Becoming* the Bionic Angel.[6]

It would be a mistake to allow the hype and irony of such declarations to obscure what they can teach us about our present situation and the direction in which we seem to be heading. The writers of *Mondo 2000* are attempting to form a bridge between Gibson's twenty-first-century cyberspace and the technocentric world of the late twentieth century.

When one roams the offices of Silicon Valley and the halls of MIT's Media Lab, the disruptive gap between the present and the future begins to fade. In many ways, we already inhabit cyberspace. Fibre optic cables, satellite up-links and down-links, telecommunications systems, Internet,

World Wide Web, and Reality Net combine to create a network of networks that is named *The Matrix*. In ways that are still only dimly visible, this Matrix is giving birth to new subjects and transforming the very structures that constitute the time and space of our dwelling. Within this net, we all become cyborgs.

The arrival of the cyborg is made possible by the gradual removal of the barriers separating the human and nonhuman as well as interiority and exteriority. This collapse of differences proceeds in two directions at once: from outer to inner and, conversely, from inner to outer. On the one hand, the body itself is progressively colonized by prosthetic devices. Implants, transplants, artificial organs, artificial insemination, genetic engineering, and synthetic drugs make it harder and harder to be sure where the so-called human ends and the nonhuman begins. On the other hand, artificial wombs, test-tube babies, artificial intelligence, and computer literacy 'externalize' bodily and mental functions to such an extent that the outer is no more merely outer and the inner is simply inner. No longer purely human, we are not quite yet replicants. When Gibson and his fellow cyberpunks extrapolate from the present to the near-future, they see a world where latter-day golems pose unimaginable threats as well as unthinkable possibilities. If 'natural' organs can be infinitely replaced by 'artificial' devices, and the contents of the mind can be preserved by being downloaded into the Matrix, then the dream of achieving immortality would seem to have been realized.

Though the technology is new, the dream is old – terribly old. Howard Rheingold, author of *Virtual Reality* (1991) and editor of *Whole Earth Review*, describes the leading edge of telecommunications research as 'the science of presence'. To underscore his point, Rheingold quotes Yamaguchi's 1989 'Proposal for a Large Visual Field Display':

> Effectiveness of visual communication and remote operation can best be achieved if the observer becomes totally involved in the displayed image through a feeling of 'being there.' The sensation of virtual existence or enhanced reality is activated by the capability of a precise pixel expression and a large visual field display. (Rheingold, 1991, p. 234)

'Being there': *Da Sein*. The *da* of *Sein* and the *Sein* of *da*: the fantasy of ontotheology is now translated to the telepresence of virtual reality. Virtual reality is, in many ways, the inevitable conclusion of what Guy DeBord (1983) labels a 'society of the spectacle'. With the inexorable expansion of the mediascape, all reality is increasingly mediaized and thus virtualized. What cultural critics so far have failed to realize is that the twentieth-century culture of simulacra extends the network of nineteenth-century speculative philosophy. Postmodernism is the idealism of the image in which the real becomes – or is revealed always to have been – the hyperreal. This hyperreal, it seems, is present – totally present – in the here and now of virtual reality. To plug into virtual reality is to jack into the Now. The presence of this present fulfils the desires of terminal faith.

Given the relays whose circuits we have been following, it should not come as a surprise that there is an important erotic dimension to emerging telecommunications technology. Nor should we be surprised to learn that in the tangled nets of this New Age the phone company becomes our surrogate mother. As Avital Ronell points out in her remarkable work *The Telephone Book* (1989), the telephone is 'a substitute for the womb'. The phone line, like the alchemist's furnace, is our link to the matrix. This is actually Freud's insight. Freud begins *Civilization and Its Discontents* (1961/1930) by rethinking the ancient question of the origin of religion. In the course of his reflections, Freud charts an astonishing course in which he argues that human beings attempt to supplement their insufficiencies first with a chemical and then with artistic, religious and technological or, more precisely, electronic 'prostheses'. His opening comments on religion are a 'response to a call' – though it appears not to have been a telephone call – of a friend who was responding to Freud's *The Future of an Illusion* (1928):

> I had sent him my small book that treats religion as an illusion, and he answered that he entirely agreed with my judgment upon religion, but that he was sorry I had not properly appreciated the true source of religious sentiments. . . . It is a feeling that he would like to call a sensation of 'eternity,' a feeling as of something limitless, unbounded – as it were, 'oceanic.' (1961, p. 11)[7]

Describing this oceanic sense as 'a feeling of an indissoluble bond of being at one with the external world as a whole', Freud traces its source to the original unity of the ego and the world. This primal identity is the psychological version of Schelling's *Indifferenzpunkt*. In the prelapsarian condition of plenitude, all desires are satisfied and all longings fulfilled. More precisely, neither desire nor need has yet emerged. The source of this archaic satisfaction is, of course, the mother. Before the beginning, mother and child are one; after the maternal bond is broken, life becomes a ceaseless *recherche du temps perdu*.

While admitting that the oceanic feeling exists in some people, Freud denies that it is the *fons et origo* of religion. Trying to salvage his argument in *The Future of an Illusion* (1928), he reasserts that religion originates in the infant's sense of helplessness and the longing for a protective father that it engenders. He is, none the less, forced to confess that his analysis might be incomplete:

The origin of the religious attitude can be traced back in clear outlines as far as the feeling of infantile helplessness. There may be something further behind that, but for the present it is wrapped in obscurity. (1961, p. 19)

What lies behind the father is, of course, the mother. The loss of the mother creates desires that can never be completely fulfilled. In the absence of true satisfaction, a series of supplements inevitably emerges. Freud identifies four 'substitute satisfactions' that represent a gradual refinement of the method for sublimating base instincts into generally acceptable cultural currency.

If, as Marx insists, religion is an opiate, then opiates are, in a certain sense, religious. By incorporating 'intoxicating drugs', Freud argues, people attempt to overcome the suffering caused by their incompletion and inadequacy:

The crudest, but also the most effective among these methods of influence is the chemical one – intoxication. I do not think that anyone completely understands its mechanism, but it is a fact that there are foreign substances which, when present in the blood or tissues, directly cause us pleasurable sensations; and they also so alter the conditions governing our sensibility that we become incapable of receiving unpleasurable impulses. (1961, p. 25)

The artist refines the strategies of the pharmacist. Art is, in effect, a drug synthesized to relieve the symptoms of loss and deprivation. In art, 'satisfaction is obtained from illusions, which are recognized as such without the discrepancy between them and reality being allowed to interfere with them'. In psychoanalytic theory, the line separating the hallucinations of the addict, and the fantasies of the artist, from the delusions of the madman is extraordinarily fine and ever-shifting. In an effort to avoid falling into madness, individuals join together to share their fantasies. One result of such communion is religion. Explaining what he regards as the definitive difference between art and religion, Freud writes:

A special importance attaches to the case in which this attempt to procure a certainty of happiness and a protection against suffering through a delusional remolding of reality is made by a considerable number of people in common. The religions of mankind must be classed among the mass-delusions of this kind. No one, needless to say, who shares a delusion ever recognizes it as such. (1961, p. 29)

But a shared delusion is still a delusion. Chemical, artistic and religious supplements remain impotent to negotiate the difference between the inner and outer, ideal and real, pleasure and reality. If desire is to be fulfilled, even partially, the fix must become technological.

Technology is, of course, as old as culture itself. To trace its origin, Freud returns to the dawn of history.

'If we go back far enough,' he argues, 'we find that the first acts of civilization were the use of tools, the gaining of control over fire and the construction of dwellings. Among these, the control over fire stands out as a quite extraordinary and unexampled achievement, while the others opened paths that man has followed ever since, and the stimulus to which is easily guessed. With every tool man is perfecting his own organs, whether motor or sensory, or is removing the limits of their functioning. (1961, p. 37)

Freud actually anticipates Eliade's claim that the founders of technology were 'the masters of fire'. Tools forged in the heat of fire function as 'extensions of their organs'. But what organs are at stake in technology? Freud supplements his myth of the origin of technology with a footnote in which he explains that 'the legends that we possess leave no doubt about the originally phallic view taken of tongues of flame as they shoot upwards' (1961, p. 36). The observation suggests that if fire is the trope for technology, the central organ extended by technology appears to be the phallus. Since the function of the phallus is to reunite the one who possesses it with the mother, the search for the phallus is, in effect, the quest for reunion with the generative matrix that bears us all. If Freud's reading of technology is right, it would not seem to be an accident that the ever-present phone company is named *Ma* Bell.

In 1879, Theodore A. L. DuMoncel published a book entitled *The Telephone, the Microphone, and the Phonograph*. This work is less interesting for the story it tells than for the images it contains. The figure of the telephone receiver that DuMoncel includes in his book makes it perfectly clear that teledildonics is more than a century old. The phone appears as a displaced phallus constructed to send messages through the matrix. In every figure depicting telephonic communication, the flow is in the same direction: from man to woman – from the mouth or tongue of the man into the ear of the woman. It is not clear whether this ear is the ear of the virgin or what Derrida describes as 'the ear of the other'. Figuring what seems to be an immaculate conception, some of the images depict a woman engaged in self-insemination or at least auto-affection. Who is this woman to whom man is always talking?

In the sentence that begins after Freud interrupts his text to explain the phallic significance of fire, he lists the technological developments that help man correct his defects and hence overcome his inadequacies: motor power, ships and aircraft, spectacles, telescope, microscope, photographic camera, and gramophone disc. His concludes his catalogue with an instrument that discloses what he believes to be the general function of technology: the telephone.

With the help of the telephone he can hear at distances that would be respected as unattainable even in a fairy tale. Writing was in its origin the voice of an absent person; and the dwelling-house was a substitute for the mother's womb, the first lodging, for which in all likelihood man still longs, and in which he was safe and felt at ease. (1961, p. 38)

The string of associations released in this passage is astonishing. The lines Freud connects suggest that the telephone, which is a synecdoche for technology, binds us back to our original 'dwelling-house'. As we know from his famous essay on the uncanny, this dwelling-house is the mother's genitals. Like the miner's tunnel and the alchemist's furnace, the telephone appears to be 'a substitute for the mother's womb'. Our deepest desire, our most profound longing is to return to the womb–tomb of Mother Earth where eros and thanatos are one. What man wants, in other words, is not only woman but *incest*. If his call goes through, if the circuit is completed, he becomes one with the mother goddess. Within this electronic economy, technology is the elixir for which we have always been searching.

'These things that, by his science and technology,' Freud proceeds to explain, 'man has brought about on earth . . . not only sound like a fairy tale, they are an actual fulfillment of every – or of almost every fairy-tale wish':

> Long ago [man] formed an ideal conception of omnipotence and omni-science, which he embodied in his gods. To these gods he attributed every-thing that seemed unattainable to his wishes, or that was forbidden to him. One may say, therefore, that these gods were cultural ideals. Today he has come very close to the attainment of this ideal, he has almost become a god himself. . . . Man has, as it were, become a kind of prosthetic God. When he puts on his auxiliary organs he is truly magnificent; but those organs have not grown on to him and they still give him much trouble at times. Nevertheless, he is entitled to console himself with the thought that this development will not come to an end precisely with the year 1930 AD. Further ages will bring with them new and probably unimaginably great advances in this field of civilization and will increase man's likeness to God still more. (1961, pp. 38–9)

The ancient dream of the alchemist is far from over. For those who have terminal faith, to become one with the matrix is to attain immortality by being transformed into the divine. The transformer is the electronic net in which we are already entangled. Freud could not, of course, begin to envision the radical changes that telecommunications would bring by the end of the century. The dream of the New Age is not only omni-potence and omniscience but, perhaps more important, the omnipres-ence that immortality bestows. 'Telepresence', Howard Rheingold (1991) insists, 'is a form of out-of-body-experience' (p. 256). If carried far enough, sublimation creates a sense of the technological sublime in which even bliss becomes immaterial as the screen and I become one. Reflecting on the implications of the Gulf War, Paul Virilio (1991) comments:

> Curiously, telecommunications sets in motion in civil society the properties of divinity: ubiquity (being present everywhere at every instant), instantaneousness, immediacy, omnivision, omnipresence. Every one of us is metamorphosed into a divine being here and there at the same time.   (p. 70)

When every where is everywhere, a New Age approaches. Or so it seems. The end is approaching . . . approaching without arriving from the ever-not-so-distant future. We are counting down or up to the end and the beginning of the new millennium. The New Age that many are proclaiming will, like all the new ages in the past, be repeatedly deferred. This non-arrival does not, however, deprive the New Age of its power. To the contrary, the very impossibility of realizing the end is what lends the apocalyptic imagination its force. Far from destroying faith, infinite deferral creates the distance that creates the time and space for faithful vision. Every faith is, in the final analysis, terminal faith.

Notes

1 Mircea Eliade (1978) develops a survey of the historical background of alchemy. I have drawn on his insights throughout my account of alchemy.
2 As Gray (1952, pp. 205–20) points out, the homunculus is actually an alternative form of the philosophers' stone.
3 Goethe's Faust is, of course, obsessed with alchemy. As Robert Gray (1952) demonstrates, Goethe's fascination with alchemy informs all of his scientific and literary works. It is not insignificant that one of Goethe's official duties in Weimar was the oversight of the Bureau of Mines.
4 The pivotal figure who links alchemy and nineteenth-century romanticism and idealism is Jacob Böhme. Böhme's complex mystico-speculative vision represents a henological translation and formalization of the central tenets of alchemy. Numerous romantic poets and idealist philosophers were deeply influenced by Böhme's vision. Böhme's writings were especially important for Hegel.
5 Quoted in Roszak (1986, p. 150). Roszak, whose book *The Making of a Counter Culture* (1970) remains the most insightful analysis of the social trends of the sixties, also stresses the importance of electronic music and light shows for the mind-expanding rituals of the youth culture.
6 Queen Mu and R. U. Sirius, editorial, *Mondo 2000*, no. 7, Fall 1989. Quoted in Andrew Ross (1991, p. 163). Ross's chapters, entitled 'New Age – A Kinder, Gentler Science?' and 'Cyberpunk in Boystown', are particularly informative discussions of the social and cultural tendencies that I am examining in this chapter.
7 Ronell's account of the telephone is deeply informed by Freud's insights.

References

DeBord, Guy 1983: *Society of the Spectacle*. Detroit: Red and Black Press.

DuMoncel, Theodore 1879: *The Telephone, the Microphone, and the Phonograph.*

Eliade, Mircea 1978: *The Forge and the Crucible: The Origins and Structures of Alchemy*. Chicago: University of Chicago Press.

Freud, Sigmund 1928: *The Future of an Illusion*. London: Hogarth.

—— 1961 (orig. 1930): *Civilization and Its Discontents* (trans. James Strachey). New York: Norton and Norton.

Gibson, William 1984: *Neuromancer*. New York: Ace Books.

Gray, Robert 1952: *Goethe the Alchemist: A Study of Alchemical Symbolism in Goethe's Literary and Scientific Works*. Cambridge: Cambridge University Press.

Hegel, G. W. F. 1970: *Philosophy of Nature* (trans. Michael Petry). New York: Humanities Press, vol. II.

McLuhan, Marshall 1964: *Understanding Media: The Extensions of Man*. New York: McGraw-Hill.

Marinetti, Filippo 1972: The Founding Manifesto of Futurism. In R. W. Flint (ed.), *Marinetti: Selected Writings*, New York: Farrar, Strauss and Giroux.

Rheingold, Howard 1991: *Virtual Reality*. New York: Summit Books.

Ronell, Avital 1989: *The Telephone Book: Technology, Schizophrenia, Electric Speech*. Lincoln, Nebraska: University of Nebraska Press.

Ross, Andrew 1991: *Strange Weather: Culture, Science and Technology in the Age of Limits*. New York: Verso.

Roszak, Theodore 1970: *The Making of a Counter Culture*. London: Faber and Faber.

—— 1986: *The Cult of Information: The Folklore of Computers and the True Art of Thinking*. New York: Pantheon Books.

Schelling 1988: *Ideas for a Philosophy of Nature* (trans. Errol Harris and Peter Heath). New York: Cambridge University Press.

Snelders, H. A. M. 1970: Romanticism and Naturphilosophie and the Inorganic Natural Sciences 1797–1840: An Introductory Survey. *Studies in Romanticism*, vol. 9.

Virilio, Paul 1991: *L'écran du désert*. Paris: Galilée.

—— 1986: *Speed and Politics: An Essay on Dromology* (trans. Mark Polizzotti). New York: Semiotext(e).

CHAPTER FOUR

postmodern religion?

Zygmunt Bauman

'Religion' belongs to the family of curious, and often embarrassing concepts, which one perfectly understands until one wants to define them. Postmodern mind, for once, agrees to issue this family, maltreated or sentenced to deportation by the modern scientific reason, with a permanent residence permit. Postmodern mind, more tolerant (since better aware of its own weaknesses) than its modern predecessor and critic, resigns itself to the tendency of definitions to conceal as much as they reveal and to maim and obfuscate while pretending to clarify and straighten up. It also accepts the fact that all too often experience spills out of the verbal cages in which one would wish to hold it, that there are things of which one should keep silent since one cannot speak of them, and that the ineffable is as much an integral part of the human mode of being-in-the-world as is the linguistic net in which one tries (in vain, as it happens, though no less vigorously for that reason) to catch it.

The arrival of postmodern serenity does not mean, of course, that the desperate attempts to 'define religion' are likely to grind to a halt. Postmodern mind did not quite live up to André Breton's pugnacious call 'to deal drastically with *that hatred of the marvellous* which is rampant in some people'.[1] The postmodern mind is too humble to forbid and too weak to banish the excesses of the modern mind's ambition. It only, so to speak, puts them in perspective – lays bare their inner springs as well as their vanity. And so the frantic efforts to 'define religion' will go on unabated, trials long ago discredited yet by now conveniently forgotten (thanks to the 'collective amnesia' and the 'Columbus complex', which, as Pitirim Sorokin observed a long time ago in his *Fads and Foibles in Modern Sociology and Related Sciences* (1956), keep the kind of speech called social sciences forever vigorous and self-confident) will be rehashed no end and with no greater chance than before of passing the test of time.

More often than not, 'defining religion' amounts to replacing one ineffable by another – to the substitution of the incomprehensible for the unknown . . . This is the case with the most popular definitions, which have served mainly to placate the scientific conscience of sociologists eager to declare the embracement of the unembraceable: the definitions which 'defined religion' pointing to its relation to the 'sacred', 'transcendental', 'enchanted' or even, in the tamed and thereby vulgarized renditions of Rudolf Otto (1959), the 'tremendous'.[2]

Define, *and* Perish

What worries the obsessive definition-makers is the belief that if we fail to coin a 'rational definition' of religious phenomena (that is, a definition which would pass the test of that rationality through which social science constitutes and legitimizes itself), we would enter the postmodern world ill-prepared to tackle the questions proclaimed central by the sociological descriptions of historical trends. Is the world we inhabit more, or less religious than it used to be? Do we witness a decline, redeployment or renaissance of religiosity? The way to resolve (or, perhaps, by-pass?) the problem leads through the tested stratagem of cleverly chosen definition. By this reckoning, two types of definitions may get us out of trouble. One removes the problem of historical trends from the agenda – by dissolving the issue of religion in some unquestionably universal and eternal traits of the human existential predicament; the other, on the contrary, tapers the definition in such a way that religiosity becomes as precisely measurable as the waist size, thereby ensuring that the elusive issue of sociocultural trends is replaced with a thoroughly manageable problem of statistical tendency.

As it happens, we find examples of both types of stratagems in the records of the European Conference held in 1993 in Amalfi. On the one hand, Jeffrey C. Alexander believes that by an expedient of circumcision (cutting off the final 'n' from 'religion') we move 'away from the mundane and commonsensical to a more fundamental understanding of religion', and then we can see better that religion (now returned to its 'latinate form' as 'religio', exotic and mysterious and thus containing presumably untapped supplies of illumination) 'is the name we give to the activity that allows us to feel we are in contact with this noumenal world "beyond our own", which to be sure is a world of the imagination, of projected fantasy and the sensibility of the unconscious mind. In this precise [sic] sense, and no other more ontological one, religion allows transcendence.' The statement that religion is 'the most omnipresent of the qualities that distinguish humankind' follows therefore as no surprise, being a foregone conclusion. Religion is the most universal of human qualities simply because everything human – from painting, through orgasm, to writing sociology – has been defined as a religious phenomenon. On the other extreme, we find in the same volume Bernard Barber's and Alan Segal's declaration of intent to make the definition 'rigorously analytic, useful for picking out the religious aspect or component in a complex of concrete activities and beliefs'. *If* such a definition is coined (not very convincingly, for reasons spelled out before, Barber and Segal want to reach it through the far from obvious concept of the 'transcendental'), then one can be satisfied that 'much that goes on in churches, synagogues and mosques is not religious by our analytical definition', and – we may say – one can compose an inventory of the things religious with something approaching the chartered accountant's standard of precision.[3]

Whether one 'defines' religion through things *transcendental*, or through things *ultimate* – practical application of the definition remains as tall an order, and in the end as contentious, as the definition itself. As Thomas Luckmann (1967) has pointed out, 'matters that come to be of "ultimate" significance for the members of later generations are likely to be congruent only to a limited extent with matters that were of "ultimate" significance to earlier generations' (p. 82). One can avoid this difficulty by trying to obtain the description of the 'transcendental' or 'ultimate' from the institutionalized religious spokesmen, but then, for practical and theoretical purposes, one ends up with a tautology: churches are about religion, and religion is what churches do. Or one wishes to walk without institutional crutches, pinpointing the relevant phenomena according to one's own interpretation or the popular intuitions of the 'transcendental' or 'ultimate' – and then one ends up with a conceptual net either too tight or too porous, catching too many, or leaving out too many human thoughts and actions in the unexplored remainder of the pool of life.

Let me repeat: the postmodern mind is altogether less excited than its modern adversary by the prospect (let alone moved by the urge) to enclose the world into a grid of neat categories and clear-cut divisions. We are somewhat less horrified today by the nasty habit things have of spilling over their definitional boundaries, or even by the premonition that the drawing of such boundaries with any degree of lasting reliability defies human resources. We are also learning to live with the revelation that one cannot articulate all one knows, and that to understand – to know how to go on – does not always require the availability of a verbalized precept. We are not all that appalled by the necessity to settle for 'family resemblances' where the modern pursuit of transparency goaded us to seek the shared 'distinctive features'. I propose therefore, that in opposition to the traditional concerns of the 'sociology of religion', what comes at the top of our list of interests when we wish to understand the phenomena of religion and religiosity is not so much the need to 'define them clearly' as the need to find out 'how up till now social mechanisms were able to operate', 'pointing out on what kinds of assumptions, what kinds of familiar, unchallenged, unconsidered modes of thought the practices that we accept rest' (Foucault, 1988, pp. 50, 154). Perhaps in the case of religion more than in all other cases, because religiosity is, after all, nothing else but the intuition of the limits to what we, the humans, being humans, may do and comprehend.

God, or Insufficiency of Self-sufficiency

In his classic and in my view unsurpassed analysis of the way in which religiosity is gestated by human existential conditions, Leszek Kołakowski (1982) proposes that religion is not 'a collection of statements about God, Providence, heaven and hell'. Rather:

> Religion is indeed the awareness of human insufficiency, it is lived in the admission of weakness. . . .
> The invariable message of religious worship is: 'from the finite to the infinite the distance is always infinite . . .'.
> [W]e face two irreconcilable ways of accepting the world and our position in it, neither of which may boast of being more 'rational' than the other. . . . Once taken, any choice imposes criteria of judgement which infallibly support it in a circular logic: if there is no God, empirical criteria alone have to guide our thinking, and empirical criteria do not lead to God; if God exists, He gives us clues about how to perceive His hand in the course of events, and with the help of those clues we recognize the divine sense of whatever happens.   (pp. 194, 199, 202)[4]

The suspicion that there are things that humans cannot do and things which humans cannot understand when left to their own wits and muscles, however stretched by the contraptions which the humans may invent using the same wits and muscles they have been endowed with, is hardly ever far removed from the level of consciousness; yet it seldom reaches that level. Most of the time we (and that 'we' includes the philosophers working full time with the 'ultimate' and unsolvable questions of being) live in the state called by Anthony Giddens (1990) *ontological security* – 'a sense of reliability of persons and things', aided and abetted by the 'predictability of the (apparently) minor routines of day-to-day life (p. 82).[5] The opposite of ontological security is that *existential anxiety* which dawns upon the trustful or merely happy-go-lucky at the rare moments when it becomes evident that the daily routine's ability to self-perpetuate has its unencroachable time limits. I suggest that by far the most seminal of daily routine's accomplishments is precisely cutting the life-tasks to the size of human self-sufficiency. In so far as the routine may go on undisturbed, it offers little occasion to ruminate on the causes and purposes of the universe; the limits of human self-sufficiency can be kept out of sight.

We have come to believe the churches far and wide which, whenever pressed, insist that they provide the service necessitated by the overwhelming human urge to get answers to 'fundamental questions' of the purpose of life and to placate the fears that arise from the absence of a good answer. One wonders, though; there is little in the daily routine which prompts such eschatological inquiry. Cattle must be fed, crops harvested, taxes paid, dinner cooked, roofs repaired; or the brief must be written or studied, letter mailed, application filed, appointment kept, video repaired, tickets bought . . . Before one has had the time to think of eternity, bedtime is coming, and then another day filled to the brim with things to be done or undone. One wonders; it may well be that churches, like other producers of goods and services, had to occupy themselves first with the production of their own consumers: they had, if not to create, then at least to amplify and sharpen up the needs meant to be satisfied by their services, and so to make their work indispensable.

Of the pastoral power, whose techniques Christianity elaborated and brought to perfection, Michel Foucault (1988) wrote that

> [a]ll those Christian techniques of examination, confession, guidance, obedience, have an aim: to get individuals to work at their own 'mortification' in this world. Mortification is not death, of course, but it is a renunciation of this world and of oneself: a kind of everyday death. A death which is supposed to provide life in another world.

It stands to reason that only when such a mortification has been implanted as a duty of the individual, when an 'everyday death' has come to be accepted as the good, 'value for money' price for the promised 'life in another world', that the shepherd's role 'to ensure the salvation of his flock' may be acknowledged, respected, and endowed with power-generating capacity (Foucault, 1988, pp. 70, 62). People have to first become concerned with personal salvation, to desire the posthumous reward and fear the posthumous punishment, to need the shepherd – and need him in *this* life, now endowed with an added value of the continuous rehearsal for the life to come. If this is the case, then 'religion' has had to be *inserted* into the *Lebenswelt* of the individual, rather than being *born out of it* or sited inside it from the beginning. The worry about eternity does not 'come naturally' (much as the philosophical worry about the ultimate foundations of knowledge is not born, as Edmund Husserl was at pains to show, from the 'natural attitude', in which we are, daily and with no interruption, 'immersed naively', taking things as 'a matter of course'.[6] Great effort is needed for that worry to outweigh the gravity of daily concerns aimed at the tasks to be performed and results to be consummated in this one and only life which men and women know directly, since they make it out of their own daily work.

The hope of eternal life, the dream of heaven and the horror of hell are not the issue of parthenogenesis, though the philosophers of religion

have well-nigh succeeded in convincing us to the contrary. That excru-
ciating terror of insufficiency which, as Kołakowski suggests, makes us
susceptible to the religious message, could only follow the setting of tasks
which went beyond the reach of tools developed to tackle the tasks of
daily life: and which therefore *created* human insufficiency. Far from laying to rest the worry about the 'ultimate', now translated as the question
of salvation, churches saw to it that it saturated every nook and cranny of
the human mind and conscience, as well as presiding over the totality
of life activities.

Modernity, or Doing Without God

I propose that the case of the 'innateness', of the 'natural' presence of
religious drive in the universal human predicament, in the species-bound
way of 'being in the world', has not been proved. It has only been relent-
lessly insinuated; explicitly, through the acceptance of the ecclesiastical
self-legitimation formula as the explanation of religiosity, or obliquely,
through describing the new (or rather newly discovered) paucity of interest in eschatology as the outcome of 'secularization' (that is, of a process
defined by its starting point, a process of 'departure' from the 'norm').
Above all, it has been 'made plausible' by the 'there must be religiosity
somehow, somewhere' attitude of philosophers and sociologists who
eagerly seek a way of re-defining modern and postmodern concerns as
religious 'in their essence' or 'in the last instance'.[7]

I propose that not all strategies of human being-in-the world must be
ultimately religious (that is, grounded in an intuition of the unassailable
insufficiency and weakness of human powers), and that not all of them
were. Most notably, the modern formula of human life on earth has
been articulated in terms of a sharply alternative strategy: by design or
by default, humans are alone to take care of things human, and *therefore
the sole things that matter to the humans are the things humans may take care
of*. Such a premise may be perceived as sad and a reason to despair, or
on the contrary – as a cause for exhilaration and optimism; both perceptions, though, are decisive only to the lives devoted to philosophical
reflection, while appearing only at the rare 'philosophical moments' in
ordinary lives.

The organization of daily life is by and large independent from philosophical sadness and joy and evolves around concerns which seldom,
if at all, include the worry about the ultimate limits of things which
humans, as humans, could be reasonably (and effectively!) concerned
about. The modern revolution consisted precisely in the rejection of that
latter type of worries, or taking them off the agenda altogether, or constructing the life agenda in such a way that little or no time was left to

attend to such worries; one may also say that it consisted in plugging the ears to the homilies of redemption and salvation and closing the eyes to pictures of posthumous bliss or doom. The concerns which fill human life since the beginning of modernity relate to *problems* – and 'problems' are, by definition, such tasks as are cut to the measure of the genuine or assumed human skills, tasks 'one can do something about' or 'one may and should find out what to do about'. It was that modern strategy which Marx extrapolated into a 'law of history', when he proposed that 'no historical era sets itself tasks it cannot fulfil'. Whether this proposition is true as a timeless principle is debatable. But it certainly applies to the modern era.

In his recent study of the cultural consequences of modern revolution, which he calls 'humanism', John Carroll (1993) composed a poignant description of that alternative strategy of life:

> Its ambition was to found a human order on earth, in which freedom and happiness prevailed, without any transcendental or supernatural supports – an entirely human order. . . . To place man at the centre meant that he had to become the Archimedean point around which everything revolved. . . .
>
> The axiom on which the humanist rock was to be forged was put as well by Pico della Mirandola in 1486 as by anyone: 'We can become what we will'. . . . So the humanist fathers put their founding axiom: man is all-powerful, if his will is strong enough. He can create himself. He can choose to be courageous, honourable, just, rich, influential, or not. (pp. 2–3).[8]

I believe that Carroll's apt description of the humanist ambition would gain from a further clarification. In that world – made to human measure and guided entirely by human needs – which the humanists proposed to create, not everything was to be subjected to human will; but that will was to be directed solely towards things which could be mastered, controlled, improved by human means. Contrary to Carroll's suggestion, that the humanist creed drew inspiration from Archimedes, who believed that he stole the secrets of the gods, it rather turned Protagoras's contemplative idea that 'man is the measure of all things' into a declaration of practical intent. No wonder that in Carroll's list of all the things men can become, one 'thing', crucial to the religious promise – that of eternal life – is missing. Humanism was not so much about being able to become whatever one may will, as about willing to become what one truly, given the ample, though not necessarily infinite, richness of human potential, can: willing only what one can do something concrete and practical about making true. Afterlife clearly did not belong in this category of things. The idea of human self-sufficiency undermined the grip of institutionalized religion not by promising an alternative way to eternal life, but by drawing human attention away from it; by focusing instead on tasks which humans may perform, and whose consequences they are able to experience as long as they are still 'experiencing beings' – and this means here, in this life.

The celebratory mood of humanist writers was not the cause of modernity. It was but a philosophical gloss over the collapse of the old order and the emergence of a new one – differing from the one it was about to replace by being understood from the start as something which needed to be *constructed* and *designed* – not found and protected. In the absence of any *given* order of things, it was clear that there would be as much sense and order in the world as its human inhabitants managed to insert into it; and that the ordering work at the top must be replicated by the work at the bottom – each individual having to shape and direct his or her own life, which otherwise would remain shapeless and bereft of purpose. The modern life strategy has been a matter not of choice, wise or foolish, but of a rational adjustment to totally new life conditions which humans had never visited before.

In this process of rational adjustment, there was little use for religion. As Alain Touraine (1974) has pointed out, the 'uses' of religion are of three kinds (pp. 213–14). First, religion may impose the dependence and routine subordination to a rhythm of life which is interpreted as natural or supernatural, but which in both cases is experienced as invariable and invulnerable. Such rhythm however, let us observe, has been most conspicuously broken, and the name 'modernity' stands for its collapse; there was not much left which religion, with its message of a pre-ordained, once-off created world, could serve.

Secondly, membership of a church or a sect may play an important role in keeping the walls of social divisions solid and impenetrable, and thus served well a social structure marked by low mobility and permanence of stratifying factors. But, let us observe again, such rigid *structure* has been gradually eroded in the ever more vigorous and flexible, diffuse and de-centred processes of *structuration*, and again, religion with its message of 'divine chain of being' was ill fitted to make sense of the new situation and new challenges. For reasons spelled out above, one can agree with Touraine's opinion that the 'importance of the first two aspects of religious life' has been greatly reduced; but in opposition to Touraine one would also point out that the reduction in question was the outcome not of 'de-christianization' but of those deep transformations in life conditions and viable life strategies of which the alleged 'de-christianization' was itself one of the effects.

The third use of religion Touraine describes as 'the apprehension of human destiny, existence, and death'. In the case of this function, Touraine notes the on-going 'isolation' of religion: 'like the dance and painting, religion becomes a leisure activity, that is, deliberate, unregulated behaviour, personal and secret'. This statement can be accepted with the proviso that it is the interest in 'existence and death' itself which has been relegated to leisure pastimes, such as bear only a marginal impact on the way the day-by-day and serious life activities are organized. Whether the extant 'churches and sects', and particularly those among them which boast the greatest and the fastest growing numbers of followers, can be similarly marginalized as leisure commodities, is debatable. The important point, though, is that in order to resist such a marginalization, churches and sects which have managed to do just that need to appropriate other functions than catering to the preoccupation with the mysteries of existence and death.

Anti-eschatological Revolution

Not unlike the late-modern modernist art, which – having pushed the modern obsession with pure and perfect form to its logical end – reached the brink of the destruction of art as such, and thereby paved the way for the postmodern aesthetic equanimity and formal tolerance, the late-premodern 'art of pious life' had pushed the church-inspired obsession with death and posthumous salvation to a radical extreme beyond which continuation of life became virtually impossible, thereby making some sort of psychological 'neutralization' of death imperative.

In his exhaustive study of the late-medieval and early-modern culture of sin and fear, Jean Delumeau (1990) found the fascination and infatuation with posthumous life, and the demands of the salvation-oriented piety, raised to heights no longer attainable by people still engaged in normal life-pursuits. The monks, preachers and other 'artists of religious life' set standards of piety which clashed not just with popular 'sinful' inclinations, but with the maintenance of life as such, and thereby cast the prospects of 'eternal life' out of reach of all but the few saints. The care for salvation turned rapidly into a luxury for the chosen few, able and willing to opt out from a life normal for the rest and practise outworldly asceticism; and by the same token ceased to be a viable proposition for the ordinary people wishing or obliged to carry on their business of life as usual.

The macabre derives from the ascetic contemplation of monks entirely turned towards the otherworld and who sought to convince themselves – and to persuade others – of the wicked character of our illusions here below. This ecclesiastical discourse then spread out of the monasteries through preaching and iconography – that is, through the evangelism of fear. . . . The insistence on the macabre, in the wake of the *contemptus mundi*, thus stood within the logic of a vast enterprise of guilt-infliction aimed toward salvation in the afterlife.   (1990, pp. 112–13)

The life of self-immolation, mortification of the body, rejection of worldly joys was what salvation, according to its prophets and devoted practitioners, demanded: they urged 'penitence and detachment from worldly things such as honours, wealth, beauty, and carnal desire'. As could only be expected, the sheer exorbitance of such demands had effects not at all resonant with the preachers' intentions. One effect was a morbid taste 'for spectacles of suffering and death', 'culminating in willfully pernicious scenes of tortures, executions, and slaughters'. 'Departing from the moral and religious lesson', continues Delumeau, 'there was a gradual sliding into sadistic pleasure.' The *macabre* turned, one might say, into an art for art's sake. On the other hand, and more seminally, *memento mori* showed the pronounced tendency of turning into *memento vivere*: 'Since life is so short, let us hasten to enjoy it. Since the dead body will be so repulsive, let us hurry to gain all possible pleasure from it while it is still in good health' (Delumeau, 1990, pp. 112–13). All the more so, as the earning of spiritual salvation by rules excruciatingly difficult to obey was becoming an increasingly nebulous prospect for most.

At their radical extreme, the inflammation of death-fright and the fomenting of the dream of eternal life proved, so to speak, counter-productive. They gave rise to altogether different yearnings, which could hardly be tied down to religious purposes and thus were blatantly unfit for employment in the service of ecclesiastical power. More importantly, they jarred with the prerequisites of daily life and of the reproduction of its conditions. If life this side of death was to continue, concerns with 'honours, wealth, beauty and carnal desire' had to gain an upper hand over such concerns with life-after-death as required their renunciation – and they did. Modernity undid what the long rule of Christianity had done – rebuffed the obsession with afterlife, focused attention on the life 'here and now', redeployed life activities around different narratives with earthly targets and values, and all-in-all attempted to defuse the horror of death. The toning down of the impact of the awareness of mortality, and – more seminally yet – the detachment of it from religious signific-ance, thus followed.

This effect has been achieved in modern times through the application of three not necessarily coherent, yet closely intertwined and in the end complementary, strategies.

Firstly, like everything else in modern life death has been subjected to the division of labour; it has become a 'specialized' concern. For the rest, the non-professionals, death has become a somewhat shameful and embarrassing affair, somewhat akin to pornography (as Geoffrey Gorer (1965) observed), an event not to be discussed in public and certainly 'not in front of the children'. The dead and particularly the dying have been removed beyond the confines of daily life, assigned separate spaces not accessible to the public, and entrusted to the care of 'professionals'. The elaborate and spectacular public ceremony of funerals has been replaced with the brief and on the whole private event of the burial or incineration of the body under the efficient supervision of the experts.

Secondly, similarly to all other 'wholes', the total and unassailable prospect of death has been sliced and fragmented into innumerable small and smaller-still threats to survival. One cannot do much with that prospect as such, and it would be utterly foolish to concern oneself with things one can do nothing about. But the little threats may be fought back, pushed aside, even defeated. And fighting them back is an activity so time- and energy-consuming, that no time or energy is left for musing on the ultimate vanity of it all. Death does not appear any more, to modern men and women, as the scythe-wielding skeleton in the black gown, who knocks on the door only once and which cannot be barred entry. Significantly, modernity has not produced another symbol to replace the sinister figure of Death; it has no need for an alternative 'unified' symbol, since death itself has lost its past unity – it is now dissolved in the minute, yet innumerable, traps and ambushes of daily life. One tends to hear it knocking now and again, daily, in fatty fast foods, in listeria-infected eggs, in cholesterol-rich temptations, in sex without condoms, in cigarette smoke, in asthma-inducing carpet mites, in the 'dirt you see and the germs you do not', in lead-loaded petrol and the lead-free, in fluoride-treated tapwater and fluoride untreated water, in too much and too little exercise, in over-eating and over-dieting, in too much ozone content and the hole in the ozone layer; but one knows now how to barricade the door when death knocks, and one can always replace the old and rusty locks and bolts and alarms with 'new and improved ones'.

Thirdly, while the death of the near and dear has become a thoroughly private and semi-secret event, human death as such has turned into a daily occurrence, too familiar and ordinary to arouse horror or any other strong emotions; just a spectacle among other spectacles which combine into the *Lebenswelt* of the modern cinema-goer and video-borrower. Like all other spectacles, death 'as seen on TV' is a drama played in *virtual reality*, no less but no more tangible and 'given to hand' than the exploits of the Startrek heroes, gun-slinging cowboys or trigger-happy Rambos and Terminators. Death game is like other games – dangerous perhaps but amusing, and amusing because dangerous. It holds a considerable measure of fascination; like the late-medieval *danse macabre*, it tends to develop into an art for art's sake. And, just as the sight of a crowd of naked bodies does not arouse sexual passions which are easily triggered by a solitary nakedness, people dying 'like flies', in droves, take the sting of dread from the sight of death. In a form yet more impressive than Aldous Huxley imagined, his vision of 'death conditioning' (showing children people in their death-throes, while feeding them their favourite sweets) has come to be practised with effects not far from those he envisaged.

The overall effect of the modern ways of responding to the factuality of death – by its domestication-cum-estrangement or by dissolving the *issue* of the inevitability of death in the plethora of practical *problems* related to the effectivity of health-protecting techniques – has been a considerable weakening of the conception of life as life-towards-death (as Heidegger famously articulated it, with a retrospective – or was it rather a posthumous? – wisdom). Death, deployed once by religion as a kind of extraordinary event which nevertheless imparts meaning to all ordinary events, has itself turned into an ordinary event – even if, admittedly, the last in the chain of ordinary events, the last episode in the string of episodes. No more a momentous happening, ushering in the existence of another, longer duration and graver significance, but merely the 'end of a story' – and stories hold interest only as long as they envelop and hold open the possibilities of surprise and adventure. Nothing happens after the story is over – and so those who put themselves in charge of that *nothing*, the religious experts, do not have much to offer to those who are engrossed in living the story . . .

And the stories lived by modern men and women are, indeed, engrossing.

Uncertainty, Non-ontological

With a good deal of simplification, we can say that the lives of premodern men and women held little uncertainty. In a world virtually unchangeable within the horizon of individual life, its residents – ascribed from their birth to clearly charted life-tracks – expected little surprise as long as they lived. The time of death, impossible to predict and coming from nowhere and unannounced, was the only window through which they could get a glimpse of uncertainty; and the uncertainty that might have been glimpsed were they brought to that window and made to look through it, was the uncertainty of existence as such; the ontological uncertainty, one uniquely suitable to be grasped and told in eschatological narrative.

With the progress of modern medicine, which has supplied virtually every instance of death with its specific, 'rational' and 'logical' cause, death is no more a caprice of blind fate, no more as utterly haphazard and unpredictable as it used to be. Having become a natural, not at all mysterious and even partly manageable occurrence, it offers little ground to eschatological ruminations. On the other hand, it is the *life before death* that offers daily insights into uncertainty. Only what is glimpsed through the many windows offered by the vagaries of modern life, by the brittleness of achievements and fragility of human bonds, is not the *ontological* variant of uncertainty: and so the eschatological narrative is ill fitted to unlock its mysteries and vent the anxieties such mysteries foment. The puzzle, most frightening and ubiquitously present in all daily pursuits, is the course of one's life, not the moment of death. It is the ebb and flow of luck, the rise and fall of values one has got used to cherishing, the eccentricity of ever-changing expectations, the capriciousness of rules which keep changing before the game is finished, the cacophony of voices in which it is hard to pinpoint the leading motif – which most painfully, with most immediate and tangible effects, defy understanding. All these challenges to understanding, to 'knowing how to go on', are human products; they bear witness not to human insufficiency, but to human omnipotence (even the sinister vagaries of climate, the premonitions of a new ice age or of the planet's overheating, are traceable to what humans do or neglect to do); and my poor response to human-made challenges is the fault of the human – all-too-human – faculties of one human being: myself. The uncertainty I suffer from is the outcome of human potency, and it is human potency that I need to guide me on the road to certainty.

Already in 1957, in *Die Seele im technischen Zeitalter*, Arnold Gehlen noted that

> fewer and fewer people act on the basis of personal, internalized value orientations.... But why are there fewer such people? Clearly because the economic, political, and social atmosphere has become hard to grasp intellectually, and hard to live up to morally, and because it changes at an accelerated pace....
>
> In a world where such things go on, any belief in constant principles of orientation is in danger of being denied that minimum of external confirmation without which it cannot survive. (1980, orig. 1957, pp. 52–3)

People whose already internalized orientations keep being devalued, even ridiculed, by the day, need authoritative guidance; but the guidance they seek and may reasonably expect, a guidance adequate to the kind of agony they experience, is one likely to call on their own resources, aimed at reforming (correcting, improving, developing) their own know-how, attitudes and psychical predispositions. 'As soon as the *polis* ceased to lay down the law about everything, the way opened up for the emergence of previously unthinkable stirrings of the psyche' – observes Gehlen (quoting Ernst Howald's *Die Kultur der Antike*) (ibid., p. 75); and the 'stirrings of the psyche' to which Gehlen alludes are the prodromal symptoms of the birth of *identity*, that most seminal of all modern creations/inventions. The birth of identity means that from now on it is the individual's skills, power of judgement and wisdom of choice that will decide (at least need to decide; at any rate is expected to decide) which of the infinite number of possible forms in which life can be lived become flesh, and to what extent desultory and wavering choice may fulfil the role once played by the *polis*-purveyed and protected 'constant principles of orientation'.

It is the uncertainties focused on *individual identity*, on its never complete construction and ever attempted dismantling-in-order-to-reconstruct, which haunt modern men and women, leaving little space and time for the worries arising out of *ontological* insecurity. It is in this life, on this side of being (if indeed there is another side at all . . .), that existential insecurity is entrenched, hurts most, and needs to be dealt with. Unlike the ontological insecurity, identity-focused uncertainty needs neither the carrot of heaven nor the stick of hell to cause insomnia. It is all around, salient and tangible, all-too-protruding in rapidly ageing and abruptly devalued skills, in human bonds entered *until further notice*, in jobs which can be taken away without *any* notice, and in the ever new allures of the consumer feast, each promising untried kinds of happiness while wiping the shine off the tried ones.

Postmodern men and women do need the alchemist able, or claiming to be able, to transmogrify base uncertainty into precious self-assurance, and the authority of approval (in the name of superior knowledge, or access to wisdom closed to the others) is the philosophical stone these alchemists boast of possessing. Postmodernity is the era of experts in 'identity problems'; of personality healers, of marriage guidance, of writers of 'how to reassert yourself' books; it is the era of the 'counselling boom'. Postmodern men and women, whether by their own preference or by necessity, are *choosers*. And the art of choosing is mostly about avoiding one danger: that of *missing an opportunity* – by virtue of not seeing it clearly enough, or not chasing it keenly enough, or being too inexperienced a runner to catch it. To avoid this danger, postmodern men and women need counselling. The uncertainty, postmodern-style, begets not the demand for religion – it gestates instead the ever rising demand for identity-experts. Men and women haunted by uncertainty postmodern-style do not need preachers telling them about the weakness of man and the insufficiency of human resources. They need reassurance that they *can* do it – and a brief as to *how* to do it.

Elsewhere, I have argued that in the postmodern, consumer-oriented society individuals are socially formed under the auspices of the pleasure-seeker or sensation-gatherer role instead of the producer/soldier role formative for the great majority of society members (at least the male society members) in the modern era.[9] I also argued that the criteria by which the performance in a sensation-gatherer role is assessed are notoriously resistant to all quantification – and by the same token defy 'objective', that is cross-individual, comparisons. Unlike the performance of a producer or a soldier, the sensation of the experience-seeker cannot – with any degree of self-assurance – be assessed as 'adequate' or 'normal', let alone as the most intense or most satisfying, accessible in principle to one's own self or particularly to other people. There is always a fly of self-doubt and suspicion of inadequacy, 'falling short of the possible', in any barrel full of the sweet sensual honey. This circumstance opens up a new, wide area of uncertainty – and generates ever growing demands for the 'teachers of experience', or their technical products, which may help to enhance, deepen or intensify sensations.

This-worldly Transcendence

Abraham Maslow (1964) pointed out that, with the benefit of hindsight, the cases of personal illumination, revelations or ecstasy recorded in the lives of the saints, and then replicated more broadly (though perhaps in a somewhat more attenuated form) in the lives of the rank-and-file faithful, can be reinterpreted as, 'in fact, perfectly natural, human peak-experiences'. Ecclesiastical institutions, one may say looking back, 'can be seen as a kind of punch card or IBM version of an original revelation or mystical experience or peak-experience to make it suitable for group use and for administrative convenience. . . . [O]rganized religion can be thought of as an effort to communicate peak-experiences to non-peakers.' (Maslow, 1964, pp. 19–24).[10]

With great insight and analytical skill, Maslow uses concepts which could be gestated and fully formed solely in the greenhouse of late-modern or postmodern culture to reinterpret *a posteriori* an experience which was lived without the benefit of the much later discovered proper names. It 'makes sense' to us to recognize in religious ecstasy of the past the intense and 'total' experience which the precepts of 'libidinal economy' (or 'conatus toward satisfaction' – Edith Wyschogrod (1990, pp. 252 ff.)), so prominent in postmodern culture, prompt us – individuals constructed as sensation-gatherers – to seek and find. The question is, though, whether the reverse procedure equally 'makes sense'? Whether one can legitimately recognize the orgasmic experience of the postmodern sensation-gatherers as essentially religious?

I propose that the postmodern cultural pressures, while intensifying the search for 'peak-experiences', have at the same time uncoupled the search from religion-prone interests and concerns, privatized it, and cast mainly non-religious institutions in the role of purveyors of relevant services. The 'whole experience' of revelation, ecstasy, breaking the boundaries of the self and total transcendence – once the privilege of the selected 'aristocracy of culture' (saints, hermits, mystics, ascetic monks, *tsadiks* or *dervishes*) and coming either as an unsolicited miracle, in no obvious fashion related to what the receiver of grace has done to earn it, or as an act of grace rewarding the life of self-immolation and denial – has been put by postmodern culture within every individual's reach, recast as a realistic target and plausible prospect of each individual's self-training, and relocated as the product of a life devoted to the art of consumer self-indulgence. What distinguishes the postmodern strategy of peak-experience from one promoted by religions, is that far from celebrating the assumed human insufficiency and weakness, it appeals to the full development of human inner psychological and bodily resources and presumes infinite human potency. Paraphrasing Weber, one may call the postmodern, lay version of peak-experience the realm of 'this worldly ecstasy'.

Obviously, it is no longer the 'religious organizations', with their message of the perpetual insufficiency of man, who are best suited to 'communicate the peak-experience to non-peakers'. Whoever comes to replace the officiants of the traditional religious organizations must first and foremost abolish the concept of 'non-peakers' altogether, declaring the peak-experience a duty and a realistic prospect for *everybody*: 'You can do it'; 'Everybody can do it'; 'Whether you do it, is entirely up to you'; 'If you fail to do it, you have only yourself to blame'. Secondly, having uncoupled the dream of peak-experience from religion-inspired practices of self-denial and withdrawal from worldly attractions, those concerned must harness the dream to the desire for worldly goods and deploy it as the driving force of intense consumer activity. If the religious version of peak-experience used to reconcile the faithful to a life of misery and hardship, the postmodern version reconciles its followers to life organized around the duty of an avid, perpetual, though never definitely gratifying consumption. The paragons and prophets of the postmodern version of peak-experience are recruited from the aristocracy of consumerism – those who have managed to transform life into a work of the art of sensation-gathering and sensation-enhancement, thanks to consuming more than ordinary seekers of peak-experience, consuming more refined products, and consuming them in a more sophisticated manner.

The promise of new, overwhelming, mind-boggling or spine-chilling, but always exhilarating experience, is the selling point of food, drinks, cars, cosmetics, spectacles or holiday packages. Each dangles the prospect of 'living through' sensations never experienced before, and more intense than any tested before. Each new sensation must be 'greater', more overpowering and exciting than the one before, with the vertigo of 'total', peak, experience looming always on the horizon. It is hoped, and overtly or tacitly suggested, that by moving along the road of quantitative accretion of sensual intensity one would arrive eventually at a qualitative breakthrough – to an experience not just more profound and enjoyable, but 'totally different'. And in that journey one would be helped by 'meta-experiential' goods and services – those aimed at the enhancement of the psychic and bodily 'sensation-receiving' powers and skills. It is not just that more sublime pleasures ought to be offered – one needs also to learn how to squeeze the potential they contain, the potential that opens up in full solely to the past masters of the art of experiencing, the artists who know how to 'let themselves go' and who have made their mind and body, through diligent training, fit to receive the full impact of the overwhelming sensation. And the purpose of such training is provided by the metaphor of multiple orgasm: a fit body, served by an equally well-trained mind, is a body capable of repeated, even continuous intensity of sensations; a body forever 'on a high', constantly open to all chances of experience which the world around may provide – a sort of *well-tempered clavier* always ready to emit tunes of sublime beauty.

It is such a 'meta-experiential' function which is performed today by numerous 'self-improvement' movements, deriving their seductive powers from the promise of developing the experiencing potential of the body through exercise, contemplation, self-concentration, breaking psychic blocks and convention-induced constraints, letting free the suppressed instincts or cleansing out hidden injuries, developing the skills of self-abandonment and passive submission to the 'flow' of sensations, or embracing the esoteric, best of all exotic, mysteries able to teach and guide all these efforts. The axiom which underpins all such movements is that experiencing, like all other human faculties, is above all a *technical* problem, and that acquiring the capacity for it is a matter of mastering the appropriate *techniques*.

It goes without saying that any similarity between such movements and religious churches or sects is purely superficial, reduced at best to their organizational patterns. Rather than sharing their character with religious institutions, they are products and integral parts of the 'counselling boom' – though they are not, like other branches of counselling, meant to serve directly the consumer choices of assumedly fully-fledged consumers, but are aimed rather at the training of *'perfect consumers'*;

at developing to the full the capacities which the experience-seeking and sensation-gathering life of the consumer/chooser demands.

Back into the Future

There is, though, a specifically postmodern form of religion, born of internal contradictions of postmodern life, of the specifically postmodern form in which the insufficiency of man and the vanity of dreams to take human fate under human control are revealed. This form has come to be known under the English name of *fundamentalism*, or the French name of *intégrisme*, and shows its ever more weighty presence all over the part of the world once dominated by Christian, Islamic and Judaist religions.

I propose that the rise of a religiously-dressed form of fundamentalism is not a hiccup of ostensibly long-chased-away yet not-fully-suppressed mystical cravings, not a manifestation of eternal human irrationality, immune to all healing and domesticating efforts, and not a form of escape back into the premodern past. Fundamentalism is a thoroughly contemporary, postmodern phenomenon, embracing fully the 'rationalizing' reforms and technological developments of modernity, and attempting not so much to 'roll back' modern departures as to 'have the cake while eating it'. It makes possible a full enjoyment of modern attractions without having to pay the price they demand. The price in question is the agony of the individual condemned to self-sufficiency, self-reliance and a life of never fully-satisfying and trustworthy choice.

It is difficult not to agree with Gilles Kepel's (1994) diagnosis, that the present-day fundamentalist movements are

> true children of our time: unwanted children, perhaps, bastards of computerization and unemployment or of the population explosion and increasing literacy, and their cries and complaints in these closing years of the century spur us to seek out their parentage and to retrace their unacknowledged genealogy.
>
> Like the workers' movements of yesteryear, today's religious movements have a singular capacity to reveal the ills of society, for which they have their own diagnosis. (p. 11)[11]

One needs to make it clear, however, that the 'ills diagnosed' are different from those once laid bare by the workers' movements, and thus the movements which diagnose them (which *are*, knowingly or unknowingly, their diagnosis) attract a different kind of converted and the faithful. True, one should not play down the role of the traditional constituency – the deprived and the impoverished, whose ranks grow rather than shrink in the world of global free trade, where all stops have been pulled and all bars de-legalized. Unlike the case of the workers of yesteryear, though, the misery of the present-day deprived (the present-day form of the 'hidden injuries of class', to recall the apt phrase coined by Richard Sennett and Jonathan Cobb (1972)) appear to them (in most cases adequately) not as the outcome of exploitation, but as a result of having been left behind in the scramble for the entry tickets to the consumers' party. The poor of today are first and foremost *flawed consumers*, unable to take advantage of the treasures displayed tantalizingly within their reach, frustrated before the act, disqualified before even trying; while they are unfulfilled producers, or people cheated at the division of surplus value, but a distant second.[12] It is this quality which makes them, potentially, a constituency from which fundamentalist movements – which are triggered and kept on course above all by the agonies of the postmodern selves, self-reliant by appointment, free agents – may draw their reserves. A message of human insufficiency, or resentment of self-sufficiency, incubating in the bitter experience of fully-fledged postmodern consumers, may be telling also to their differently tuned ears.

The bitter experience in question is the experience of *freedom*: of the misery of life composed of risky choices, which always mean taking some chances while forfeiting others; of incurable uncertainty built into every choice; of the unbearable, because unshared, responsibility for the unknown consequences of every choice; of the constant fear of foreclosing future and yet unforeseen possibilities; of the dread of personal inadequacy; of experiencing less and not as strongly as others perhaps do; of the nightmare of being not up to the new and improved formulae of life which the notoriously capricious future may bring. And the message arising from that experience is: no, the human *individual* is not self-sufficient and cannot be self-reliant; one cannot go by one's own judgement, one needs to be guided, and directed, and told what to do. This is a message of insufficiency; but unlike the message carried by premodern religion, it is not the message of the weakness of human *species* – but of the irreparable weakness of the human *individual*, compared with the human species' omnipotence.

In this respect, fundamentalism brings into the open the underground anxiety and premonition normal and well-nigh universal under the postmodern condition. It gives public expression to what many people have suspected all along, though are authoritatively told not to believe or led not to think about. On the other hand, the framework of life offered by fundamentalism merely brings to its radical conclusion the cult of specialist counselling and guidance and the preoccupation with expert-assisted self-drill, both of which the postmodern consumer culture daily promotes; in this respect, fundamentalism is the supreme (though radically simplified) embodiment of a tendency aided and abetted by the whole

thrust of postmodern culture. One may conclude that religious fundamentalism is a legitimate child of postmodernity, born of its joys and
torments, and heir to its achievements and worries alike.

The allure of fundamentalism stems from its promise to emancipate
the converted from the agonies of choice. Here one finds, finally, the
indubitably *supreme* authority, an authority to end all other authorities.
One knows where to look when life-decisions are to be made, in matters big and small, and one knows that looking there one does the right
thing and so is spared the dread of risk-taking. Fundamentalism is a radical remedy against that bane of postmodern/market-led consumer society,
the risk-contaminated freedom (a remedy that heals the infection by
amputating the infected organ – abolishing freedom as such, in so far as
there is no freedom free of risks). Fundamentalism promises to develop all
the infinite powers of the group which – when deployed in full – would
compensate for the incurable insufficiency of its individual members, and
therefore justify the unquestionable subordination of individual choices
to the rules proclaimed in the group's name.

Islamic *intégrisme* of ayatollas' or Muslim Brothers' style, the Lubavich
sect of the present-day chassidic movement, evangelist churches of the
Bible belt, belong to a wider family of postmodern responses to those
postmodern fears which have been visited upon the individuals *qua* individuals by the progressive de-regulation and privatization of all 'secular'
insurance/protection nets, once state-provided through the entitlements
of state citizenship. In a world in which all ways of life are allowed, yet
none is safe, they muster enough courage to tell those who are eager
to listen what to decide so that the decision can remain safe and stand
up in all courts that matter. In this respect, religious fundamentalism
belongs to a wider family of totalitarian or proto-totalitarian solutions
offered to all those who find the burden of individual freedom excessive
and unbearable. And apart from religious fundamentalism, this family
includes many forms of ethnic, race-oriented, or tribal fundamentalisms,
all constituted in opposition to the secular state and to the indiscriminate
and non-discriminating (denigrated as 'abstract') citizenship which has
come to replace the by-and-large discredited political totalitarian movements (like Communism or fascism) – thoroughly modern (or pre-
postmodern) in their appeal to state-managed solutions and the state
legislative and ordering powders.

For from being an outburst of premodern irrationality, religious fundamentalism, much like the self-proclaimed ethnic revivals, is an offer of
an *alternative rationality*, made to the measure of genuine problems beset-
ting the members of postmodern society. Like all rationalities, it selects
and divides; and what it selects differs from the selection accomplished
by deregulated market forces – which does not make it less rational (or

more irrational) than the market-orientated logic of action. If market-type rationality is subordinated to the promotion of freedom of choice and thrives on the uncertainty of choice-making situations, the fundamentalist rationality puts security and certainty first and condemns everything that undermines that certainty – the vagaries of individual freedom first and foremost. In its fundamentalist rendition, religion is not a 'personal matter', privatized as all other individual choices and practised in private, but the nearest thing to a *compleat mappa vitae*: it legislates in no uncertain terms about every aspect of life, thereby unloading the burden of responsibility lying heavily on the individual's shoulders – those shoulders postmodern culture proclaims, and market publicity promotes, as omnipotent, but which many people find much too weak for the burden.

Religious fundamentalism, Kepel (1994) has suggested, has 'a singular capacity to reveal the ills of society'. How true. With the market-induced agony of solitude and abandonment as its only alternative, fundamentalism, religious or otherwise, can count on an ever-growing constituency. Whatever the quality of the answers it supplies, the questions which it answers are genuine. The problem is not how to dismiss the gravity of the questions, but how to find answers free from totalitarian genes.

Notes

1 Cited by Susan Gablik (1985, p. 66).
2 Rudolf Otto's fundamental *The Idea of the Holy* (first published in 1917, here quoted from John Harvey's 1923 translation (1959)), is in actual fact a closely argued statement about the *impossibility* of a 'rational definition' of religious experience. We may only try to approximate to it in our descriptions, remembering all the time that its complexity cannot be really grasped: 'like every absolutely primary and elementary datum, while it admits being discussed, it cannot be strictly defined' (Otto, 1959, p. 21). Imagery of that experience cannot be 'taught'; it can only be 'evoked'. What appears in the religious experience is given the name *'mysterium tremendum'*: 'it may burst in sudden eruption up from the depths of the soul with spasms and convulsions, or lead to the strongest excitements, to intoxicated frenzy, to transport, and to ecstasy. It has its wild and demonic forms and can sink to an almost grisly horror and shuddering' (p. 27). The absence of structural logical coherence is paralleled by the absence of associated behavioural logic. *Mysterium tremendum* is at the same time 'daunting' and 'fascinating' – these two qualities combining 'in the strange harmony of contrasts, and the resultant dual character of the numinous consciousness', a consciousness which brings together what cannot be rationally tied together – 'horror and dread' on the one hand, 'potent charm' on the other (p. 45). And according to Mircea Eliade (1956), the sole thing one can say about the nature of hierophany (and everything can acquire hierophanic value, that is, become the 'expression' of the *sacrum*) is that it always signals a *selection*: it divides

the world into the 'sacred' and the rest. One is tempted to say that by this description, all attempts at definitions also contain a sizable measure of hierophanic value . . .

3   See Carlo Mongardini and Mariele Ruini (1994, pp. 15, 31). In the same volume, Johan Goudsblom rightly points out that most of our discussion of religious phenomena remains, even if unknowingly, under 'the influence of theology' – hopelessly mixing 'emic' and 'etic' elements in how the pheno-mena are described (p. 89). We may add that the same applies to the 'rationalizing ideology', which also weighs heavily, even if as a tacit premise, on all attempts to define religious phenomena. Accordingly, the discourse finds itself in a virtual 'double bind', forced or cajoled to absorb elements from two mutually exclusive cognitive universes. In the 'religious science' discourse, the emic elements drawn from theology co-exist uneasily with emic elements inserted by the 'rationalization' discourse, which for the last couple of centuries strove to estrange and reify religious experience as the *wholly other* of reason. The present-day efforts to 'define religion' bear all the signs of the influence of the Enlightenment war against superstition – *a rebours* . . .

4   These are, of course, statements describing the common and distinctive attributes of *religion*, not necessarily those of the manifold religious *institutions*. The latter would be better described by a reference to their functions, rather than their constitutive creeds or recruiting slogans – and functions are more varied that the essentially intellectual response of 'explanation' or 'making sense' of the genuine or induced confusion, queries or fears of the faithful. Thus churches and sects may perform integrative/assertive/enabling political functions towards politically and economically oppressed minorities; and parishes, chapels and congregations are known for the important sociating role they play in cementing closely-knit communities and securing their continuous self-reproduction.

5   As Giddens (1990) points out, 'philosophers pose questions about the nature of being, but they are not, we may suppose, ontologically insecure in their ordinary actions' (p. 93). Indeed, Arthur Schopenhauer (1966), while overwhelmed with issues like 'why there is not nothing at all rather than this world', and agonizing over the fact that 'no ground, no final cause can be found' (p. 637), led an orderly and secure *bürgerliche* life and was truly appalled when its leisurely rhythm was abruptly broken by the events of the 1848 revolution. Schopenhauer went far beyond the call of duty to restore the 'groundless' world without a final cause to the routine pursuit of its daily causes – including inviting government soldiers to his house, from which location the insurgents were well visible (and could accordingly be shot with ease) (see Schopenhauer, 1978). He returned to eschatology and ontological security when the revolution had been safely put down.

6   See Edmund Husserl (1967, p. 14; 1968, p. 13).

7   Statements to this effect abound to such an extent that one is all too often misled into taking the frequency of repetition for a sign of self-evidence. They are all shaped according to a similar pattern: true, religion has changed its form beyond recognition, and people live their lives without giving religious signification to what they do, but this is only because they do

not see through their motives as well as we – the social scientists – are able to do.... Thus Jeffrey C. Alexander (1994) writes that 'sacrality and the demand for experience of transcendence remain fundamental features of life.... The referents are no longer in heaven, but the signifiers and the signifying processes remain religious: their aim [whose aim? – Bauman] is to place an actor, group or society in touch with the pure and impure forces from which the world seems, in the mythic and existential imagination [whose imagination? – Bauman], to ultimately derive' (p. 19). Thomas Luckmann (1967), on his part, suggests that it is 'religious themes' that have been 'taken up' by virtually all those institutions which now serve the running of daily life: 'syndicated advice columns, "inspirational" literature ranging from tracts on positive thinking to *Playboy* magazine, *Reader's Digest* versions of popular psychology, the lyrics of popular hits, and so forth, articulate what are, in effect, elements of models of "ultimate" significance' (p. 104).

8   John Carroll (1993) sees the humanist upheaval as ushering in a relatively brief, and certainly time-limited period which now comes to its end. He also considers its consequences as uniformly disastrous for the quality of Western Civilization. I propose to separate Carroll's perceptive diagnosis of the humanist strategy from both these – highly contentious – opinions.

9   See Zygmunt Bauman (1995), chapter 4, 'A Catalogue of Postmodern Fears'.

10   Abraham Maslow left ample accounts of the narratives he obtained from people reporting their 'peak-experiences'. Among the elements which keep repeating in their reports we find many features which characterize the ideal type of experience as promoted by postmodern culture: for instance, sensations of unusual concentration of attention, gathering all spiritual powers; the effacement of the difference between figure and ground (that is, the impression of 'wholeness'); ego-transcendence; the self-justifying nature of the moment which feels like 'end-experience' rather than 'means-experience'; lack of consciousness of time and space; the perception of the world as beautiful, good and desirable – and, above all, the experience of 'a loss, even though transient, of fear, anxiety, inhibition, of defense and control, of perplexity, confusion, conflict, of delay and restraint' (Maslow, 1964, p. 66): a loss of all the most sinister nightmares haunting postmodern individuals afflicted with identity-anxiety.

11   I also fully endorse Gilles Kepel's (1994) working assumption that 'what these movements say and do is meaningful, and does not spring from a dethronement of reason or from manipulation by hidden forces; rather it is the undeniable evidence of a deep malaise in society that can no longer be interpreted in terms of our traditional categories of though' (p. 11).

12   For a fuller argument, see the chapter entitled 'Two Nations, Mark Two: the Oppressed' in Bauman (1987).

References

Alexander, Jeffrey C. 1994: in Carlo Mongardini and Marieli Ruini (eds), *Religio: Ruolo del sacro, coesione sociale e nuove forme di solidarietà nella società contemporanea.* Rome: Bulzoni Editore.

Bauman, Zygmunt 1987: *Legislators and Interpreters*. Cambridge: Polity Press.
—— 1995: *Life in Fragments*. Oxford: Blackwell.
Carroll, John 1993: *Humanism: The Wreck of Western Culture*. London: Fontana.
Delumeau, Jean 1990: *Sin and Fear: The Emergence of a Western Guilt Culture, 13th–18th Centuries*. New York: St Martin's Press.
Eliade, Mircea 1956: *Traité d'histoire des religions*. Paris.
Foucault, Michel 1988: *Politics, Philosophy, Culture: Interviews and Other Writings 1977–1984* (ed. Lawrence D. Kritzman). London: Routledge.
Gablik, Susan 1985: *Magritte*. London: Thames and Hudson.
Gehlen, Arnold 1980: *Man in the Age of Technology* (trans. Patricia Lipscomb). New York: Columbia University Press.
Giddens, Anthony 1990: *The Consequences of Modernity*. Cambridge: Polity Press.
Gorer, Geoffrey 1965: *Death, Grief, and Mourning in Contemporary Britain*. London: Cresset Press.
Goudsblom, Johan 1994: in Carlo Mongardini and Marieli Ruini (eds), *Religio: Ruolo del sacro, coesione sociale e nuove forme di solidarietà nella società contemporanea*. Rome: Bulzoni Editore.
Husserl, Edmund 1967: *The Paris Lectures*. The Hague: Martinus Nijhoff.
—— 1968: *The Idea of Phenomenology*. The Hague: Martinus Nijhoff.
Kepel, Gilles 1994: *The Revenge of God: The Resurgence of Islam, Christianity and Judaism in the Modern World* (trans. Alan Braley). Cambridge: Polity Press.
Kołakowski, Leszek 1982: *Religion: If there is no God . . . On God, the Devil, Sin and Other Worries of the so-called Philosophy of Religion*. London: Fontana.
Luckmann, Thomas 1967: *The Invisible Religion*. London: Macmillan.
Maslow, Abraham H. 1964: *Religions, Values and Peak-Experiences*. Columbus: Ohio State University Press.
Mongardini, Carlo and Ruini, Marieli (eds) 1994: *Religio: Ruolo del sacro, coesione sociale e nuove forme di solidarietà nella società contemporanea*. Rome: Bulzoni Editore.
Otto, Rudolf 1959: *The Idea of the Holy* (trans. John W. Harvey). London: Penguin.
Schopenhauer, Arthur 1966: *The World as Will and Representation*. New York: Dover.
—— 1978: *Gesammelte Briefe* (ed. A. Hübscher). Bonn.
Sennett, Richard and Jonathan Cobb 1972: *The Hidden Injuries of Class*. New York: Knopf.
Sorokin, Pitirim 1956: *Fads and Foibles in Modern Sociology and Related Sciences*. Chicago: Regnery.
Touraine, Alain 1974: *The Post-Industrial Society: Tomorrow's Social History: Classes, Conflicts and Culture in the Programmed Society* (trans. Leonard Mayhew). London: Wildwood House.
Wyschogrod, Edith 1990: *Saints and Postmodernism: Revisioning Moral Philosophy*. Chicago: University of Chicago Press.

CHAPTER FIVE

tradition, retrospective perception, nationalism and modernism

Ninian Smart

The only thing perhaps that we can change is the past and we do it all the time. Of course we cannot alter everything about the past: our retrospective perceptions have to be plausible. Without a real Battle of Hastings, English history could not supposedly start there. The simplest way of changing the past is by category. For instance, there is now such a thing as Native American Religion, but in an important sense it did not exist, say, in the eighteenth century. Our concept now subtly changes all the 'thens'. The new collective neo-tradition has more clout than the piecemeal religious and ethnic groupings of the past. Again, we have the emergence, in the last two centuries or more, of the nation-state. Nations themselves are newly invented, but of course out of plausible existing materials. An old peasant language is reshaped by intellectuals, and through a nation's educational system becomes official. The land becomes defined by borders and thus sacred. Old heroes are adopted into the gallery of the nation's saints.

Some traditions, however, are perceived as relatively new: royal France was replaced by revolutionary France – the one being as it were the Old Testament and the other the New. The USA sees itself as a young country. The Soviet Union was seen as a new revolutionary creation, replacing decadent Tsarism. But even these new traditions are, or were, traditional. In short we may see the modern world as involving retraditionalization.

We can see all this against the background of the eighteenth and nineteenth centuries, when the world effectively came under the sway of Western powers, and the process of imperialism spurred a new self-consciousness in Asia, Africa and elsewhere. The basic project of existing cultures – for instance in India, China and Japan – was to transform themselves enough to respond to and fight off the colonial powers. In one way the most successful such change was that of the Japanese, who in forty years between the Meiji restoration and the Battle of Tsushima became an equal and honorary Western power. Of course, the traditionalism of the period of Japanese revolutionary transformation had to be modified. The samurai class was transformed; Buddhism and Shinto were split apart, and the latter reinvented as State Shinto, ironically declared not to be a religion in order to maintain the fiction of the imperial period that the Japanese had freedom of religion. In the time after the Second World War the social and political changes continued, though large elements of traditional Japan were preserved. No and the Tokyo String Quartet lived together, and the kimono and Gucci.

The challenges from the West to other cultures were also in part challenges to its dominant Christianity. Modern Western culture questioned one of its main creations. We can set out these challenges as follows:

There was the new ethos of capitalism with its industrial motor, born of the steam engine and *The Wealth of Nations*, and elaborated in new technologies.

There was a new form of education, especially higher education aimed at elites (including the colonial), emphasizing science, engineering, new forms of administration, and liberal democratic ideas as a vital ingredient.

There was evangelical and proselytizing fervour: in short the missionary critique (and occasional defence) of indigenous cultures.

There was nationalism, which in imperial and aggrandizing guise was a wonderful transmitter of itself.

The consequence of these challenges was the invention of neo-traditions. Many of these were newly shaped nationalisms often calling on ancient resources. Some of the new traditions were re-formed religions. For instance, modern Hinduism managed to synthesize various motifs from the past. There are still scholars who deny that there is such a thing as Hinduism ('reification' and 'essentialism' are words often muttered), but if you try to deny that there is anything called Hinduism in the presence of modern Hindus you get a dusty answer. It may not have existed, but it does now. Let us dwell then on seeing how the challenges of the modern world were met, by contemplating the Indian case, which has been maybe the most successful culture in modernizing without sacrificing much of its tradition. China under Maoism, by contrast, was much less effective, since so much of Chinese tradition had to be sacrificed in the course of a social reconstruction which was supposed to make China strong. It was powerful militarily; but in economics and politics it was long in a state of rigidity and oppression.

It is doubtful whether we can speak of Indian nationalism until late in the nineteenth century. Moreover there were regional competitors, such as Bengali and Maharashtrian patriotism. The new self-consciousness was expressed in the formation of the Congress in 1885. Of all the leaders, such as Lokamanya Tilak and Surendranath Banerjea, the most effective in framing a nationalist ideology was Swami Vivekananda. The essence of his ideas surrounded much later thinking, such as that of Gandhi and Radhakrishnan. The pluralism of Vivekananda's worldview was important in accommodating the important minority religions – Islam, Christianity and so on. In reaching back into the Hindu heritage, Vivekananda picked on Advaita Vedanta, which he modified into a modern form. This argued that the eternal Self in each being is identical with the Divine Being, Brahman. While in its classical form it argued that the universe as perceived by us as consisting of separate beings is in the higher truth illusory, made of *māyā*, Vivekananda was more realist and world-affirming. Truths about the world remain true, though at a lower level. The higher truth signifies the identity of *Brahman* and *Ātman*, the Divine Being and the Self. All religions, he affirmed, point to the same ultimate: the Gods are so many lower-truth symbols pointing at the One Reality. All this he perceived as the essence of Hinduism. Moreover, Hinduism should take credit for having long perceived this unity of all religions, taken in their ultimate meaning. Vivekananda called on Hindu and Christian mystics, Sufis and Buddhist contemplatives to bear witness. So first of all Vivekananda shaped a pluralistic Indian nationalism.

Secondly, his philosophical stance could, through its notion of levels of truth, accommodate both transcendental claims and scientific ones; and this in turn could create a hospitality to the new capitalist order, and encourage socialist versions of industrialism.

Thirdly, Swami Vivekananda expressed himself in fluent English and was therefore the spokesperson of a new Indian English-speaking elite. His ideas fitted in with democratic ideals, and even had a resonance with utilitarianism, itself influential in the management of the Indian Empire. Vivekananda's utilitarianism was deeper, because he had a more profound (and spiritual) sense of what human happiness consists in. He was able to take a reformist stand: and indeed a number of the Hindu nationalists saw the necessity of changing some Indian social traditions.

Fourthly, he was able to combat Christian criticisms by pointing out that evangelicals and others had a singularly negative and dispiriting view of other traditions; while Hinduism had long been plural and tolerant. So some forms of Christianity were strict and narrow-minded, not having the expansiveness of true spirituality.

Fifthly, Vivekananda's nationalism could take advantage of the forces which gave rise to modern Indian nationalism: the unification of the subcontinent by the imperial conquest and the creation of a national communication system, notably through the railways; the spread of higher education in English and its use in the administration; and the counter-presence of British nationalism in the rather arrogant form of imperialism, which created the reflex of Indian patriotism. This made Indian national-ism strong enough to combat the centrifugal dynamics of the many lan-guages and cultures – though ultimately it did not wholly overcome the fissiparous tendencies of communalism (hence the Partition in 1947, with its tragic consequences). But all in all Vivekananda's worldview was an impressive ingredient in and shaper of the new sense of India, and ultimately of the Indian constitution after Independence.

Actually, Vivekananda's Neo-Hinduism was a vision dialectically cre-ated at the intersection between two cultures – British and Indian. It was a new India and a new Hindu heritage that were being fashioned. It was an effective ideology in that it enabled India to modernize and to retain her customs and traditions. Of all the major cultures, India did best in balancing modern effectiveness and older values. A glance at an Indian street shows this clearly; by contrast a Japanese street is more orderly and Westernized.

Since we have been examining the creation of a new tradition and one which incorporates nationalism, let us pause at this point to con-sider the varieties of nation-creation. Some nations are based on history and language; others differentiate themselves on the basis of religion; others are chiefly marked by history alone. As examples of linguistic nations, there are Italy, Norway, France, Wales . . . As examples where religion or ideology differentiate countries, consider North and South Korea, Pakistan and India, China and Taiwan, Croatia and Serbia . . . As countries differentiated by history alone, Argentina and Chile, Iraq and Syria, South Africa and Zimbabwe . . . In all these cases there may be minor factors modifying my bold distinctions.

Because history in all cases is important in the creation of new national traditions, the apparatus of allegedly scientific history from Hegel onwards has proved important. Although many modern historians are critical and like to debunk, others contribute to the myth-making simply by acceding to the categories of national tradition. You can take classes in so many modern universities in British, Italian, Nepalese, Indonesian and Turkish history. These histories go back before the times of the modern entities in question. What can it mean to say that Julius Caesar was Italian, the Buddha Nepalese, or Darius the Great Iranian? Yet the tradition projected by the category is almost ineluctable, is it not?

Yet there are ways in which the new traditions can begin to crumble: there is after all a measure of detraditionalization at work in the evolu-tion of modern individualism. This has varying roots: the rejection of infant baptism among the Anabaptists, which signalled a certain individualism in religion (though in practice it was combined with strong communal pressures in faithful congregations); the tradition of rights from Locke onwards; the emergence of nineteenth-century utilitarianism; capitalist attitudes, treating each person as a unit of production and consumption; and general trends in the separation of religious organizations from the State. All this allows a weakening of traditional patterns of behaviour. Who is afraid of excommunication any more? We have in the Western world and elsewhere a large growth in a New Age type of religion in which individuals make up their spiritual 'traditions' out of elements of older religions, etc. There is a phenomenal growth, over the last fifty years, of new religious movements, especially in Africa. Often these involve a novel symbiosis of features of differing traditions: in the case of Africa a blend of classical African religious traditions and, typically, Christianity. A much stronger element of choice is available in much of the modern world: such choice being mediated by rational considerations, taste, and religious experience.

Moreover, the modification of existing religious traditions has been great in the last half-century, and we have only touched on some of the factors. To be more explicit: the globalization of the world as a result both of the Second World War and of new technologies brings traditions into increasingly intimate (and sometimes hostile) contact with one another. Already in the 1950s one could come across Catholic monks trying out Zen, and other phenomena of blending. Against such innovations, and the often important liberal tendencies in modernizing religions, there are of course backlashes – typically supposedly 'conservative' movements, whether evangelical in kind or scripturally potent – movements which often are based on a kind of experiential individualism impelling people to join tightly knit organizations (for instance, Pentecostal churches, the Islamic Brotherhood, etc.). Such organizations are knit together typically by the glue of emotion, rather than by the bonds of customary tradition. So although often people gather together in a backlash against modernizing trends, they too are shaping new traditions. Conservatism is simply one variety of novel traditionalization. Though in theory conservative movements are doctrinally and philosophically traditionalist, they often have many new features – new concerns with ritual, dispensing with existing authorities, a certain energy in pursuing social concerns, vigour in organization using the technical methods of today, etc.

As indicated above, conservatism is chiefly a reaction to liberal trends within modernizing religion. The latter phenomenon is the result of some degree of blending between liberalism and traditional faith. Thus modern Christianity in the West has had to accommodate itself to scientific discoveries which force non-literalism on mainstream interpretation of the Bible; democratic movements, which require some opening up of religious governance; and the revision of family and other law, which loosens older values. Obviously the way in which these factors have an impact on a religion will depend on the configuration of that faith. For instance, modern scientific cosmology makes the scale of Genesis obsolete, but not that of the Buddhist scriptures, while it may favour *creatio ex nihilo* rather than the Buddhist pulsating universe. Generally speaking, liberal modernism is a kind of syncretism between a given tradition and the liberal ethos. It is of course natural for worldviews to affect one another in all kinds of ways.

Despite the importance of growing individualism, and not only in the West, the new national traditions have great power. When E. M. Forster stated that he would rather betray his country than his friends, he was met with contumely. Most nations put you to death for treason. The new national traditions are often reinforced by ideology or religion – worldviews which more generally can contradict the national idea. However nicely phrased, patriotism implies the practical inferiority of others. This contradicts the stated values of many religions. It is contrary to democratic liberalism, socialism and other secular philosophies. Fascism is more complaisant and often incorporates such motifs as 'Because I am German I can kick you non-Germans around.' If you are blond and Norwegian, by the way, you are *really* German. But all the major worldviews which blend with nationalism are ultimately in contradiction with the main thrust of the worldviews themselves, for they tend to be universalist. Britain in the latter days of its Empire tried to rationalize this situation by saying that Britain represented Christian civilization and liberal democratic ideas – obviously in contradiction in the last resort with the practicalities of Empire. Poland is Catholic, but contains un-Christian anti-Semitism, as well as a past love of the greed of conquest. Sri Lanka is supposedly Buddhist but justifies its strictly un-Buddhist treatment of the Tamils on the grounds of its historical destiny to maintain Buddhism (including the four holy states of love, compassion, joy in others' joy, and equanimity).

In fact, claims that a nation is Christian, or whatever, are themselves expressions of a new interpretation of both the religion and the nation. Since the nation is a new tradition the national religion is new, however old it might have been. And not just the religion but also the ideology (I do not greatly differentiate between the two). For example, Marxism becomes different in China: if it had not it might not have 'won'. Croatian Catholicism is transformed somewhat by becoming Croatian.

So far the nisus of these remarks is that traditions are being reformed, and most are young. It would have been hard to imagine Brahmins of the Veda period arguing for their antiquity. It would be ridiculous to claim that Christ knew that a Christian would take a view on nuclear bombs. All religions are modern religions, even if they want to deny that they are *modernist*. In speaking of traditions here I am referring to those that roughly correspond to Tillich's account: he talked of humans' ultimate concern. Religion and ideology on the one hand, and national identity on the other, seem in most cases to correspond to this definition. The combination becomes even more strongly ultimate (of course, Tillich himself failed to consider the quantification of ultimacy!).

But the new traditions may not command loyalty. I have already mentioned the consumerism of modern capitalism. The consumer in Britain, let us say, may buy a Sony portable and a Volvo, regardless of occasional campaigns to buy British. Moreover, companies that create such products become increasingly transnational. Futhermore, travel and migration increasingly unhinge the individual from his or her past. This may of course, among diasporas, generate nostalgia for the roots (leading to greater nationalism among those abroad from the main entity: consider the role of overseas Sikhs in the campaign for Khalistan, and diaspora Tamils in the struggle for Tamil Eelam, and of course overseas Jews in the Zionist sight for Israel). Even so, the migrant is more open to choice: the South African Indians are much into the Arya Samaj, rather than truly traditional Hinduism.

It may also be mentioned that the modern era has seen racist interpretations of nationalism. So it is that Scots vaguely think that they all descend from the same people (actually Picts, Celts, English, Vikings and heaven knows whom, just as the English descend from Celts, Danes, Anglo-Saxons and so on). Croats think that they are descended from Croats, and Serbs from Serbs, Tamils from Tamils, and Jews from Jews: but actually there are plethoras of diverse genes in each population. The cultural characteristics of a given population are interesting, but recent. The projection into the past involves false thoughts.

Though ethnicism is confused, invoking elements of racism, it is important in so-called modern thinking. When I say it is confused, let me take the controversial issue of the Jews. If you take the official view of who is Jewish, namely someone with a Jewish mother, that allows for huge numbers of non-Jewish genes (and anyway a Jewish woman will have those too, as passing on through motherhood the property of Jewishness). So anti-Jewish (e.g. Nazi) accusations of race make no sense. Basically, what makes Jewishness is feeling, or (following Sartre) being regarded as Jewish. And then of course there is the added complication of religion. You can obviously be Jewish without being Jewish in the religious sense: but, by an irony, you probably recognize your Jewishness by rules laid down by the Jewish religious tradition. It is altogether a confused situation, like so many human ones. At any rate, the ethnic group known as Jews is not properly speaking racial; it is only national because of recently invented nationalism; it is imperfectly, and retrospectively projected, religious. It is one of the awful flaws in the whole concept of race; and the Jews have suffered horrendously from that idea in practice.

But ethnicism (the prejudice of one ethnic group towards another) is also equally flawed. Nations and ethnes are real, but egregiously artificial. The main purpose of this essay is not so much to criticize modern traditions of religion and nationalism as to stress that these new traditions are indeed new. In the name of traditions we have killed each other, conquered, resisted. We have died for these entities. So they have great psychic power.

Since it appears that traditions have kept changing over the centuries, and that traditions we regard as somehow ancient and ineluctable are fairly recent, it does not seem reasonable to think that we are in a mode of detraditionalization. Rather we are as busy as ever retraditionalizing. Our most important new traditions are nations, and sometimes connectedly new versions of old religions – typically, as we have seen, responses to the colonial and modern period.

Let me expand a bit on this last point. Extraordinary changes have occurred in the fabric of religions in the modern period – so much so that in my book *The World's Religions* I have divided each religion into its ancient and medieval period on the one hand and its post-colonial and modern period on the other. Sometimes ancient traditions could not be used easily for reconstruction, as in China, where Maoism took over instead; but elsewhere cultures could be radically reshaped, as in Meiji Japan, and among Jews after the Enlightenment. Islam was later, at least in the Arab world, in experiencing colonial rule, shielded up until the First World War by the Ottoman Empire (though not in Egypt and North Africa). Islam is still digesting the challenges; and I believe that contemporary Islamism, though not without modernizing tendencies, will be short-lived, and Islam will rediscover Islamic modernism from the beginning of the twentieth century, together with a redeveloped Sufism, which finds it easier to cope with modern science. We have noted some of the changes in Hinduism in the last two centuries; and Africa pullulates with new religions and churches (over 10,000 in sub-Saharan Africa, for example).

What then is a tradition? It is of course something handed down, but also interpreted and projected back. Provided you can suppose that what is handed down is forgotten you can shape it as you please. Although modern historians may occasionally make life difficult in the reinvention of what has gone before, on the whole the past is (roughly) the period predating your grandparents. Few of us remember our great-grandparents; and most have only a rather dim remembrance of our grandparents' times. Intellectuals tend to have a clearer perception of the past because they have read books about the First and Second World Wars and the Victorian era before them. They have a less than vivid perception of the cloud that stands between most folk and the past. For most people the reinvention of the past can become easily plausible.

My conclusion therefore is as follows. While on the one hand a modern individualism makes it easier for people to change or abandon what they perceive as traditions (though it is not simple to evade nationality), on the other hand this era is, like others, one of the invention and reinvention of traditions, not one of detraditionalization *per se*. A younger colleague of mine at the University of California once looked gloomy in an outdoor café we both frequented on campus. He was depressed because his students had no knowledge of goings-on in Berkeley in the late 1960s. I tried to cheer him up by pointing out that anything that happened before a freshman reached the age of twelve was ancient history. In other words, now even Mrs Thatcher was ancient history, and Ronald Reagan. And another thing has to be said: all ancient history is equally ancient. The collapse of the Soviet Union and the Resurrection of Christ occurred in the same miasma of old time. So by the same token, anything emanating from ancient history is a tradition. And because we have the freedom to swim deeply in the miasma, we can make of tradition what we will: though always remembering to be plausible, since historians supply us with rocklike records which we cannot quite wipe out in the fogs of reminiscence.

CHAPTER SIX

from fundamentalism to fundamentalisms: a religious ideology in multiple forms

Bruce B. Lawrence

There is but one fundamentalism yet there are many forms of fundamentalist self-expression. The move from singular to plural is the move from participant emphasis to critical analysis. For fundamentalists Truth is always and everywhere one. Hence there can only be one true text, one true reading of that text and one true community. The very notion of fundamentalisms disconfirms the heart of each fundamentalism: one group, and one group alone exists as the repository of Truth; it reflects scriptural verities; it and it alone knows, advocates and defends God.

By this logic, there can never be a fundamentalist study of fundamentalisms. Students of fundamentalisms must be outsiders because only outsiders can weigh the evidence of each insider who is at the same time a claimant to truth. Yet even among students there are tough choices. How does one decide which communities deserve to be studied as fundamentalist? Are they only the most familiar, the close at hand, that is to say, Christian, Jewish and Muslim? Or are they also the very distant, the dimly known, such as Hindu, Buddhist, Sikh?

Whichever choice is made, one must begin by being clear what is meant by fundamentalism. The term was already much contested before the Fundamentalism Project, based at the University of Chicago, began holding annual meetings on the subject in the late 1980s. The Fundamentalism Project has since produced five hefty volumes, each addressing one facet of fundamentalism, their total corpus exceeding 3,000 pages of printed text.[1] By contrast, my own book, *Defenders of God: The Fundamentalist Revolt against the Modern Age*, is a mere 325 pages. Since it was published before the appearance of Volume One of the Fundamentalism Project, I can still claim to speak with a bit of detachment about pluralizing the f-word, as it is sometimes called.

Since 1989, when *Defenders of God* was first published, and in part as a result of the conversations it fostered, the very word fundamentalism has been increasingly pluralized. In the mid-1990s fundamentalism is no longer seen as limited just to the United States or just to Protestant Christian groups; at least not in academic circles, where almost no-one still claims that fundamentalism is but a single species occurring in a single religious tradition. The central premise of *Defenders of God*, accepted now by most scholars, is that fundamentalism has mushroomed into fundamentalisms, not just locally but globally, not just in the United States and Europe but also in Africa and Asia. Even when researchers focus on mostly Euro-American movements which are also Protestant Christian, they retain in the back of their mind a comparative notion of fundamentalism, suggesting its applicability to other religions and to other non-Christian groups.

The critical first step is to recognize the nature of what we define as fundamentalism. Some have claimed that the very term is at once 'too embracing and too restrictive', simultaneously 'demonizing its referents and also homogenizing them'.[2] Yet no one has devised a better term to refer to a phenomenon that all agree constitutes part of the current period in world history, a period which I, in the spirit of Marshall Hodgson, call the High Tech Era.[3] Instead of apologizing for the term fundamentalism or refusing to use it, I prefer to nuance it and I do so by identifying and then exploring three types or brands of fundamentalism: literalist, terrorist, and political activist. Though they may look alike, they are not the same, and it makes a big difference which brand of fundamentalism you are pursuing, whether as a participant or as a student.

Christian Literalist

The literalist stand is the best known. It acknowledges fundamentalism as a peculiar, albeit restrictive, kind of discourse. It looks at the term 'Bible believer', and asks: whose Bible? what kind of belief? For a sociological exploration of this approach one can do no better than Nancy Ammerman's superb monograph *Bible Believers: Fundamentalists in the Modern World* (1987). The issues that Ammerman addresses can be recast in literary critical terms. Though there is a book called the Bible, there is no consensus about what it means, since interpretive communities make of the Bible what they want for their own preconceived, often tacit agendas. Their notion of belief has very little to do with faith or social justice. Instead, it harks back to the Scottish enlightenment notion of

'just plain common sense'. Once decoded, the common sense, fundamentalist sorting out of Biblical propositions sounds very much like
a back-door retrieval of early-modern abstractions, such as objectivity,
certainty, reason and, of course, the most valent and vague of all,
science.

Those who study Bible believers often accept their logic even while
seeming to criticize them as imperfect readers. Kathleen Boone, for
instance, situates her subjects within the scope of reader-response theory.
Her study *The Bible Tells Them So: The Discourse of Protestant Fundamentalism*
(1989) applies literary criticism to the teachings of televangelists such as
Jerry Falwell, Pat Robertson, and Jimmy Swaggart. She produces a kind of
postmodern gloss on literalism, advocating the benefit of drawing a circle
around those who draw circles around others. Boone affirms the value
of literalism in order to make Falwell et al. accessible to others unlike
them. Despite its artful dalliance between the open classroom and the
bully pulpit, this approach underscores how narrowly scripturalist is
the favourite American brand of fundamentalism. Far from looking to a
golden past, it anticipates a fiery future; it confirms that judgemental
consequences apply to all, with the faithful few being spared only at the
moment of millennial conflict, otherwise known as Armageddon.

Fundamentalists do not accept other believers as kindred souls open
to salvific glory, and they could not imagine other believers whose apocalyptic vision and social advocacy would also qualify them as fundamentalists. Protestant American fundamentalists, arguing among themselves
about who are the 'real' fundamentalists, would never locate fundamentalist movements beyond the two oceans, whether looking westward across
the Pacific to East and Southeast Asia or alternatively, eastward across the
Atlantic and beyond Europe, to the Middle East and also South and
Central Asia.

Yet scholars have long been tracking another species of fundamentalism. During the 1980s, well before *Defenders of God* appeared, one could
find several books that located fundamentalism in a part of the world
beyond Europe and in a religion other than Christianity. The area was
the Middle East, the religion Islam.

Muslim Terrorist?

While literalist motifs were woven into many books on the Arab/Muslim
Middle East, most authors preferred to speak of Islamic fundamentalism
as a distinct species, and the cognate term for this distinct species was
not literalism but terrorism. Scholars might have empathy for literalists
but not for terrorists. Terrorists kill, and religions that foster them are to
be opposed with relentless vigilance. Since 1979, coinciding with the

Islamic revolution in Iran, Islamic fundamentalism has become an enemy of the West, and of all humankind.

Let me give but one example of this approach, though elsewhere I have noted more than fifty scholarly or semi-popular books that echo the same theme.[4] The political scientist Richard Dekmejian published *Islam in Revolution: Fundamentalism in the Arab World* in 1985; and Dekmejian presumes fundamentalism to be a core attribute of the Islamic mindset at all times and in all places. Invariant and unchanging, it has two manifestations, one passive, the other militant. Looking at over a thousand years of Middle Eastern history, Dekmejian traces fundamentalism as an instinctual, inevitable response characteristic of all Muslims. The latest episode, datable from 1948 with the creation of Israel, merely confirms a recurrent, timeless phenomenon. 'As in centuries past,' writes Dekmejian, 'the Islamic community generated its own culturally nativist response to crisis – a return to Islam and its fundamental precepts' (1985, p. 3).

The presuppositions embedded in such an assertion are as false as they are slanderous. Muslims, like Christians and Jews and Sikhs, have changed over the centuries, even over decades. There is no infinite regression of sameness, unless one ignores empirical evidence. While the Islamic community does share some common emphases, they are channelled through geographically disparate and often culturally dissimilar expressions of communitarian loyalty. The most recent expressions of difference among Muslims have become rife in the multiple nationalisms of Africa and Asia, often giving rise to intra-Muslim warfare as in the case of the nine-year-long Iran–Iraq war of the 1980s.

There also can be no 'return' to Islam. The so-called Islamic revival amounts to a selective re-emphasis of some features of the Muslim past, but the Islamic community can never be said to have left its past, and so it cannot 'return' to Islam. Muslims, like non-Muslims, invoke different parts of beliefs and practices, cultural artifacts and symbols, in response to present moments. And like the great empires of premodern Islamic history, contemporary Muslim communities experience a variety of triumphs and defeats; there is no Islamic crisis that separates Muslims from the rest of humankind or debars them from a global nightmare – whether due to nuclear conflagration or ecological disaster – that would forever change the world as we know it.

What Dekmejian wants to highlight is the equation of fundamentalism and terrorism as a precondition to understanding the Arab/Muslim world. In his lexicon the two terms are synonymous: even though Iranian and Lebanese Shi'ites might resist being so closeted, they become extensions of a Sunni fundamentalist mindset that is unremittingly anti-Western, hostile to cultural tastes, dress styles, but especially military actions or diplomatic initiatives that derive from the Great Satan, to wit, the USA. This approach makes no allowance for the play between public and private spheres, gender variations, and generational shifts. It favours lists and charts over factual analysis. All Muslims become potential fundamentalists; all who honour Islam – its beliefs and rituals, rhythms and tones – are not only Islamic activists or revivalists but extremists capable of hijacking planes and blowing up airports or trade centres. Funded by the Defense Intelligence Agency, *Islam in Revolution* is designed to trigger a single response from every reader: Muslims are dangerous, Islamic fundamentalists are killers. Even before the World Trade Center bombing, which quickly prompted a second edition of *Islam in Revolution* (1995), most Americans came to link radical Islam with hatred of the West and the killer instinct. If any single word can suffice to recall this deformation of logic and experience, it has to be terrorist.

It would be unfair to deduce that Dekmejian represents the sum total of current scholarship on Islamic fundamentalism. The series of suppressed referents that riddle and falsify his approach recurs in far too many other works, yet others signal new, more hopeful directions. The best on Sunni Islam remains Emmanuel Sivan, *Radical Islam: Medieval Theology and Modern Politics* (1985). The Continental literary style of the author, marked by frequent excursi, complex puns, and large doses of self-criticism, has made the work less accessible than the Anglo-American mixture of plodding and carping that suits Dekmejian. Yet Sivan's book continues to engage the dogged inquirer, for beneath his patina of rhetorical moves and countermoves Sivan puts forth a consistent thesis: Islamic fundamentalism is not the whole of Muslim history, nor is it the sum total of current worldviews expressed by Muslims, even those in countries labelled by Western policy makers as 'radical', 'anti-Western', 'terrorist'.

The Shi'i counterpart to Sivan is not another Israeli historian but an Austrian anthropologist. Reinhold Loeffler's field study, *Islam in Practice: Religious Beliefs in a Persian Village* (1988), captures the range of outlook among 21 character types in a south Iranian village. These are individual voices of Muslims peripheralized within their own society. They are rural, often tribal, semiliterate or nonliterate, premodern as also pre-Enlightenment in their worldview. Yet they do not project as dumb masses swaying in response to daily pronouncements from Tehran where urban, literate, anti-Enlightenment mullahs now happen also to control the instruments of political/military power. There is a fundamentalist voice in this chorus; it is, however, but one of many. It says that the Qur'an lays down all the laws for government and society and that Imam Khomeini, aided by other, equally devout Shi'i clerics, was trying to enact these laws in post-1979 Iran. Yet others say: 'We have been told, "Woe to the day when the mullahs should come to power." I knew there would be disaster if this Khomeini should come back and the country become a playground of the mullahs.' And about the Iran–Iraq war, another remarks: 'Paradise has become full with all the martyrs. There is no more room for us ordinary people in Paradise. That's the way things are nowadays.' The most gripping exchange takes place between a father and son. The father laments:

> My son now is telling me about the true Islam; they have to fight a holy war and if necessary get killed. I tell him there is no holy war in the absence of the Last Imam. He shouts at me saying I do not understand a thing. These young ones are like unfledged birds. When they try to fly, they fall from the tree and a cat eats them. They cannot discern the right road. I tell him to stay out of everything, to mind his own business, and do his studies; it's not the right time. But he won't listen. He will get hurt.[5]

Though beginning from variant approaches with opposite target groups, Sivan and Loeffler come to the same conclusion: don't generalize about all Muslims or about any particular group in a discrete historical time frame. People are pragmatic. They do weigh options. They do value their lives. Muslims are no different from others, and having just returned from Iran in January 1996, I can confirm that Loeffler's 7-year-old prediction rings truer today than when he first published his pioneering study: the mullahs control political power but not civil society in post-Khomeini Iran, and the much touted hatred of the USA is a chimera that could disappear overnight with some bold initiative from Washington.

Jewish Political Activist

Concerning Jewish fundamentalists, we again face not one but several contestants for the banner proclaiming 'the Jewish truth about the divine plan for the current age'. One contestant is Yigal Amir, the zealot assassin of Yitzak Rabin, who has recently been sentenced to life-imprisonment. He shares with many other West Bank settlers an all-or-nothing view of Israel as *eretz Israel*, a space sacred only for Jews and intended for them alone. But even before Rabin's assassination, there was a tendency, at least among journalists and globe watchers, to see more than one group of Jewish fundamentalists, and at the same time to recognize that Judaism, like Islam, did not have an inherently fundamentalist tendency, one that had always to be held in check by countervailing forces.

Unfortunately some scholars tend to embrace the restrictive outlook of their subjects. In a dense monograph, titled *For the Land and the Lord: Jewish Fundamentalism in Israel* (1988), the political scientist Ian Lustick has argued that Gush Emunim (or the Bloc of the Faithful), the main advocates of *eretz Israel*, or Israel for Jews only, are nothing less than quintessential Jewish fundamentalists. They are not terrorists but activists, and indeed in Lustick's view anyone who acts on religiously motivated principles is a fundamentalist. Lustick defines fundamentalism as both a belief system and an ideology: fundamentalism, according to him, describes any movement whose 'adherents regard its tenets as uncompromisable and (providing) direct transcendental imperatives to political action oriented toward the rapid and comprehensive reconstruction of society' (1988, p. 6).

By such a broad definition all political activists whose programme invokes utopian goals, whether they be the IRA, the Red Brigade, or Gush Emunim, become fundamentalist. Within Israel it also means casting the fundamentalist mantle over avowed secular ideologues, such as Yuval Neeman and his supporters in the right-wing Tehiya Party. It also means excluding and labelling as non-fundamentalists all religiously motivated persons whose primary agenda is not political. By this criterion, the *haredim*, who happen to be the most militantly observant sector of contemporary Israeli society, are not fundamentalist. It is hard to agree with Lustick that the 10,000–20,000 devotees of Gush Emunim will determine the future of Israel, pre-empting the fundamentalist potential that exists elsewhere in the complex diaspora of world Jewry. A phrase that epitomizes Lustick's approach, though it is not restricted to him, is 'political activist'.

Let me not compound the sins of others by making an equally suspect totalizing claim of my own. There are more tangents of definitional equivalency in fundamentalism than the three which I have cited, but these three form a convenient set of referents for considering multiple fundamentalisms. No matter what the religion or location, fundamentalists may be literalist, terrorist, or just plain political activist. Each definitional option depends on the context which you choose to explore and, even more, on the interpreter whose reading of religious data you choose to follow.

Fundamentalists as Anti-modernists and Anti-nationalists: The Sikh Case

None of the above definitions are finally serviceable, however, unless one provides an additional perspective sorely lacking in most studies of fundamentalism: diachronic historical investigation. Why did fundamentalists emerge only at that conjunction in the experience of humankind called the modern age or the High Tech Era? Are there no premodern, pretechnological fundamentalists, and if not, why not? What do fundamentalists share with one another that separates them from other potential terrorists, political activists, or scriptural literalists? How can one make sense of all the varieties of fundamentalism without succumbing to a form of stereotyping reductionism that precisely mirrors the accusation which others level against fundamentalism?

To answer such questions we need to ask a still bigger question: How did the modern world come into being? What limits did it pose to pre-modern elites, and to traditional values? What are the 'real' revolutions that continue to shape the world in which we all live, fundamentalists and non-fundamentalists alike?

In my view, there is one theorist who more than any other helps to set the stage for considering the emergence, the threat, and the limits of fundamentalism. His name is Marshall Hodgson. Well known to Islamicists, Hodgson was actually a member of that rare breed of scholars who tried to escape the ghetto existence of his own guild: he studied Islam but he studied it as a global historian with a truly ecumenical view of human-kind. He believed in modernity. He traced its origin to a basic transforma-tion of the world order, beginning with the Enlightenment. He termed this transformation the Great Western Transmutation, or GWT for short. The GWT was a process that was, coincidentally, not inevitably Western. The GWT began in one part of the globe, the West, but in time it affected everyone everywhere on the face of the earth. The GWT had economic, political and social manifestations but it was also religious in its counter-threat. The GWT became a threat to *all* religion because it stressed the human rather than the divine, rationality rather than faith, efficiency rather than value, meaning rather than truth, quantity rather than quality, science rather than superstition, and change rather than continuity.[6]

The GWT, as exposited by seminal figures like Thomas Jefferson, Karl Marx, Friedrich Nietzsche, and Michel Foucault, claimed to be non-religious. It was, in fact, anti-religious, excising the God-factor from all cognitive understandings of the historical process or contemporary exist-ence. Just as the GWT became worldwide, so did the reaction against it by those who were moderns but not modernists. Though modernized in their social pursuits and instrumental skills, they refused to relativize their worldview. They became known as 'fundamentalists'.

Chief among the attributes of all fundamentalists is opposition to the cognitive core of modernism, that is, the relativization of every human value, the framing of a spectrum analysis that includes all viewpoints within itself and so asserts itself as the ultimate point of reference. The constitution becomes the scripture, the supreme court, the church of America – that is the argument of proponents of civil religion, and it captures the extent to which, as the sociologist John Wilson (1987) has observed, America is still the pioneer standard-bearer of global seculariza-tion (p. 21). Global fundamentalisms reject not only civil religion but all its trappings. Fundamentalists are anti-relativists, opposing the corrosive acid of modernism with values that they uphold as eternal and absolute, God-given and scripturally empowered. Once framed in its global perspective, fundamentalism makes sense. It is an ideology. It is countercultural. It is often political, but it is above all religious in that it derives from charismatic leaders who uphold a particular interpretation of scripture as the only fail-safe device for protesting against the phalanx of modernism, which is also the umbrella of nationalism.

There are multiple relationships – more oppositional than complementary, but necessarily both – which characterize fundamentalism and nationalism. It is a major topic explored in *Defenders of God*, where I look at the symbiosis of the religious and political Islamic Republic of Iran, as also the Gush Emunim and the National Religious Party in Israel. Beyond these cases, let me introduce a further case, the case of Sikhs, in order to highlight both the possibilities and the limits of talking about global fundamentalism or multiple fundamentalisms.

The Sikhs stand apart. They stand apart because Sikhs, besides requiring their men to wear distinct headgear or turbans, often migrate abroad and almost always prefer to live in cities. They are internationally engaged as traders, middlemen, entrepreneurs in a wide range of communicative, technological and electronic industries. Fourteen million strong, the majority of Sikhs continue to dwell in a single region of South Asia, the agricultural heartland of present-day North India, the Punjab. Sikhs are Punjabis, by ethnic background, linguistic training, and cultural outlook. They are also deeply religious in their private and public profile.

Sikhs trace their ancestry back to a North Indian protest movement that produced a string of warrior saints known as *gurus*. Two of these gurus, Guru Nanak and Guru Gobind Singh, dwarf others in the historical and symbolic force that they have imparted to current Sikh perceptions of collective identity. While Guru Nanak is lauded as an apostle of ecumenical engagement, Guru Gobind Singh is heralded as the exemplar of communitarian separatism, demanding loyalty to the insider-group above and against all others. The ideal Sikh community, according to Guru Gobind Singh, is the *khalsa*. But aspirations of the *khalsa* have been thwarted by the GWT, first by eighteenth-century Mughal officials who prevented Sikh agriculturalists from acquiring land tenure in the Punjab, then by nineteenth- and early twentieth-century British administrators who harnessed both Hindu and Sikh commodity export producers to the cyclical demands of a new world capitalist system, and finally by post-Independence Hindu nationalists who denied Sikhs the benefit of the only territorial patrimony they ever claimed, the Punjab.

Since 1947 Sikhs have had special cause to be bitter about the winds of historical change. Consider the most long-suffering Sikh agriculturalists, those who migrated to eastern Punjab from western Punjab, joining their

destiny to the newly independent, secular state of India. Told to subordinate their interests to the multiple strands of Indian national identity, they
were not granted the same measure of autonomy as Hindus in adjacent
Kashmir. Neither in 1947 nor in the decades immediately after did Sikhs
get either a separate state or its psychological equivalent. In 1961 Tara
Singh coined the rhetorical query: 'The Hindus got Hindustan, the Muslims
got Pakistan, what did the Sikhs get?'[7]

Among the many answers to this riddle, some were humorous, even
obscene. Five years later, however, the Sikhs got a positive answer, or
so it seemed. In 1966 the Sikh leader, Sant Fatch Singh, threatened to
fast until death unless his group's demands for a separate state were
granted by the Government of India. The result was a compromise: the
former state of Punjab was divided into two states, one Haryana with a
majority of Hindus, the other a rump state of Punjab with a majority of
Sikhs. The victory proved to be pyrrhic, however, since Sikhs did not
constitute a decisive majority and their demographic margin slipped to
barely 52 per cent by the early 1980s. Also there continued to be rural–
urban demographic disparities, with Hindus maintaining their plurality
in the major cities of the Punjab. Even the unprecedented increase in
Punjabi wheat production during the late 1970s did not benefit all Sikhs,
nor did it translate into greater political power, either at the national
level or in the jockeying for influence at the principal gurudwara sites.

It was in response to these circumstances of alienation and distrust
that one sub-group of Sikh cultivators, the Bhindranwale Jat, began to
call in increasingly strident tones for spiritual restoration. The Bhindranwale Jat never spoke for the majority of Punjabi Sikhs, and many other
Sikhs openly opposed their leadership throughout the 1970s. But the
Indian government chose to ignore the potential danger of intra-Sikh
factionalism; some have even argued that government officials tipped
their influence toward the underdog Sant Bhindranwale, presuming
they could always outmanoeuvre or outlast him. The result of that fatal
miscalculation, whether due to deliberate neglect or malevolent intervention, was a bloody moment of state-sponsored terrorism, so bloody
that its culmination in 1984 has been labelled by Sikh observers as the
Holocaust of the Punjab. It involved a direct military assault by Indian
Army shock troops on Sant Bhindranwale and his supporters after the
latter had cloistered themselves with a vast arsenal of modern weapons
in the holiest of holy Sikh shrines at Amritsar. Thousands were killed,
including Sant Bhindranwale, and massive damage was done to the
major structures of the Amritsar complex. The outrage of Sikhs was not
quelled until Mrs Gandhi, who had ordered the assault, code named
Operation Bluestar, was assassinated by her own Sikh bodyguards in
November of the same year. Equally appalling was the carnage visited

upon the Sikhs by revenge-minded Hindu nationalists after Mrs Gandhi's assassination. Though scarcely mentioned in the same breath with Operation Bluestar, it may be more fittingly titled a holocaust. The official toll of Sikhs killed in Delhi alone in the first four days of November 1984 was 2,146, most through random acts of mob violence, which also led to damage or destruction of over 400 Sikh temples (gurudwaras). In addition to the official toll of those brutalized or murdered, there was the fear-induced migration of more than 50,000 Sikhs from different parts of India to the Punjab: they sought, but seldom found, refuge from further acts of violence by aggrieved Hindus.[8]

As a result of Operation Bluestar and the chain of events it unleashed, the agitation for a separate Sikh nation that the Operation was intended to quell persists, however muted, till the present day. Through the Indian government's action Sant Bhindranwale became not only a martyr but a focal point for all the longings of Sikh separatists. Dissent from non-separatists became increasingly less tolerated, especially after the major accommodationist, Sant Harchand Singh Longowal, was assassinated in 1985.

Even from such a brief narration one can see how Sikh fundamentalism conforms to the general pattern of global fundamentalism that fits the activist/terrorist model, at the same time that Sikh protests have an internal logic justified by the most recent history of the Punjab and the Republic of India. A beleaguered sub-group within a marginalized minority embraces a religious ideology of protest against the dominant oppressor. In this case, as in most others, the oppressor is deemed to be the modern nation-state (e.g., the Republic of India) because it subordinates all ideologies to its own and projects its power through coercive structures, at once economic and political, journalistic and military, overt and covert.

Conclusion

The more one investigates global fundamentalism(s), the more contradictions proliferate, and preformulated stereotypes have to be adjusted or abandoned. There is not a single brand of global fundamentalism but three major brands and countless hybrid forms of each brand. It is better to speak of global fundamentalisms than a single worldwide fundamentalist movement, and to acknowledge the agenda of each as both discrete in its local context and inter-connected through the contradictions of late capitalism.

What are the contradictions of late capitalism? Above all, they are the indices of global inequities that persist within as well as between the independent nation-states that dominate late twentieth-century political and economic, as also cultural and religious, exchange. For many, the optimism of pre-First World War Europe was dashed by that war and the subsequent events of man-made mass death (Wyschogrod 1985), with the Second World War prefiguring 'the age of total war' (Hobsbawm, 1994, pp. 21–53).

Yet it is necessary to recall the extent to which Euro-American elites remain wedded to a notion of teleological perfectionism. Technological advances in production, communication and medicine, combined with the triumph of global capitalism, are still imagined to be determinative, and despite the faddish fascination with transnational religion as a prelude to fading national identities (Rudolph and Piscatori (eds), 1997), divisions engendered by nationalism remain as fierce as when Tagore first warned of their danger (Tagore, 1917/1991).

In short, one must agree with the fundamentalists of every stripe that there is no imminent prospect of a value-neutral utopia where all races, creeds and viewpoints will find with all classes, generations and genders a better world order – at once more just and durable. Fundamentalists never believed such a utopia was possible, and their ideological protest against modernists/secularists/nationalists draws on circumstances of not just alienation but deprivation that afflicts much of humankind. What I once said about Afro-Asian Muslims also applies to the majority of non-Muslims in Africa, Asia and much of Latin America: with the exception of social and political elites, most are compelled 'to seek the basic staples of survival, to wit, food, water, clothing, shelter, and only rarely have they had the "luxury" to pursue secondary concerns like better employment for themselves, higher education for their children, religious conformity for their country, or (in the case of women) status revision for their gender' (Lawrence, 1989/1995, p. 203).

The future looks to be still more dystopian than utopian for the world's inhabitants outside the all-too narrow information highway and the cosmopolitan bourgeoisies who both benefit from, and are sustained by, its magical allure. East and West elide, but in a single age-old global economy that perpetuates inequality: even as resources, services and benefits of the High Tech Era flow toward Asia. Religious protestors will surface within the societies of most rapid change, and their vehement opponents will also be their immediate targets: secularists who share belief in the continuous growth of a world system marked by cultural diversity and political pluralism as well as persistent rivalries (McNeill, 1995).

Hence the sociocultural gaps of our uneven, modern world will continue to evoke varied responses from both religious and secular ideologues. Though those of us who are secularists, or at least non-fundamentalists, can never erase the challenge posed by fundamentalists, we should have strategies for coping. The first step in coping is to appreciate the fundamentalist dilemma; it is integral to the same world disorder that plagues all of us and prods us to be imaginative as well as compassionate in our dealing with others unlike us.

On that score scholarship is as pragmatic as computer programming, yet it is less susceptible to homogenization than the Netscape. It requires attention to moods and motivations that Clifford Geertz perhaps did not imagine when he framed his much quoted definition of religion (1973; discussed and critiqued by Asad, 1993, pp. 29f.). It suggests that the symbolic and emotive power of fundamentalism is as authentically modern as it is persistently disruptive. The lessons are not easy to learn but they need to be learned and then applied again and again, especially as a new millennium dawns not merely with the failed predictions of apocalypticists but also with the lowered expectations of much of humankind.

Notes

1 The five volumes, with their publication dates, are: *Fundamentalists Observed* (1991), *Fundamentalists and Society* (1993), *Fundamentalists and the State* (1993), *Accounting for Fundamentalists* (1994), and *Fundamentalists Comprehended* (1995). All were co-edited by Martin Marty and Scott Appleby. All were published by the University of Chicago Press.

2 The quotation is excerpted from p. 2 of an articulate programme summary announcing a 26–7 April 1996 international conference, 'Challenging Fundamentalism: Questioning Political and Scholarly Simplifications', convened in Kuala Lumpur under the joint auspices of the Institute for Malaysian and International Studies (IKMAS), Universiti Kebangsaan Malaysia and the Friedrich Naumann Foundation, Germany.

3 See Bruce Lawrence, *Defenders of God* (pp. 48–9), for the rationale behind this choice of temporal marking, both aligned to and distinct from Hodgson's GWT, or Great Western Transmutation.

4 Bruce Lawrence, Religious fundamentalists: a bibliographical survey, Part 1: Islam – Khomeini and after (1993), a review of over 75 books on Islamic fundamentalism(s), mostly from the 1980s and early 1990s.

5 All these quotations come from the last section of Loeffler's carefully structured and highly nuanced book (1988), the section being entitled 'The Effect of the Revolution' (pp. 225–44).

6 See especially Marshall G. S. Hodgson, *The Venture of Islam* (1974), vol. 3 for an elaboration of his several arguments on the distinctive character of the modern period.

7 See Harjot Oberoi, 'Sikh Fundamentalism: Translating History into Theory' (1993, p. 260). A superb analytical essay on both Sikhism and the fundamentalist phenomenon, it lays out the features of scriptural absolutism and its oppositional force better than any comparable study of a fundamentalist movement.

8 See Harjot S. Oberoi, 'From Punjab to Khalistan: Territoriality and Metacommentary' (1987, p. 39).

References

Ammerman, Nancy 1987: *Bible Believers: Fundamentalists in the Modern World*. New Brunswick: Rutgers University Press.

Asad, Talal 1993: *Genealogies of Religion*. Baltimore: Johns Hopkins University Press.

Boone, Kathleen 1989: *The Bible Tells Them So: The Discourse of Protestant Fundamentalism*. Albany: State University of New York Press.

Dekmejian, Richard 1985: *Islam in Revolution. Fundamentalism in the Arab World*. Syracuse: Syracuse University Press. (2nd edition, 1995)

Geertz, Clifford 1973: *The Interpretation of Culture*. New York: Basic Books.

Hobsbawm, E. J. 1994: *Age of Extremes. The Short Twentieth Century, 1914–1991*. London: Michael Joseph.

Hodgson, Marshall G. S. 1974: *The Venture of Islam*. Chicago: University of Chicago Press, vol. 3.

Lawrence, Bruce 1989: *Defenders of God: The Fundamentalist Revolt against the Modern Age*. San Francisco: HarperSanFrancisco; 1995, with new Preface, Columbia: University of South Carolina.

—— 1993: Religious fundamentalisms: a bibliographical survey, Part 1: Islam – Khomeini and after. *Choice*, February, pp. 923–32.

Loeffler, Reinhold 1988: *Islam in Practice: Religious Beliefs in a Persian Village*. Albany: State University of New York Press.

Lustick, Ian 1988: *For the Land and the Lord: Jewish Fundamentalism in Israel*. New York: Council on Foreign Relations.

McNeill, William H. 1995: The rise of the West after 25 years. In Stephen K. Sanderson (ed.), *Civilization and World Systems: Studying World-Historical Change*. London: Sage.

Oberoi, Harjot 1987: From Punjab to 'Khalistan': territoriality and metacommentary. *Pacific Affairs* 60 (1): 26–41.

—— 1993: Sikh fundamentalism: translating history into theory. In Martin Marty and Scott Appleby (eds), *Fundamentalisms and the State*, Chicago: University of Chicago Press, pp. 256–85.

Rudolph, Susanne H. and James Piscatori (eds) 1997: *Transnational Religion and Fading States*. Boulder: Westview Press.

Sivan, Emmanuel 1985: *Radical Islam: Medieval Theology and Modern Politics*. New Haven: Yale University Press.

Tagore, Rabindranath 1917/1991 (with a new introduction by E. P. Thompson): *Nationalism*. London/New Delhi: Macmillan.

Wilson, John F. 1987: Modernity. In M. Eliade (ed.), *The Encyclopedia of Religion*, New York and London: Macmillan, vol. 10, pp. 17–22.

Wyschogrod, Edith 1985: *Spirit in Ashes. Hegel, Heidegger and Man-Made Mass Death*. New Haven: Yale University Press.

CHAPTER SEVEN

from pre- to postmodernity in Latin America: the case of Pentecostalism

Bernice Martin

Introduction: Postmodern Theorizing – Some Reservations

According to many of its current theorizers, postmodernity is not a neatly definable, unified concept. Indeed, postmodern theory proclaims the demise of watertight, unified categories, especially those in the binary mode, since the Cartesian (modernist) mafia which used to patrol their boundaries have all been dismissed from office as charlatans engaged only in 'legitimating the rules of their own (language) game', as Lyotard (1984) puts it. Thus postmodern theory itself has to be recognized as a series of only partly overlapping 'discourses' or 'language games' sharing, at best, a 'family resemblance' (*pace* Wittgenstein) which enables us to group them loosely together under that evocatively imprecise heading.

This is not the place to engage in detail with the philosophical premises of the various postmodern theorists except in order to make clear what this essay is *not* attempting, and to assert a thoroughly late- and reflexive-modernist view about the nature of the social and the status of evidence, not least because the substance of this chapter is the obstinately burgeoning state of (Protestant) Christianity – at least in Latin America – one of those Grands Récits dismissed as obsolete (intellectually untenable? mere relativized preference rather than Universal Truth? empirically fragmented and declining?) by the most influential (French) strand of postmodern theory. Indeed, I am almost tempted to suggest that much postmodern theory, as it relates to religion, looks more like a continuation of the

Enlightenment secularization metanarrative than like a really radical break with that supposedly discredited discourse of Western power and bourgeois intellectual dominance.

Postmodern theories primarily concerned with philosophical abstraction tend to focus on *how* human beings 'know' rather than *what* they know. Such theories are epistemologically based critiques of what passes for knowledge. Starting from the ineradicable positionality of the observing subject they proceed to destabilize the claims to objectivity, neutrality and universality which have been made for 'scientific' and 'expert' knowledge of all kinds, including that of the social sciences. Both the French structuralist and poststructuralist tradition and the Marxist strand of critical theory, deriving largely from the Frankfurt school, tend to represent knowledge (and, indeed, cultural and material practices) as 'discourse' which is inescapably 'ideological'. Both knowledge and the knowing subject are regarded as fragmented, partial (in both senses of the word), discontinuous and radically disintegrated. The idea of a unified, objectively knowable social reality 'out there' is exposed as the mythic construct of bourgeois rationalism, itself a product of the discourse of the Enlightenment metanarrative. The premise of the integrated, unified, individual subject, central both to Enlightenment rationality and to bourgeois individualism, meets the same fate. Individual subjectivity, constituted in and through language and symbolic communication, is seen as the site on which multiple, discontinuous discourses collide, creating dissonance, fragmentation and eloquent but unacknowledged absences.

Postmodern culture, the construct of postindustrial electronic and computerized communication and information, mimics these philosophical aperçus in its own fragmented, discontinuous and fluid character. In a style which itself demonstrates the excess and ambiguity he attributes to postmodern culture, Baudrillard (1988), for example, claims that all 'objects' and 'functions' are abolished and 'there remains only a single dimension, communication': culture becomes an obscene 'ecstasy of communication'; the human self no more than a television screen on which the entire universe is forever arbitrarily projected, while the interior of the self is flattened and eliminated through its exposure, in turn, to the entire universe.

According to this postmodern vision of culture, all the walls and boundaries are collapsed – between interior and exterior, public and private, the imaginary and the real – while signifiers float loose from the signified, meanings are destabilized, everyday life is aestheticized, and culture is marked by the fusion and confusion of 'high' and 'popular' forms, and by the prevalence of simulation, spectacle and a commercialized nostalgia.

Baudrillard's particular version of postmodernity is markedly dystopian, even nihilistic. Many other theorists of the postmodern, notably those influenced by Foucault, are also fatalistic about the ever mysterious efficacy with which the 'state', or 'power', or what Lyotard bathetically calls 'decision makers', deploy coercive discourses which serve to make individuals the 'willing' agents of their own oppression and exploitation. (This, for many, is where religion comes in – as an obsolete but still coercive discourse, especially if it can plausibly be tarred with the brush of 'fundamentalism'.) Some, more dependent than they often admit on the shattered fragments of Enlightenment reason, persist in hoping for revelation and emancipation through the (essentially intellectual) exercise of deconstructing 'dominant' discourses. (Feminist critical theory like that of Catherine Belsey (1985) comes to mind here.) Others rely on the protean, disruptive, carnivalesque manifestations of Desire in postmodern culture to perform the same emancipatory, liberating miracle which the bohemian *avant-garde* has been hoping for since at least the *fin de siècle*.[1]

I have problems with much of this, not least with the inconsistencies – the continuing aspiration to reveal what was hidden by the old meta-narratives while denying the possibility of arriving at any better approximations to an unobtainable truth; the epistemological turn which denies any possibility of access to a reality beyond situated discourse but which nevertheless traces cultural transformations to documentable, observable technological changes; and most of all the postmodern assertion that such contradictions are simply not a problem because inconsistency and incommensurability are inherent in the postmodern condition and not resolvable through an outdated bourgeois rationality which anyway misses the point of the postmodern self as inescapably multiple, protean and fragmented.

Fortunately there are other ways of conceiving of postmodernity which retain a foothold in philosophical realism, that is, in the assumption that there is indeed a social reality 'out there', not, to be sure, quite so unified nor so totally transparent and amenable to demonstration as the classical social sciences sometimes supposed, but documentable nevertheless, even allowing for the inevitable distortions in that documentation which arise from the situated 'blick' of the observer, even, sometimes, open to alteration by intentional human action. Indeed, the (postmodern) *recognition* of the positionality of the observer, far from destroying the very possibility of rationality and science, itself demonstrates the quality of reflexivity, that is, the human capacity to learn new lessons, to hear voices which have before been inaudible, to recognize absences when they are brought to the attention, in short, to *adjust* the position from which we observe in the light of new evidence and new approaches to what constitutes *evidence*. Postmodern theory has not in fact eliminated the *practice* of mainstream empirical social science, however much its rhetoric is inclined to relativize the truth claims of so dull and dated an enterprise.

Thus, an influential text such as Ulrich Beck's *Risk Society* (1992) operates from an implicit premise of philosophical realism. Indeed, all those comparative sociologists like Beck who remain more concerned with *what* we know about the new global social and economic dispensation, rather than being solely concerned with the philosophical basis of *how* we know anything at all, largely by-pass the epistemological dilemma and continue working within adaptations of classical sociological frameworks. David Harvey, whose *The Condition of Postmodernity* (1989) has become an indispensable source, continues to work out of the classical Marxist Grand Récit into which he has – reflexively, of course – incorporated insights from Simmel and others. Other sociologists combine Weberian models with the phenomenological tradition: thus, for example, Hansfried Kellner, starting from Weber's observations about the application of technical rationality to ever more human enterprises, empirically anatomizes the postmodern itch to tinker with the structures of 'the lifeworld' by constantly unstitching the taken-for-granted in the pursuit of individuation, novelty, and the extension of the capitalist marketplace (see Kellner and Heuberger, 1991).

Yet others draw, in a thoroughly eclectic way, on several sociological traditions; for example Anthony Giddens (1991), Krishan Kumar (1995), Scott Lash and John Urry (1987, 1993) and Mike Featherstone (1990, 1991, 1995), as well as Ulrich Beck, all make use of Weber, fragments of Marx, much Simmel, Elias, and any other theorists who can conceptually facilitate a systematic empirical and comparative sociology of the world we currently inhabit. (See also Beck, Giddens and Lash, 1994.) Such social realist approaches are fundamentally concerned to map the interplay between economic, technological, social and cultural change in the contemporary world and to elucidate the senses in which that world is evolving into a 'global' system. It is such versions of the postmodern debate on which I shall primarily draw in my own substantive analysis below.

All these writers have noted many of the same cultural traits celebrated/demonized by the philosophical postmodern theorists – fragmentation, contradiction, the symbiosis of the local and the global, the contraction, or, in Anthony Giddens's term, the 'distanciation' of time and space, the fusion of 'high' and 'low' culture, the prevalence of spectacle and so on – and relate them back to empirical phenomena, notably to the new structures of global capitalism, the communicative logic of the technologically new systems of information and communication, and the pivotal role of cultural as well as other kinds of technical experts within post-industrial capitalism. They *situate* the philosophical project of postmodern theorizing, as well as the marks of postmodern culture, within a matrix of documented empirical change. In *Economies of Signs and Space*, Scott

Lash and John Urry (1993) offer a neat summary of recent global processes which have resulted in the emergence of postmodern cultures and
postindustrial economies worldwide. The primary components of their
model are: globally circulating objects, that is, capital, goods, services,
information and communication; mobile subjects, that is, a global labour
market involving large-scale migrations of both permanent and temporary
sorts at all levels of skill; steady increments of both cognitive and aesthetic
reflexivity; and an ever greater individualization in both economic and
social life. All these developments are facilitated, perhaps even necessitated,
by the pervasiveness and pivotal role of information and communication
structures located both at the control centres of economic and political
activity and at the level of everyday life, accompanied by a radical transformation of the configurations of time and space. With such a model
it then becomes possible to deploy comparative empirical analysis, as in
their earlier book, *The End of Organized Capitalism* (1987), to account for
the variety of approximations to the model in actual societies, to trace
different routes to postmodernity and to delineate the alternative articulations of the local and the global.

Religion, Modernity and Postmodernity: a Preliminary Empirical Note

I shall attempt to show below how such a model illuminates the recent
history of Latin America and its progressive incorporation into global
capitalism since the 1960s. Crucially, I shall argue that the mass movement of Latin American Protestantism has been an integral part of a
dramatic transformation of the continent in a postmodern direction. This
latter point calls for some preliminary glossing, since, before the event,
the emergence of such a movement on such a scale would have been
regarded as thoroughly implausible in the most influential sociological
circles. *Nobody* expected a new Protestant Reformation! In fact modernist – Enlightenment – sociology got it badly wrong so far as religion is
concerned: Durkheim, as an anti-Enlightenment thinker, is an honour-
able partial exception here. Far from fading away as modernity bit, religion has acquired a new lease of life in the postmodern era, sprouting
vigorous revival movements in Islam and a vast, worldwide expansion
of 'third force' Christianity based on the 'Gifts of the Spirit'. This latter movement has spread widely through Africa, Asia and the Pacific
Rim as well as Central and South America, and is currently appearing
among the ruins of the eastern European Communist experiment and
even in parts of western Europe itself. Indeed, as Peter Berger (1992)
insists, far from being the type case of the future, western Europe, with
its Scandinavian vanguard of secularity and 'post-material values' (see

Inglehart and Granato, 1996), looks ever more like the *exception* so far as religion goes. Thus an increasingly religiously indifferent western Europe faces a global system in which religious identity is still deeply etched at both individual and (local) collective level and in which serious revival movements are occurring in all three World Religions of the Book *as part of the globalization process.*

It seems to me to be misleading, mischievous even, to characterize all of this as 'religious fundamentalism' – an unmistakably pejorative term in the vocabulary of the European intelligentsia – as Zygmunt Bauman does in this volume, and to place these movements within 'a wider family of totalitarian or proto-totalitarian solutions offered to all those who find the burden of individual freedom excessive and unbearable' (p. 74). I suggest that this fundamentally [sic] misrepresents the reality of the new Pentecostal Protestantism of Latin America, and does so partly because it derives from an over-determined and over-systematized view of belief systems *in the abstract*, with insufficient understanding of how beliefs operate in an everyday context where 'individual freedom' and 'totalitarian solutions' are seldom so conveniently or neatly polarized. I contend, moreover, that it is only by descending to the quotidian and the empirical that one can observe the ways in which such movements operate to *empower* individuals in new ways and open up to them freedoms which have never before shown up on the radar screen of self or of society in the regions and among the social groups most affected by these movements in the new global context.

The point holds equally at the level of persons and at the level of social and cultural systems. David Martin (1996) has comprehensively exposed the category mistake involved in grouping all theologically conservative 'revival' movements in the contemporary world under the rubric of 'fundamentalism', either through their supposed 'totalitarian' ambitions or through their doctrine of Biblical (or Koranic) inerrancy: in any case, third force Christianity is more centrally marked by the importance of the gifts of the Spirit than by the doctrine of Biblical inerrancy. As Martin shows, the recent wave of Pentecostal Christianity, in reality, has opened up large cracks in all the old 'sacred canopies': in other words it is a major element in a massive worldwide shift – a shift not unrelated to the impact of (post-)modern communications – away from religious/cultural monopolies and towards a pluralism based on the voluntary principle. Thus, whereas it may well be that the Afghan Taliban are indeed seeking to eliminate that gap between church and state in which civil society might grow, in the case of Latin American Pentecostalism the movement is instrumental in *opening up* just such a space. Latin American Protestants assuredly do hold to strict rules of life and throw up a stratum of powerful pastors, but neither feature makes them a 'totalitarian' movement. What they are equally essentially doing is 'walking out' from the *old* coercions of what Rowan Ireland (1991) refers to in Brazil as a suffocating combination of 'national security authoritarianism' in the political sphere and *'coronelismo-paternalismo'* (clientelism) in the cultural sphere. Instead, the new Protestants create what David Martin (1996, p. 10) calls their own 'autonomous spiritual space over against comprehensive systems' and there nurture new cultural and personal potentialities.

The global importance of this emergence of pluralist options will be clearer if we consider a further aspect of the picture. Most of the areas of mass religious revival today are located in what until very recently we would have called the Third World. In general these are places where, to put it broadly and without nuance, there has been or there is currently occurring a swift transition from *pre*modern to *post*modern conditions with barely any classically modernist phase intervening. Such is certainly the case in Latin America. Classical models of 'development' derived from the history of *industrialization* in western Europe may, therefore, be less than helpful in illuminating these new situations, though empirical models of *postindustrial* economies and *postmodern* culture may have a relevance and analytic value.

Certainly the coincidence of mass religious revivals with this shift from pre- to postmodernity was not anticipated by *any* theoretical tradition in the social sciences. In the case of Latin America few social scientists of any persuasion would have been surprised to see a slow erosion of Latin American Catholicism by secularizing forces on the lines of western Europe. A handful, it is true, eagerly anticipated the mass impact of a radicalized Catholicism following liberation theology's 'option for the poor'. In fact neither of those things happened and no-one predicted what did occur, that is, the rise, between the 1960s and the present, of a powerful Protestant movement, largely (70 per cent) Pentecostal in character, beginning among the poor but spreading steadily into the middle classes. It currently involves around 10 per cent of the Latin American population, some 40 million to 50 million people in all, and it is still growing. It ranges from almost a third of the population in Guatemala, through Chile at 20 per cent, Brazil at 15 per cent, Mexico at 10 per cent, to Venezuela where Protestants are so far a negligible figure. Overall, this development has effectively eroded the cultural monopoly of Catholicism which persisted in Iberia's New World territories long after they had acquired independence and even after the formal separation of church and state, and has finally ushered in an era of creeping religious pluralism. This incipient pluralism perhaps 'fits' the condition of postmodernity more easily than would a continuing religious monopoly, but it is important to recognize the half-hidden *cultural* diversity within the richly syncretic colonial Catholic monopoly of premodern Latin America, since it provides a rich soil for the volatile postmodern cultural developments. Catholicism may have monopolized *power*, but it has always concealed a potentially explosive *cultural* diversity beneath its strained baroque façade.

Indeed, if postmodern culture is characterized by 'floating signifiers', then a good case can be made for regarding the culture of most of Latin America, but pre-eminently that of Brazil, as having been postmodern *avant la lettre*. The ethnic and cultural mix of the continent has produced a riotous syncretism of mix-and-match, or perhaps more accurately, of hide-and-seek symbolism. Historically, the Portuguese imperium in Brazil was even more ramshackle than its Hispanic counterpart in the rest of the New World, and the Catholic Church, spread thinly, reliant on foreign man-power and funding, was subject to endemic laxity and corruption over several centuries. The result was a patchwork of syncretic beliefs and cultural practices which incorporated much of the religion of the con-quered indigenous peoples and of the imported African slaves in a variety of more or less transmuted forms. Despite periodic suppression, the religion of the subject peoples has shifted shape and contrived some kind of con-tinuous existence over five hundred years, sometimes underground, often under the guise of folk Catholicism, sometimes in its own right. The cross-fertilization of elements has been so extensive that, in the contemporary context, attempts to recuperate some long-lost 'pure' culture – of negritude, of spiritism, even of Latin American Catholicism or an 'uncorrupted' Pro-testantism – are bound to resort to the pious fictions familiar to theorists of postmodernity. They become instances of (often politicized) 'nostalgia', cultural constructs of a desired 'authenti-city' located in a mythic past which elides the compromises and messy co-existences of the real history of ethnic conquest and cultural survival-against-the-odds.

It is crucial to recognize that Latin America has remained relatively untouched by the Enlightenment, and, apart from a tiny minority of secu-lar liberal intellectuals, the population at all status levels has remained thoroughly 'inspirited': Latin American society is still 'enchanted' in Weber's sense. Its 'magical realist' fiction, so popular on the global liter-ature market, is one expression of this. What the continent shares with its superpower northern neighbour, the USA, is the weakness of that popular secularization which was supposed to arrive with 'modernity'.[2] The Latin American culture, which is currently accommodating itself to a traumatic shift towards a postindustrial economy and postmodern soci-ety, still takes for granted the religious ground of individual and social being. We should not be surprised, therefore, if religious movements accompany the social and economic upheavals which have convulsed the continent in recent decades.

Western secular intellectuals, who tend to regard *political* protest as the only proper (rational? secular?) response to dramatic social change, have simply failed to recognize the *religious* movements of the poor as genuine *mass* movements. It is remarkable, for example, how few of the many volumes of research on social movements in Latin America ever refer to Protestantism even when they include Catholic base communities within their purview; and the few that do not totally ignore Protestantism seem to have noticed it mainly because their focus is women (60 per cent of the new Protestants are female) rather than because they have a more adequate perspective on what constitutes a social movement (see, for instance, Jelin, 1990). It is doubly important, therefore, to take note of the accounts of Protestants themselves, who eloquently attest the many ways in which conversion brings them an increased measure of control over their individual and communal destiny and expands the options realistically available in their everyday lives. They are very clear that their faith and their churches together revolutionize their lives and prospects. The new Protestantism is thus intensely relevant to this-worldly concerns and not merely an other-worldly hope or a sectarian 'religion of the oppressed'. Indeed, it is often precisely what makes the practical difference between riding the wave of social change and being swamped by it.

In what follows, I shall first outline the structural changes in Latin America which herald postmodernity; then examine the role of the new Protestant movement in this transformation; and finally point to some recent developments within Brazilian Protestantism which display exuberantly postmodern cultural features by contrast with the classic (modernist, European) Protestantism on which Weber, Troeltsch and other sociologists of religion have based their models. I shall argue that these features are both genuinely postmodern and at the same time continuous with aspects of the premodern folk religiosity of Latin America. They are also in sharp tension with some of the hedonistic assumptions of postmodern popular culture.

The Arrival of Postmodernity in Latin America

Since the 1940s, and more swiftly since the 1960s, Latin America has experienced a huge economic and cultural transformation which has attracted less notice than the violent political upheavals which have accompanied and, in important ways, facilitated the change – the usurpation of leftist regimes by rightist military dictatorships, some with US backing, in the 1960s and 1970s, and the eventual return (mostly) to civilian democratic government in the 1980s. Over these decades Latin

America has become integrated into the global capitalist economy and the global culture of communications – for example, as Barney Warf shows (1995), unlike Africa and most of the Middle East a large part of Latin America in on the Internet today and can boast a number of 'global cities' which form important nodes on the worldwide trading and information network.

Latin America has acquired a postindustrial economy and a postmodern cultural sphere in a remarkably short time. Certainly there remain differences between the Latin American and the North American/European economies but they are differences of scale and balance rather than of kind. Indeed, as Nigel Harris (1987) among others has argued, although a vocabulary of Third World/First World contrasts still pervades the development literature, this terminology is increasingly unsatisfactory as a way of de-signating whole regions of the world. The global economy today distributes employment and capital without much reference to societal borders, and the global winners and losers in the capitalist game are increasingly differentiated *within* rather than straightforwardly *between* societies and regions.

It is normal to find ever-growing pockets of First World conditions within so-called Third World societies: indeed there is little to differentiate the lives of the new middle classes, the postmodern technocrats, communications experts, business managers and the rest as between, say, São Paulo and London. Conversely, in First World societies subject to stiffening global economic competition and its associated economic shake-ups – deindustrialization, corporate downsizing, high unemployment and underemployment especially among the least skilled and the young – an underbelly of marginalized sectors has appeared, marked by conditions which until very recently we would have associated exclusively with Third World 'underdevelopment'. Certainly there remains a difference in the scale and intensity of poverty and marginalization among the poor in the shanty towns of, say, Rio as against their counterparts in the 'sink estates' of, say, Liverpool, but the similarities have become striking enough to provoke a thesis of global 'underclass' convergence (see for example Seabrook, 1993). Lash and Urry (1993) have gone so far as to suggest that even the most (post)-modern societies today harbour a potentially 'ungovernable' class festering in 'impacted ghettoes' which differs only in scale from its counterpart in the megacities of the so-called Third World. Jeremy Rifkin's (1995) apocalyptic warnings make the point even more strongly.

This development in Latin America, in both its benign and its malign features, has been so swift as to be inescapably traumatic. A brief account of the process may help us to situate the equally dramatic and unanticipated growth of Protestantism which occurred in parallel with the economic and political transformations.

Beginning typically in the 1960s the states of Latin America were, as a matter of political policy, opened up to world trade. This brought inward investment but also a swift erosion of the import substitution industries on which the mostly leftist regimes of the immediately preceding period had based their policies of state-initiated industrialization, modernization and corporatist economic management. In a number of cases, notably Chile and Brazil, the free-trade policy was inaugurated by right-wing military juntas who had violently displaced the leftist regimes of the sixties. Their free-trade policy was part of a wider strategy of economic development which involved dismantling the protectionist apparatus of the regimes they had replaced. Multinational corporations flooded into the booming megacities of the 1970s along with the inward investment. At the same time, much of traditional agriculture was transformed into large agribusiness enterprises, as in the case of the Chilean fruit industry, for example. Simultaneously, Latin American governments began to apply policies of privatization and deregulation to domestic markets, emulating the neo-liberal economic ideas which were becoming dominant in North America and Europe in the seventies.

By the time that the transition back to parliamentary democracy occurred in the late 1970s or early 1980s, most of the states in the region were so deeply integrated into the global economy that a radical withdrawal from international capitalist competition behind a protectionist fence was no longer viable: after the fall of Communism such a reversion was perhaps less ideologically persuasive anyway. Crucially, however, the new civilian governments were prisoners of the debt crisis of the early 1980s, which was itself, at least in part, brought about by the free trade policies of the previous decade, exacerbated by recurring currency crises and a disastrous collapse of world commodity prices in 1980. Latin American indebtedness put effective control of economic policy in the region into the hands of the experts in the international financial institutions, who were managing the debt and who were thus able to insist on further instalments of neo-liberal economic policies as the condition for debt rescheduling and development assistance. Only in the early 1990s, after a decade of austerity in Latin America, have these international financial institutions, notably the World Bank, begun to soften their controls and encourage investment in human resources as a priority, notably through education, health, and pension schemes.[3]

The consequence of all this has been to fix the Latin American economies firmly inside the new global patterns of distribution of capital and labour. It has created a typically postindustrial labour market, particularly in the cities, largely by-passing the European stage of urban *industrialism* with its mass proletariat, for a hi-tech, information-based economy with a large tail of routine service-sector workers and a significant underbelly in the 'informal economy' which accommodates, typically, around a quarter of the labour force. Notwithstanding the (in reality, very limited) export of manufacturing from North America and elsewhere to the *maquiladoras* south of the Rio Grande, industrial manufacture remains a minority sector even in the most industrialized countries, such as Mexico and Brazil, where there is a significant manufacturing export trade. Moreover, the majority of manufacturing enterprises remain small scale and labour intensive (see Gwynne in Preston, 1987) – that is, pre-Fordist – while much of the recent manufacturing development is thoroughly post-Fordist (see for example Shaiken, 1994). And neither creates an industrial proletariat of the classic modernist kind. In little more than thirty years this process has transformed a premodern agrarian economy, structured on corporatist and clientelist lines, into a postindustrial capitalist system approximating ever more closely to the individualistic, venture-capital model of Latin America's major trading partner and powerful neighbour, the USA.

What does such a change mean for social organization? Its simplest narrative elements are: first, mass movements of population over space and over a changing occupational hierarchy, movements which have entailed the creation of the megacities, the continuous flow of labour to and from North America, and a widespread experience of upward occupational mobility among the new urbanites; secondly, a dramatic shift from the boom of the sixties and seventies to the post-debt recession of the eighties which not only interrupted the benevolent thrust of expanding opportunities but brought further traumas as the recession made possible an accelerated restructuring of the labour market into a now globally familiar 'flexible' shape with lower wage rates, greater insecurity and higher unemployment; and thirdly, the political traumas entailed by the history of repressive military regimes and their aftermath – at worst, continuing civil strife and guerrilla struggle, as until recently in Guatemala and Peru, or, at best, as in Chile or Argentina, a civic culture still coloured by the long shadow of political violence, repression and everywhere, endemic corruption and the widespread perception of the state as predatory. One obvious paradox is that the repressive juntas presided over the peak of the economic boom while the democratic regimes have had to take responsibility for the austerity measures. Let us take these elements and examine them more closely.

First, consider the mass movements of population, the emergence of what Lash and Urry (1993) call the 'mobile subjects' of the postmodern dispensation. The movement of population from the countryside to the towns began as early as the 1940s but speeded up sharply in the 1960s. As Alan Gilbert (1994) shows, from being only one-third urban in 1940 Latin America's population today is typically two-thirds urban while in the most advanced economies, including Mexico, Chile and Brazil, three-quarters of the population live in settlements of over 20,000. Moreover, most Latin American societies are economically and socially dominated by one or two mega-cities such as Mexico City with its 20 million inhabitants or São Paulo with nearly 18 million. While these cities are structured around a hi-tech heart, indistinguishable from similar quarters in Paris or Frankfurt, they have also spawned extensive shanty towns – housing and planning has never kept pace with the needs of the flood of rural migrants, and the most common mode of acquiring tenure in these pullulating spaces remains the 'invasion' or squatter settlement, and not only for the poorest segments.[4]

There is evidence that until the recession of the 1980s the migrants to the city were typically the more ambitious and better qualified people, and that their expectations of improved quality of life and occupational advance were well founded, despite the disorder and squalor of much of the shanty town development. Even the poorest in the city were better off than their rural relatives, whom they typically subsidized (see Gilbert, 1994). Even the most convinced Marxist scholars recognize the reality of a widespread experience of upward mobility and improving standards of living for the larger part of the urban population in the 1960s and 1970s (see for example Scott, 1994; Madeira and Singer, 1975; Gillespie, 1990).

It was, of course, the changes in the occupational structure itself which brought about this far-reaching pattern of net upward mobility. By the time of the debt crisis, the Latin American economy had come to look remarkably like that of the capitalist West. The service sector was unequivocally dominant, the core sector was firmly based in the most up-to-date systems of information and communication, with an extensive network of transnational corporations dominating the city and extending into agribusiness. The eighties recession merely added the finishing touches to this structure by further deregulating and 'flexibilizing' the labour market, expanding the practice of subcontracting and firming up the distinction between core and peripheral employment (see Gilbert, 1994; Gilbert and Gugler, 1992).

The growth of the service sector, here as elsewhere, has created a new middle class of white collar employees and postindustrial professionals in a brief couple of generations. The expansion was too swift for the offspring of the existing urban elite to fill the gaps, the deficit being made up by rural migrants converted in short order into clerks, salesmen, catering employees, computer experts, mass-media workers, teachers, government officials, social workers, managers and the rest. Gilbert (1994) notes that by the late seventies white collar workers in Latin American cities typically accounted for between 40 and 50 per cent of the formal labour force while industry seldom provided more than 30 per cent of employment. Commerce and services employed half to three-quarters of the workforce while the two largest categories of urban employment were, and remain, domestic servants (up to one-third of all employed persons) and sales staff (around 20 per cent). It is worth noting here that, though the evidence overall remains inconclusive, a number of studies such as that of Margo Smith (1973, in Pescatello) have suggested that domestic service has provided a particular channel of upward mobility, not so much for first-generation women migrants themselves as for their children. (The preference of middle-class professionals for Protestants as domestic help is a point we shall come to below.)

Despite this expansion of opportunities, however, there has remained a substantial segment of the poor at the bottom of the pile, many of them outside the formal economy altogether, creating work for themselves in the 'informal sector', selling bootlaces, sweets, cigarettes on street corners, shining shoes, collecting cardboard, 'ravelling' waste textiles to make cleaning rags, scavenging the garbage dumps and so on.

This concept of the 'informal sector' was introduced by PRELAC (the Latin American Programme of the International Labour Office) in the 1970s to cover employment in the myriad of very small-scale enterprises: in practice it has come to designate 'activities oriented towards the logic of subsistence' by which those who can find no formal work attempt to scrape a living (see Pérez Sáinz and Menjívar Larín, 1994). Although there is some evidence that, particularly in the 1970s, some of these enterprises managed to accumulate capital and graduate into the small business sector in the manner so claimed by De Soto (1987) – indeed some of the Pentecostal lives documented in our recent research fall into that category – this has been rarer since the recession of the eighties. Moreover such success falls predominantly to men. The women in the informal sector are notably struggling for bare subsistence. (For documentation of the point see Pérez Sáinz and Menjívar Larín, 1994; Brydon and Chant, 1989.)

While the informal sector had been relatively easy to enter in the boom years, after the debt crisis, as formal unemployment rose and average wage rates fell dramatically, it became harder to find a niche in the informal sector which could guarantee basic subsistence even for an isolated individual let alone a family. Moreover the structural adjustments of the 1980s changed the composition of the informal sector, bringing in far more heads of households from the least skilled and most precarious employment sectors: more women and children, and, above all, more women who were lone parents, as John Humphrey (1994) has shown. In the mid-1980s, for instance, United Nations estimates suggest that the size of the informal economy in Brazil was around 27 per cent, yet as Lynne Brydon and Sylvia Chant (1989) demonstrate, half of all women workers in Belo Horizonte were self-employed, compared with one-fifth of their menfolk, while 85 per cent of female household heads worked in the informal sector. In the absence of effective welfare provision, people have few other choices in economic hard times: when there is no formal employment for them they must beg, steal or create their own work. The dividing line between penny capitalism at one end and criminality at the other is also notoriously thin. Furthermore, the two main criminal growth industries, drugs and prostitution – which recruit most easily when the poor have few other options – are themselves part of the postmodern global economy, in which goods and persons easily circulate transnationally, not least through international tourism (see Dimenstein (1991; 1994), Scheper-Hughes and Hoffman (1994) and Scheper-Hughes (1992) for the harrowing details of the life and death of Brazilian street children).

What all this adds up to is the multiple paradoxes of a fast transition from pre- to postmodernity in Latin America. On the one hand there is a series of processes which open up opportunities for mobility of all kinds and for modes of existence and self-consciousness far removed from the rural, quasi-feudal clientelism in which 'the individual', as Durkheim would understand the term, barely existed. The new middle classes acquire all the self-motivation and 'reflexivity' that Giddens, Beck and others have noted as characterizing the global postindustrial professional, who works at the interface with electronic international communication and control systems. The poor, too, display new forms of self-reliance, self-motivation and initiative in the struggle for survival. At least up to the end of the seventies, the stimulus for most migrants, whether as temporary workers in North America or as first-generation urbanites, has been a *realistic* expectation of material betterment and new freedoms. The mobile have, at least to some degree, have *had* to break out of the traditional patterns of mandatory mutual dependency in rural family, class and clientage relationships: to discover a new self-dependency and a new individualization and to create new *voluntary* networks of mutual support. It has been an era of effective new opportunities and, just as crucially, of emerging new forms of selfhood.

By the same token, however, the traditionally guaranteed networks of mutual dependency cannot any longer be expected to come to the rescue when times are hard: neither the extended family nor the clientage system can necessarily offer protection against the new vicissitudes. Indeed, this 'shorn lamb' aspect of the new mobile individual is one of many new costs entailed by the fast transition to postmodernity. Social change, especially at this accelerated pace, is a Pandora's box which lets out new ills along with novel potentialities. Perhaps the most seriously dystopic features of change are, first, the intensification of poverty and marginalization at the bottom of the heap, in a context of increased general affluence and exponential rises in expectations fuelled not only by actual experience especially in the pre-debt society, but also by the cornucopia of mass-media images; and secondly, the near collapse of the family as the primary institution of mutual support, especially, but not exclusively, among the poor. Both features merit closer attention, not least because they are directly addressed by the new Protestant reformation.

Evidence such as that reviewed by John Welch (1993) suggests that, even in the growth period of the 1960s and 1970s, the gross gap between the top and bottom of the income scale did not narrow and in some cases may even have widened; the absolute numbers of the poor did not decline though a more differentiated middle class emerged between the income extremes. All of this is as true of the successful economies like Chile as it is of the more troubled ones. Furthermore, the economic stagnation of the 1980s seems to have reversed many of the indices of improvement, notably those relating to the infrastructure of education, health, sanitation and housing, and to have reduced the expenditure on social service provision as a proportion of GDP. The 1980s also saw certain clear signals of trouble in these societies, notably a rising incidence of youth crime and of child abandonment. Yet, as Eliana Cardoso and Ann Helwege (1995) have shown, with the exception of very poor countries such as Haiti and Peru, life expectancy, infant mortality and literacy rates in the Latin American/Caribbean region continued to improve right through the post-debt recession and into the nineties. The picture, therefore, is of a volatile combination of benevolent and highly problematic tendencies.

Lash and Urry (1993), among others, have noted the increased polarization between the 'losers' and 'winners' in the postindustrial economy, that is between the unemployed and underemployed, and the 'underclass' hustlers of the 'black' economy on the one hand; the upwardly mobile, the new middle classes and the securely employed 'core' workers on the other. They emphasize two particular features of this polarization: the spatial separation within the city, and the 'institutional deficit' within the 'impacted ghettoes' of the poor and marginalized. Both features merit some comment. The spatial separation of the prosperous and the poor is a striking feature of the Latin American mega-cities as indeed are the many devices which the prosperous devise to protect themselves from the indigent and importunate – from walled and guarded residential enclaves to the death squads that periodically rid the streets of inconvenient bands of street children. Jeremy Rifkin (1995) makes much of this kind of spatial segregation in his exploration of the dystopic implications of the new global employment structures. It is important to recognize, however, that such spatial separation cannot be consistently sustained.

The poor inevitably spill over from their shanty towns into the public, commercial heartlands of the global cities in order to hustle a living by offering services and/or begging/preying on the prosperous who work, live or shop there. Moreover, it is increasingly necessary to admit some of the poor into the precious and vulnerable domestic space of the prosperous – that figure quoted above of up to one-third of the formal urban work-force who are in domestic service says it all. The new dual-career, middle-class couples have to trust the nanny or housekeeper with their children and their housekeys – hence the preference for the Pentecostal domestic whose religious formation, with its emphasis on honesty, sobriety and self-discipline, will guarantee her employers' most intimate haven against incursions of underclass disorder.

The 'institutional deficit' within the residential ghettoes of the poor is the second point Lash and Urry (1993) make in their argument about social polarization in the postmodern city. Because Lash and Urry derive their argument mainly from the European and North American cities – deindustrialization following industrialization – their pattern does not perfectly fit the Latin American case. They see it as a process of the pro-gressive *abandonment* of deindustrialized areas by institutions of employ-ment, distribution, social control and cultural formation. In the case of the Latin American shanty towns in the mega-cities, it would be more accurate to point to the *failure to develop* such an institutional infra-structure in the first place. The institutional vacuum in the do-it-yourself squatter settlements is most easily filled by the criminal mafia, a sys-tem which among other things perpetuates the old clientelage pattern. Where the endemic disorder of these areas is challenged, the challenge almost always comes from religious institutions. There is always a Catholic presence, sometimes in the form of 'base communities', and there are efforts at neighbourhood organization, but of all the voluntary institutions which seek to create institutional and cultural order within the chaos of the ghetto, the Protestant movement is easily the most numerically sign-ificant and culturally effective. In many of the enclaves of the urban poor there are as many *practising* Protestants as there are *practising* Catholics in spite of the minority status of Protestantism overall. The dense net-work of independent, store-front churches within the honeycomb of the ghetto acts as the main bulwark against Lash and Urry's 'institutional deficit'. It constitutes a major experiment in self help through the volunt-ary principle, and a significant step away from clientelism towards plural-ism as the organizing principle of social, cultural and economic life.

Much the most urgent of the 'institutional deficit' suffered by the poor concerns the family. It is important not to misrepresent the situation, either by assuming that the traditional Catholic family ideal embodies an actual past reality for the poor rather than a rhetorical ambition;

or, at the other extreme, by hailing current family behaviour, in the fashion of Judith Stacey (1990), as an unproblematic transition to a postmodern mix-and-match family system or as the beginnings of a release for women from an oppressively patriarchal institution. It is probably at least half true, as one of our Chilean research collaborators suggested, that the one-parent family has been the archetypical family of the poor ever since the beginning of the colonial era, simply because it is the product of the sexual politics of conquest (personal communication with Arturo Fontaine Talavera). Certainly lone-mother headed families are nothing new, nor is a culture of *machismo* which accepts violence against women as normal and invests masculine honour in men's successful control and domination of women.[5]

I would argue that the gender culture of the Latin American poor is a tattered remnant of the Mediterranean culture of honour and shame, imported with the colonial elite and quite literally cross-fertilized by the sexual politics of conquest. Poor men – indigenous, black or mestizo – have always been as powerless to protect the chastity of 'their' women from the predations of more powerful males as have the women themselves. Masculine honour and status among the 'popular classes' have therefore clustered around other expressions of male power and liberty, notably the pleasures of the street and the bar and the man's right to spend his earnings on drink, drugs, women, gambling and other personal gratifications. None of this is new. What *is* new stems from the swift transition from pre- to postmodern life, from mass mobility, from the endemic disorder of the ghettos of the mega-cities and the disruption of the old rural social system, not least by political violence and selective migration, and from the intensification of poverty and marginalization for significant segments of the postmodern 'losers' in the recession.

The demographics of what has been happening to the institution of the family in the Latin American region are fairly clear. The marital and quasi-marital tie has become increasingly fragile, the incidence of cohabitation ('informal marriage'), which was always a large but uncertain figure among the poor, has increased at all class levels, and the illegitimacy rate, especially among teenage mothers, has risen. All these trends can be traced back to the 1960s but clearly they were intensified in the 1970s and even more so in the 1980s. They run strikingly parallel to similar trends in the West though the Latin American pattern shows an even greater prominence of the indicators of family dislocation among the poorer sectors. The dramatic increase in the numbers of 'street children' must be included as a striking index of these changes. It is significant, as Scheper-Hughes and Hoffman (1994) have shown, that the terms popularly used to describe these children have mutated from relatively benevolent or playful ones roughly translated as 'ragamuffin' or 'urchin' in the 1960s to the current usage, 'the abandoned', which indicates a widespread sense that too many of the poor do not or cannot support and protect their offspring. The actual scale of the problem is difficult to establish. Alan Gilbert (1994), for example, is sceptical about United Nations claims that there are as many as 30 million street children in Latin America as a whole, and even more critical of the World Council of Churches' figure of 50 million, which would imply that one in three of all children under 16 fall into the category. Gilbert, like Scheper-Hughes (1992), notes that these enormous figures include all children who work or do odd jobs in the street, many of whom do have homes to go to: even some of those who live on the streets remain in contact with family, especially with mothers, and, indeed, are often 'street children' because stepfathers refuse to feed and house them though mothers often try to sustain some continuing tie. We noted above that the recession of the 1980s drove more women and children to seek work, especially in the informal economy, when unemployment and falling wage rates made it increasingly necessary for individual family members to support themselves in the absence of a 'family wage', and in ever more instances, the absence of any male breadwinner in the family at all.

The indices of family dislocation, especially the rise in the proportion of lone mothers, has attracted much attention and concern. An article in 1992 eloquently expressed the mounting anxiety about these developments. Rubem Katzman, Principal Social Affairs Officer in the Social Development Division of the United Nations Commission for Latin America (ECLAC), under the title 'Why Are Men So Irresponsible?', reviewed the evidence for increased male irresponsibility particularly among the 'lower class urban sector'. By irresponsibility he meant:

> a type of behaviour which involves avoidance of the obligations associated with the formation and maintenance of a family . . . reflected in an increase in rates of illegitimacy, the proportion of adolescent pregnancies, and in rates of abandonment of families with children. (Katzman, 1992, p. 79)

Katzman is here identifying a phenomenon which has excited anxious debate about the emergence of a new 'underclass' throughout the global capitalist world. His own interpretation, based on the rather uncritical deployment of a functionalist model of the family, has all the same weaknesses as, say, that of Norman Dennis and George Erdos (1993) for Britain, especially in leaving him wide open to feminist caricature as an advocate of more female economic dependence on men as a cure for wholesale male irresponsibility. Katzman does, however, and also like Dennis and Erdos or Charles Murray (1990), point to a real phenomenon in citing the existence of 'a generation of males of whom a substantial proportion are simply not fitted to play the roles of husband and father'. Having been set up by (economic) circumstance to fail both as bread-winner and as head of household, every failure to live up to traditional obligations serves to speed up his abandonment of these obligations.

While it is clear that the group most affected by these developments is the urban poor, it would be a mistake to assume that the matter rests there. The level and speed of geographical and social mobility over the last three generations has inevitably had an impact on older family systems, partially disrupting the extended family and rendering ever more contingent the normative ideal of lifelong monogamy. The range of social experience and alternative options has been irreversibly broken open by swift social change. Moreover, even the most benevolent trends towards mass upward occupational mobility and free geographical movement create casualties as well as new opportunities. Our own research threw up a significant sector of the new middle classes anxious to strengthen the nuclear family in a context where rising expectations, easy mobility, unprecedented affluence and the communications fiesta of postmodern society so easily turn everything to flux and fluidity.

There is considerable evidence that Latin American women, especially among the poor, have long regarded the irresponsible *machismo* of their menfolk as a chronic problem. The Catholic Church has traditionally recommended patience to them and they have turned to the Virgin for solace. In Brazil many have also used the spiritist cults, in which women are prominent leaders and mediums, as magical means to control their recalcitrant menfolk, or, if necessary, to wreak vengeance on their lovers, husbands and sons. An anthropological study conducted when the power of the Peruvian Maoist movement, Sendero Luminoso, was at its height, showed similar preoccupations. Carol Andreas (1991) found that in a rural area of Peru, where as many as a third of families were headed by women who had to scrabble for a living in the informal economy, such women were disproportionately attracted to the Shining Path movement. Moreover, where they came to prominence in the movement's 'people's committees' the first thing they did was to 'put an end to delinquency, drug addiction, prostitution and domestic violence' by the introduction of draconian measures against these typical scourges inflicted by poor men on poor women. Yet of all the available prophylactics, only the new Protestantism can claim serious success in putting the family back together again. Indeed it is becoming increasingly clear that one of the great positive attractions of the Protestant movement, and one which it parades prominently in its self-presentation, is its ability to eliminate the double standard and restore a moral order in the relations of men and women which the Catholic Church preached and promised but failed to deliver for centuries past.

The Growth of Protestantism and the Transition to Postmodernity

What we see, then, is a continent in accelerated transition from pre- to postmodernity with a population facing major structural changes in the economy, the political sphere and in culture: changes which entail a paradoxical and bewildering combination of beneficent, novel possibilities and massive new strains. In its chronology, the growth of Protestantism strikingly parallels this trajectory of change. Starting from seeds planted, by European as well as North American missions, in the nineteenth century and further stimulated by the worldwide radiation of Pentecostal revival out of Azusa St in 1906, Latin American Protestantism took off on a spectacular new expansion around the 1960s as the great population migrations got under way and the mega-cities began to take shape. As David Martin (1990) has shown, this movement was swiftly and definitively *indigenized*.

In so far as it received stimulation from North American Protestantism, this came crucially not from missionaries despatched south from the Bible Belt but through Latin American migrants to North America who found Protestant, often Pentecostal, churches the natural home of blacks and other outsiders like themselves in the big cities north of the Rio Grande, and who brought the message back to the southern continent, occasionally along with a taste for tele-evangelism. The movement was spread by the human resources of the Latin American poor themselves.

The movement swelled the historic Pentecostal churches such as the Assemblies of God in Brazil and the Methodist Pentecostal Church in Chile, while largely by-passing the mainstream Protestant churches of European origin. It began among the mobile poor where it spread like wildfire for two decades, mostly by fission via the do-it-yourself storefront churches which dot every street in the urban ghettoes. By the late 1970s it was also expanding into the urban middle classes, especially among the new postmodern professional and business sector, and at the same time penetrating deeper into the poorest and most disorderly urban sectors, for example, through the explosive success of Brazil's Cura Divina movement (of which more below), which has had a remarkable appeal among casualties of the drug culture. From the 1970s it also took fire in some rural areas, notably those with heavy concentrations of indigenous peoples such as the Maya of the Yucatán and Guatemala or the Quechua of Ecuador; in remote rural areas long neglected by the Catholic Church, such as the Chiapas in Mexico (discussed in Bowen, 1996); in rural areas which were clear losers in the new economic game (Chiapas again, or Bahia in Brazil as documented in Ireland, 1991) or where agribusiness had destroyed the old neo-feudal relations and created a new sector of landless casual labour, as in the fruit-growing areas south of Santiago in Chile.

A clear pattern emerges from this picture, highlighting particular groups whose structural situation in some way predisposes them to consider the new cultural option of Protestantism. The mobile poor, often mobile both geographically and socially, are the largest such category. They were far from being unambiguous beneficiaries of the old clientelist networks and the traditional power structures, and as socioeconomic change broke up these old structures and left displaced individuals and families to fend for themselves as best they might in the favellas and barrios of the heaving mega-cities, an enterprising minority made a virtue of necessity and took their fate into their own hands, turning to new religious experiments for salvation in its broadest sense. The case of the indigenous and, in Brazil especially, the black peoples of the continent is also less than mysterious. Many of these were barely Hispanicized (Lusitanianized) even after over four hundred years of colonial domination – the Mapuche of southern Chile offered continued military resistance until the 1890s for instance. It is not fanciful to see Protestantism as an obvious anti-colonial option for such groups in the same way that Islam today appeals to segments of the black populations of North America as a symbolic refusal of colonial Christianity. Furthermore, many of the concentrations of the new Protestantism in Latin America – some of which are also, of course, concentrations of indigenous peoples – are located in peripheral areas like the Yucatán, or in borderlands or remote areas: all of which are notorious among sociologists for their tendency to harbour resistance to the cultural hegemony of the centre.

These cases also illustrate very clearly one of the processes widely recognized as characteristic of the postmodern global condition. They display a direct connection between the local and the global which leapfrogs over the national level, and is greatly assisted in doing so by (post)modern communications. There is little doubt that an important source of pride and validation among many of the new Protestants is a sense of being part of a worldwide movement of *winners*, however humble and obscure their particular group may seem. This has both a theological dimension, which can include a sense of shared genealogy with the Reformation theologians of northern Europe, and a broader geopolitical dimension, which involves a consciousness of being on the same side as the biggest and most successful players in the global development game, notably, though not exclusively, the USA. As one Mexican Bible translator put it: 'We have been held back by Catholicism for too long on this continent.'

The historic position of the Catholic Church is itself a factor predisposing the poorer sectors of the population to the Protestant option, as also is the current of syncretic folk religiosity lying beneath the surface of official

Catholicism. With regard to the latter it is important to recognize that, even apart from areas where the indigenous population remains ethnically homogeneous, among mestizos the genetic and cultural admixture of black and indigenous elements is stronger at the lower end of the status hierarchy – the poor are everywhere less 'white' than their social betters, and, as Roger Lancaster (1992) has shown for Nicaragua, even within families the pecking order tends to place individuals in a colour hierarchy. My point here, however, is that the strength of the pre-Christian indigenous traditions and of strands of African spiritual sensibility within the syncretic mix is greatest among the least privileged groups. The colonial role of the Catholic Church, together with the continuing strength of this strand of folk sensibility, work together to pave the way for what on the surface appears to be an aberrant cultural development in a 'historically' Catholic culture.

The Catholic Church has been an instrument of colonial power and control ever since the days of the *conquistadores*: this is one reason why so many Protestant groups explicitly try to reverse the process by sending missions to Spain and Portugal. For example, in the medieval university town of Coimbra in Portugal, I was told by members of the Universal Church of the Kingdom of God (the largest of Brazil's Cura Divina churches) that the black Brazilian missionary preaching that morning in June 1994 was a 'Warrior of the Holy Spirit' come to conquer the once conquering Portuguese. The Light of the World Church in Guadalajara, Mexico, has a mission to Rome for the same reasons. The Catholic Church in Latin America started as an instrument of imperial domination and actively supported the dominance of a narrow, culturally Iberian elite over many centuries. Moreover, it was further associated with foreignness, especially perhaps in Brazil, since a considerable proportion of the priesthood has always come form abroad, usually from Europe. The paradox of the current situation is that the very efforts at reform which the church has made in order to rid itself of this legacy in the twentieth century, have often served to drive a further wedge between it and the poor. The church's attempts to eliminate laxity by Romanizing the Latin American church in the early part of the twentieth century had already disturbed some of the syncretic accommodations to the folk practices of these diverse populations, for example placing the traditionally semi-autonomous black brotherhoods for the first time under serious clerical control. The reforms of The Second Vatican Council in the early 1960s – which was, perhaps not coincidentally, the moment of Protestant take-off – backfired seriously.

Among other innovations, the Latin American church began to clear out the cultic paraphernalia of syncretic folk Catholicism along with the baroque clutter which was increasingly regarded by the educated, international opinion-formers of Catholicism as being in dubious aesthetic taste and obsolete theological fashion. As Rowan Ireland (1991) has shown, this did much to sever the link with the tradition of folk Catholicism for many of the poor, who found the plain washed church interiors, the abandonment of Mary's month, the banishment of the healing cults and of the statues of demoted saints, all very hard to accept. More recent positive valuation of 'enculturation' among enlightened cadres of worldwide Catholicism has not, thus far, succeeded in remedying these losses.

Pentecostalism, by contrast, had powerful continuities with those very folk elements which were being purged from the Catholic Church in the sixties and seventies. These included the exuberance of the worship, the transmuted elements of spirit possession gathered up into liturgical practice centred on the Third Person of the Trinity, and above all, the healing and exorcism which Pentecostalism offered just at the point when the cults of folk healing, especially those associated with the Virgin and the saints, were being discarded as superstition by the Catholic Church. David Martin (1997) has even suggested that the Holy Spirit directly takes over from the Virgin as the source of succour and healing for the new Protestants. Indeed, as several recent studies confirm, it is hard to overestimate the importance of the search for healing in the process of conversion (see for example Bowen, 1996; Burdick, 1993; Chesnut, 1996).

Moreover, despite the Catholic Church's many centuries of preaching a Christian doctrine of exemplary suffering, one powerful assumption of Latin American folk religiosity remains the view that the primary business of religion is to seek out and clear away whatever hinders the well-being of persons, whether the hindrance is located in their own sin, in external malevolence, in the action of negative spirits or whatever. This conception of well-being makes little distinction between its physical, material and spiritual dimensions, and healing is thus understood as involving all these facets with little of the material/spiritual dichotomy so characteristic of Western thought. Pentecostalism is more hospitable to such an assumption than is the purified and increasingly intellectualized Catholicism of the period since the Second Vatican Council. John Burdick (1993) has further commented on the particular appeal which Pentecostalism has for the unlettered as compared with the bookishness of much mainstream Protestantism and the intellectualism of recent Catholic catechetics. The gifts of the spirit can fall as easily on the illiterate as on the educated, and glossolalia can bless the monoglot as effortlessly as the gifted linguist. This demotic and incipiently democratic character of the Pentecostal tradition gives it an edge over the Catholic Church, in which the charismatic tendency is largely confined to an educated stratum and is anyway kept under tight clerical rein.

Even liberation theology, the Catholic 'option for the poor', has not succeeded in drawing in the Latin American 'popular classes' in significant numbers. In any case, the Catholic Church in Latin America remains predominantly conservative and has been too deeply implicated in the historical structures of elite domination to throw off easily its popular association with old patterns of power and oppression. Even the Catholic base communities are more often devotional than political in focus, as William Hewitt (1992; 1996) and Manuel Vásquez (1997) have shown; and, as David Martin has argued, might best be seen as a part of the same groundswell which has nurtured Pentecostalism: most base communities look in many ways like Pentecostal groups in that they focus on the reformation of individual and family life, and, in so far as they are political at all, they concern themselves pragmatically with local community issues like housing, the provision of utilities and so forth.

It has sometimes been supposed (contrary to the weight of evidence) that Pentecostalism was in some way deployed as an instrument of American capitalist cultural imperialism to strangle liberation theology at birth. In reality, the deployment of liberation theology by a radical sector of the Catholic Church in the late 1960s was, at least in part, an attempt to compete with the already successful growth of what the church pejoratively calls 'the sects'. William Hewitt (1992; 1996) has concluded that the reasons for liberation theology's lack of appeal for the poor themselves include the intellectualist mode in which it was promoted and the distant nature of its goals. One might add the persistence of clerical control to the list. The poor, caught up in the maelstrom of the transition to global capitalism and postmodernity, respond with more enthusiasm to the Pentecostal option because they see with their own eyes its capacity to transform individual lives, here and now, for the immediate better. This is surely the crux of the matter. Pentecostalism grows because it offers two valuable things: to many, including some of those who gain worldly success, it offers an anchor in the face of dizzying new possibilities; to many more it offers hope and lived solutions to problems arising out of structural conditions which it is beyond the power of individuals to alter.

Global capitalism, mediated through high-level political and economic choices made by the big players in the geopolitico-economic game, has set the structural limits but does not minutely determine the range of responses to them. In the discussion which follows it is essential to retain a picture of 40 million or more *persons with real power of agency actively choosing* this Pentecostal option, on the basis of perfectly reasonable, if not purely rational (in the Enlightenment sense), motivations and assessments. These myriad choices form a pattern clear enough to tempt the sociologist to risk a structural analysis. What I want to avoid as far as possible in this analysis is any implication of determinism. None of this was irreversibly foreordained, and certainly not in its devilish detail by some mechanical process of structural adjustment. Even the cultural conditions discussed above, which may have lubricated the slipway into Pentecostalism, are no more than predisposing factors.

Nevertheless, at the structural level it is clear that Pentecostalism operates as one, perhaps the most successful, among several cultural and institutional prophylactics acting against the obviously dystopic features of the transition to postmodernity – the disorder and squalor of the urban settlements in the absence of an effective institutional infrastructure; the strains on the family as the baseline unit of mutual economic and interpersonal support; the characteristic entrapments of despairing poverty which are the nemesis of so many males, those so-called 'underclass' vices which mirror and are mirrored by the hedonistic excesses of certain styles of postmodern affluence – that is, alcoholism, drug addiction, compulsive gambling, sexual promiscuity, street violence, all being fed by global consumption industries both legal and criminal.

The argument that Pentecostalism offers middle-range solutions to these problems owes something to a Durkheimian view of religion as a hedge against *anomie*, both the *anomie* of social and institutional disorder and the normlessness accompanying suddenly expanded horizons, mass mobility and the decay of older systems which had held the individual tightly within familial, communal, class and patronage networks. In this sense, the new Protestantism looks like a form of *resistance* to precisely those aspects of the postmodern condition which most clearly display the postmodern qualities of fluidity, uncertainty, contradiction and excess. This might seem dangerously close to an endorsement of the Bauman argument (earlier in the present volume) that religion in the postmodern era acts as a refuge for those who cannot cope with 'freedom'. Certainly the new puritan rules of life, which outlaw alcohol and drugs and all participation in the hedonistic entertainments of postmodern media and contemporary culture (film, theatre, television, football and so forth) and which insist on chastity and modesty for *both* sexes, are the key to the success of the movement in counteracting the dystopic effects of the transition to postmodernity. Yet before conceding anything to Bauman's view we need to examine the situation more closely, and in particular to be a little sceptical of using a term like 'freedom' to characterize the undeniably oppressive chaos which engulfs the poor. Equally significant, perhaps, is the suspicion that we have been here before, in that there may be little that is distinctively 'postmodern' in these problems or their solutions.

It is hard to resist the conclusion that the Pentecostal revolution in Latin America is performing the same miracle as that by which Methodism tamed the wild American frontier and created civic institutions *ex nihilo* as described by A. Gregory Schneider (1994), or that better known case in which early Methodism and popular Nonconformity stemmed the chaos of first-stage industrialism in England and claimed a crucial sector of the unchurched masses for Evangelical Christianity – the Protestant work ethic and active citizenship rather than revolutionary class politics. The argument, from Weber and Halévy, is familiar and underlies the most comprehensive account of the recent Latin American story (see Martin, 1990). As in the earlier instances, Protestantism has once again created a critical mass of persons for whom self-discipline, a work ethic and the values of domestic rectitude have become second nature. Far from constituting a *retreat* from 'freedom', this is precisely what enables them to wrest some control over their own lives out of conditions created by local manifestations of global change, which trap them in powerlessness and insecurity. As individuals, especially if they are near the bottom of the social pile, they cannot alter the macro-structures within which they have to contrive their own survival. But they can alter their responses to these limiting conditions. In converting to Pentecostalism they empower themselves in ways which have concrete consequences for themselves and for society.

The societal consequences may well include easing the path of the latest capitalist transformation, though individuals emphatically do not follow the Holy Spirit *in order* to help capitalism *per se*. Individual persons become Pentecostals because they are in search of healing and hope in a world turned upside down. Among the commonplace consequences of giving up alcohol, tobacco, drugs, prostitutes and violence, working more thoroughly and consistently, restoring family relationships and becoming an active member of a church congregation, one can observe many forms of all-round betterment, very often including more regular income and better management of the household economy – the evidence suggests, for instance, that it is common for men to devote 30 or more per cent of their earnings to their own pleasures before conversion (see, for example, interviews conducted in Santiago by Centro de Estudios Públicos, 1994). After conversion the family will almost inevitably eat and dress better, and children will get at least some schooling.

The consequences of all this *for capitalism* are, perhaps, as unintended as was the entrepreneurial foundation laid by Weber's capitalist pioneers on the rack of the Calvinist doctrine of election. Pentecostals, however, like the early Methodists, do intend to improve social conditions. They conduct vigorous campaigns against 'the vices' and all the disorder they foster, and they deliberately try to strengthen and stabilize the family: these issues are the routine theme of sermons and teaching in the churches. In this sense they directly address the social and, as they firmly maintain, the moral ills around them: but with the primary purpose of healing and restoring individual souls. As one Methodist Pentecostal pastor in Chile said when we asked whether his church had any social work outreach programmes: 'Yes we call souls to repentance: that *is* our social work.'

I have argued elsewhere (1995) that the dynamic of mutual inter-penetration between Latin American Pentecostalism and postmodern capitalism differs in certain significant ways from the dynamic of Non-conformity and early industrial capitalism. The current transformation of capitalism in Latin America, as we saw above, involves a postindustrial, post-Fordist labour force for whom assembly-line docility, deference to hierarchical authority or the clock-time disciplines of the factory would be anachronistic. What this postmodern economy requires from them is micro-entrepreneurial initiative, an individualized and more feminized psyche, a high level of self-motivation, and the flexibility with which to face insecure employment and self-employment, mobility, and the twenty-four-hour working day. This applies even, indeed especially, to the informal economy (in which Burdick (1993) and others have found Pentecostals over-represented) as well as to the new service occupations at the interface with information technology and modern communications (where middle-class Pentecostalism is currently fast expanding).

Adjusting to all this is a very tall order indeed for a workforce cata-pulted into postmodern conditions out of a premodern, rural world, with no serious transition via industrial modernity. A cultural and social system based on patron–client relations within which the poor were of no polit-ical account and were socially defined by their ascribed roles, has rather suddenly given way to a system in which the opportunities and the costs fall ever more directly on the individual as an atomized unit of social as well as economic labour: as both the protections and the constraints of the old dispensation are stripped away. The need to operate *as an individual* at the level of the psyche, as well as in terms of social and economic roles, becomes ever more imperative and universal. Indeed, in some ways this affects the poor even more than the privileged, who are often able to transfer those aspects of the clientelist system which benefit them into the new structures – hence so much of the notorious corruption – while the poor are left to face the new economic dispensa-tion as best they may.

Pentecostalism is uniquely poised to effect this cultural transition, not least because its fundamental conception of the human person is as a unique, individual soul, named and claimed by God. Its business *is* the business of selfhood. As Salvatore Cucchiari (1988) expresses it, Pente-costal conversions are 'mythologies of the new self'. Furthermore, Pente-costalism simultaneously contains elements compatible with both the pre- and the postmodern. It carries forward enough of the premodern and the local to enable it also to carry the global and radical possibilities of individualized self-consciousness without causing vertiginous confusion. It is able to re-package premodern religious sensibilities and to transform familiar elements of ethnic, familial and other habits of collective solidarity within a movement which also inaugurates new experiences of postmodern individualism, autonomy, mobility and self-determination.

The secret lies in the paradoxical combination of these contradictory elements. The new Protestantism offers converts a novel experience of *spiritual* autonomy which also makes for a deeper sense of the individualizing tendencies in the wider world; it energizes the irreducible human motivation to survive even in the most unpropitious circumstances, by harnessing that motivation to transcendent ends. At the same time it roots and supports the individual within a face-to-face, voluntary community of believers; the old ascribed solidarities may help to provide the template but it is the *voluntary* nature of belonging which is new. Within this voluntary community there have grown up practices of mutual help, the encouragement of education and modes of participation in the practical organization, in the pastoral work and in the evangelism of the church which serve to spread widely among the mass of believers the actual experience of individual responsibility and leadership. *Individualization* and the *voluntaristic, collective* creation of new social capital thus occur in tandem.

This is only the first of the paradoxes within the Pentecostal movement which are inseparable from its success. They are also the basis of a refutation of Bauman's one-dimensional characterization of 'fundamentalism' as a refusal of 'freedom'. Let us outline a few of these crucially fruitful paradoxes. First let us press a little harder on the individual/collective freedom/authority paradoxes touched on above. Bauman is not alone in assuming that Pentecostals and other 'fundamentalists' are under authoritarian rule rather than being 'free' individuals: David Lehman (1996) makes similar charges. This view is based on a misconception of how such voluntary religious groups work. It is certainly the case that Pentecostal pastors are typically authoritarian in tone, but their authority is deployed both to protect the boundaries of the believing community and to reinforce the active mass participation noted above as the mark of the voluntary religious group. Moreover the pastor's authority is limited by the freedom of anyone who dissents, to secede and set up a new, autonomous congregation. Indeed, fission of this kind is the lifeblood of the movement and probably the secret of its huge success. It is this do-it-yourself character of the new Protestantism which offers the sharpest contrast to the high level of clerical authority which seems to be inseparable from even the most progressive initiatives of the Catholic Church. Indeed clerical control is probably the main factor limiting the success of *Evangelization 2000*, the Latin American Catholic

Church's belated attempt in the 1990s to copy the winning formula of the Pentecostal movement. This factor may even go some way to explaining why it has become commonplace in the 1990s to find whole base communities converting *en masse* to Pentecostalism.

A belief in Biblical inerrancy by no means results in a uniformity enforced from on high (or even internationally, as Lehman has suggested), in that it is accompanied by an extreme form of the classic Protestant insistence on the right, even the necessity, for each individual believer to read his or her own Bible and be his or her own theological authority. Latin American Pentecostals certainly read the Bible literally, though they do so less as a matter of settled principle than because they actually share the mental world of the writers of the New Testament. The main effect of this is, as one Chilean Catholic scholar remarked with amazement, that they regard the Apostles as their own familiar friends, people just like themselves with whom they converse on intimate terms in their prayers (Carmen Galilea, private communication). It is important, too, to remember that narrative is a far more common usage than generalized theological or dogmatic formulae among the new Pentecostals: telling and retelling the stories of their own, personal, individual salvation is at the heart of their evangelism, their worship and their self-understanding; their testimonies are, as Cucchiari (1988) puts it, 'the mythic idiom through which they validate their new religious and social identities' (p. 418). The immediacy and literalness of their faith can also be a source of spontaneity and innovation. For example, one Pentecostal service which we attended in rural Chile included an entirely impromptu liturgical dance of rapt beauty and great seriousness offered as a Thanksgiving by a middle-aged woman, a casual farm labourer like everyone else in that congregation, who had recently been cured of a paralysis. Spontaneous acts of this kind come with the territory: they are part of the *expressive* empowerment brought with the gifts of the Spirit, a world away from caricatures of dour, regimented Puritan conformity which disdain for 'fundamentalism' so often conjures up.

The strict Pentecostal moral code is another superficially plausible source of the notion that the new Protestantism is a form of totalitarianism and a denial of individual freedom. These rules are both fierce and detailed. They encompass the avoidance of all stimulants, a dress code designed to avoid sexual titillation, a strict code of sexual morality and public modesty, and the avoidance of the temptations habitually offered by the 'permissive' entertainment media, by parties, football and other such occasions of alcoholic and other excess. They are vigilantly policed by pastors and congregations who most certainly do view themselves as their brothers' and sisters' keepers. These rules, however, are essentially *self*-imposed. And in a very important sense they represent an optimism about the possibility of radical alterations of lives. The purpose of the rules, as many Pentecostals explain it, is to save individuals from themselves until such time as they have learned to Walk in the Way with full confidence. They willingly embrace the *discipline* of the new faith precisely because they have rejected the *fatalism* which marked the culture of the unregenerate poor and which was reinforced, especially in the women, by the official, clerical Catholic view of exemplary suffering.

We met the argument many times among Pentecostal converts that the rules of conduct, especially for men, have to be unreasonably harsh not because, say, football is intrinsically evil (except through its association with alcohol) but because habits of self-destructive indulgence – often quite literally addictions – can only be broken by the strongest countermeasures, which depend for their effectiveness on communal policing and sacred authority. The collective maintenance of the rules, along with the authoritative leadership of the pastorate, serve to protect the boundaries of the voluntary group and the integrity of the redeemed self from the incursions both of the old corruption and of the new disorder which prevails all around. Far from signalling a retreat into totalitarianism, the puritan code of conduct backed up by the authority of the pastorate is the indispensable foundation on which *self*-determination and a measure of real control over one's own life can be built up. Cucchiari (1988) again understands the significance of the apparent contradiction when he describes Pentecostal conversion as 'a paradoxical process implying a more autonomous self achieved *through* surrender or recommitment to the claims of a moral order' (p. 418).

Within the protected enclave of the voluntary religious group, the actual experience of life, moreover, begins to nurture new principles and, even more important, new practices of participation. Typically this will grow out of small beginnings – teaching in Sunday School, taking some responsibility in the choir, preaching in your own street, prophesying in church, visiting the sick, praying aloud in the women's meeting, giving public witness to your faith, running a small savings scheme, helping to keep the church accounts. All of this fosters initiative rather than deference and passivity, creating transferable skills in exactly the same way that early Methodist class meetings have been shown to do – the ability to speak in public, to organize, to take responsibility both *for* and *with* others, to develop a facility in interpersonal communication, even to learn to read and write for the first time. Far from being an escapist ghetto for the powerless, these self-governing Pentecostal congregations offer a route to new possibilities, to new experiences of selfhood, new patterns of individual *and* co-operative action, to skills and modes of response which have a real survival value in the secular world beyond the voluntary group. At the most concrete level, we encounter church

initiatives teaching everything from building skills to rudimentary accounting, screen printing to domestic science: Pentecostalism is more than Bible
reading and speaking in tongues. Indeed it is a boundary-breaking movement: just as tongue-speaking itself breaks the bounds of languages, so
Pentecostals everywhere are prepared to attempt the impossible in all
kinds of eminently practical ways.

The argument will be clearer if we apply it in two crucial areas where
the energizing paradoxes work most effectively, that is, in relation to the
family and to postmodern education and technology. Pentecostal policies
in relation to the family are too easily slotted into the Bauman approach:
they seem on the face of things regressively patriarchal, anti-feminist
and sexually repressive, in fact the very antithesis of the postmodern.
The new Protestantism preaches the strict Pauline doctrine that the man
is the head of the woman, that wives should be subject to their husbands,
that sex should be confined to monogamous wedlock. Yet studies of the
new Pentecostal groups demonstrate that the everyday reality of gender
relations in the family and in the church is that women are empowered
and their lives are improved while men experience a new dignity and
sense of responsibility as well as a new integration into the domestic
sphere. Even the insistence on lifelong monogamy is less restrictive
than it seems since it is usually held to apply to *new* Christian marriages
and offers a fresh start to many, especially to lone women who are
the casualties of the intensified marital instability of the postmodern
transition.

Elizabeth Brusco (1986) was perhaps the first to note the extent to
which a new Christian patriarchy, in practice, served to *feminize* the male
personality. The man is drawn away from the *machismo* world of street
and bar, he is pacified and domesticized. As heads of families and mono-
polizing the official authority roles in the church, men are reined in by
new responsibilities, or, more accurately, by a real requirement to live
up to responsibilities always recognized in theory but habitually violated
in practice. For the first time the Protestant churches achieve what the
Catholic Church has preached but not been able to deliver for centuries
– it has eliminated the double standard of sexual morality and substi-
tuted mutual and equal responsibility between men and women. The
dominance of the male is, after all, the commonplace of Latin American
gender culture at all class levels: it would be very extraordinary to find
an overtly feminist religious movement growing out of such a cultural
soil, especially among the poor. What has in fact happened is a movement which accepts the premises of male dominance but transforms a
culture which routinely expects unrestricted male licence to one in which
the necessary corollary of male authority (rather than domination) is
the responsibility of leadership and the duty of consultation with those

for whom men take responsibility. As Brusco (1993, in Garrard-Burnett and Stoll) has noted, what this demonstrates is not the principle of unrestricted individualism, but an individualism rooted in *voluntarily shared* responsibility within the primary group of the family and the voluntary group of the church. As one Brazilian Pentecostal woman told us: 'Before he became a believer my husband just used to do whatever he liked but now he takes trouble to find out what I and the children want.'

Recent research on Pentecostalism in Africa by Ruth Marshall (1991; 1993) and Rosalind Hackett (1993), and among first-generation Afro-Caribbean migrants in Britain by Nicole Toulis (1995), replicates this finding. As Cucchiari (1991) writes of Sicilian Pentecostalism, it is 'an attempt to re-establish a stable patriarchal order within the boundaries of the church community [which] . . . in seeking to achieve this conservative goal actually undermine[s] it' (p. 688). It operates as a 'transformative system' within which the old (in our terms premodern) comes to incorporate the new (the postmodern). Pentecostal women successfully struggle against patriarchy in their everyday lives and in their theological understandings while actively supporting an official Christian patriarchy. Pentecostal men make enormous concessions to the interests and needs of their womenfolk in the way they actually manage the relations of the sexes and quite fundamentally in what they come to see as the locus of masculinity and femininity, while still enjoying the security of an official gender code which enacts male superiority. The right hand does not know what the left hand does.

Just one illustration will suffice. The Pentecostal churches characteristically locate the authority of the male in his (Pauline) monopoly of the ministry of the Word. Yet Pentecostalism values the gifts of the Spirit even more highly, and it is here that women come into their own as prophets and inspired tongue speakers, healers and visionaries, the best beloved of the Holy Ghost. In short, there are two modes of spiritual authority held in creative tension within the movement, each with its special arena and each transforming the other. Although Cucchiari's argument has been developed out of his research on Sicilian Pentecostalism it has a far wider relevance. He postulates a crisis in gender relations as new conditions undermine the foundations which made an older patriarchal hegemony more-or-less sustainable. A contradiction appears between a decaying hegemonic system of patriarchal gender relations based on honour and shame (within which the male and female routes to 'salvation' were different) and an emergent system in both secular and religious contexts in which there is gender equality: in Pentecostalism salvation is essentially and explicitly the same for men and women. He suggests that, caught at the point of transition, both men and women suffer nostalgia for a lost past of harmonious difference, status, security and mutual respect. Cucchiari's Sicilian Pentecostals 'did not long for the poverty and overt class oppression of the past but for what they perceived to have been the more satisfying and validating cultural order of their youth or of their parents' youth' (1991, p. 701). There are, however, differences between male and female idealizations of this non-existent golden age. For men it was:

> a time when masculine authority went unchallenged and public interaction was shaped more by the moral politics of manly honour *than by the commercial politics of jobs and bank accounts.* . . .

> The women, on the contrary, may see it as a time when women, as wives and mothers, achieved a prestige akin to that of the Virgin herself as high priestess of the family. That is, women's nostalgia may be for a kind of *domestic redemption that seems neither viable nor achievable today.* (1991, p. 701, my emphasis)

Cucchiari emphasizes the importance of the search for a system of 'gender integrity', in which gendered identity embodies a moral order. As we see in the above quotations this is important precisely because it is a *different* order from that of the new commercial marketplace which has become the dominant arena, in which status and public identity are forged and in which poor males are of little account. 'Gender integrity' can act as an alternative order of self-definition in which dignity and status are actually achievable. For males, it needs to offer a validation of the masculine sexual identity, which is itself threatened by the crisis in the honour/shame hegemonic system. The *de jure* Pauline patriarchy of Pentecostal authority structures helps to solve this problem, while the actual experience of recognition and validation in home and church makes palatable, even satisfying, the *de facto* feminization and pacification of the male personality. At the same time, women, who form over 60 per cent of Pentecostals, and who are frequently the casualties of failed sexual and family relationships, are able to transfer their need for what Cucchiari (1991) calls 'domestic redemption' to the sacred family of the church, in which they become 'the moral, activist centre' (p. 701). The emergent system, though full of tension and ambiguity, is thus able to respond to the needs of both men and women.

Cucchiari's model of Pentecostalism as a 'transformative system' is directly applicable to Latin America. Moreover, the crisis there encompasses far more than just the gender order. Indeed, the evidence presented above about the traumatic nature of Latin America's transition to postmodernity as part of the system of global capitalism strongly suggests an across-the-board crisis – in the economic order itself, in the political order, in the social order, in the cultural order, including the cultural construction of identity and selfhood. It is beyond the scope of this chapter to deal in any detail with all these areas, but a case could certainly be made for regarding Pentecostalism as a 'transformative system' in regard to most of them. The beginnings of such a case lies in the argument above about the paradoxical ways in which Pentecostalism nurtures individualism within the voluntary collective, and develops the potentiality for freedom, initiative and self-determination within an enclave whose boundaries are protected by the authority of the pastorate and by the sacred character of the disciplinary rules. Acting essentially as a means to religious salvation through the healing and reconstitution of the personhood of the believer, Pentecostalism nevertheless serves to develop attributes, motivations and personalities adapted to the exigencies of the deregulated postmodern labour market, as I have shown elsewhere (1995). Even the pacification and feminization of the male personality, rooted firmly in a religiously based moral order, can have a pay off in the job market of a service-based economy. That same moral order can also exact an economic price when it dictates opposition to the corruption endemic in the transition between two economic orders.

Dilemmas of this kind are one reason why Pentecostals have a marked preference for self-employment. That preference may also arise out of the Protestant habit of independence, which begins in reading and interpreting The Word, and perhaps also out of the convenience of self-employment for folk who punctuate the working day with prayer and evangelism. At all events it encourages precisely the kind of micro-entrepreneurship so prevalent both in the informal economy and in the new high-tech consultancies of the flourishing new business sector. Tensions pervade the interface between religious and economic orders, not least the problem of whether believers should expect economic miracles, but Pentecostalism is remarkably successful in holding these tensions in an ambiguous but effective balance which assists believers to negotiate the transition from a decaying corporatist–clientelist economic order to one characterized by deregulated market competition.

David Martin (1990; 1996) has marshalled the evidence on which a similar case might be made in respect of the political order; much of Rowan Ireland's (1991) work would also fit into such a framework. Here the paradox concerns the Pentecostal rejection of politics as corrupt (the 'Walk Out') and the question of whether an incipiently democratic set of principles and practices is merging within the cocoon of the 'apolitical' or politically 'passive' or 'conservative' Pentecostal community.

The features journalistically pigeonholed as 'conservative' or 'regressive' in Pentecostalism all signal that same 'nostalgia' cited by Cucchiari as a crucial element in the transformative system. A framework of conservatism derived from a transcendent moral order can stabilize the situation both in symbolic and in actual ways for people who must cope with unprecedented insecurity and volatility, especially when that moral order is experienced as continuous with the local past. The vaulting leap from pre- to postmodernity is more easily managed where it takes off from a sense that the group is *restoring* a lost or never-fully-realized ideal. Something of this kind lies behind the piquant finding of Chilean opinion polls in the late 1980s which showed that the Catholic bishops' conservative moral stance was most strongly supported not by active Catholics but by evangelicals. The sociology of religion is forever finding fresh instances of the new, emerging disguised as the restoration of a pristine past dispensation. Pentecostalism is no exception.

It remains to confront one final paradox: Pentecostalism's general enthusiasm for contemporary technology, which exists alongside Pentecostalism's well-developed distrust of precisely those features of mass communication and information most central to theorizing about postmodern culture – its refusal of moral certainty; its sexual hedonism; its fluidity and ambiguity; its delight in excess, contradiction and spectacle; its aestheticization of culture; its protean destabilization of signification, of meaning; its implicit drift to relativity; its cornucopia of images and of affluence; its hollowing out of real life in favour of simulacra; its flattening and fracturing of individual identity. Are we here encountering another 'transformative system' or is this a stark contradiction, demonstrating that Pentecostalism is engaged in cultural resistance to postmodernity?

There is no doubt whatever about Pentecostalism's appetite for new technologies, including the technologies of mass communication as the means to ever more effective evangelism. The microphone is a *sine qua non* of evangelical services and street preaching, and in the dirt-poor storefront churches which cannot afford electronic hardware one often sees improvised megaphones, sometimes mounted on a supermarket trolley for outdoor use. There is much evidence, too, of the importance of the cassette as an instrument of mission, with instances of whole remote communities converted by cassette tape. Every group of any size tries to get access to a radio channel, seriously rich churches aspiring to owning television companies or buying regular television time. The Universal Church of the Kingdom of God has even successfully challenged the monopoly of Roberto Merinho and Globo Television in Brazil in a bruising political contest which sent charges of corruption and criminal involvement with laundered drug money flying between the two corporate contestants, but in the end the Universal Church achieved its own TV channel as well as having its own national and regional newspapers and local radio outlets. Obscure pastors of all denominations in rural as well as urban areas become autodidacts in the arts of journalism, photography and public relations; congregations depute members to acquire technical training so that the church can make use of video cameras and recorders, PA systems, computers and so on; some churches in poor areas are guardians of the only locally available telephone or cassette player.

The enthusiasm for new technology is more than just an acceptance of the means to a desirable end, that is, getting the message of salvation across to the largest possible audience. It is part of a wider tendency, particularly among the pastorate, to value highly all kinds of practical knowledge as a way of improving their control over the material conditions of their lives. It is our experience that the Pentecostal pastor is as concerned with drainage, plumbing and building in the work of establishing new churches and developing the community of believers as he is with theological debate. This widespread enthusiasm for useful knowledge can also give rise to a desire for advanced technological education as a means of catching up with the more economically and scientifically advanced societies. One Chilean Methodist Pentecostal pastor was particularly eloquent on this theme, dreaming of a Pentecostal university of technology and space science.

It is perhaps relevant to note that most pastors, and more especially those in the tiny autonomous churches, are unpaid and must earn their living in the secular world alongside the members of their congregations. The Methodist Pentecostal pastor referred to above had been an upholsterer all his working life. Few of them have received a full-time professional training for the pastorate, although a small minority may have worked their way through Bible College in the United States or attended courses in the college of a more established denomination in Latin America. This has two important effects. First, it limits the social and educational distance between pastor and congregation to only that which results from the self-education typical of this hidden intelligentsia. Secondly, much of the Pentecostal movement has self-consciously refused the institutionalization of a process – the separate theological formation of the pastorate – which it has observed in the mainstream Protestant churches as the typical route to liberalism and apostasy.

What Pentecostals mistrust about advanced education, including theological education, is the insidious secularizing tendencies associated with humanistic subjects and pedagogies, yet they want education for themselves and, above all, for their children. For a similar reason they deeply fear the secular output of the very mass media they passionately desire to employ in their evangelism. The ubiquitous TV soap operas are regarded with special loathing as a source of sexual corruption and moral subversion. There is a very instructive story found in several variants all over the Latin American Pentecostal world. It recounts that somewhere – in Brussels or Geneva, or New York – there is a super-computer, the Beast of the Apocalypse, ready to stamp all our identity cards with the mark of the Anti-Christ, 666, and poised to make every last radio and television automatically translate into the language of the individual listener and viewer every piece of filth which spews out from the set: a reverse babel; a demonic Pentecost. In some ways, it seems, they agree with the negative verdict of Baudrillard and others about the cultural effect of the mass media, though the vocabulary and metaphoric structure in which they say so is rather different from that of the gurus of postmodern theorizing.

Pentecostals know they are in a dilemma over the taming of the all-powerful media of mass communication. They try to solve it by confining believers to the news programmes and the evangelical output, but once the television or radio set is in the home the impulse to graze is powerful and they have to rely on self-censorship. It is impossible to know how effective this is. When we visited one pastor's wife in Santiago (she was an ex-prostitute, now a noted healer in her little congregation), she was watching an Elvis Presley film, one of the down-home, sentimental offerings from his army years. She showed no embarrassment so we supposed this counted as wholesome, but the incident illustrates the problem. This, of course, is what fuels the ambitions of Pentecostal churches of any size to create a whole alternative Christian media output – not just preaching but Christian music, news and documentary programmes.

There are signs that Pentecostals are becoming ever more sophisticated in their understanding and deployment of the media and of popular cultural styles. It is true that the main body of Pentecostals are among the poor and their cultural style continues to reflect this fact. The typical dress code, for example, is not merely caught in a fashion time-warp but remains the unmistakable mark of respectable poverty. The same is true of speech patterns. Yet, since the late seventies two new sectors have emerged within the movement who tend to deploy a much more up-to-date cultural style and use of language. These are the new postmodern Pentecostals and Neo-Pentecostals. One layer is the inner city poor drawn out of the culture of drugs, the night-time economy of brothels, gambling houses, petty crime and the street folk. Their style comes straight out of the secular mass media and popular culture. The second sector is the new middle-class professionals and small business class, many of them working with information and communication technology. Their style too is as postmodern as that of their unconverted peers.

The 1980s saw the growth of new churches reflecting the recruitment of these new sectors. Of particular note, there appeared in the mega-cities an unknown number of upwardly mobile new professional and educated products of a strict Pentecostal upbringing. Many of these, uncomfortable with the restrictive class and cultural *style* of their churches of origin, have formed house churches and the like, or float loose of institutional anchors, retaining most of the moral and theological core of Pentecostalism but, in terms of appearance and surface style, indistinguishable from the rest of the postmodern city professionals with whom they work. They represent one 'lifestyle option' among the many in the postmodern cultural marketplace. It is worth glancing at two Brazilian examples of the new postmodern Pentecostal churches just to see how far they have come in their use of postmodern media and their incorporation of contemporary style.

The Universal Church of the Kingdom of God, centred on Rio and São Paulo, is part of the Cura Divina movement. It buys up redundant cinemas for its churches, planting itself in the entertainment sectors of cities, handy for the night-time economy and its many casualties. The churches are barely altered and minimally decorated, but they stay open for twenty-four hours. There is a sequence of services every day and counsellors are available at all times for individuals to approach. After dark, troops of missioners go out into the streets to recruit the street children, drug dealers, prostitutes and criminals and offer them new life. Its key ritual is exorcism – 'liberation' from the demons which cause ill health, distress, poverty. It offers miracles, including the miracle of prosperity, to those who believe. Although, or perhaps because, the demons are identified as the old Afro-Brazilian gods, the church has had a powerful attraction for poor blacks. Rather than leaping to the conclusion that this is a form of self-inflicted racism ('internal colonialism'), it may be useful to reflect that Africa is currently full of similar Christian groups and, further, that pre-Christian African religion was often marked by a willingness to abandon one's own gods for those of a more powerful rival group. Certainly the Universal Church's style and liturgy is continuous with the Afro-Brazilian tradition. It is perhaps another case of the local leaping to the global.

Crucially, for the present argument, the other stylistic component of the church's liturgy is drawn from contemporary media and popular culture. The pastors themselves, young men half of whom claim to have come out of the drug economy, are sharply dressed holy hustlers, a combination of rock star/DJ and television game show host. The music too is Brazilian pop and the services culminate in a samba-like dance of thanksgiving. The church has abandoned the Pentecostal dress code: in this matter 'it is forbidden to forbid' and sinners are invited in, dressed just as they are. It offers healing first, totally free except for the need to believe. Only then are the moral disciplines of Pentecostalism introduced through a slow induction and training. The church has grown from a handful in the late 1970s to around 2 million today.

The Universal Church has built up its own media empire as I indicated above. Its media professionals make sure that the church's output is highly polished, fully comparable with secular populist taste in its presentational values. It also mounts regular spectacles – mass healings in central city stadiums and the yearly Battle of the Gods on New Year's Eve, when church members challenge the Afro-Brazilian spirits on the beaches of Rio at midnight, when the feast in honour of the goddess of the sea is held. The media, of course, report these events. The Universal Church seems to have found a style of religious presentation as effective in its populist appeal as the *Sun* newspaper in Britain: it is all in the worst possible taste and wonderfully popular.

The *Renascer* church in São Paulo is an upmarket version of much of this, although without the special ethnic Afro-Brazilian content. This is a mega-church with a special mission to educated young professionals, especially those in the media, the entertainment and culture industries, and the information and communication business – the heart of the postmodern revolution itself. It attracts young adults whose lives are in danger of disintegration through overdoses of hedonism – drugs, alcohol and the other excesses of bohemian affluence. It offers marital 'encounter' and support for the family along with the whole moral programme of Pentecostalism. Its style and liturgies, however, remain fully postmodern. It runs a weekly spectacular, based in Christian rock music, and on other days of the week may feature orchestral musicians, artists, dancers. It has its own Christian popular music channel on radio, it runs its own publishing house, screen-printing company, and a shop which sells the products of these enterprises for profit. Its media output is highly sophisticated and fully professional. Its members dress fashionably and speak the *lingua franca* of global culture: they are as ironic, reflexive, goal oriented and concerned with future planning as their peers but they practise Christian patriarchy and Pentecostal moral absolutism, just like their humbler brethren in the shanty towns. They have the full postmodern credentials without the moral relativism.

It is possible, of course, that postmodern culture will hollow them all out, but it is as well to recall that the United States, postmodern pioneer though it is, is perfectly able to contain its Bible Belt 'fundamentalists' within the vast range of lifestyle chores on offer. It may be salutary, too, to remember those old Marxist critiques from the early seventies, of Daniel Bell and other supposed 'technological determinists': it is not the technology itself that matters (*pace* McLuhan, Baudrillard and the rest) but who owns and controls it and the uses to which it is put. Without necessarily knowing the theory, the Latin American Pentecostals appreciate the argument. That is why they are so intent on owning and controlling their own postmodern technology of information and communication. Reflect, too, on that aspect of postmodern theory which argues that the new information and communication media make visible and audible many publics which the political Centre was unaware of: postmodernity makes manifest the Other, the Local, and draws the attention of the Centre to them. This has happened with the Pentecostals. They have become visible not only to the old power and culture brokers, but *to themselves* as, collectively, a power to be reckoned with. They are using their newly discovered muscle to challenge postmodern culture not merely as little people from the margins but from *within the heartlands of that culture itself.* We await the outcome with curiosity and risk no hasty prediction.

Acknowledgement

Where evidence and arguments are not otherwise attributed they come from research conducted with David Martin in Mexico, Chile and Brazil and funded by the Pew Foundation through the Institute for the Study of Economic Culture, under its Director Peter L. Berger, Boston University, Massachusetts. The research will be published shortly under the title *Betterment from On High: Pentecostal Lives*, Oxford University Press, Oxford.

Notes

1 A good example of this view was a paper/performance presented by Barbara Kennedy at the conference *Shouts from the Street*, at Manchester Metropolitan University, in September 1995. Entitled 'The Cool Fascinations of the Last Seduction', the paper argued for the liberating potential of certain kinds of extreme expressions of violence and sexuality in art forms, especially film, and focused on a presentation which combined extracts from two films, images from *The Last Seduction* (in which a *femme fatale* uses her sexuality to engineer the murder of a number of adulterous men) with the sound track of *Natural Born Killers* (in which a couple of glamorous young psychopaths inflict motiveless murder on random victims).

2 In their review of the data from the 1990–91 World Values Survey, Ronald Inglehart and James Granato (1996) demonstrate the surprising closeness of North and South America on a range of values, and more particularly the continuing salience of religion in the whole region as against the relative secularity and preference for 'postmaterialist' values which mark northern European and Scandinavian societies. The maps of value distribution in this essay are particularly illuminating.

3 Armando Linde (1995), writing on 'Latin America and the Caribbean', makes a strong case for beginning to invest in 'human resources'. Indeed the World Bank is currently attempting, so far unsuccessfully, to get the prosperous nations to pursue a policy of debt remission and slackened monetary discipline in Africa as well as Latin America in order to encourage health and welfare 'investment'. The strongest recent critique of the neo-liberal policies of international financial institutions can be found in Catherine Caufield (1997), *Masters of Illusion: The World Bank and the Poverty of Nations*.

4 While Alan Gilbert (1994) gives the statistical documentation, a more vivid description of the detailed human consequences can be found in journalistic records such as that of Guillermoprieto (1994).
5 Two particularly concise and instructive historical arguments on this point can be found in Verena Stolcke's (1991) essay on 'Conquered Women' in *Report on the Americas*, and Magnus Morner's (1973) chapter on 'The Conquest of Women'. Roger Lancaster's (1992) brilliant dissection of the gender culture of contemporary Nicaragua has relevance for the whole continent.

References

Andreas, Carol 1991: Women at work. In North American Congress on Latin America, *Report on the Americas*, vol. 24, no. 4: 19–24.
Baudrillard, Jean 1988: *The Ecstasy of Communication*. Brooklyn, New York: Autonomedia.
Beck, Ulrich 1992: *Risk Society*. London: Sage.
—— Anthony, Giddens and Lash, Scott 1994: *Reflexive Modernization*. Cambridge: Polity.
Belsey, Catherine 1985: Constructing the subject: deconstructing the text. In J. Newton and D. Rosenfelt (eds), *Feminist Criticism and Social Change*. London and New York: Methuen.
Berger, Peter 1992: *A Far Glory*. New York: Anchor/Doubleday.
Bowen, Kurt 1996: *Evangelism and Apostasy*. Montreal and Kingston: McGill/Queen's University Press.
Brusco, Elizabeth 1986: The Household Basis of Evangelical Religion and the Reform of Machismo in Colombia. PhD dissertation, City University of New York.
Brydon, Lynne and Chant, Sylvia 1989: *Women in the Third World*. Aldershot: Edward Elgar.
Burdick, John 1993: *Looking for God in Brazil*. Los Angeles: University of California Press.
Cardoso, Eliana and Helwege, Ann 1995: *Latin America's Economy*. Cambridge: MIT Press.
Caufield, Catherine 1997: *Masters of Illusion: The World Bank and the Poverty of Nations*. London: Macmillan.
Centro de Estudios Públicos 1994: *Interviews: La Pintana Case*, Serie Andecendentes, no. 15. Santiago, Chile.
Chesnut, Andrew 1996: *Born Again in Brazil*. New Jersey: Rutgers University Press.
Cucchiari, Salvatore 1988: 'Adapted for Heaven': conversion and culture in western Sicily. *American Ethnologist*, vol. 15: 417–41.
—— 1991: Between shame and santification: Patriarchy and its transformation in Sicilian Pentecostalism. *American Ethnologist*, vol. 17: 687–707.
De Soto, H. 1987: The Other Path. New York: Harper & Row.
Dennis, Norman and Erdos, George 1993: *Families without Fatherhood*. London: Social Affairs Unit.

Dimenstein, Gilberto 1991: *Brazil's War on Children*. London: Latin American Bureau.

—— 1994: Little Girls of the Night. In North American Congress on Latin America, *Report on the Americas*, vol. 27, no. 6: 29–34.

Featherstone, Mike (ed.) 1990: *Global Culture*. London: Sage.

—— 1991: *Consumer Culture and Postmodernism*. London: Sage.

—— 1995: *Undoing Culture*. London: Sage.

Garrard-Burnett, Virginia and Stoll, David (eds) 1993: *Rethinking Protestantism in Latin America*. Philadelphia: Temple University Press.

Giddens, Anthony 1991: *Modernity and Self-Identity*. Cambridge: Polity.

—— 1992: *The Transformation of Intimacy*. Cambridge: Polity.

Gilbert, Alan 1994: *The Latin American City*. London: Latin American Bureau.

—— and Gugler, Josef (eds) 1992: *Cities, Poverty and Development*, 2nd edn. Oxford: Oxford University Press.

Gillespie, Charles 1990: Changing Brazil: etiologies and strategies. *Luso-Brazilian Review*, vol. 27, no. 2.

Guillermoprieto, Alma 1994: *The Heart that Bleeds*. New York: Knopf.

Hackett, Rosalind 1993: The symbolics of power discourse among contemporary religious groups in West Africa. In L. Martin (ed.), *Religious Transformations and Socio-Economic Change*. Berlin: Mouton de Gruyter.

Harris, Nigel 1987: *The End of the Third World*. London: Penguin.

Harvey, David 1989: *The Condition of Postmodernity*. Oxford: Blackwell.

Hewitt, William E. 1992: *Base Christian Communities and Social Change in Brazil*. Lincoln and London: University of Nebraska Press.

—— 1996: The changing of the guard: transformations in the politico-religious attitudes and behaviours of CEB members in São Paulo 1984–1993. *Journal of Church and State*, vol. 38, no. 1: 115–36.

Humphrey, John 1994: Are the unemployed part of the urban poverty problem in Latin America? *Journal of Latin American Studies*, vol. 26, pt 3: 713–36.

Inglehart, Ronald and Granato, James 1996 (June): Culture and economic development in Latin America: evidence from the World Values Surveys. Paper presented at Symposium on 'Cultural Values and Economic Development in Latin America', INCAE, Alajuela, Costa Rica.

Ireland, Rowan 1991: *Kingdoms Come*. Pittsburg: University of Pittsburg Press.

Jelin, Elizabeth (ed.) 1990: *Women and Social Change in Latin America*. London and New Jersey: UNRISD/Zed Books.

Katzman, Rubem 1992: Why Are Men So Irresponsible? *Comisión Económica Para América Latina Review*, no. 46: 79–87.

Kellner, Hansfried and Heuberger, Frank (eds) 1991: *Hidden Technocrats*. New York: Transaction.

Kennedy, Barbara 1995 (Sept.): The cool fascinations of the last seduction. Conference paper/performance, *Shouts from the Street*, Manchester Metropolitan University.

Kumar, Krishan 1995: *From Post-Industrial to Post-Modern Society*. Oxford: Blackwell.

Lancaster, Roger N. 1992: *Life is Hard*. Berkeley: University of California Press.

Lash, Scott and Urry, John 1987: *The End of Organized Capitalism*. Cambridge: Polity.

—— 1993: *Economies of Signs and Space*. London: Sage.

Lehman, David 1996: *Struggle for the Spirit*. Cambridge: Polity.

Linde, Armando S. 1995: Latin America and the Caribbean in the 1990s. *Finance and Development* (March): 2–5.

Lyotard, Jean-François 1984: *The Postmodern Condition*. Manchester: Manchester University Press.

Madeira, Felicia and Singer, Paul 1975: Structure of female employment and work in Brazil 1920–1970. *Journal of Interamerican Studies and World Affairs*, vol. 17, no. 4 (Nov.).

Marshall, Ruth 1991: Power in the Name of Jesus. *Review of African Political Economy*, no. 52: 21–37.

—— 1993: 'Power in the Name of Jesus': social transformation and Pentecostalism in Western Nigeria 'Revisited'. In T. Ranger and O. Vaughan (eds), *Legitimacy and the State in Twentieth Century Africa*, London: Macmillan.

Martin, Bernice 1995: New mutations of the Protestant ethic among Latin American Pentecostals. *Religion*, vol. 25: 101–17.

Martin, David A. 1990: *Tongues of Fire*. Oxford: Blackwell.

—— 1996: *Forbidden Revolutions*. London: SPCK.

—— 1997: The Gunning Lectures, University of Edinburgh (unpublished).

Morner, Magnus 1973: The conquest of women. In L. Hanke (ed.), *History of Latin American Civilizations: Sources and Interpretations*, vol. 1, New York: Little, Brown, pp. 137–41.

Murray, Charles 1990: *The Emerging British Underclass*. London: Social Affairs Unit.

Pérez Sáinz, J. P. and Menjívar Larín, R. 1994: Central American men and women in the informal sector. *Journal of Latin American Studies*, vol. 26, pt 2: 431–7.

Pescatello, Ann (ed.) 1973: *Female and Male in Latin America*. Pittsburg: University of Pittsburg Press.

Preston, David (ed.) 1987: *Latin American Development*. London: Longman.

Rifkin, Jeremy 1995: *The End of Work*. New York: Deep Books.

Seabrook, Jeremy 1993: *Victims of Development*. Guildford: Verso.

Scheper-Hughes, Nancy 1992: *Death without Weeping*. Berkeley: University of California Press.

—— and Hoffman, Daniel 1994: Kids Out of Place. North American Congress on Latin America, *Report on the Americas*, vol. 27, no. 6: 21–4.

Schneider, A. Gregory 1994: *The Way of the Cross Leads Home: The Domestication of American Methodism*. Bloomington: Indiana University Press; distributed in UK by Open University Press, Buckingham.

Scott, Alison M. 1994: *Divisions and Solidarities: Gender, Class and Employment in Latin America*. London: Routledge.

Shaiken, Harley 1994: Advanced manufacturing and Mexico. *Latin American Research Review*, vol. 29, no. 2: 39–71.

Stacey, Judith 1990: *Brave New Families*. New York: Basic Books.

Stolcke, Verena 1991: Conquered women. *Report on the Americas*, vol. 24, no. 5: 23–8.

Stoll, David 1990: *Is Latin America Turning Protestant?* Berkeley: University of California Press.

Toulis, Nicole 1995: Belief and Identity: Pentecostalism among First Generation Jamaican Women in England. Cambridge: PhD thesis.

Vásquez, Manuel A. 1997: Structural obstacles to grassroots pastoral practice: the case of a base community in urban Brazil. *Sociology of Religion*, vol. 58, no. 1: 53–68.

Warf, Barney 1995: Telecommunications and the changing geographies of knowledge transmission in the late twentieth century. *Urban Studies*, vol. 32, no. 2: 361–78.

Welch, J. H. 1993: The new face of Latin America: financial flows, markets and institutions in the 1990s. *Journal of Latin American Studies*, vol. 25, pt 1: 1–24.

CHAPTER EIGHT

secularization and citizenship in Muslim Indonesia

Robert W. Hefner

There are times when world events move with such stunning speed that they challenge our images of the past and our models for the future. We are living through one of these periods of intensely destabilizing change right now. The collapse of Communism in eastern Europe, the international drive for democratization, the clamour over human rights, the contest between secularist and religious visions of government and society – these and other things have forced observers in many societies to wonder whether there are not important commonalities to modern social development. Can cultures be compared? Are modern societies developing in a similar manner? Is it possible to talk about human rights across cultures? And, of most direct relevance for the issues to be addressed in this chapter, can we say that the modern era brings secularization or some other cross-culturally convergent process of religious change?

Not since the years following the Second World War have such broadly comparative issues been in the air. At that time, Western social scientists were confident that one could talk abut a range of modern social traits, the historic achievement of which was referred to as, of course, 'modernization'. Theories of modernization dominated the social sciences during those same years, and coloured popular understandings of modern social change. During the late 1960s and 1970s, however, the 'orthodox consensus' (Giddens, 1984, p. xv) that supported this perspective collapsed, and with it went the shared confidence that there are broad commonalities to modern social change. During the 1980s and 1990s, no analytic orthodoxy succeeded in imposing itself in the social sciences, but, among some social theorists, there was growing scepticism about universalist preachments. Universalism seemed to give way to relativist affirmations of the incommensurability of cultures and the playful, even ironic, indeterminacy of modern social change.

It is against this background of relativist ferment that I want in this chapter to reopen the question as to whether secularization is intrinsic to or, at the very least, widespread in modern religious change. For the moment let me note that by 'secularization' I mean the processes whereby domains of social activity and human experience previously organized around religious norms are 'desacralized' by their reinterpretation and reorganization in terms of ideals of a less sacral nature (Berger, 1967, pp. 106–8; cf. Wilson, 1985). The issue of secularization is not merely an academic one, of course. It has serious consequences for a host of policy issues, including, most notably, the question of the appropriate role of religion in government, the marketplace, and modern civil life as a whole.

The practical relevance of this question is all the clearer in the case of the country whose situation I want to address in this chapter, the Southeast Asian nation of Indonesia. Though less familiar to the Western public than its Middle Eastern counterparts, Indonesia is the largest majority-Muslim country in the world, with some 88 per cent of its almost 200 million people officially professing Islam. In addition to its demographic girth, Indonesia is significant because, after a quarter-century of sustained economic growth, it is about to emerge as an influential voice in the political and cultural affairs of the larger Muslim world.

Indonesia was once regarded by many of its Muslim brethren as a bastion of secularism and religious heterodoxy. In the early 1960s, it was renowned for its syncretic mystical movements, and for the fact that it had the largest Communist Party not only in the Muslim world, but in the non-Communist world as a whole. However, over the past fifteen years this nation has experienced an Islamic revival of historically unprecedented proportions. Unlike some of its Middle Eastern counterparts, however, a key feature of this revival has been the emergence of an intellectually vital and politically influential community of liberal or, as I have termed them elsewhere, 'civil pluralist' Muslims (Hefner, 1993a; cf. Barton, 1995). Civil pluralist Muslims deny the necessity of a formally established Islamic state, emphasize that it is the spirit and not the letter of Islamic law (*shariah*) to which Muslims must attend, stress the need for programmes to elevate the status of women, and insist that the Muslim world's most urgent task is to develop moral tools to respond to the challenge of modern pluralism (Effendy, 1994, pp. 141–228; Madjid, 1994).

In the case of Indonesia, a curious feature of the emergence of this civil pluralist tradition was a debate in the 1970s over the meaning and relevance of secularization for Muslims. As in most of the Muslim world, the great majority of Muslim intellectuals view secularization in extremely negative terms, as a feature of Western as opposed to Muslim modernity. In the West, they argue (citing a host of Western experts who say just this), the process of secularization drove religion from public life, reducing it to a matter of personal ethics and 'individual choice'. In as much as this is the case, secularization is the very antithesis of the Islamization of state and society to which many Muslims aspire. However, for some among the civil pluralist leadership, secularization is regarded not merely as compatible with Islam but as vitally necessary for its modern development. In the early 1970s, one of the most influential spokespersons of Indonesian civil pluralism, Nurcholish Madjid, linked secularization to the deepest of Islamic values, *tauhid* or the affirmation of God's absolute oneness. For Madjid and like-minded intellectuals, secularization is not Westernization but a means to realize this most compelling of religious ideals.

In this chapter I want to look at the idea and process of secularization from this Muslim Indonesian perspective. To do so, I will first briefly examine earlier discussions of secularization in Western social theory. Having done so, I will then summarize a few well known arguments as to how religious change in the modern Muslim world compares with that of the West. In the interest of brevity, my point of entry into this last issue (effective analysis of which would require more extensive case analysis than can be done here) will be the remarks of the late Ernest Gellner. In several books written during the last fifteen years of his life, Gellner made a forceful case for the idea that the Muslim world is the 'great exception' to secularization (Gellner, 1992, p. 18), in that it alone among the world's core civilizations 'totally and effectively defies the secularization thesis'. This is the question I examine here, not merely from the perspective of general theory but in relation to religious politics in Indonesia.

As Gellner might have predicted, recent developments in Indonesia seem at first to defy the secularization thesis and suggest that Islam is a 'great exception'. Over the past fifteen years, there has been a far-reaching Islamic revival, and its projects have included the extirpation of heterodox folk traditions and the 'Islamization' of areas of everyday life previously regulated by non-Islamic norms. At a deeper level, however, these developments are less exceptional relative to the Western experience than might first appear to be the case. In particular, I will suggest, a basic challenge to religion in both regions has been, and remains, the question of how simultaneously to develop a shared national culture, with its associated ideals of cultural citizenship, while still being responsive to the nation's pluralism. A key issue for Muslims attempting to devise such a response has been the question of whether Islam provides fixed ethical formulae for such a project, or values of a more generalized sort. Seen from the perspective of this debate, I will suggest, there are profound affinities between modern religious developments here and in the Western world.

Whether these similarities allow us to speak of a common process of 'secularization' in the Muslim and Western worlds depends on our characterization of this most slippery of analytic terms. My point in this chapter is not to adopt a position one way or another on this matter, but to suggest that the questions raised by the secularization debate are still deeply vital for the comparative sociology of religion and, more generally, of modernity.

Secularization Revisited

Secularization theory is less a theory in the technical sense of the word than it is a loosely structured set of assumptions as to the contours of religious development in the modern era. From an intellectual historical perspective, what is most remarkable about these assumptions is less their analytic rigour or depth of insight than their breadth of appeal. Despite the great differences that separate the approaches, secularization assumptions filtered into each of the twentieth century's great schools of Western social thought: Marxism, liberalism, and postmodernism.

As is well known, the 'inherited model' (Wilson, 1985) of secularization theory drew most heavily on the writings of Emile Durkheim. From Durkheim, the model developed its image of societal modernization as the progressive differentiation and specialization of social structures. In this view, commerce and industrialization bring about a growing division of labour, and this in turn promotes a generalized 'differentiation' (separation and specialization) of social institutions. Kinship, politics, education, and employment all separate from an original unity and assume a dizzying variety of specialized forms. In the process, human society is transformed from a simple, homogenous collectivity into the pluralistic entities we know today.

For Durkheim and later secularization theorists, this process of structural–functional differentiation involves not just adjustments in social organization but the fragmentation or pluralization of life-worlds, meanings, and experience. Where previously there was a shared 'sacred canopy' (Berger, 1967) stabilizing human experience, in modern times the canopy is rent and the collective bases of morality and identity are lost. Unlike the German philosopher Nietzsche (and the many postmodern theorists who reference him for their work), Durkheim believed that this loss of religion was but a temporary dysfunction of early modernization (see Beckford, 1989, p. 25). No society can survive without a collective moral consciousness, he thought, and eventually a new, though more individualized, 'civil religion' would emerge to play the role earlier assumed by religion. Centred on Durkheim's 'cult of the individual', this civil religion would provide coherence and stability even in the absence of a theistic canopy.

With the related concept of civic culture, this idea of civil religion played a key role in models of modernity developed by such leading figures as Edward Shils (1960), Robert Bellah (1975; Bellah and Hammond, 1980), and, early in his career, Clifford Geertz (1973). Later proponents of secularization theory, however, tended to regard this feature of the theory with decided ambivalence. These more sceptical approaches looked beyond Durkheim to Max Weber and Friedrich Nietzsche to reach a bleaker conclusion on the modern prospects for a civil morality. Borrowing from Weber's ideas on instrumental rationalization, these theorists emphasized that science, technology, and modern capitalism have worked not merely to differentiate our world, but to depersonalize and disenchant it. Having initially relied on a religious ethic to institutionalize capitalism and bureaucratic government, modern Western society discovered that it could work well enough without an overarching ethical consensus. Modernity's challenge to religion and civic morals, it seemed, has been more severe than Durkheim had imagined (cf. Fenn, 1978).

In sum, though one wing of secularization theory remained, of the possibility of a collective moral consciousness of at least limited scope, the other echoed Weber and Nietzsche in affirming modernity's destabilization of all foundational certitudes. Though during the 1960s and 1970s secularization theory vacillated between these Durkheimian and Weberian poles, in the 1980s social theorists (especially of the postmodern variety) leaned more toward the Weberian or Nietzschean view, emphasizing the irrecoverable fragmentation of modern life-worlds and the resulting privatization or decline of religion. Of course, during these same years other, less mainline theories of religious modernization continued to affirm the potential for spirituality even in a postmodern age (Berger, 1992; Cox, 1990). More surprisingly, in the early 1990s there was a veritable deluge of sociological and anthropological research suggesting that rumours of modern religion's demise were premature (see Casanova, 1994; Juergensmeyer, 1993; Martin, 1990; van der Veer, 1994). These studies heightened our appreciation of the modern world's diversity, but did not manage to bring about a new consensus on the nature of modern religious change.

In retrospect, however, what was especially intriguing about mainline secularization theory was the ease with which it so often moved from a sober, descriptively neutral view of religion to a prescriptively hostile one. The modest version affirmed that, as a result of society's structural–functional differentiation (or some equally radical process of life-world pluralization), the scope of religious institutions is progressively narrowed, until religion becomes a matter of personal belief rather than public consciousness. Sometimes this argument was linked to a second thesis: that the modern search for salvation had retreated to the realm of personal self-expression, and this search for expressive realization, rather than conventional spirituality, was the real religion of modernity (Luckmann, 1967).

Even where this latter theme was not appended, this view of modern religion's privatization often slipped from straightforward description to normative prescription. The tendency is well illustrated in the following quote from one of the most distinguished of secularization theorists, the British sociologist Bryan Wilson:

> The secularization thesis implies the privatization of religion; its continuing operation in the public domain becomes confined to a lingering rhetorical invocation in support of conventional morality and human decency and dignity – as a cry of despair in the face of moral panic.   (Wilson, 1985, p. 19)

As this quote unwittingly illustrates, it is a slippery slope from a soft secularization thesis to a hard one. One moves from comments about the desacralization of the public and the pluralization of beliefs to generalizations about the 'irrationality' of religion. Thus, in the same work, Wilson (1985, p. 18) describes religion as 'deep-laid in man's essential irrationality' and implies that it is only because of this 'essential irrationality' that the inexorable progress of secularization has not advanced further. On the evidence of a country such as the United States, where the great majority of citizens continue to profess a religious faith (Wuthnow, 1988), this characterization of religion as irrational and culturally descendant seems curious, to say the least. But it was typical of the tendency among early secularization theorists, and among a portion of the Western public, to confuse the varied theses implicit in secularization theory with proof of religion's demise.

The Great Exception?

Given the severity of their forecasts, it is not surprising that many secularization theorists have been perplexed by the phenomenon of modern Islam. While the Judaeo-Christian tradition is represented (as we have seen, much too simplistically) as in irreversible decline, religion in the Muslim world seems as vibrant as ever. Ernest Gellner aptly summarized this paradox:

> It is possible to disagree about the extent, homogeneity, or irreversibility of this trend [i.e., secularization] . . . but, by and large, it would seem reasonable to say that it is real. But there is one very real, dramatic and conspicuous exception to all this: Islam. To say that secularization prevails in Islam is not contentious. It is simply false. Islam is as strong now as it was a century ago. In some ways, it is probably much stronger.   (Gellner, 1992, p. 5)

Speaking from a different theoretical tradition, the distinguished Turkish sociologist Bassam Tibi has also argued that secularization is inevitable in all contemporary societies, since it is a necessary feature of the functional differentiation of modern social structures (Tibi, 1990, p. 127). Not surprisingly, when he turns to the Muslim world, Tibi is disturbed to see that much Islamist discourse insists on a 'congruence between the sacred and the political' (p. 131). Rather than seeing this as an effort to exercise ethicopolitical control over a disordered world, he characterizes it as an essentially preindustrial, 'organic' form of politics, incompatible with the modern era's demand for autonomy and functional specialization. Citing the European experience, he notes that Protestantism eventually came to be 'primarily domiciled within the sphere of interiority' (p. 139); consistent with this experience, he predicts that 'The future of Islam seems to lie in a parallel direction'. Thus what began as an oversimplified understanding of religion's fate in the West is quietly generalized to the Muslim world.

While Ernest Gellner agrees with Tibi in seeing Islam as out of step with what he believes are the secularizing and privatizing imperatives of the modern world, he is much less optimistic about the long-term prospects for the kind of liberalizing change Tibi has in mind. Modern Islam, Gellner insists, has evolved a social organization and ideology unique among the world religions in its ability to adapt to the challenges of modern nation-building. More particularly, Gellner asserts, Islam has been able to play a role in nation-building akin to that of ethno-nationalism in the West, but with quite different consequences for religion. In the West, Gellner argues, nineteenth-century nationalism revived and idealized, and thus ultimately transformed, ethnic culture. Though in a few countries such as Ireland, Poland, and Spain, religion played a role in nationalist movements, in most of the West, Gellner notes, nationalism looked to ethnic and folk culture rather than Christendom for its core symbols. In this manner it displaced Christianity from its role as the key emblem of European political identity (cf. Anderson, 1983, p. 24).

Like Christianity, Gellner continues, Islam too had long been split into a high and a low variant. The high tradition was associated with the trans-ethnic and trans-political clerisy, or *ulama*, while the low or folk tradition was grounded in kinship politics and localized shrines to Muslim saints (Gellner, 1981, pp. 75–6). Throughout history the two traditions flowed into and influenced each other. Periodically, however, they also erupted into conflict, when reformers 'revived the alleged pristine zeal of the high culture, and united tribesmen in the interests of purification and of their own enrichment and political advancement (Gellner, 1983, p. 76). With its industries, education, and above all, powerful state, the modern era, Gellner argues, has irreversibly altered this 'flux and reflux' (Gellner, 1981; 1992, p. 14) of localization and reform. Today, modernizing reformists stigmatize the folk variant of Islam as the cause of the

Muslim world's backwardness, and work with considerable success for its extinction. In reformers' eyes, Gellner claims, the twin challenges of modernization and Western dominance demand that this backward tradition be replaced once and for all with a purified, high Islam.

For Gellner, Islam is unique among the world's historic religions 'in that it allows the use of a pre-industrial great tradition of a clerisy as the national, socially pervasive idiom and belief of a new style community' (Gellner, 1983, p. 81). Whereas in the Western world the rise of the modern state diminished Christianity's role in political life, in the Muslim world nation-state development has revitalized religion. Though Gellner shies away from making social forecasts, he hints that things are not likely to change in the near future. 'So far', he comments, 'there is no indication that it [Islam] will succumb to secularization in the future either' (1992, p. 18).

Islam and Pluralism in Indonesia

For want of space I will not assess the adequacy of Gellner's overall characterization of secularization (but cf. Munson, 1993, pp. 82–7). Narrowing focus, I want to examine the putative exceptionalism of the Muslim world in light of Indonesian Islam. Indonesia is rather far from the historic heartlands of the Muslim world. However, it is the most populous of Muslim nations and, over the past two centuries, has witnessed movements of political and religious reform like those in other Muslim countries. By way of illustration, let me focus attention on religious change in one portion of the vast Indonesian archipelago, the island of Java, where some 60 per cent of Indonesians live.

The standard characterization of Javanese Islam is that provided by Clifford Geertz (1960) in his *The Religion of Java*. Whatever its shortcomings, this work succeeds brilliantly at capturing the extraordinary pluralism of Javanese Islam in the 1950s and the forces animating its change. Geertz identified three strains of Javanese Islam: the *abangan* or folk variant, which he saw as a ritualistic mélange of indigenous, Hindu, and Muslim elements; the *santri* tradition, a more or less orthodox variant of normative Islam; and the *priyayi* or aristocratic variant, which Geertz characterized as deeply influenced by Java's earlier Hindu–Buddhist tradition.

Marshall Hodgson (1974, p. 551) and, more recently, Mark Woodward (1989) have demonstrated that in distinguishing Hindu–Buddhist from Islamic elements in Javanese religion Geertz used an unjustifiably narrow conception of Islam. As a result, a good deal of what he identified as Hindu–Buddhist is more properly understood as derived from Islamic Sufism and courtly ceremonial styles adapted from Indo-Persian Islamic precedents. For the purposes of our present discussion, however, whether Geertz's analysis is philologically on the mark is of secondary importance to what his work reveals as to the dynamics of Islamic reform in the mid-twentieth century. Conducting research at a time when Indonesia had the freest parliamentary democracy in all Southeast Asia, Geertz describes a situation in which class and ideological conflicts were super-charged with religious antagonisms pitting *abangan* Javanists, who tended to support Indonesia's nationalist and Communist parties, against *santri* Muslims. Though religious issues were but one influence on this bitter polarization, the conflict had a profound effect on the subsequent development of Indonesian religion.

The religious component in this struggle centred on *abangan* Islam's predilection for mysticism and cults of local saints, earth spirits, and revered ancestors. Reform-minded *santri*, Geertz showed, regarded all these activities as polytheistic deviations from Islam, and used Muslim political parties to advance the cause of religious reform. Muslim reformers also bitterly attacked spirit-mediums, magicians, healers, herbalists, and anyone else who appeared to traffic in magical powers or tutelary spirits. Reports from other times and places in Java paint a similar portrait of a sustained Muslim drive against *abangan* traditions (Hefner, 1987, 1990; Kim, 1996; Pranowo, 1991).

Forty years after Geertz's research, we can assess the results of the *santri* reformation effort. The evidence is overwhelming: the reformist initiative has proved astoundingly successful, suppressing heterodox cults and canalizing public expressions of popular spirituality away from the *wujudi* (mystical) pantheism once characteristic of folk Javanese religion and into more *tauhidic* or monotheistic devotional forms. To provide a brief but concrete illustration of this achievement, let me quote a passage from the recently completed dissertation of a young Korean anthropologist trained at the Australian National University. Based on his research in a Central Javanese village, the passage concerns the well-known *abangan* habit of invoking earth and ancestral spirits in their most famous of rituals, the ceremonial meal known as a *slametan* or *kendhuri*:

> If all sorts of supernatural beings of different origin such as local spirits, dead ancestors, Hindu deities, and Islamic prophets were previously invoked . . . , it is now only the name of Allah which can be heard. . . . The same is true when villagers were asked to point out to whom this ritual was directed and of whom they asked a *slamet* [blessing]. They only talked about Allah. (Kim, 1996, p. 156)

What Kim is describing here is a reformation event taking place in villages and towns across Java. A region long renowned for its syncretic appeals to Hindu, animist, and Muslim spirits has been swept up in an Islamic resurgence as profound as any in the modern Muslim world. The transformation is every bit as powerful as that which David Martin (1990) has described among evangelical Protestant converts in Latin America. Though, by comparison with other Muslim societies, Javanese Islam remains vigorously pluralistic, there can be no question that reformist Muslims have carried out nothing less than a great transformation, bringing popular religion into closer conformity with Islam's monotheistic ideals (see Hefner, 1987; Pranowo, 1991).[1]

Is this secularization? Clearly if our ideas on secularization are based on the 'hard' version of the thesis that I described above, this is not secularization at all, but simply a delegitimation of old religious practices and the sacralization of others. Religion has not been banisher to the realm of the personal, exposed as 'essentially irrational', or pushed down a slippery slope towards extinction. On the contrary, while attacking spirit cults and shamans, Muslim reformers promote daily prayer, mosque attendance, payment of alms, and other expressions of Islamic piety. From a normative Islamic perspective, the Javanese appear more religious than ever.

If, however, what we mean by secularization is more the 'soft' version to which I earlier referred, with its desacralization of the concrete in favour of an abstraction of the divine, I think it is clear that the efforts of Islamic reformers contain elements similar to what is conventionally known as secularization. In attacking guardian spirits, belittling the spiritual efficacy of ancestors, and contesting the morality of magic, Muslim reformers have desacralized domains that previously fell under the spell of magical and spiritist technique, and relocated divinity to a higher or more abstract plane. In so doing, the reformers have enacted an ethic consistent with the Islamic emphasis on God's absolute oneness (*tauhid*). At the same time, they have brought popular religion in line with more general notions of spiritual agency, displacing the immediate, manipulable spiritualism of animist cults with a unitary appeal to Allah.

Let me pause for a moment on this last point, because it is central to our task of distinguishing what is useful and what mistaken in earlier versions of secularization theory. The process of 'desacralizing' certain worldly acts while relocating divinity away from the manipulable concreteness of curing, cultivating, etc., is, I believe, a widespread (though by no means universal) form of religious change in modern monotheistic religions. As with an earlier generation of Christian reform, this Islamic reformation does not disenchant the world, but distances its spiritual agency from the immediacy of this-worldly space–time events. Rather than a cure being achieved because a spirit can be cajoled, blessing comes to those who live in the way of an all-powerful, but also more remote, Allah.

Though theorists inclined to a 'hard' version of secularization theory may have difficulty distinguishing this kind of religious change from their own notion of desacralization-slipping-into-disbelief, the difference is profound. By conceiving of God in less manipulable, more abstract terms, this softly secularized religious experience can resonate with more generalized ethical appeals and more empirical vehicles of explanation and control. As this resonance deepens, we should not be surprised to hear believers explain local moral issues in terms of universalistic ethical ideas, such as the interests of the community of Muslim believers (*ummat*). Similarly, we should not be surprised if, like post-Reformation Christians, some Islamic reformists affirm that there is no contradiction between belief in God's majesty and the efficacy of most (though not all) modern science.

In as much as this type of change has taken place in large portions of the Muslim world,[2] it bears a striking resemblance to the earlier efforts of Christian and post-Christian philosophers to carve out a space for empirical science by insisting that the book of nature was as legitimate a way to God as the Book of Revelation (Casanova, 1994, p. 24; Outram, 1995, p. 45). Whether, in fact, we want to continue to use the term 'secularization' to refer to this type of religious change should not concern us as much as the recognition that such rationalization has occurred in places other than the modern West. Whether it is intrinsic to *all* modern religious traditions (which I believe it is not), we none the less see here a striking convergence in the historical experience of a significant segment of modern Christianity and Islam.

If Islam in modern Indonesia has been a powerful agent of something resembling secularization, however, it has also been linked to what might appear to be a rather different project. In the 1950s, the drive for Islamic revitalization centred on not just monotheistic repudiation of spirit cults, but efforts to Islamize the Indonesian state. Failing a full Islamization of the state, Muslim activists pressed for enforcement of an agreement known as the 'Jakarta charter'. This charter was a statement that had originally been appended to the preamble to the 1945 declaration of Indonesian independence, but was dropped after protests from Indonesia's Christian and Hindu minorities (Boland, 1982). According to the charter, the government was to work to 'carry out' (I., *menjalankan*) Islamic law (*shariah*) among the Muslim portion of the Indonesian populace. In other words, rather than building a high wall between church and state, Muslim reformers sought to link the two with a solid, stable bridge.

The effort to achieve an Islamic state was opposed, of course, by secular-minded Muslim leaders, as well as by the leadership of the powerful nationalist and Communist parties. Supercharged by a deteriorating economic situation, the struggle between Muslim parties and the

Communists came to a tragic climax during 1965–6. Then, in the aftermath of a failed left-wing officers' coup, Muslim organizations joined forces with the military to destroy the Indonesian Communist Party, resulting in the death of 250,000–500,000 people (Cribb, 1990; Hefner, 1990). Though the motives that fuelled the killing were varied, some Muslim political organizations sacralized the campaign, calling it a holy war or *jihad* (see Boland, 1982, p. 146).

From this abbreviated history, we can see that whatever may have been occurring in the realms of curing and spirit worship, Muslim politics were not animated by a similar commitment to the desacralization of the mundane. On the contrary, Muslim politicians saw themselves as engaged in a sacred struggle to recapture the Indonesian nation from secularist and atheistic rivals. On the surface, then, the Muslim campaign conformed rather nicely to Ernest Gellner's 'exceptionalist' vision of modern Islam. A purified high Islam was posed in opposition to the corrupted Islam of the *abangan* community. Rejecting Communism, secularism, and liberalism, political Islam was to provide an alternative basis for the terms of cultural citizenship.

Muslim efforts did not end, of course, with the destruction of the Communist Party. In the aftermath of 1965–6, the military-dominated government announced that its first priority was the political and economic stabilization of the country. It moved quickly to restrict the activities of political parties, including Muslim ones. In the face of the government's restrictions on political Islam, the Muslim community split into two camps, some supporting co-operation with the government and others favouring principled opposition. The debate which ensued among Muslim intellectuals is interesting for our purposes, because it came to focus on the highly charged question as to whether the modernization of Islam required its 'secularization' (*sekularisasi*) (Madjid, 1984). Several leaders called for an innovative programme of Islamic renewal (*pembaruan*). They criticized the identification of Islam with party politics, implying that the earlier politicization of Islam (through its association with formal political parties) had only undermined popular piety. The campaign for a Muslim state, they added, confused a profane preoccupation with a sacred one.

There is nothing in scripture, these critics argued, to indicate that Muslims must establish an Islamic state. Hence these and related political efforts must be viewed in a relativist light and as 'secularized'. In a limited sense, Madjid and others meant that Muslims should repudiate narrow partisanship and work for the greater religious good. More generally, however, the renewal groups' call for secularization was a bold affirmation of their belief that Muslims must come to terms with Indonesia's pluralism, and develop a normative charter for the nation inclusive of all of its citizenry (see Madjid, 1994).

In the years since this initial appeal, Madjid and others sympathetic to the ideals of Indonesia's movement for Islamic 'renewal' (*pembaruan*) have not ceased in their promotion of theological and practical reforms. They have consistently rejected the notion that women should play a second-class role in religion or public life, and called for a 'contextual' understanding of Quranic injunctions on such matters as inheritance and divorce. In the mid-1980s, they were among those most ardently urging the Muslim community to give up the struggle for an Islamic state and accept the non-confessional state ideology or *Pancasila* as the basis for Muslim social and political organizations. In the aftermath of several anti-Christian incidents (including church burnings) in 1991–2, Madjid and his supporters launched a bold appeal for religious tolerance, basing it on, among other things, the highly controversial argument that people of other faiths could and should be properly regarded as 'Muslim' when professing faith in God. More recently, civil pluralist Muslims have been at the centre of efforts to promote the democratization of Indonesia's still tightly controlled political system, calling for, among other things, a loosening of controls on the press, an end to government manipulation of elections, and official tolerance of a political 'opposition' (a policy the government rejects on the grounds that it is contrary to Indonesian cultural tradition).

For the moment, however, let me return briefly to the controversy surrounding Madjid's original appeal for secularization in the 1970s, and explore its implications for our understanding of religious politics here in Indonesia. Madjid's appeal for secularization provoked disbelief among some in the Muslim community. Nurcholish Madjid was attacked for trying to transform Islam into what one Muslim critic called a 'spiritual personalist ethical system' akin to modern Western Christianity (Hassan, 1980, pp. 114, 123). Madjid and his associates took care to emphasize that they rejected the ideology of *secularism*, with its privatization of religion, while supporting *secularization* construed as the desacralization of things wrongly sacralized. Critics dismissed such arguments as academic sophistry. Any move towards secularization, they insisted, violates the essence of Islam. Islam is a 'total way of life', and thus a complete and self-sufficient 'system' unto itself. Its components, therefore, cannot be arbitrarily separated one from the other. This image of Islam as a complete social order (*al-nizam al-islami*) has been a recurrent theme in the discourse of conservative Islamists in much of the modern Muslim world (see Moussalli, 1992, pp. 69–70, 87; Mitchell, 1969, pp. 234–45).

Though Madjid's influence temporarily declined following this controversy, the government's wariness toward the politicization of religion made any kind of mass-based mobilization difficult during the 1970s and 1980s. As a result, whether they agreed with the civil pluralists or not, most of the national Muslim leadership channelled their energies during these years away from party politics into programmes of social and educational reform. It is clear that many Muslim leaders viewed such efforts as the proper focus for a pluralistic Islam that had renounced once and for all the 'myth' (as some intellectuals called it) of an Islamic state. However, other Muslim leaders viewed this apoliticism as a mere temporizing strategy, hoping to win time and mass support before pressing forward with another campaign to Islamize the state.

It would take me beyond the confines of the present chapter to describe events during the 1970s and 1980s in any detail (but see Hefner, 1993a). Let me say simply that the depoliticization of Islam did not diminish popular piety but helped to promote it. The Muslim leadership's forswearing of party politics reassured military officials opposed to political Islam. At the same time, and with the support of the Department of Religion (which had long been dominated by Muslim officials), the Muslim community was able to embark on a bold programme of religious revival. It doubled the number of mosques in the country in just ten years, introduced mandatory religious education into all schools, established a network of Islamic teacher-training colleges, and, in brief, reversed the decline in Muslim piety that had resulted from the politicization of Islam in the Old Order (pre-1966) period. For those of us familiar with the Indonesia of an earlier era, the results of this campaign have been astonishing. Public culture in Indonesia is today far more Islamic than it was in the 1950s.

The ascent of this politically low-profile, cultural Islam had a decisive impact on Indonesian politics and society. It created a Muslim middle class with greater initiative than at any time since the founding of the New Order. It has left unresolved, however, the difficult question of which variant of Islam is to guide the Muslim community into the next phase of Indonesia's national development. Though the civil pluralist version of Islam remains popular among the new middle class, the ruling elite – which throughout the 1960s and 1970s had done its best to deflect any kind of Islamic politics – has reacted to the resurgence with a high-risk strategy of co-optation and control. On the one hand, like leaders of many Middle Eastern states in the 1980s (Roy, 1994, p. 125), the regime has made sweeping concessions to Muslims in such cultural fields as religious education, mosque construction, and public proselytization. It has done so, however, while attempting to separate reform-minded democrats from Islamic conservatives less concerned about such issues as minority rights, the rule of law, and social justice (see Feillard, 1995, pp. 289–306). The government's policies will prove crucial over the next few years to the determination of which vision of Islam, and which formula for modern citizenship, will prevail.

Conclusion: Religion and Cultural Citizenship

By way of conclusion, let me return to my earlier comments on secularization and determine just what the Indonesian example can tell us, first about pluralism and secularization, and secondly about whether or not Islam constitutes, as Gellner argued, a 'great exception' to modern processes of religious change.

The first and most general comment we can make is that, here in Indonesia, the processes that correspond most closely to what Western theorists once identified as secularization are a good deal *less* mechanical, and a good deal *more* ethico-political, than our generalizations about 'structural differentiation' would imply. Certainly, in a round-about way the changes sweeping the Indonesian Muslim community can be traced back to the achievements of modern science, an industrial division of labour, and modern differentiation. However, the Muslim effort has also been abetted by forces more specifically religious and political than such organizational generalities imply. To put the matter in too-polar terms, one could say that religious change here has been affected as much by the related struggles for a modern Islam and Indonesian citizenry as it has by generic processes of structural differentiation.

With their Durkheimian emphases on socioeconomic differentiation, mainline variants of secularization theory tend to overlook this more complex play of forces, and portray secularization as the more or less mechanical consequence of changing socioeconomic organization. Yet we know that even in the West the making of modern religiosity was deeply affected by the variable circumstances of different Christianities and political struggles over the form and meaning of national citizenship. To cite a familiar example, we know that in the early-modern era France and England came to institutionalize very different relationships between Church and state despite having achieved similar levels of economic development. In France, a monopolistic clergy opted in the pre-Republican era for a strong alliance with the royalist state; it used this alliance, in turn, to suppress religious pluralism, especially that represented by the Protestant Huguenots. As so often happens in human history, however, this gesture of apparent strength – which, to borrow terms from Indonesia's civil pluralists, involved the 'sacralization' of an all-too-human political establishment – proved over the long run to weaken religion in French civil life. Identified as they were with a monolithic state system, the Church's policies helped to ensure that popular social movements would show an equally monolithic hostility to the clergy and religion. And as David Martin (1978) has observed, this same pattern of polarization, pitting a state-allied clergy against anti-clericals hostile to all religion, has been a recurring feature of religious politics in many parts of the Latin-Catholic world.

The Church of England, of course, was also an established church. At times its leadership displayed aspirations every bit as monopolistic as its French counterpart. Catholics and Nonconformist Protestants were sometimes persecuted and even killed. At a critical moment in its historic development, however, the Church had to decide what to do with the growing number of Protestant Nonconformists who rejected church authority. The stand-off between establishment supporters and their Nonconformist rivals was long and hard, and its outcome was not determined by the sheer weight of modernizing social structures. In the end, rather than choosing to suppress pluralism, the Church and the state blinked and ended up tolerating it. As we all know, this failure of England's elite to push for a decisive suppression of Catholics and Protestant Nonconformists provided a precedent for a more general tolerance and, eventually, a more inclusive form of cultural citizenship.

The point here is that in England, France, and the rest of Europe, the precise role of religion in government and society has been considerably more varied than is implied in mainline variants of secularization theory. Religion's role in public life has been influenced by the decisions of religio-political elites in the face of pluralism and political dissent. Structural variables have also been critical; the social costs of murdering religious dissidents were much lower when those dissidents were concentrated in, say, a marginal community of peasants or petty traders rather than in the upper echelons of an ascendant bourgeoisie. However, ruling elites regularly make bad choices, and societies pay the price. Thus, while growing differentiation may have increased the social costs of religious repression, it was not itself sufficient to guarantee that elites would make the 'right' choice, and opt for a less repressive union of religion and state.

A similar contest over the direction of politics and society is one of the primary influences on religious change in Indonesia and other parts of the modern Muslim world. Some rivals in this contest reject religious disestablishment and insist on a direct and literal application of Islamic law to all aspects of government and social life. Others insist that such a view distorts the true meaning of Islam, attributing a fixed and closed quality to what is supposed to be a universal and thus open ethical system. For these latter critics, Islam in a pluralistic era must serve as the source of a generalized or civil ethics, inspiring the public's sense of social justice, rather than providing a finished blueprint for government and law.

Relative to many other Muslim countries, what is remarkable about Indonesia is that, at the moment, so many Muslim leaders endorse this civil pluralist understanding of religion rather than the establishmentarian view. In part, of course, this reflects the success of Indonesia's national elites at marginalizing more radical Islamist options. But the full explanation for Indonesia's Muslim pluralists is more complex than this. Many pious Muslim leaders have willingly opted for the pluralist option, as have broad segments of the Muslim public. In part, I believe, this reflects Indonesian Islam's rich pluralist heritage.

Though an earlier generation of Western scholars identified its most distinctive trait as the strength of so-called 'pre-Islamic' survivals, the more distinctive quality of Indonesian Islam has long been its remarkable tradition of intellectual and organizational pluralism. Even in an earlier era when virtually all Javanese, Malays, or Minangkabau called themselves Muslims, neither the courts nor religious scholars (*ulama*) exercised monopoly control over the Muslim community. There were always different Muslim rulers, diverse Muslim associations, and alternative ideas as to how to be a good Muslim.

Unlike many Middle Eastern countries, this pattern of cultural pluralism and pluricentric organization was reinforced rather than diminished during the colonial era. The Dutch colonial government placed strict limits on Islamic activities, and provided little of the support for legal and intellectual systematization which, for example, the British provided in colonial Malaya (Ellen, 1983; Roff, 1967). Rather than reinforcing a union of religion and state, colonialism pushed Muslims out of the corridors of power into villages and marketplaces. In the nineteenth century, a vast network of Quranic schools spread across Java and other parts of Indonesia. The leaders of these institutions were contemptuous of Europeans and native aristocrats, and did their best to locate their institutions both physically and culturally at far remove from government (Dhofier, 1982). The pattern was repeated in the early twentieth century, when the first modern Muslim organizations were established. All of these organizations were obliged to operate outside rather than within the channels of state, and developed a strong spirit of civic independence.

Reform movements of the early independence era (after 1945) and the more recent New Order (after 1966) have no doubt altered this pattern of Islamic pluralism. In particular, as we have seen, there have been powerful pressures against heterodoxy and for an Islamic state. In addition, rather than being 'privatized', Islam has come to be an ever more pervasive feature of public life, as evidenced in the recent proliferation of Islamic greetings, television shows, dress styles, study groups, and cuisines. Yet even as public piety has come to conform to Muslim norms, Muslim politics has remained decidedly pluricentric. Despite the government's establishment in 1976 of a council of *ulamas* (Majelis Ulama Indonesia) and its recent efforts to co-opt Muslim leaders, Indonesia still has no unified organization of *ulama*-scholars and no hegemonic Islamic political organization. Though some Muslim leaders occasionally lament this pluralism, seeing it as a fatal political weakness from a democratic perspective, it is really a blessing in disguise. Much as with Christian leaders in an earlier north-western Europe, it has led some Muslims to the realization that hegemonic aspirations must be renounced in favour of pluralism, tolerance, and the generalization of Islamic values into a civic culture.

There are more contemporary influences on this Islamic tradition of tolerance as well. The experience of Muslims since independence has impressed upon many the dangers of too direct a linkage between religion and power. It was, after all, during the Old Order period, when religious issues were politicized to an extreme, that one heard the loudest cries among some in the nominal Muslim (*abangan*) community for a turning away from Islam. Similarly, it was in the aftermath of the anti-communist killings of 1965–6 that one saw some 2 million nominal Muslims (most of whom had been affiliated with the Communist Party) turn from Islam to Hinduism and Christianity (Hefner, 1993b; Lyon, 1977). Conversely, there has been an unprecedented deepening of Islamic piety since the 1980s, a period during which political Islam has been far less influential than civic-cultural Islam. In the eyes of some Muslim Indonesians, this dampening of political passions, which is to say, the 'desacralization' of party politics, was necessary to allow a deepening of Islamic values.

Though this historical experience may seem a fragile basis on which to build a principled consensus on the merits of pluralism, it is exactly the kind of heritage that provided the initial impetus for the development of civil pluralist ideologies in the West. The critical question now is whether this social precedent can be rationalized and institutionalized within a legal–political framework so as to deepen and reinforce it, or, alternatively, whether short-term interests will prompt Indonesia's elite to waste this precious cultural capital.

Let me return, finally, to secularization theory and modern religious change. What I have tried to suggest in this chapter is that we must reject 'harder' versions of secularization theory, especially those that understood secularization as an inevitable and universal process of religious privatization or decline. Having done so, we are in a better position to understand the variable nature of religious change not just in the developing world, but in the Western world as well (cf. Casanova, 1994; Martin, 1978). From this revisionist perspective, the situation of Muslims in Indonesia and elsewhere seems less exceptional than was implied in earlier theories of modernity and secularity.

While rejecting elements of secularization theory, however, it is important to retain that tradition's conviction that there are commonalities to religious change in the modern age. Modernity has ushered in a host of common problems. Foremost among these is the thoroughly modern conundrum of how to balance pluralism with the ethico-political need to devise culturally viable terms for national citizenship. Though Muslim responses to these challenges show the imprint of their own civilizational experience, they also indicate that their range of options is not entirely different from those available in the early-modern and contemporary West. In an era when certain Western and Muslim leaders speak of an inevitable 'clash of civilizations', it is useful to remind ourselves of these shared challenges, and of the fact that on all sides there are people of good will struggling to devise and defend a modern civility.

Notes

1 This is *not* to say that mysticism of a pantheistic or polytheistic sort has disappeared entirely in Java, least of all in private circles. My point is instead that religious discourse and practice in the *public* sphere have changed decisively as a result of the Islamic resurgence. Paul Strange (1986), an historian and one of the most astute Western observers of Javanist mysticism, has also noted this change, emphasizing that since the early 1980s mystical groups have been placed on the defensive, with the result that many have sought to reorient their ritual and doctrine in a more explicitly Islamic direction. He concludes an important article with the observation, 'Islam may not have established itself as "the" religion of Indonesia, but it seems clear that its sense of what "religion" is defines, shapes and constrains all discourse about religion and spiritual life' (Strange, 1986, p. 110).

2 Let me emphasize that my point is that this pattern of desacralization of the concrete and abstraction of the divine is one that is *widespread* in modern monotheistic religions; however, it is but one general type of re-formation among several that we can recognize as taking place in modern religions. I do not mean to imply, therefore, that this type of reform is universal or dominant, even in monotheistic traditions. Within Islam itself, the modern era's destabilization of established hierarchies and pluralization of lifeworlds has at times resulted in a curious re-enchantment of the local and concrete. Perhaps the most dramatic example of this phenomenon has been the spread of the so-called *zar* cult across large portions of North Africa and the Middle East. While invoking a category of spirits (*jinn*) legitimate with orthodox Islam, the *zar* cult comes dangerously close to openly challenging the tenets of reformist monotheism. In its most typical form, *zar* ritual includes women cultists' possession by *jinn*, and their acting out of the sometimes outrageous requests of those spirits. Among other things, the whole affair provides for a rather dramatic assertion of women's ritual voices (see Boddy, 1989). Studies from other modern or postmodern settings which suggest a similar compatibility between modernity and what we might call a 'segmented' enchantment include, among many others, David Martin's (1990) research on Latin American evangelicals, Winston Davis (1992) on Japanese religion, and Gananath Obeyesekere (1981) on Sri Lankan Buddhist ecstatics.

166   *Robert W. Hefner*

References

Anderson, Benedict 1983: *Imagined Communities: Reflections on the Origin and Spread of Nationalism*. London: Verso.

Bakker, F. L. 1993: *The Struggle of the Hindu Balinese Intellectuals: Developments in Modern Hindu Thinking in Independent Indonesia*. Amsterdam: VU University Press.

Barton, Greg 1995: Neo-modernism: a vital synthesis of traditionalist and modernist Islamic thought in Indonesia. *Studia Islamika: Indonesian Journal for Islamic Studies* 2 (3): 1–71.

Beckford, James A. 1989: *Religion and Advanced Industrial Society*. London: Unwin Hyman.

Bellah, Robert N. 1975: *The Broken Covenant: American Civil Religion in Time of Trial*. Chicago: University of Chicago Press.

—— and Phillip E. Hammond 1980: *Varieties of Civil Religion*. San Francisco: Harper & Row.

Berger, Peter L. 1967: *The Sacred Canopy: Elements of A Sociological Theory of Religion*. Garden City: Doubleday.

—— 1992: *A Far Glory: The Quest for Faith in an Age of Credulity*. New York: Free Press.

Boddy, Janice 1989: *Wombs and Alien Spirits: Women, Men, and the Zar Cult in Northern Sudan*. Madison: University of Wisconsin Press.

Boland, B. J. 1982: *The Struggle of Islam in Modern Indonesia*. The Hague: Martinus Nijhoff.

Casanova, Jose 1994: *Public Religions in the Modern World*. Chicago: University of Chicago Press.

Cox, Harvey 1990 (orig. 1965): *The Secular City*. New York: Macmillan.

Cribb, Robert (ed.) 1990: *The Indonesian Killings: Studies from Java and Bali*. Clayton, Victoria: Center for Southeast Asian Studies, Monash University.

Davis, Winston 1992: *Japanese Religion and Society: Paradigms of Structure and Change*. Albany: State University of New York Press.

Dhofier, Zamakhsyari 1982: *Tradisi Pesantren: Studi tentang Pandangan Hidup Kyai* [Pesantren Traditions: A Study of the World View of Traditional Islamic Scholars]. Jakarta: LP3ES.

Effendy, Bahtiar 1994: Islam and the State: the transformation of Islamic political ideas and practices in Indonesia. Columbus, Ohio: Ph.D. dissertation, Department of Political Science, Ohio State University.

Ellen, Roy F. 1983: Social theory, ethnography, and the understanding of practical Islam in South-East Asia. In M. B. Hooker (ed.), *Islam in Southeast Asia*. Leiden: Brill, pp. 50–91.

Feillard, Andrée 1995: *Islam et armée dans l'Indonésie contemporaine*. Paris: L'Harmattan.

Fenn, R. K. 1978: *Toward a Theory of Secularization*. Storrs, Conn.: Society for the Scientific Study of Religion.

Geertz, Clifford 1960: *The Religion of Java*. New York: Free Press.

—— 1973: *The Interpretation of Cultures*. New York: Basic Books.

Gellner, Ernest 1981: Flux and reflux in the faith of men. In E. Gellner, *Muslim Society*, Cambridge: Cambridge University Press, pp. 1–85.

—— 1983: *Nations and Nationalism*. Ithaca: Cornell University Press.

—— 1992: *Postmodernism, Reason and Religion*. London: Routledge.

Giddens, Anthony 1984: *The Constitution of Society*. Berkeley: University of California Press.

Hassan, Muhammad Kamal 1980: *Muslim Intellectual Responses to 'New Order' Indonesia*. Kuala Lumpur: Dewan Bahasa dan Pustaka.

Hefner, Robert W. 1987: Islamizing Java? Religion and politics in rural East Java. *Journal of Asian Studies* 46 (3): 533–54.

—— 1990: *The Political Economy of Mountain Java: An Interpretive History*. California: University of California Press.

—— 1993a: Islam, state, and civil society: ICMI and the struggle for the Indonesian middle class. *Indonesia* 56: 1–35.

—— 1993b: Of faith and commitment: Christian conversion in Muslim Java. In R. Hefner (ed.), *Conversion to Christianity: Historical and Anthropological Perspectives on a Great Transformation*, Berkeley and London: University of California Press, pp. 99–125.

Hodgson, Marshall G. S. 1974: *The Venture of Islam*. Chicago: University of Chicago Press.

Juergensmeyer, Mark 1993: *The New Cold War? Religious Nationalism Confronts the Secular State*. Berkeley and London: University of California Press.

Kim, Hyung-Jun 1996: Reformist Muslims in a Yogyakarta village. Canberra: PhD thesis, Department of Anthropology, Australian National University.

Luckmann, Thomas 1967: *Invisible Religion: The Problem of Religion in Modern Society*. New York: Macmillan.

Lyon, Margaret L. 1977: Politics and religious identity: genesis of a Javanese-Hindu movement in rural Central Java. Berkeley: PhD dissertation, Department of Anthropology, University of California.

Madjid, Nurcholish 1984: *Islam, Kemodernan, dan Ke-Indonesiaan* [Islam, Modernity, and Indonesian-ness]. Bandung, Indonesia: Mizan.

—— 1994: Islamic roots of modern pluralism: Indonesian experience. *Studia Islamika: Indonesian Journal for Islamic Studies* 1 (1): 55–77.

Martin, David 1978: *A General Theory of Secularization*. Oxford: Blackwell.

—— 1990: *Tongues of Fire: The Explosion of Protestantism in Latin America*. Oxford: Blackwell.

Mitchell, Richard P. 1969: *The Society of the Muslim Brothers*. New York: Oxford University Press.

Moussalli, Ahmad S. 1992: *Radical Islamic Fundamentalism: The Ideological and Political Discourse of Sayyid Qutb*. Beiruit: American University of Beiruit.

Munson, Henry, Jr 1993: *Religion and Power in Morocco*. New Haven: Yale University Press.

Obeyesekere, Gananath 1981: *Medusa's Hair: An Essay on Personal Symbols and Religious Experience*. Chicago and London: University of Chicago Press.

Outram, Dorinda 1995: *The Enlightenment*. Cambridge: Cambridge University Press.

Pranowo, Bambang 1991: Creating Islamic tradition in rural Java. PhD thesis, Clayton, Victoria: Department of Anthropology, Monash University.

Roff, W. R. 1967: *The Origins of Malay Nationalism*. New Haven: Yale University Press.

Roy, Olivier 1994: *The Failure of Political Islam*, trans. Card Volk. Cambridge, Mass.: Harvard University Press.

Shils, Edward 1960: Political development in the new states. *Comparative Studies in Society and History* 2: 265–92, 379–411.

Strange, Paul 1986: 'Legitimate' mysticism in Indonesia. *Review of Indonesian and Malaysian Affairs* 20 (2): 76–117.

Tibi, Bassam 1990: *Islam and the Cultural Accommodation of Social Change*. Boulder: Westview.

van der Veer, Peter 1994: *Religious Nationalism: Hindus and Muslims in India*. Berkeley and London: University of California Press.

Wilson, Bryan 1985: Secularization: the inherited model. In Phillip E. Hammond (ed.), *The Sacred in a Secular Age*, Berkeley: University of California Press, pp. 9–20.

Woodward, Mark R. 1989: *Islam in Java: Normative Piety and Mysticism in the Sultanate of Yogyakarta*. Tucson: University of Arizona Press.

Wuthnow, Robert 1988: *The Restructuring of American Religion*. Princeton: Princeton University Press.

CHAPTER NINE

religion and national identity in modern and postmodern Japan

Winston Davis

The identity of traditional society is generally a function of its totems, spirits, ancestors, heroes and gods. Even in the modern world, the construction of national identities in such countries as Greece, Poland, Ireland and the United States continues to depend to a large extent on religion. In countries like Japan, however, national identity seems to have relatively little to do with conventional, institutional religion. Even if one can never safely say that the gods are dead even in Japan, it would appear that they are presently related to the national identity in a rather round-about way. The religion that remains important for the identity of the Japanese today is one that manifests itself in para-institutional, diffuse forms. We shall see that while Japanese identity does not necessarily depend on religion, religion continues to be used to bear witness to the alleged uniqueness of the 'Japanese spirit'. At the end of the essay, I shall raise some questions about the viability of this 'spirit' as it prepares for its rendezvous with the twenty-first century.

To chart the development of the self-identity of modern (and putatively postmodern) Japanese, I shall examine a body of literature variously known as Japan Theory (*Nihon-ron*), the Theory of Being Japanese (*Nihonjin-ron*), or the Theory of Japanese Culture (*Nihon-bunka-ron*). This 'Theory' (which actually is not usually very theoretical) refers to a barrage of popular books, newspaper and magazine articles, and even scholarly works, devoted to such questions as 'Who are we Japanese?', 'What makes us unique?', 'Why doesn't the rest of the world understand us [or our trade policies]?', and more recently, 'What is there about our culture that makes us so successful?'

To convey a vivid impression of the flavour and pervasiveness of Japan Theory, Peter Dale (1986), in a passage worth citing at length, asks us to imagine dozens if not hundreds of works pouring from the presses of Oxford and Cambridge, in which the Hare Professor of Moral Philosophy discussed the uniqueness of the English ethical tradition, or Wittgensteinians examined at book length hundreds of terms in the Oxford English Dictionary to derive concepts of Englishness in such terms as 'fair play', 'good form', 'gentleman', 'guvner', etc., or wrote books on the influence of bad weather on parliamentary institutions and democracy, of cricket on the outlook of the English people, on matriarchy as a constant element underlying British institutions from the times of Boadicea through to Mrs Thatcher; treating everything under the English sun as consequences of some peculiar mentality unchanged since one's ancestors first donned woad and did battle with Caesar; imagine this as something which filtered down through newspapers and regional media to everyday life, and you have something of the picture of what has taken place in Japan, where almost any discussion from the formally academic to the colloquial market-place exchange can reflect this ideology of nationhood.   (Introduction, n.p.)

Since most Japanese seem to be affected in one way or another by the images generated by this discourse, Japan Theory deserves to share some of the attention lavished on the country's New Religions, movements which seem to concern a smaller segment of the population. BEFU Harumi and MANABE Kazufumi have shown that as many as 82 per cent of the residents of suburban Nishinomiya (located between Osaka and Kobe) have read some Japan Theory (mostly in newspapers) and that they largely approve of its contents (pp. 97–111).

For Japanese, the term *Nihon-ron* is a neutral expression. While some Japanese scholars want to make a distinction between the more academic and well-researched field called Japan Studies (*Nihon kenkyū*) and Japan Theory (a more popular, even entertaining kind of literature), the distinction escapes the notice of many writers and most readers. Among foreign scholars, however, Japan Theory is anything but neutral. Indeed, it has become a highly charged symbol for renascent Japanese nationalism and old-fashioned racism. To the foreign scholar, Japan Theory represents a highly tendentious concentration on the uniqueness of Japanese culture, society and personality. In place of genuinely comparative model-building, Japan Theorists seem to be engaged in the generation of fanciful symbols that will catch the 'essence' of being Japanese. Japan is the 'society of Protean Man', or 'Moratorium Man', the 'vertical society', the 'miniaturizing society', the 'society of the eternal child', the 'maternal society'.[1] One could add to this list ISHII Takemochi's 'holonic path' Theory, YAMAZAKI Masakuzu's 'tender individualism', HAMAGUCHI Eshun's 'contextualism', KAMISHIMA Jirō's 'convergence society', and ITAMI Hiroyuki's 'corporate humanism' – all professorial contributions to the buzz-words of the Theory. All of this – the essentialism, the overemphasis placed on uniqueness, the implicit nationalism and the occasionally outrageous instances of racism – naturally raise the ire of Japan watchers in the rest of the world. Peter Dale (1986), for example, refers to Japan Theory sarcastically as a tangle of 'cozy mendacities', 'the intellectual fast food of consumer nationalism', and to the Theorists themselves as the 'sleuths of autochthony' (pp. 9, 16, 21).

As unofficial responses to (literally) self-seeking questions, Japan Theory creates national self-images which probably – to speak for a moment in its defence – satisfy the universal human craving for identity and 'belonging'. But the Theory seems to have several other strategic functions as well. Internally, it creates a set of norms which reinforces a traditional ethic of conformity and obedience; externally, it serves as a defence against criticism of Japan by foreigners and their governments. In the 1980s, as a result of the furore in the West over Japanese-managed trade, Japan Theory has become increasingly defensive. In general, the neo-nativist mandarins of Japan Theory seem less concerned about injustice than they are about the legitimation of the Japanese Way of Life. Like the Confucian biographers of the past, they try to create ideal images of a people embodying the ideals of loyalty, hard work, sincerity, and harmony. While they try to describe Japanese culture and character, description is neither their end nor their *forte*. By telling the Japanese who they are, the Theorists indirectly are telling them who they *should be* – if they want to be *real* Japanese. But, what kind of people are they and should they be?

The Development of Japan Theory

In the Tokugawa period, nativist scholars like MOTOORI Norinaga (1730–1801) and HIRATA Atsutane (1776–1843) tried to spell out what it meant to be Japanese in terms that were explicitly religious. As the descendants of the Sun Goddess, Amaterasu, and other ancestral deities, the Japanese were naturally superior to other races. The True Way, lost in ancient times in other countries, had been preserved only in Japan. MOTOORI insisted that, unlike the Chinese – who were forced to resort to artificially contrived Confucian principles to lead a decent life – the Japanese *naturally* have a 'sincere heart' (*magokoro*). According to HIRATA,

Japanese differ completely from and are superior to the peoples of China, India, Russia, Holland, Siam, Cambodia, and all other countries of the world, and for us to have called our country the Land of the Gods was not mere vainglory. It was the gods who formed all the lands of the world at the Creation, and these gods were without exception born in Japan. (In TSUNODA et al. (eds), 1958, p. 39)

There was an obvious cosmological ring to the arguments of the nativists. HIRATA thought that the 'fact' that every morning the sun shines on Japan before it shines on the rest of the world was proof of the country's global superiority. Cosmology also figured in the negative images the Japanese had of other countries. Another Tokugawa scholar, AIZAWA Seishisai, noted that

> our Divine Land is situated at the top of the earth. Thus, although it is not an extensive country spatially, it reigns over all quarters of the world, for it has never once changed its dynasty or its form of sovereignty. The various countries of the West correspond to the feet and the legs of the body [of Japan]. That is why their ships come from afar to visit Japan. As for the land amidst the seas which the Western barbarians call America, it occupies the hindmost region of the earth; thus, its people are stupid and simple, and are incapable of doing things.   (In Keen, 1954)

After the Meiji restoration (1868), the Japanese quickly developed a more realistic view of what people in other parts of the world *were* capable of doing. At the beginning of the period, the writers of the Japanese Enlightenment criticized their fellow countrymen for being overly curious about trifles, servile in the face of authority, naive, superstitious, passive, shallow and sensuous. NAKAMURA Masanao wrote in the *Meiroku Zasshi* that many of his fellow countrymen were

> people rooted in servitude, the people who are arrogant toward their inferiors and flattering toward their superiors, the ignorant and uneducated people, the people who love sake and sex, the people who do not like reading, the people who do not reflect on their duties and who know not the laws of Heaven, the people of shallow wisdom and limited capacity, the people who avoid toil and do not endure hardships. . . .   (Braisted et al., 1976, p. 372)

The list goes on and on. It would, in fact, be hard to find a more self-critical Japan Theory until the 'deficiency theories' (*ketsujo riron*) of MARUYAMA Masao and his disciples in the early postwar period.

By late Meiji, as a symptom of the rising nationalism associated with wars successfully waged against China and Russia, a more positive Theory began to emerge. Increased tension between capital and labour, rice riots and other social and economic tensions prompted the government and its intellectual supporters to develop a more compelling ideology. European theories of progress, race and nationhood were imported to reinforce nativist convictions already in place. The result was the prewar Emperor System (*tennō seido*), often called 'emperor worship' in the West. By the Taishō period (1912–25), fixation on national exceptionalism was becoming intellectually fashionable. In his book *Climate and Culture*, first drafted in the 1920s, the philosopher WATSUJI Tetsurō wrote:

> When asked for my impressions of anything unusual after my first visit to Europe, all that I could do was reply with a very firm 'no'. There was a great deal that impressed me of the Egyptian or Arabian deserts that I saw en route. However, on my return to Japan at the end of my travels, I was made suddenly and keenly aware of the strange character in Japan, a strangeness in no way inferior to that of the Arabian desert, *a strangeness which makes Japan unique in the world.* (1961, p. 156, my emphasis)

At the heart of WATSUJI's Theory is his concept of *fūy thisdo* or climate. By this he means not just meteorological phenomena, but a powerful (and ambiguous) mixture of climate (in its usual sense), history, culture, values, and national character. Understood in this way, WATSUJI's climate becomes the means of 'self-apprehension', or 'a means for man to discover himself' (ibid., p. 8). He divides the world into the climates (and cultures) of desert, meadow and monsoon. Monsoon culture, for example, includes India, the South Seas and all of East Asia. China and Japan are both said to have monsoon climates and cultures. This, however, poses a problem for WATSUJI as a Japan Theorist. It is not enough to locate Japan geographically and meteorologically in East Asia. That, after all, would simply underscore Japan's unexceptional Asianness. The problem was to extricate Japan from the world of the monsoons and demonstrate her unique climate and culture. WATSUJI had to show Japan's difference not only from the meadow climate of the West and the desert climate of Arabia, but also from the rest of monsoon Asia. In general, WATSUJI says, the oppressive heat and humidity of monsoon cultures encourage a spirit of resignation and passivity. Thanks to the climate, the Indian, while experiencing a 'fullness of feeling', lacks any significant 'historical awareness'. His logic is 'intuitive', his learning 'stifled', his sentimentalism 'cringing'. India's monsoon culture was the cause of the country's political submission to the English imperialists. In the South Seas, the 'monotony' of the monsoon climate discouraged 'productivity'. This is why one finds 'no cultural monuments' there. While the natives are 'ever agitated and burning with violent passions', like the Indians, they have become 'easy prey for and ready lackeys of the Europeans' (ibid., p. 23).

But China is the crucial case. As a Japan Theorist wanting to prove the uniqueness of Japanese culture, it was imperative that WATSUJI establish Japan's *Theoretical* distance from China. This, of course, was no mean feat since Japan's cultural dependence on China was obvious to the whole world. The contrast he draws between the contentment of the Chinese and the restless ambition of the Japanese is intentionally stark. Chinese cultural artifacts display, he tells us, a 'marked absence of emotional content' and have 'no delicacy of texture'. The Chinese people are content to gamble and smoke their opium. 'The picture of the Chinese, birdcage in hand, gazing up blankly at the sky all day long is strange in Japanese eyes, for, to the latter such a leisurely rhythm of life seems to lack all sensitivity' (ibid., p. 127).

Thus, by a simple stroke of his Theoretical brush, WATSUJI removes Japan from her climatic moorings in Asia and assigns her in a more progressive, indeed 'unique', place in the world. Japan, he says, has been blessed by nature with a unique mixture of climates and therefore has a unique culture. By virtue of her 'heavy rains and snows, Japan's climate is by far the most distinctive within the whole monsoon zone; its nature can be said to be dual, combining both that of a tropical belt and that of a frigid zone' (ibid., p. 134). With their mixed climate in their blood, the Japanese are filled with 'emotional vitality and sensitivity' and are completely *'lacking all continental phlegm'* (ibid., p. 135; my emphasis). Anticipating the dualism of Ruth Benedict's (1977, orig. 1946) 'chrysanthemum and sword', WATSUJI (1961) believed that Japan's mixed climate gave rise to a 'fusion of a calm passion and a martial selflessness' (p. 143). While capable of 'gentle affection', the Japanese could also give vent to 'typhoons' of emotion. The occasional violence of Japanese temperament and the deliberate honing of a martial spirit enabled the Japanese to rise above the usual resignation and submissiveness of monsoon culture.

WATSUJI began his academic career as a specialist on Nietzsche and Kierkegaard. After the 1920s, when he claims to have 'discovered' the significance of Buddhism, he turned to the investigation of things Japanese. Even though WATSUJI was never close to the military leaders of fascist Japan, the political (or nationalistic) structure of his thought had a decidedly reactionary slant.[2] For example, he uses the traditional Japanese home to create the image of a perfectly homogeneous (and morally regimented) society. Unlike the Western house, where the hallway is virtually an extension of the street outside, and where door locks prevent access to private rooms by other members of the family, the Japanese home, while closed to the outside world, is completely open within. Fragile, sliding doors which cannot be locked symbolize 'a division within a unity of mutual trust, and [are] not a sign of a desire for separation'. Thus, the Japanese house 'exhibits an internal fusion that admits of no discrimination' (WATSUJI, ibid., p. 145). The house mirrors, and also helps to create, the unity of the family which lives in it. Unlike the Western family – which he claims is merely 'a gathering of individuals to serve economic interests' – 'all distinction disappears' in the Japanese household (ibid., p. 144). Like other Japanese ideologues, WATSUJI extends the ideal unity of the family to the 'family-state' (*kazoku kokka*). Since at least the Meiji period, the Japanese have been

> one great family which regarded the Imperial House as the home of its deity. The people as a whole are nothing but one great and unified house, all stemming from an identical ancestor. . . . Within the borders of this state as a whole, there should be the same unreserved and inseparable union that is achieved within the household. (ibid., p. 148)

WATSUJI believed that the 'indissoluble unification' of the Japanese state was the work of religious ritual, i.e., the imperial rites conducted at the Grand Shrine of Ise. Because war was related to this ritual activity it had a similar impact. 'It was through war that a single ritual had been attained and in the same way war showed the path to inseparable union. The achievement of the latter was made possible by the selflessness that lay beneath the martial spirit' (ibid., p. 152).

While he apparently did not believe literally in Shinto mythology, WATSUJI recognized the essential role of Shinto in the imperial system. Robert Bellah (1965) argues that he

> turns the tables on those who would hold Shinto to be inferior to the world religions and who would stigmatize early Japanese culture as inferior because primitive. WATSUJI was fully aware that early Japan was primitive, but he believed that Japan's primitiveness was the seed of its vitality, its sense of living community. . . . (p. 580)

Primitive communities of this sort demand commitment and obedience from the individual. In such a 'climate', the 'individual never thought of standing on his rights' (WATSUJI, 1961, p. 166). Individuals subordinate themselves to groups, groups to the state. There is, of course, no room for opposition, loyal or disloyal. WATSUJI believed that the Japanese proletarian movement itself was merely a 'coterie' of self-serving leaders followed by 'hardly any or at best only a handful of people . . .' (ibid., p. 169). His political fundamentalism reached its apex in his wartime writings. In these essays, as Bellah (1965) puts it, he draws a vivid contrast

> between the particularistic Japanese *gemeinschaft* community (*kyōdōtai*) in which all persons and groups are taken up and both included and negated in reverence for the emperor as the expression of the absolute whole, and the American *gesellschaft* society [WATSUJI's Japanese term is literally 'profit society' (*rieki shakai*)] based only on naked utilitarian self-interest: between Japanese culture (*bunka*) and American [materialistic] civilization (*bunmei*). Though this is perhaps a starker statement of the basic confrontation in

terms of which WATSUJI interpreted contemporary world history than is to be found elsewhere in his work, it is in almost every element foreshadowed in his writings dating from well before the war, in some cases even from the early nineteen twenties. It is not a conception produced to order for wartime consumption. It has roots deep in some of the main currents of Japanese thought, and that is its interest to us. (Bellah, 1965, p. 583)

Bellah concludes that WATSUJI was wholly committed to a primitive, cultural particularism based on the 'fusion of Japan, emperor, society and individual'. 'Fusion' resulted in a moral and political system that recognized no transcendental standpoint from which the individual could analyse or criticize society. According to WATSUJI, a Japanese human being (*ningen*) is never an individual in the Western sense of the word; he or she is always defined in terms of a set of relationships with others (*hito no aida*). While symbolic interactionists the world over would probably applaud this insight, WATSUJI applies it to the Japanese alone. The salient characteristics associated with 'modern' society are defined out of existence. We are left with a recipe for political fundamentalism, a programme that aims at the de-differentiation of a complex society in the name of a totalitarian 'togetherness'.

Needless to say, after the end of the Second World War, Japan Theories of this sort fell out of favour.[3] During the intense suffering of the early postwar years, most Theorists could see only the vast negative outcome of Japan's 'uniqueness'. Both Marxists and 'bourgeois' sociologists (primarily Weberians) tended to explain the country's recent débâcle in terms of the persistence of the traditional: the values of familyism, feudalism and village. Like other ideologues, WATSUJI himself underwent a conversion to a more liberal, democratic point of view. He, too, began to think more seriously about his country's shortcomings, attributing these deficits to the 'closed country (*sakoku*) policy' of the Tokugawa regime.

The foremost example of the self-critical Japan Theory of the early postwar period was the work of the celebrated political scientist MARUYAMA Masao. MARUYAMA decisively attacked Japan's fascist ideology by describing the subordination of the individual to the group as an idolatrous suppression of individual autonomy. He argued that modernity (which he explicitly defined along European lines) presupposes: (1) a Kantian split between what is and what ought to be, (2) the development of social criticism based on a sense of individual autonomy (*shutaisei*), and (3) the rejection of 'metaphysically guaranteed' political institutions.[4] At the heart of his liberal political philosophy was an explicit rejection of all forms of political fundamentalism, for, as he put it, 'the internally divided consciousness [Hegel] can no longer accept the innocent premodern continuative consciousness' (1974, p. 184). MARUYAMA's work is of such high quality that it probably should not even be mentioned in this review of Theories celebrating Japanese exceptionalism. I mention it here only because it does represent an important turning point in the history of those Theories.

In 1958, Japan regained her independence and the country's economy began its postwar 'take-off' – thanks to the stimulus of the Korean War. Independence and economic recovery inspired a new Japan Theory which placed less emphasis on the negative outcomes of the Japanese tradition. Works of scholars like KATŌ Shūichi and UMESAO Tadao softened MARUYAMA's critique of Japanese culture by examining the country's development from a comparative, relativistic point of view. For KATŌ, Japan was a 'mongrel culture' composed of Western and Japanese elements – a *zasshu bunka*, an epithet not intended as criticism. UMESAO went further still, showing that Japan's development at the eastern edge of the Eurasian landmass paralleled that of Europe at its western edge. Convinced that Japan belonged to the First World – not, of course, by geography, but by the trajectory of her own historical development – UMESAO, in effect, reversed MARUYAMA's critique. UMESAO has also made his mark on Japan Theory by insisting that, unlike Thailand, Indonesia and other 'Small Civilizations', Japan, like India and China, is a 'Great Civilization' (*daibunmei*) in her own right. In one respect, UMESAO's thought seems to have an outcome similar to WATSUJI's. Both Theories remove Japan from her historical setting in Asia and elevate her to the ranks of her Western rivals.

Beginning around 1964, Japan Theorists largely abandoned the historical relativism of KATŌ and UMESAO and returned to their basic staple: the country's cultural uniqueness. As self-confidence rose and the memory of war faded, Theorists began to appreciate anew the blessings of their cultural heritage. The Theory reached a new plateau of self-confidence in 1970 when NAKANE Chie published her highly influential book, *Japanese Society*. NAKANE's work was soon recognized as a classical description of Japan's allegedly unique group orientation and hierarchical organization. About the same time, DOI Takeo (1971/1981), KIMURA Bin (1972) and HAMAGUCHI Eshun were laying new emphasis on the uniqueness of the Japanese psyche. KIMURA (1972) pictured the Japanese self (*jibun*) not as an autonomous entity, but merely as that *part of a relationship* which happens to be temporarily held by a person (pp. 137–54). Unlike the Western self, which is predicated on clearly defined ontological boundaries, the Japanese self expands and contracts to fit shared relationships or situations. What was remarkable about psychological Theories of this sort – which obviously are closely related to WATSUJI's – was their denial of individual autonomy (*shutaisei*) as a personal virtue. The lack of autonomy – a cultural deficit bemoaned by thinkers like FUKUZAWA Yukichi in the Meiji period and MARUYAMA Masao after the war – was celebrated as a pre-requisite for the cultivation of other Japanese virtues such as consensus and loyalty. The prewar ideal of the subordination of the individual to the group was trotted out again as the 'secret' behind Japan's economic miracle.

Since we have now reached what might be called the high point of postwar Theory, we should note that one of the major differences between contemporary Japan Theory and the propaganda of the fascist period is that the former is not yet official government ideology. There are exceptions, however. The Foreign Ministry, for example, used to distribute a free, condensed version of NAKANE's (1970) book in its overseas embassies, obviously hoping to capitalize diplomatically on the book's idealistic view of Japan as a co-operative, classless society. Even official government documents are occasionally written over the watermark of Japan Theory. A good example is a report prepared for the Ōhira Cabinet in 1980 called *Economic Administration in the Age of Culture*, a study that was deeply influenced by the 'overcoming the modern' ideology of the fascist period and by the thought of WATSUJI Tetsurō in particular. In general, however, Japan Theory remains a popular, spontaneous product of the country's 'opinion leaders', and not the work of official government scholars.

In the 1970s, Japan Theory spawned a new sub-discipline devoted to the explanation of Japan's economic success – again, in terms of the country's allegedly unique culture. Here the Japanese admittedly have much to be proud of, and proud they are. As KARATSU Hajime, one of Japan's neo-nationalists, puts it, '[Japan's] machine tools, best in the world; metal molds, best in the world; steel sheets and plastics, also best in the world'. All of these technological achievements are explained in terms of the country's singular mentality. In KARATSU's own words: 'The Japanese are geniuses at developing applications, which is the core work in the field of technology. This aptitude comes from their *unique way of looking at things free of the fixed concepts that Westerners get hung up on*' (in KOMORI Yoshihisa, 1990, p. 46, my emphasis).

A classic example of the Theory of Japanese Management is YAMAMOTO Shichihei's *The Spirit of Japanese Capitalism* (1979), a title seemingly inspired by Max Weber's *Protestant Ethic and the Spirit of Capitalism*. Intended for a popular rather than a scholarly audience, the book is nearly pure Japan Theory. In fact, the author warms up many of the old chestnuts that WATSUJI and wartime intellectuals used to peddle. Like Japan Theory in general, YAMAMOTO's book creates an idealized self-image of Japanese institutions, contrasting them with more realistic assessments of those of the West. The Japanese firm, we are told, is both a functional group and a community or 'Gemeinschaft'. For YAMAMOTO, as for WATSUJI, the Japanese home is an important national symbol. Unlike his American counterpart, the Japanese employee does not have to leave his community when he goes to work. His apartment is owned by the company, making his fellow workers his neighbours. Because American firms are only functional groups (and not communities), Americans do not care about the moral image of their companies. The Japanese live to work, while Americans count the days until they can retire. Indeed, retirement for the American is 'liberation'.

Specialists on the Japanese economy will find little new in YAMAMOTO's book, and much that is questionable. The familiar, idealized images are all piously reaffirmed in terms of Japan's unique culture: permanent employment, the seniority system, loyalty to the firm, the application of (fictive) kinship concepts to the workplace, and a critical attitude toward labour unions and the use of foreign labour. According to YAMAMOTO, the Japanese are an open and gentle race. They value etiquette and are sensitive to the views of others. This, however, does not mean that Japanese society is open. Foreign workers are incapable of entering into the fictive kinship relationships of Japanese industry and therefore can never become part of Japanese society (YAMAMOTO, 1979, pp. 88–9).

YAMAMOTO maintains that the differences between the Western and Japanese economies originate in two very different *religious* traditions. The ultimate source of Japanese capitalism is a 'unique religiousness' which is socially diffuse, relatively secular, and mildly anti-clerical. In this religion, there is nothing more sacred than belief in the human heart. In this sense, all Japanese are 'religious'. YAMAMOTO explains that it would be patently absurd to say that the Japanese are not religious simply because most no longer believe in the gods or Buddhas. In the West, the covenant-centred religion of the Bible ultimately gave rise to a business world of laws and contracts. In Japan, where man and the gods are not bound by covenants, business is based on 'understandings' (*hanashiai*) reached through mutual consultation.

Lying behind the values of Japanese industry are the teachings of SUZUKI Shōsan, the warrior-turned-monk of the early Tokugawa period. YAMAMOTO (1979) sums up SUZUKI's worldview as follows: the order of our hearts, of society and the universe must be harmonized and made one. This can only be done by 'realizing' the Buddha or universal order implicit in the human heart. The impediments to spiritual realization are the Three Poisons of classical Buddhism: greed, anger and illusion. As the doctor of the soul, the Buddha has given us a prescription to ward off these Poisons. Above all, one must follow one's own occupation with honesty and devotion. Secular occupations, SUZUKI believed, are forms of Buddhist practice enabling the individual to become a Buddha himself. For him, work is a 'pilgrimage', society the Buddha. These, YAMAMOTO contends, were the teachings that made SUZUKI Shōsan, the Founder of

Japanese Capitalism! They are the doctrines which created the 'spiritual structure' and 'unseen principles' of the modern Japanese economy, for example, the principle that profits are legitimate only when they are the 'natural result' of virtue and hard work. Japan's economic miracle owes nothing to Western economics or management science. On the contrary, it is the direct outcome of patterns of employment established in the Tokugawa period and of such values as the 'unity of loyalty and filial piety' (*chūkō itchi*) and the 'consciousness of the extended household' (*dōzoku ishiki*).

In 1979, the year YAMAMOTO's book appeared, KUMON Shumpei, SATŌ Seizaburō and MURAKAMI Yasusuke published their influential work, *Kintractual Society as a Pattern of Civilization*.[5] Here Japanese self-confidence reached a new high-water mark. Again we are presented with a 'multi-linear', evolutionary theory in which Japanese development independently parallels that of the West. The implication of the Theory is that since each nation has its own way of development, modernity is not the monopoly of the West – a statement which is certainly true. As in WATSUJI's *Climate*, Japan is 'Theoretically' distanced from China. While China and India meander into the *cul de sac* of Third World poverty and stagnation, Japan proudly marches off toward postmodernity ahead of her First World compeers. Too long and complex to summarize here, the book seeks to explain the evolution of the principles of the *ie* ('kintractual' household system) which, together with the values of the traditional *mura* (village), inform Japanese institutions today. The failures of the 1930s and 1940s are attributed to the failure of political institutions; the successes of the postwar period to the adroit implementation of *ie* principles and values. What worries those outside the 'kintractual system' is, of course, the fact that '*ie* principles' were also at work in the 'family state' of the fascist period.

Japan Theory, the New Religions and the Spirit of Postmodernism

In spite of their obvious differences, Japan Theory and the country's New Religions have several things in common.[6] Both are keenly interested in questions of identity. Both are the products of anecdotal rhetoric and revelatory bricolage. Both Theorist and Messiah are enthralled by virtually the same eschatology – the same vision, incidentally, that captivates Japanese politicians, bureaucrats and intellectuals – namely, the beatific vision of the coming twenty-first century as the 'Age of the Pacific Rim', or more explicitly, the 'Century of Japan'. When intellectuals on Japanese TV recently opined that Emperor HIROHITO's death was a 'farewell to modernity', they were, so to speak, 'talking eschatology'. Looked at from an historical perspective, their farewells seemed to be a fulfilment of the prophecy of the fascist ideologues of the early 1940s that Japan would 'overcome modernity'. For contemporary Theorists, the emperor's death was a sign portending not only the messianic birth of the world's first postmodern society, but the beginning of Japan's financial, cultural and political hegemony.

Both Messiah and Theorist are deeply concerned that the Japanese do not mess up their millennium at the last minute by catching what, in Japan, is called the 'English Disease' – a malady associated with laziness, low productivity and deindustrialization. One 'disease' some Theorists *have* caught is the very one that has been spreading among the New Religions, i.e., the 'bug' of postmodernism. Indifference to logic (even in critical thought), the ahistoric orientation of Buddhism and Shinto, fascination with futurology, and the recent triumph of 'technopunk' in science fiction and TV commercials are all cited as 'proof' that Japan has become the world's first postmodern culture. In Japanese literature, decentred authorial voice; indifference to plot or sustained character and meaning; fascination with surfaces, forms, parody, and pastiche are said to be other indications of postmodernism. Some even argue that the country was postmodern before it became modern – since, say, the eighteenth century. Because Japan never had a 'structure' or a 'construction' to begin with, it is not obliged to submit to the humiliating surgical procedures of 'deconstruction'.[7] According to some of Japan's *avant garde* Theorists, Western postmodernists, deconstructionists and poststructuralists (people like Derrida, Barthes, Foucault, Deleuze and Guattari) are simply trying to catch up with Japan's 'dispersed, fragmented, and decentred' culture.[8] Some Theorists today tend to regard the appearance of deconstruction and other neo-Nietzschean modes of thought as omens pointing to the appearance of a new civilization based on Buddhist Emptiness.[9] Such Theoretical metaphors for Japan as the 'hollow onion' or the 'shell-less egg' express the same meontological ideal.

In a playful, but somehow humourless piece, ASADA Akira (1988) concocts a postmodernist Theory by pasting together philosopher NISHIDA Kitarō's 'place of non-being' (*mu no basho*), DOI Takeo's (1981, orig. 1971) psychological theory of dependence (*amae*), and the fascist notion of 'overcoming the modern' (*kindai no chōkoku*). Claiming that Japan's postmodern culture is the product of a playful, 'infantile capitalism', ASADA asserts that the country's economy is quite unlike that of the West (which allegedly has been made 'senile' by its archaic belief in God). The emperor (the 'passive medium') sits enthroned somewhere in the middle of ASADA's postmodernity – presumably right in the middle of NISHIDA's 'place of non-being'. As in the fascistic civil religion of the 1930s and early 1940s, the emperor is regarded as a silent demigod embodying a

realm of absolute purity above and beyond state, politics and history. In
ASADA's postmodernism, we therefore have a position completely opposite
from the self-critical stands of intellectuals like MARUYAMA Masao, IENAGA
Saburō, and ISHIDA Takeshi. Not only are the symbols and principles of transcendence and autonomy not regarded as the source of political health;
they are seen as cultural lags which slow down the economy and spoil
the fun.

As ideological and ethnocentric as some Japan Theory is, its authors
are trying to say something important. In a largely secular society, they
play the role priests and theologians used to play in religiously based
civilizations. They purvey a sense of large (if not ultimate) meanings
and meaningful (if not absolute) identities. They are obviously right
when they insist there is more than one road to modernity, and therefore
more than one way to be modern, or postmodern. Ironically, however,
while they stridently call for a social science based on indigenous categories, they often continue to speak in terms borrowed from the West.
Dale (1986) argues that the better part of the Theory is based on the
scribblings of German nationalists. However that may be, they have
also assimilated such concepts as Ruth Benedict's 'shame culture' (1977,
pp. 156–7), Erik Erickson's 'adolescent moratorium', Robert Jay Lifton's
'Protean Man' (1968), as well as the more recent intellectual fads of postmodernism, poststructuralism and deconstruction that I have just discussed. They have transformed this imported intellectual property into
new self-images which purport not to be beholden to the West. The result
is not only a new bevy of images, but a new ideological game pitting
Westerners against fresh and aggressive Japanese ideologists eager to leap
ahead of their opponents, leaving them with the modernity the Theorists
have always claimed as their own. At the end of the game, the score-
board presumably will read: 'West: modern; Japan: postmodern'. This, of
course, is another way of saying: 'West loses; Japan wins'. Winning this
ideological game has some rather serious political implications. Not only
are Theorists trying to create new rationales for national self-confidence;
they are also generating the image (and therefore the ideal) of a nation
which once again can go its own way. Already, Japan Theory is being
marshalled defensively around a wide spectrum of foreign and economic
policies.[10]

Japan has not been well served by games of this sort in the past – just
as the West has not been well served by some of its Theorists, thinkers
(some as eminent as Max Weber himself) who have claimed that modernity could only have developed in the West. Japanese culture – reduced
by postmodern Theory to fashion, collage, and pastiche, offers Japan no
genuine spiritual, moral or political guidance. A discourse which delights
in fragmented 'meta-masses' and a 'mosaic of culture styles' is not going

to produce a sense of national identity for the Japanese any more than dilation on multiculturalism by English professors in the United States will produce a responsible concept of nationhood for Americans. The triumph of Japanese postmodernists therefore seems to be a Pyrrhic victory. Like Mahayana Buddhism itself, postmodernism seeks to overcome dualisms of subject and object, thought and action, good and evil, sacred and pro-fane. The collapse of subject and object, thought and action – long the aim of Japanese philosophers – may be innocent enough as epistemology or Buddhist soteriology – but it can have a devastating effect when applied to politics.[11] Applied to the state, what does this imply if not the abdica-tion of all political awareness, criticism and responsibility? One can best appreciate the importance of critical thinkers like MARUYAMA Masao who call for more personal autonomy by contrasting them with Theorists who celebrate the absorption of the Japanese soul by the emperor, or – what is just as appalling – by Japan, Incorporated.

In the West, the political implications of postmodernism have not gone unnoticed. Jürgen Habermas, for example, warns that postmodernism, while seemingly apolitical, actually harbours deeply reactionary ideas. Daniel Bell (1990) characterizes the movement as 'a revolt against con-temporary liberalism' which substitutes 'pastiche for form and clever-ness for creativity'. In Europe, postmodernism seems to train its playful, antilogocentric guns on all projects originating in the eighteenth century, from the humanities to the nascent social sciences.[12] One could argue that if the postmodernists take their idea of 'incommensurable language games' to its logical conclusion, the very notion of a constitutional political order – one of the most notable 'logocentric' products of the Age of Enlightenment – must also be targeted for deconstruction.

Notes

Whenever appropriate, Japanese family names have been put first. The only exceptions concern Japanese authors whose translations have been published, in the West, by publishing houses who have put family names last, or who have otherwise decided to adopt this convention. To help the reader, all family names have been placed in small capitals.

1 See my *Japanese Religion and Society* (1991, p. 258).
2 See Robert Bellah (1965, p. 589).
3 For the historical development of Japan Theory in the postwar period, I rely largely on discussions by AOKI Tamotsu (1989) and KAMISHIMA Jirō (1990). The most judicious treatment of Japan Theory in English is Kosaku YOSHINO's *Cultural Nationalism in Contemporary Japan: A Sociological Enquiry* (1992).
4 See Andrew Barshay (1992, p. 382).
5 This opus can also be classified as part of the new Theory of Japanese Management. In this regard, see MURAKAMI Yasusuke (1987, pp. 33–90).

6   The Japanese New Religions are groups founded in the course of the nine-
    teenth and twentieth centuries. They generally combine charismatic or sham-
    anistic leadership with articulate, syncretistic gospels, intense evangelism,
    and an emphasis on faith healing and other this-worldly benefits.
7   See MIYOSHI Masao (1988, pp. 525–50) and KARATANI Kōjin (1988, pp. 615–
    28).
8   See David Pollack (1989, p. 76) and Marilyn Ivy (1988, pp. 419–44).
9   The Research Project Team for Japanese Systems (HAMAGUCHI Eshun, Repres-
    entative), *Japanese Systems: An Alternative Civilization?* (Yokohama: SEKOTAC
    Ltd, 1992), p. 93. See also ASADA Akira (1988, pp. 629–34).
10 See my *Japanese Religion and Society* (1991, pp. 263–7) for examples.
11 In the writings of WATSUJI Tetsurō for example, NISHIDA Kitarō's concepts of
    emptiness and nonbeing are transformed into the 'absolute negation' (*zettaiteki
    hiteisei*) of the self, which in turn translates as absolute devotion to a divine
    emperor. Gino K. Piovesana (1969) characterizes his position as 'totalitarian
    state-ethics' (p. 143).
12 See Allan Megill (1985, p. 340).

References

AOKI Tamotsu 1989: Sengo Nihon to 'Nihonbunkaron' (Part I), *Chūō kōron*, (June),
    pp. 156–73; 'Nihon-tataki' no arashi no naka de (Part II), (July) *Chūō kōron*,
    pp. 158–83.
ASADA Akira 1988: Infantile capitalism and Japan's postmodernism: a fairy tale.
    In Masao MIYOSHI and H. D. Harootunian (eds), Postmodernism and Japan, *The
    South Atlantic Quarterly* 87 (3) (Summer): 629–34.
Barshay, Andrew E. 1992: Imagining democracy in postwar Japan: reflections on
    MARUYAMA Masao and modernism. *Journal of Japanese Studies* 18 (2).
BEFU Harumi and MANABE Kazufumi: Empirical status of Nihonjinron: How real is
    the myth? *Kwansei Gakuin University Annual Studies*, vol. XXXVI (Nishinomiya,
    Japan), pp. 97–111.
Bell, Daniel 1990: Resolving the contradictions of modernity and modernism
    (Part Two). *Society* 27 (4) (May/June): 66–75.
Bellah, Robert N. 1965: Japan's cultural identity: some reflections on the work
    of WATSUJI Tetsurō. *Journal of Asian Studies* 4 (August): 573–94.
Benedict, Ruth 1977 (orig. 1946): *The Chrysanthemum and the Sword: Patterns of
    Japanese Culture*. London: Routledge & Kegan Paul.
Braisted, William Reynolds, ADACHI Yasuchi and CHIKUSHI Yuji (trans.) 1976: *Meiroku
    Zasshi: Journal of the Japanese Enlightenment*. Cambridge, Mass.: Harvard Univer-
    sity Press.
Dale, Peter 1986: *The Myth of Japanese Uniqueness*. New York: St Martin's Press.
Davis, Winston 1991: *Japanese Religion and Society: Paradigms of Structure and Change*.
    Albany: State University of New York Press.
DOI Takeo 1981 (orig. 1971): *The Anatomy of Dependence*. Tokyo: Kodansha
    International.

Ivy, Marilyn 1988: Consumption of knowledge in postmodern Japan. In Masao MIYOSHI and H. D. Harootunian (eds), Postmodernism and Japan, *The South Atlantic Quarterly* 87 (3) (Summer): 419–44.

KAMISHIMA Jirō 1990: Society of convergence: an alternative for the Homogeneity Theory. *The Japan Foundation Newsletter* XVII (3) (January): 1–6.

KARATANI Kōjin 1988: One spirit, two nineteenth centuries. In Masao MIYOSHI and H. D. Harootunian (eds), Postmodernism and Japan, *The South Atlantic Quarterly* 87 (3) (Summer): 615–28.

Keen, Donald 1954: HIRATA Atsutane and Western learning. *T'oung Pao* 42: 353–80.

KIMURA Bin 1972: *Hito to hito to no aida [Between Person and Person]*. Toko: Kobundo.

KOMORI Yoshihisa 1990: A critique of Japan's neonationalists. *Japan Echo* XVII (2) (Summer).

KUMON Shumpei, SATO Seizaburo and MURAKAMI Yasusuke 1979: *Bunmei to shite no ie-shakai [Kintractual Society as a Pattern of Civilization]*. Tokyo: Chuokoronsha.

Lifton, Robert J. 1968: Protean man. *Partisan Review* 35 (Winter): 13–27.

MARUYAMA Masao 1974: *Studies in the Intellectual History of Tokugawa Japan*, trans. Mikiso Hane. Tokyo: University of Tokyo Press.

MIYOSHI, Masao 1988: Against the native grain: the Japanese novel and the 'Postmodern' West. In Masao MIYOSHI and H. D. Harootunian (eds), Postmodernism and Japan, *The South Atlantic Quarterly* 87 (3) (Summer): 525–50.

Megill, Allan 1985: *Prophets of Extremity: Nietzsche, Heidegger, Foucault, Derrida*. Berkeley: University of California Press.

MURAKAMI Yasusuke 1987: The Japanese model of political economy. In Kozo YAMAMURA and Yasukichi YASUBA (eds), *The Political Economy of Japan*, vol. I: *The Domestic Transformation*, Stanford: Stanford University Press, pp. 33–90.

NAKANE Chie 1970: *Japanese Society*. Berkeley: University of California Press.

Piovesana, Gino K. 1969: *Contemporary Japanese Philosophical Thought*. New York: St John's University Press (Asian Philosophical Studies no. 4).

Pollack, David 1989: Modernism minceur, or Is Japan postmodern? *Monumenta Nipponica* 44 (1): 75–97.

TSUNODA Ryusaku et al. (eds), 1958: *Sources of Japanese Tradition*. New York: Columbia University Press, vol. II.

WATSUJI Tetsurō 1961: *Climate and Culture: A Philosophical Review*. New York: Greenwood Press.

YAMAMOTO Shichihei 1979: *Nihon shihonshugi no seishin [The Spirit of Chinese Capitalism]*. Tokyo: Kobunsha.

YOSHINO Kosaku 1992: *Cultural Nationalism in Contemporary Japan: A Sociological Enquiry*. New York: Routledge.

CHAPTER TEN

the construals of 'Europe': religion, theology and the problematics of modernity

Richard H. Roberts

Introduction: 'Divinity' and Its Discontents

My topic, that of the conflicting identities of Europe (a theme that I have apostrophized as the 'souls of Europe'), is one which shows how 'divinity' might operate today, in what has been influentially represented by Jean-François Lyotard as the 'postmodern condition'. I am also concerned to show how 'divinity' understood as the study of religion and theology, whilst fraught with difficulty, is simultaneously and equally a task full of promise; that is when, as I shall argue, the term 'divinity' is rightly understood.

Given my experience as a Professor of Divinity in Scotland, this chapter has a relative focus through which an array of major issues can be refracted, in part at least, on the basis of participant observation. What, then, is 'divinity'? In the ancient Scottish university divinity faculties as founded, or refounded at the Reformation, this term came to comprise dogmatic or systematic theology, philosophy of religion and 'apologetics'. Through this subdisciplinary triad it was possible to articulate 'faith' in dogmatic or systematic theology; to explore the nature and limits of 'reason' as applied to central conceptions of faith in the philosophy of religion; and then to articulate *both* in forms answerable to the world in 'apologetics'.

One purpose here is to show how the disciplinary range and remit of 'divinity' has in effect been changed and extended almost beyond recognition by force of circumstance, not least through cultural transformations taking place at the heart of European culture and society in which the quest for and the rebuilding of identities has become a matter of central importance. From the early-modern period, and certainly since the Enlightenment, a gradual and increasingly complex process of secularization has taken place which has involved not only the marginalization of religion and theology but also the occultation and migration of the sacred. The immediate context of the study of religion and theology has, furthermore, also been radically affected, in particular since 1989, by a largely unanticipated global resurgence of religion and of forms of religiosity. Thus on the levels of locality, Europe, and the world system, there are interconnected phenomena which have to be understood and interpreted within a common theoretical framework.[1]

The contemporary situation now confronts us with a fundamental challenge which may be expressed in the form of a dilemma: *either* retreat ever more into the diminishing and fragmented redoubts of traditional religious discourse, forced by secularization to the margins of social life and problematically rebirthed in the subcultures of fundamentalism and New Age; *or* redefine in a comprehensive way the remit and tasks of divinity.[2]

In our era, in which, as Karl Marx once remarked, 'All that is solid melts into air', it is not, however, religion and theology alone that have experienced crises of identity and relevance. For the representation of 'life' itself in the human and social sciences is also in a relatively fluid and undecided state.[3] The French philosopher-historian Michel Foucault has put it thus: the 'death of God' is attended by the death of man:

> Rather than the death of God – or rather in the wake of that death and in profound correlation with it – what Nietzsche's thought heralds is the end of his murderer; it is the explosion of man's face in laughter and the return of masks. (1970, pp. 385–6)

The *explosion of man's face in laughter* and the *return of masks* are terrifying and perplexing features of our age. Moreover, the *religious* condition is affected. In the resonant image of the distinguished literary critic and comparativist George Steiner: 'It is to the ambiguous after-life of religious feeling in Western culture that we must look, to the malignant energies released by the decay of natural religious forms' (1971, p. 46). We now live in the 'after-life' of religion, an era of 'post-religion'. Under these conditions 'tradition' quales in the face of 'detraditionalization'; and new religious growths, *masks of identity*, return, not least in forms of fundamentalisms and new forms of religiosity which all in their turn invite critical interpretation.[4] The student and teacher of divinity are, however, faced with a further challenge: whilst new religious growths sprout fungi-like on the stumps and trunks of the fallen trees of tradition – and humanity dances with its new spiritual masks – the traditional mainline denominations of the Christian Church in Western Europe culture are for the most part in decline.[5]

As Richard Dawkins (1989) has recently – and in a certain measure rightly – pointed out, the institutional functionalization of a mere dictionary definition of 'theology' (in his case the *Oxford Dictionary*) as the study of God, his nature and attributes, is scarcely defensible as it stands.[6] For we live in an era in which the existence of God is widely disputed, and the presence of many gods (or even in some quarters of goddesses) is asserted.[7] Furthermore, we now operate in an environment in which budget-centre and managerial methods demand well-defined remits. In consequence, what is now at stake is the presuppositions and composition of the inner core of the designated zone of the study of religion and theology, and how this is to be addressed by competences, which – in the absence of an explicit and publicly justifiable remit – might just as well be broken up, and, where possible, redistributed.

The 'Souls of Europe' and the Postmodern Problematic

If we grant in initial terms the reality of the new constraints and possibilities introduced above, then what might a problem look like to which 'divinity' could legitimately address itself? It is to this end that we examine the topic adverted to in the metaphorical title of this text, the 'souls of Europe': that is, the problem of European identity, or rather of a range of European *identities*, understood from a standpoint in which religious and theological factors are acknowledged as significant. And this *despite* the marginalization and migration of the sacred in European culture evident during the last two centuries.

It is precisely the changed status, the diminished sociocultural and societal space of religion and theology, that must become fully part of any critical, yet positive, argument designed to sustain the continued pursuit of the study of religion *qua* religion, and theology *qua* theology in the academic setting. Both the context, and changes in approach, do, of course, have consequences for the Church and for ministerial training which are in the longer term inescapable.

'Divinity' now appears to lack a defensible *episteme* or 'the total set of relations that unite, at a given period, the discursive practices that give rise to epistemological figures, sciences, and possibly formalised systems' (Foucault, 1972, p. 191). We set out on the assumption that underlying the politics of representation involved in the formation and practice of all disciplines there is a universal problem concerning the nature of the human. This crisis is commonly associated with poststructuralism and the depiction of the human as a *postmodern* condition. This implies tacit knowledge. Again in the words of Michel Foucault:

> Man has not been able to describe himself as a configuration in the *episteme* without thought at the same time discovering, both in itself and outside itself, at its borders yet also in its very warp and woof, an element of darkness, an apparently inert density in which it is embedded, an unthought which it contains entirely, yet in which it is also caught . . . (that is) the Other and shadow. (1970, pp. 326–7)

Religion and theology – and thus divinity – have much thinking of their as-yet *unthought* to do.

The image of the 'souls of Europe' resonates with the conflictual identities that both afflict 'Europe' in an extended and as yet unspecific sense, and also affect Scotland as a relatively small, yet important – we may add *paradigmatic* – country on the geographical periphery of Europe.[8] Indeed for present purposes, Europe and Scotland may be understood as the macrocosm and microcosm, respectively, of a series of interrelated problems. Both dimensions can be analysed as regards the historic and sequential emergence of conflicting identities; and both contexts demand methodological self-awareness. Such self-awareness requires theorization, which in turn permits the comparison of types based upon the isolation of historical stages in traditions (and the classification of such periodizations) to be transformed into a discussion of *metanarratives* operating in the *conflictual field of forces* that gives rise to identities in the contemporary world. This is a world which now manifests the *postmodern condition*.

The French writer Jean-François Lyotard expresses the contemporary state of *metanarratives* in a well-known passage to do with 'incredulity towards metanarratives':

> This incredulity is undoubtedly a product of progress in the sciences: but that progress in turn presupposes it. To the obsolescence of the metanarrative apparatus of legitimation corresponds, most notably, the crisis of metaphysical philosophy and of the university institution which in the past relied on it. The narrative function is losing its functors, its great heroes, its great dangers, its great voyages, its great goal. It is being dispersed in clouds of language narrative elements – narrative, but also denotative, prescriptive, descriptive, and so on. Conveyed within each cloud are pragmatic valencies specific to its kind. Each of us lives at the intersection of many of these. However, we do not necessarily establish stable language combinations, and the properties of the ones we do establish are not necessarily communicable. (1979, p. xxiv)

What is at stake here is this: what happens to identities when traditions pass into an era of *detraditionalization* (see, for example, Bauman, 1991; Beck, 1992; Giddens, 1991) and into *postmodernity*, in which such identities become 'clouds of language narrative elements' which we can only strive to hold together as pragmatic valencies in language combinations? Moreover, how should we transmit and negotiate identities composed of artifacts (including those of religion and even theology) that are exchanged as cultural or symbolic capital in the European marketplace of a globalized world system?[9] This presentation of the context of the problem of identity presupposes a set of fundamental cultural insights implicated in the modern/postmodern problematic, which we shall approach in stages.

We therefore now investigate under the rubrics of 'archeology' (Michel Foucault) and 'genealogy' (Friedrich Nietzsche) the historic emergence of the 'souls' or cultural identities of 'Europe' as a way of construing in a contextualized way the problematic interactions of *premodernity* (Christendom, tradition and the *ancien régime*), *modernity* (the dialectic of Enlightenment, Communism, instrumental reason and European integration), and *postmodernity* (inaugurated by the progressive triumph of the market, fluidity of identities, the collapse of Communism and the 'End of History'). A thread that links the themes of tradition, conflictual metanarratives and dialectical contemporaneity can be found in the thought of the philosopher Hegel; it is no accident that on an international scale a movement *back to Hegel* is now taking place. So to a brief depiction of Hegel's prefigurement of the present confrontation of premodernity, modernity and postmodernity.

In the Hegelian parable of the Lord and Bondsman to be found in the *Phenomenology of Mind* (1807/1910), Hegel provides an extraordinary and compelling account of the growth of consciousness into a mature and tested self-consciousness. The *Phenomenology* underlies and is received in the work of such thinkers as Karl Marx, Friedrich Nietzsche, Edmund Husserl, Jean-Paul Sartre and Michel Foucault, who all in their respective ways recapitulate and resolve the 'moments' in the knowledge/power nexus.[10] In Hegel's text the dialectical conception of the achievement of full personhood over against the 'other' is represented as a 'trial by death', for,

> The individual who has not staked his life, may, no doubt, be recognised as a Person; but he has not attained the truth of this recognition as an independent self-consciousness. In the same way each must aim at the death of the other, as it risks its own life thereby; for that other is to it of no more worth than itself; the other's reality is presented to the former as an external other, as outside itself; it must view its otherness as pure existence for itself or as absolute negation. (Hegel, 1910, p. 233)

What is true of consciousness may now also be applied to the emergence of cultures in an era in which cultural identity and cultural agency (or lack of it) appears to displace class as a medium of analysis and empowerment. In Hegel's *Phenomenology* the traditions of *premodernity* (associated with ancestral sacralized social hierarchy) come into conflict with *modernity* (the total – and totalizing – emancipation of reason and ambiguous *Geist*); yet in Hegel's early dialectic the agonistic emergence of the metanarratives in an unresolved consciousness also prefigures the dynamics of self-creation characteristic of the *postmodern self*. The contrasting receptions and resolutions of the Hegelian dialectic permit insight into the problematic that has worked itself out in the events of the later nineteenth and twentieth centuries. A renewed Hegelian interpretation of European culture after the fall of Marxism may facilitate the thinking of the 'unthought' – and the uncovering of what some of a Eurosceptical turn of mind might well prefer to remain the *politically unthinkable*.

We here touch upon what George Steiner has called the 'theory of aggression' (1971, p. 46) residing in the very heart of European culture. It is the depiction of this dialectic discerned in the successive and then layered identities of 'Europe' that is the focal point of our analysis. It is this problematic that in turn has burdened – and still afflicts – the inner core of Christian theology in the Western world, for 'All recognition is agonistic. We name our own being, as the angel did Jacob, after the dialectic of mutual aggression' (Steiner, 1970, p. 46).

'Europe' as Periodization and Typology

Approached from the standpoint of history, 'Europe' is a deeply ambiguous term. On the one hand it may be understood as the 'New Europe', in which a configuration of nation-states cede sovereignty, and elements of cultural identity – and thus hegemony – to a greater whole, to the extent required by political and economic integration. 'Europe' also, however, implies an uneasy confrontation with the conflictual identities of the 'Old Europe'. As part of a greater conflictual totality these identities emerged, differentiated themselves, enjoyed a near global triumph, and then 'declined'.

In the contemporary context, then, complex tensions now arise between the modernizing conformity required by multinational capitalism expressed in European integration and its 'Europe', on the one hand, and, on the other, the 'old' Europe of nationalisms, ethnic diversity, anti-Semitism, fear of Islam, and the renewed Roman Catholic ideology of 'Christendom'. Religious and theological elements have been of importance (both positive and negative) in the successive transformations of the 'idea' and the identities of the 'old' Europe.

The origins of the idea and of the identities of Europe are shrouded in myth.[11] In particular, the myth of Europa presented in its fullest form in the poem of Moschos of Syracuse (*c*.200 BC) represents the earliest manifestation of a persisting mythopoeic or myth-creating tendency.[12] In the time of Homer the name 'Europe' applied to Middle Greece, but also according to other texts, to Thrace and Epirus. Gradually the designation spread to the whole Greek mainland, and then in the colonization period it referred to one of the three great journey directions away from the homeland (the others being Asia and Libya). Through the later Greek and then the Roman period the sense of this known mainland extended north and west. The historical evolution of Europe prior to the Christian era was profoundly influenced by migrations of Indogermanic peoples and population movements. There is now lively argument stimulated by Martin Bernal's monumental two-volume work *Black Athena* (1987/1991), in which he argues for the non-European origins of the civilization that extended itself from mainland Greece throughout Europe and beyond.

However, neither investigation of the question of historical origins, nor the mythopoeic transmutation of those origins, are our central concern at this point.[13] Whilst the various constructions placed upon the historic emergence and geographical consolidation of Europe in late antiquity, the so-called Dark Ages and the early Middle Ages mapped, amongst others, by Judith Herrin (1987), Denys Hays (1968), and most recently by Robert Bartlett (1993), inform our approach, our focal point is the decipherment of what we shall call the 'politics of representation'. In other words 'Europe' is always *someone's* representation, and designed to construe, to include – and to exclude.

An awareness of the complexity of the task of isolating European identity is not new. Systems of management of this complexity that involve periodization are normative in this domain. Thus 'tradition' (*paradosis, traditio*), the paradigm of premodern European identity, may be understood as an active 'handing on' that can be traced and constructed through a sequence of linked events. These 'events' are subsequently prioritized, thus becoming the *topoi* or commonplaces of an identity which may achieve normative status for a community, ethnic group, or even, more ambitiously, for an entity as large as that of 'Europe' itself. Such transhistorical identities, when they purport to attain universal status in the face of modernity, may be construed in the terminology of contemporary theory as competing 'metanarratives'. Each such metanarrative seeks to appropriate authority and hegemonic status as a bearer of the authentic European identity.

The passage from premodern tradition to modernity was experienced in theology above all as a crisis of history, expressed in the doctrine of *historicism.* In historicism the connection with a secure past becomes problematic: all historical events were seen to be part of a seamless causal chain of probabilities, from which revelation and the supernatural were banished *a priori.* The relation of modernity to postmodernity is never, however, a sequential *transition,* but rather a *dialectical* relation. This is expressed with brilliant economy by Lyotard: 'A work can become modern only if it is first postmodern. Postmodernism thus understood is not modernism at its end but in the nascent state, and this state is constant' (1979, p. 79).

Pre-Modernity Identity: Catholic Tradition

Two representative Roman Catholic figures, the English historian Christopher Dawson (1932, 1948, 1952) of the mid-twentieth century and the present Pope, John-Paul II, may be used in order to illustrate the *thesis* of a European premodernity grounded in tradition as opposed to the *antithesis* of modernity. Even within the Roman Catholic apologetic standpoint, it is, however, important to note significantly different resolutions of the problem of identity as periodization. Christopher Dawson (1952) has expressed an extreme Eurocentric standpoint:

> The existence of Europe is the basis of the historical development of the modern world, and it is only in relation to that fact that the development of each particular state can be understood.   (p. 24)

In the aftermath of the then recent European disaster of the Second World War, Dawson argued that consciousness of nationality and the nation-state had tended to leave 'Europe in the background as a vague abstraction or as nothing more than a geographical expression' (p. 24). Furthermore, he maintained that the conception of *Europe* as such never held a definite place in a tradition of education that had been effectively dominated, on one level, by the history of the ancient world of Greece and Rome, and at a much lower level, by consciousness of an individual's own country. These were factors unfortunately linked in the British public consciousness by such works as Gibbon's *Decline and Fall of the Roman Empire.* Indeed, Dawson directly attributed the European catastrophe to this misguided double focus:

> To ignore Europe and to concentrate all our attention on the political community to which we belong, as though it was the whole social reality, leads in the last resort to the totalitarian state, and National Socialism itself was only this development carried out with Germanic thoroughness and Prussian ruthlessness.   (1952, p. 25)

For Dawson, democratic European states had ignored the 'existence of Europe as a social reality' and they thus stood irresolutely between the nation-state and the 'ideal of a cosmopolitan liberal world order' (p. 25). The latter, embodied in the League of Nations and its failure in the inter-war period, was theoretically co-extensive with the human race. But in practice it was dependent on the realities of international trade and finance. Thus according to Dawson:

> Europe is more than the sum of the nations and states of the European continent, and it is much more than a subdivision of the modern international society. In so far as a world society or a world civilization can be said to exist, it is the child of Europe, and if, as many peoples believe today, this ideal of world civilization is being shipwrecked before it has achieved realization, then Europe remains the most highly developed form of society the world has yet known. (1952, pp. 25–6)

Dawson developed his distinctively Eurocentric standpoint in the broad 'Christendom' tradition. Europe as such is defined as

> a community of peoples who share in a common spiritual tradition that had its origins three thousand years ago in the eastern Mediterranean and which has been transmitted from age to age and from people to people until it has come to overshadow the world. (1952, p. 26)

For Dawson, Europe can only be understood by the study of *Christian* culture: for 'it was as Christendom that Europe first became conscious of itself as a society of peoples with common moral values and common spiritual aims' (p. 26). Dawson then develops a seven-stage account of the history of Western culture which is dominated by transitions that become the *topoi* or *loci* – the commonplaces – of a tradition that aspires to the status of a total trans-national cultural system.[14]

Dawson's stages are: (i) the Pre-Christian (and thus pre-European), which is to be regarded as the source of the intellectual and social traditions of the West; (ii) the time from Alexander to Augustus, and from the death of Augustus to the conversion of Constantine, which saw the growth of Rome and a co-operative effort between the two great Mediterranean peoples that enabled Christianity successfully to transplant a sacred tradition of immemorial antiquity into the Roman–Hellenistic world; (iii) the formation of Western Christendom through the conversion of the barbarians and the subsequent transmission of Mediterranean culture by the Church; (iv) the expansion of Christendom from the eleventh century onwards through cultural activity inspired by the Carolingian conception of Christendom as a social unity, the society of the Christian people, which transcended the lesser unities of nation and kingdom and city in an ideal of the universal Christian empire which (although corrupted) survived long enough to inspire the fourteenth-century poet Dante.

After reaching the high point of European development in the work of Dante, the remaining stages in Dawson's periodization constitute a regrettable falling away from the ideal of Christendom. Thus: (v) both the Renaissance and the Reformation, (vi) post-Renaissance Europe until 1914, and (vii) the period from 1914 to 1950, are lesser adjuncts.[15] These are all a record of contingent imperfection, against which the authentic would-be bearer of European identity has to respond through a *return to*, or *recovery of,* Christendom.

Any contemporary scheme of periodization undertaken in strictly diachronic and sequential terms would now of course require the addition of (viii) the Cold War and European integration in the EC (1949–89); and (ix) the era from 1989 onwards, with the reality of a renewed but unresolved greater Europe, in which the question of identity once more holds centre-stage.[16] But the simple addition of further contemporary periods is pointless if it is not attended by a theorization which recognizes that the recent transitions involve *qualitative disruption* and the subsequent *dialectical interaction,* indeed the *functionalization* of premodernity and modernity in the postmodern condition. Here our concern is above all with the critique of a particular peridodization and typology.

The Roman Catholic Church has of course traditionally invested heavily in the conception of a unified Christian Europe, and this idea has undergone systematic renovation and indeed reassertion on a number of levels during the pontificate of Pope John-Paul II. To take one example, an important and unambiguous expression of Papal strategy is to be found in two statements concerned with the spiritual patronage of the European totality, 'Cyril and Methodius' (John-Paul II, 1981) and 'Europe and the Faith' (John-Paul II, 1985), issued in 1981 and 1985, respectively.[17]

In the earlier document the Pope set up the theological ground-rules for a historic decade during which several important anniversaries of the millennium of the conversion of Eastern Europe would take place (e.g. the Rus of Kiev 988). Thus in 'Cyril and Methodius', the Pope made a strategic ideological pre-emptive strike by bringing into conjunction the patronage of Western Europe by St Benedict, declared by Paul VI in 1964, with his own declaration of the patronage of Eastern Europe by the Thessalonican brothers Cyril and Methodius (who died in 869 and 885, respectively). Subsequent developments have indicated the apparent wisdom of this commitment, now that interdenominational and inter-religious struggles – suppressed by Marxism–Leninism and exascerbated by economic crisis – have once more broken out after the collapse of Communism in 1989–90.

Few contemporary institutions can claim such historic legitimation as that grounded in the undivided Church, that is the Church prior to the Photian Schism and the separation of Rome and Byzantium in the ninth century.[18] Constantinople (which sent the brothers) and Rome (which confirmed their mission) are thus presented as *one in intent and purpose*; and when this partnership is placed in the same context of co-patronage with Benedict, 'protection' is seen to apply to the 'whole of Europe'. It is at this juncture that Europe appears in its true form:

> Europe, in fact, as a geographical whole, is, so to speak, the fruit of two currents of Christian traditions, to which are added also two different, but at the same time deeply complementary, forms of culture. (John-Paul II, 1981, p. 17)

The proclamation of the co-patronage of Cyril and Methodius combines historical justification with the future eschatological reference of the 'signs of the times'. Thus the new-born Europe of the Dark Ages 'ensured the Europe of today a common spiritual and cultural heritage' (John-Paul II, 1981, p. 18). Now in a new Dark Age of Europe that primal resource must be reasserted. And all these levels of legitimation combine in a highly distinctive form of discourse:

> Therefore, with certain knowledge and my mature deliberation, in the fullness of apostolic authority, by virtue of this Letter *and for ever*, I constitute and declare saints Cyril and Methodius heavenly co-patrons of the whole of Europe before God, granting furthermore all the honours and privileges which belong, according to law, to the principal Patron Saints of places. (Jean-Paul II, 1981, p. 18; my emphasis)

The second Apostolic Letter, 'Europe and the Faith', is a document that provides a fuller account of the Papal understanding of contemporary Europe and the relevance to it of its 'Christian roots'. The Pope begins with a characterization of the contemporary Europe whose destiny is at stake:[19]

> The Europe to which we are sent out has undergone such cultural, political, social and economic transformations as to formulate the problem of evangelization in totally new terms. We could even say that Europe, as she has appeared following the complex events of the last century, has presented Christianity and the Church with the most radical challenge history has witnessed, but at the same time opened the way today to new and creative possibilities for the proclamation and incarnation of the Gospel. (1985, p. 279)

The programme of the Roman Catholic Church implied in these documents is not so much dialogical as *evangelistic* in orientation. The consistent lack of allusions to any fundamental crisis affecting the Church, or indeed to Protestantism, is remarkable: the latter is here seemingly regarded as an irrelevance, an aberration over which Catholicism leaps without great effort back to a primal unity, a cultural *fons et origo*.

It is significant that here once more a succession of distinctive *topoi* (involving both exclusions and inclusions) articulate a narrative identity grounded in tradition. The Roman Catholic discourse of identity undergoes rhetorical development in preparation as it were for the last battle at the 'End of History'. A binary scission is acknowledged; plurality is eschewed in the sphere of Christian values, as living tradition confronts modernity. It is, however, Pope John-Paul II's apparent 'resistance to theory', expressed in a *retreat* from periodization of the history of the divided church – the Renaissance, the Reformation and the Enlightenment – that tends to isolate and consolidate contemporary Catholic teaching at some distance from the dynamics of *self*-creation that constitute *postmodernity*. The postulation of a seamless trans-historical identity is itself an act of spiritual and theological politics, part of whose rhetoric is to be the *ars theologia artem celare*: the theological art that seeks to conceal its artfulness.

The Roman Catholic and Papal vision is that of ancestral tradition, the inner principle of the *ancient régime*, a conception of continuity and interpretative *topoi* that constitutes the *premodern* thesis in our argument, and, if we once more appropriate Hegel's parable, may be regarded as the *mentalité* of unconscious spiritual Lordship (*Herrschaft*) that sees no real need to recognize the other, other than to negate it through evangelical love – and the exacting of 'docility in the Spirit'.

Before we turn to the real antithesis of Catholicism, the European *modernity* of the unambiguous Faustian and Promethean self-assertion of Marx and Nietzsche, and for our purposes, Oswald Spengler, we must briefly touch upon the uneasy and unstable accommodation effected by Liberal Protestantism. Both the original Protestant Reformation, and the later accommodating synthesis between premodern tradition and modernity in the guise of 'progress' attempted by Ernst Troeltsch's 'Liberal Protestantism', are effectively ignored in the Papal documents in question. The constructive processes underlying this Papal strategy are perhaps best seen in the fate of the 'Others' that fall outside tradition, and thus outwith the now newly *re-created* Roman Catholic metanarrative of the European spiritual, as well as the cultural *unity* of East and West (and the elision of historical discontinuity), which is secured on the level of theological ideology and religious cultural politics.

Identity as Accommodation: Liberal Protestantism[20]

In 1912, when confronting the then contemporary significance of the Reformation for Germany – and for civilization itself – the historian and sociologist Ernst Troeltsch considered the question of cultural identity at the high point of European self-confidence. In *Protestantism and Progress* (1912; see also 1922b), Troeltsch touched upon the deepest currents of the specifically German and thus Protestant contributions to the identities of Europe. In 1912, when the old order was about to disappear, Troeltsch sought to gain insight into the intellectual and religious situation of his day, assessing it as that 'from which the significance and the possibilities of development possessed by Christianity might be deduced' (pp. v–vi).

In outright contrast to the representative Roman Catholic commentators we have considered above, Troeltsch held that 'the living possibilities of development and progress are to be found on Protestant soil' (p. vi), and thus specifically *not* within Catholicism, which remains for him an essentially non-progressive phenomenon. Troeltsch sought to distinguish the perennially valuable elements in modern civilization from the temporary, and on this basis to establish a position of stable compromise:

> to give the religious ideas of Christianity – which I hold to be the sole really religious force in our European system of civilisation, and which I also believe to be superior to the religions of the East – a shape and form capable of doing justice to the absoluteness of religious conviction, and at the same time in harmony with the valuable elements in the modern spirit. (pp. vii–viii)

Troeltsch proceeds to expound the ambiguous role of Protestantism in the history of western Europe and North America. Protestantism appeared as a 'revival and reinforcement of the ideal of authoritatively imposed Church-civilisation' which served to revive the Catholic idea and relaunched the 'medieval spirit' (pp. 85–6) for a further two centuries.[21] It was only in the late seventeenth and the eighteenth centuries that the struggle for freedom took place which effectively terminated the Middle Ages. There is thus an ineradicable paradox embedded in the historical career of Protestantism, and this is best explored if 'we seek its influence at first not in a universal regeneration or reconstruction of life as a whole, but mainly in indirect and unconsciously produced effects, nay, even in accidental side-influences, or again in influences produced against its will' (p. 87).

The Protestant heritage in Europe is therefore consistently ambiguous. It recapitulates Christian identities in forms fraught with compromise.

Even as Luther had abandoned the world to the worldly authority, so Troeltsch accepted that the world as such fell under the unchallengeable sway of historicism.[22] He consequently believed that an uneasy tension existed between historicism and a residual inner conviction that Christian values were superior to those of other cultures. In contemporary terms, we might say that as a provisional synthesis made between Christian antiquity and modernity, Protestantism purported to hold the middle ground: but this does not now furnish the dialectical integration that is an imperative requirement in the face of *postmodernity*.

The political and existential weakness of the *retreat* or *turn to the subject* characteristic of Protestantism was not lost on one strident commentator whose work has recently come once more to wider public attention in the new *Zeitgeist* of postcommunism (see Fukuyama, 1992). The redoubtable cultural historian and disciple of Nietzsche, Oswald Spengler, wrote in *The Decline of the West* (1926):

> I have the same view that the cause of all our troubles is Christianity . . .
> As a view of life, Protestantism in comparison with Judaism, Catholicism, and Bolshevism, is a nullity. Nevertheless, it carries with it the immense danger that it has a passive effect upon people. From this comes the lack of self interest, of independence, of capacity of self defence, of instinct for danger.   (p. 62)[23]

What is then about modernity, with its instinct for danger, with which Troeltsch had to strike his compromise? What is the modernity against which Roman Catholicism now directs itself in fundamental antithesis? What is this reality in relation to which Protestantism is but a mere interlude – or, in Spengler's terms, a *nullity*? It is here that we encounter that other Europe, a Europe that repudiates its Christian heritage in order to strike back into different bedrock. This is a 'Europe' that advocates explicit power, a Europe that is unambiguously Promethean – and modern.

Promethean Modernity: the Negation of 'Europe'[24]

In characterizing European, indeed global 'modernity', as Promethean, it is possible to adopt a number of approaches. Thus both Marx and Nietzsche afford receptions and developments of Enlightenment reason that emphasize the recovery of the lost, thwarted grandeur of man. I have chosen instead to focus upon the lesser known and ambiguous figure of Oswald Spengler (1880–1939). (See Hughes, 1952; Dray, 1980.)

Spengler, a former gymnasium teacher turned private scholar, published *Der Untergang des Abendlandes* in Munich (2 vols, 1918–22). *The*

Decline of the West was conceived before and finished during the First World
War, and had an immense impact upon a defeated German population,
which had – with unprecedented unity – fought and lost the War. Spengler
has never been a fully respectable figure in academic terms, but his significance is none the less very considerable. Spengler's advocacy of Goethe
and Nietzsche, his endorsement of ruthless entrepreneurial capitalism
(epitomized by Cecil Rhodes), and his hatred of Bolshevism resonated
strongly with the then *Zeitgeist*, a *first postmodernity* of Weimar culture,
and thus with our own era – the *second postmodernity*.[25] Spengler expresses
what is now a topical post-Marxist perspective *prior* to the full-flowering
of Marxism–Leninism and Stalinism and the collapse of Communism. As
Francis Fukuyama has rightly discerned, Spengler *pre*-thought those parts
of the once *unthinkable* that now re-surface in the Neo-Darwinian warrior ethos of resurgent capitalism.[26]

Many of the major German-speaking Protestant theologians of the
first half of the twentieth century, for example Karl Barth, Emil Brunner,
Rudolf Bultmann, Paul Tillich and Friedrich Gogarten (all collaborators
in the journal *Zwischen den Zeiten*, 1922–33), were inescapably aware of
the impact of Spengler's text as *'the* philosophy' (Spengler, 1926, p. xv)
of their time.[27] Spengler's success stemmed not least from his presentation of the history of the West as a 'natural philosophy', so that responsibility for national failure is attributable neither to the nation nor the
individual but to the cyclic character of the historical process itself.[28]

All branches of a culture are bound together in the 'morphological relationship', in what Spengler calls the 'logic of space' (1926, pp. 6–7) within
which 'Man' is a meaning-forming conscious organism faced with the
ongoing problem of securing 'world-formation'.[29] Spengler dismisses the
traditional subdivision of history into 'Ancient', 'Medieval' and 'Modern'
which universalizes the ancestral Christian time-scale. These are terms
which distort the immensity of world history as the history of many
cultures. The very word 'Europe' comes in for pointed attack. Spengler
stresses the constructed and transient character of all characterizations of
Europe. Indeed:

> The word 'Europe' ought to be struck out of history. There is historically
> no 'European' type, and it is sheer delusion to speak of the Hellenes as
> 'European Antiquity' ... It is thanks to the word 'Europe' alone, and the
> complex of ideas resulting from it, that our historical consciousness has
> come to link Russia with the West in an utterly baseless unity. ... 'East'
> and 'West' are notions that contain real history, whereas 'Europe' is an
> empty sound.   (1926, p. 16)[30]

Spengler's historical Copernican revolution involves a radical decentring
of the European subject and its conceits. This is a form of deconstruction

avant la lettre which, moreover, presages in a 'first postmodernity' the contemporary dynamics of the so-called 'postmodern condition'. For Spengler, the self-assertion of a culture in its own context becomes the blameless norm; the organic growth of a particular cultural species takes place in a competitive environment:

> I see in place of that empty figment of one linear history . . . the drama of
> *a number* of mighty Cultures, each springing with primitive strength from
> the soil of a mother-region to which it remains firmly bound throughout
> its life-cycle; each stamping its material, its mankind, in *its own* image; each
> having *its own* idea, *its own* passions, *its own* life, will and feeling, *its own*
> death. (1926, p. 21)

The 'Decline of the West' has thus become the problem of 'Civilization. The latter state is the routinized petrifaction of that which *has become*, and it succeeds the vitality of *becoming* expressed in a true Culture. Thus 'Civilizations' are external and artificial, the death that follows life. With a challenging and unadorned honesty casting his mind as it were beyond the interlude of Bolshevism, Spengler remarks that in 'Civilization' it is *money* that comes to the fore as the dominant cultural phenomenon. For Spengler it is Cecil Rhodes (rather than, as has been the case in our own time, Margaret Thatcher, Richard Bransòn, Ivan Bowsky or Rupert Murdoch) who is the symbol of the woman or man of Imperialism and capitalism. In Civilization the energy of such hero– leaders is directed outwards, rather than inwards, as in the case of the outdated, even effete 'culture-man' (Spengler, 1926, p. 37) – that is, what in England right-wing politicians might designate a member of the 'chattering classes'. As a then present-day Caesar, Rhodes exemplified the power that precedes the inevitable Nemesis of the over-extension, petrification and decay that will ultimately result from the slogan 'Expansion is everything'. Like Francis Fukuyama in *The End of History and the Last Man* (1991), Spengler concentrates upon the apotheosis of the capitalist conqueror, the economic and technological warrior-hero, the veritable *master* for whom others will be *slaves* in the aggressive social Neo-Darwinianism of post-Marxist modernity.

According to Spengler, West European man must re-learn his place within a general cultural scheme, be warned, and devote himself pragmatically to 'technics instead of lyrics, the sea instead of the paintbrush, and politics instead of epistemology' (1926, p. 41) in the *early winter* of Civilization. In this particular 'Back to Basics', renewed scepticism is informed by the 'universal symbolism' of the 'Morphology of world-history' (p. 46), and thus the World War itself becomes part of a greater scheme, 'the type of a historical change of phase occurring within a great historical organism of definable compass at the point preordained for it hundred of years ago' (1926, p. 47).[31]

It now becomes apparent that our investigation of the identities of 'Europe' involves a struggle for the very soul of a continent and its cultures. Spengler's identification of the modern evolution of Western civilization with the single motif of the Faust legend and the organic naturalism of Goethe, combined with the subversive impulse of Nietzsche and energized by rampant technological capitalism, leads to a *caesura*:

> The insatiable historical voracity of the Western mind began with Hegel. He himself relied entirely on the traditional view of history (antiquity–Middle Ages–Modern Times). Actually an extensive knowledge of history finally leads of necessity to a perception of the void – in the artistic language of Goethe 'the beautiful purposeless game of Living Nature' . . . The standard of knowledge in 1820 supported the belief in something 'Absolute' behind single individual historical events. Today, however, we see India and China and Mexico with their dead cultures. (Helps, 1966, pp. 72–3)

With historical hindsight, modernity – and instrumental reason – have now to be reconceived after the Third Reich, the Holocaust, the discovery and use of atomic weapons and the collapse of Communism. In the midst of the iniquities of the present we require a more dialectical and theoretical representation of the nature of European identity, that is if 'Europe' is not, in Spengler's words, to be *struck out* of history. In order to attempt this, we return to the radical Hegelian impulse and trace out anew the representation of 'Europe' from the standpoint of its 'others', that is from the standpoint of the *slave* rather than the Lord or Master.

'Europe' and the Other

'Christendom' as a conception exists most powerfully in the constructive imagination of those who propound its virtues. The defence of 'Christendom' has from the time of Augustine involved coercive enforcement as a means of sustaining its integrity. As regards Europe's and Christendom's 'others', two important areas of concern stand out: the treatment of the Jews, and the relationship with Islam.[32] With respect to the former, some feminist theologians – for example Rosemary Radford Ruether in *Faith and Fratricide* (1974) – have argued that Christianity is deeply and irrecoverably anti-Semitic. This argument is now being played out in a most acute form in the diverse Jewish, Christian and secular responses to the Holocaust.[33] Outcomes are intrinsically related to recent discussion of modernity, and its expressions in the 'dialectic of Enlightenment' and its cultural antecedents.[34]

It is, however, the 'Orientalism' debate provoked by the distinguished Palestinian Christian literary critic Edward Said (1978/1991) which affords us a vital clue in the present argument, in which we seek to go beyond the mere periodization of traditions – or even – as with Troeltsch and Spengler, to go beyond the typologies of consciousness or *mentalités* into the dynamics of cultural agency.

In thinking the *unthought* implicit in the formation of the identity of Islam as presented in 'Orientalism', Said makes explicit reference to Hegel in his analysis of the *construction* of a cultural identity and its *imposition* upon a living culture. Said thus subjects the construction of *discourses of representation* of both 'Orientalism' and the resultant scholarly method to deconstructive analysis, out of which emerges his understanding of the politics of representation.[35] Said begins by designating the Orient and its special place in European experience in the following way:

> The Orient is not only adjacent to Europe; it is also the place of Europe's greatest and richest and oldest colonies, the source of its civilizations and languages, its cultural contestant, and one of its deepest and most recurrent images of the Other. In addition, the Orient has helped to define Europe (or the West) as its contrasting image, idea, personality, experience. (1978, pp. 1–2)

Said's designation of the Orient as 'the Other' resonates with Hegelian overtones and the explicit assimilation of the dialectics of lordship and bondage drawn from *The Phenomenology of Mind* (1910, pp. 228–67; see also Roberts, 1988).[36] The metaphors and the parable provide the language and interlocking conceptions used to designate and represent the discourses of culture and identities as *constructions* based on *interest*. Thus Orientalism, which presents itself as an allegedly scientific and purely objective study, is dealt with

> as the corporate institution for dealing with the Orient – dealing with it by making statements about it, authorizing views of it, describing it, by teaching it, ruling over it: in short Orientalism as a Western style for dominating, restructuring, and having authority over the Orient. (Said, 1978, p. 3)

The representation and interpretation of Islam within the ambit of Orientalism is thus understood as the exercise of a form of cultural hegemony, in Gramsci's (1971) understanding of the term, through *self-assimilated* ideological control. Conversely and reciprocally, this is directly relevant to the formation of *European* identity itself, for:

Orientalism is never far from what Denys Hay has called the idea of Europe, a collective notion identifying 'us' Europeans as against all 'those' non-Europeans, and indeed it can be argued that the major components in European culture are precisely what made that culture hegemonic both in and outside Europe: the idea of European identity as a superior one in comparison with all non-European peoples and cultures. (Said, 1978, p. 7)

Said maintains that the flexible strategy of cultural dominance through definition of the 'other' is closely associated with anti-Semitism: 'I have found myself writing the history of a strange, secret sharer of Western anti-Semitism' (p. 27). The rise of Orientalism as the charged study of the 'other' culture is traced back to the Council of Vienne (1312). The Islamic invasions beginning in the seventh century served to shift the centre of European culture northwards away from the Mediterranean and into a form of enclosure: the Romano-German civilization of the Holy Roman Empire. Consequently, 'Christendom' became the 'one great Christian community, conterminous with the ecclesia. . . . The Occident was now living its own life' (Pirenne, 1939, pp. 234, 283).

Said regards Orientalism as the product of a political master–slave relationship, the terms of which are applicable, by direct transfer, to the decipherment of the construction of the idea of 'Europe' as such. In the Enlightenment, and in particular in that side of the German Enlightenment imbued with Romanticism, the construction of the Oriental and Islamic 'other' took place. Yet we must recognize that this was the same intellectual and social context which gave rise *both* to modern post-Enlightenment German Liberal Protestant theology *and* to the poly-aspectual Romantic quest for primal sources of *European* identity and the possibility of a cultural dynamic freed from Christianity. Here the tensions between the inner-European struggle for cultural hegemony (exemplified supremely by the nineteenth-century conflict between France and Germany), the formation of modern disciplines in the humanities, and imperialism (both political and cultural), converge within a context characterized by rapid and pervasive industrialization and the secularization of culture (Chadwick, 1975/1990).[37] Here is a central nexus in the struggle for the 'soul of Europe'.

Said argues that with the loss of confidence in the Biblical texts as the primal source and justification of the cultural hegemony of Christendom, the Romantics and their associates turned eastwards and applied in transplanted form the Christian motif of dying and rising to a renascent Orient. Thus (and this is surely not without irony) a culture of Indo-European origin, exposed and displayed through the paradigmatic discipline of philology, could in turn service the needs of a culture in crisis. Increasingly deprived of its ancestral epistemological assumptions through Kantian thought in the Enlightenment, and of its Christian mythic history through historicism, the declining metanarrative of 'Europe' needed to draw upon and assimilate the 'others' it had both created and imposed (Said, 1978, p. 115). Thus the negation of the Other was simultaneously a creative act – the creation of the Other (Said, 1978, p. 120). Such procedures of negation and creation are an *intimation of postmodernity*, the era in which the capacity to self-create is the condition of cultural existence. Indeed, according to Said, 'the Orientalist could celebrate his method, his position, as that of a secular creator, a man who made new worlds as God had once made the old' (1978, p. 121). At the foundation of a *discipline*, a collection of texts – in effect a 'canon' of normativity – emerged, which was a social and cultural creation executed in what Ernest Renan called the *laboratoire philologique*, often at a remove from the 'reality' it purported to represent. In terms of a basic *leitmotif* of nineteenth-century European scholarship and intellectual life, *the ideal had displaced the real*.

The strategy of the construction of the 'other' outlined above, equally fits the era of the poet Novalis, who (by contrast with Heine) in *Die Christenheit und Europa* (1799), accused the Reformation of enthroning reason through the admission of literalism into the philological study of the *word* of God, thereby losing hold of the spiritual unity of Europe (in Taylor, 1970, pp. 131ff).

Far from being unquestionable givens, the various identities of Europe are the products of the politics of representation. In terms of the Scottish microcosm of the European problematic it would doubtless be possible to generate a similar analysis of Scottish cultural identity as assimilable to a 'Britishness' created as an imposed, or partially acknowledged, identity. To imagine that any of these processes is simply bipolar would be simplistic: all such processes of identity involve collusions as complex and intimate as the evolution of *both* Master *and* Slave within a single self-consciousness as found in Hegel's parable. Contemporary Scottish cultural politics, for example, amply exemplify these convoluted difficulties.[38]

The 'New Europe' and a 'Greater Europe'[39]

The 'New Europe' which has evolved since the Second World War was created in order to resolve a historic problem: the conflictual character of a continent divided by the Rhine corridor. In the relatively reduced circumstances of the postwar Europe, William Nicoll and Trevor Salmon (1990) have traced the idea of the 'New Europe' back to its sources, not least, for example, to Carlo Cattaneo (1801–69) and his idea of 'subsidiarity' as a means of reconciling conflicts of interest in which decentralization and federation are combined in a layered distribution of competence, responsibility and power. The career and writings of Cattaneo (1888–1977) provide essential commentary upon these processes of integration.

In the course of European integration the question of the *identity* of Europe has been until now a relatively peripheral issue. It is precisely the historic identities of Europe which have made the *pragmatic* transnationalism of the processes of European integration so important. The 'European Identity' document published in Copenhagen in 1973 (*The European Identity*, 1973) spoke of a definition of identity, but little was done. The Single European Act of 1985 refers to 'a European identity in external policy matters' (Article 36 (a)), and even this has proved extremely difficult to sustain, as the Maastricht Summit of 1991 and its painful aftermath continue to show. Although the ideas of Sully, Penn, Simon and Cattaneo 'have been transformed into living institutions and systems' (Nicoll and Salmon, 1990, p. 232), Nicoll and Salmon remark that 'the European destination is still unknown' (p. 229). Since 1989 the destabilization of this vision of gradual (if slow and painful) progress is now crisis-laden by the collapse of the Soviet Union. Yet at the heart of the European endeavour the word 'community' has not been excluded or abandoned. In the era of *glasnost* and *perestroika*, Mikhail Gorbachev wrote in 1987 of a new Europe constructed of 'enlightened' principles which was co-extensive with the papal 'greater Europe':

> Europe 'from the Atlantic to the Urals' is a cultural-historical entity united by the common heritage of the Renaissance and the Enlightenment, of the great philosophical and social teachings of the nineteenth and twentieth centuries. These are powerful magnets which help policy-makers in their search for ways to mutual understanding and cooperation at the level of interstate relations. A tremendous potential for a policy of peace and neighborliness is inherent in the European cultural heritage. Generally, in Europe the new, salutary outlook knows much more fertile ground than in any other region where the two regions come into contact.   (1987, p. 198)

The collapse of Communism has been attended by marked, but locally differentiated, changes in religious activity throughout the former socialist countries of eastern Europe and the former Soviet Union. The interpretation of these phenomena is, however, not a simple matter. Many kinds of religious and theological identity are now struggling for survival in a situation reminiscent in certain respects of that in defeated Germany after the First World War. Far from being the 'end of history', as Francis Fukuyama has argued, this new situation brings with it myriad renewals of national and ethnic identity, often with highly disruptive consequences which fall far short of the idealized vision of European identity ventured earlier by Mikhail Gorbachev.

The situation in the re-emergent Europe following the 1989–90 revolutions invites a range of theoretical explanations. But no one interpretative scheme would appear to suffice. The processes within the overall scheme of things might, for example, be theorized in terms of globalization and world system theory, international relations and European integration theory, social psychology and social identity theory, and so on. But we have argued that the construction of the 'idea' and the identity of Europe also involves the dynamics of religious and theological change and transmutations of chthonic myth grounded in problematic historical constructions and justifications.

We conclude that the only adequate methodology will be one which operates on the level of the *politics of representation* and takes account of the global and local factors we have outlined. This in turn may serve to enhance *cultural agency* and the just distribution of *cultural capital*, that is, to promote the *emancipation* of the human condition. It is only upon such a basis, which makes human freedom a central consideration, that the claims to inaugurate *theological* argument should be grounded.

Our analysis leads us to conclude that our concern should not be solely with political relations between states, nations and peoples, or indeed with such a problematic and dangerous conception as 'Europe', but with human relations as embedded in local and national cultures and with the 'cultures' and root paradigms of all human communities, which are rapidly becoming colours to be reworked on the palette of resurgent, transnational and globalized capitalism.

What, however, in more specific terms, does 'divinity' potentially have to offer? What is the positive dimension that religion and theology might add to the problem of European identity, construed, as we have attempted, as a major manifestation of the premodern, modern and postmodern problematic?

'Divinity' and Its Tasks

We have attempted to respond to the question: 'What, then, is "divinity"?' We have proceeded on the assumption that the traditional formulation of its remit and tasks needed to change, and to change for good reason. Through the presentation of a single, but interestingly complex, issue, that of the 'souls of Europe', we have explored the identities of a continent, showing how these originated in premodern traditions, which then entered into metanarrative conflict, with the onset of modernity. It would, however, be sociologically misleading to represent the *tertium quid* of a postmodern reconstitution of European identities in the religious field in the sloganistic terms of the detraditionalized circulation of narrative fragments. The reality is more complex.

In the parable of the Lord and Bondsman in Hegel's *Phenomenology of Mind*, we found a metaphorical and real representation of this conflict, and, moreover, a prefiguration of the possibility of an active *postmodern translation* (in effect an *Aufhebung*), that is, a passing beyond sterile opposition into the realm of *supercession* or *sublation*. The Scottish intellect and sensibility (with its instinctive lust for contradiction) is probably better equipped than the English mind (with its residual love of *via media*) to cope with this contingency. In the zone of the critically reflexive, *self-creating* self, the responsibility of *becoming* is grounded; in a trial by death, consciousness strives for full self-consciousness or accepts the negated status of *thinghood* (*Dingheit*). This is a universal dialectics which resists the totalizing appropriation of the possibilities and rewards of persecution by any one interest group, be it identified with ethnicity, gender, or sexual orientation.

We have argued that the *thesis* of ancestral Catholic Christian tradition (as well as Janus-faced Protestant Reformation) and the *antithesis* of secularizing modernity were uneasily reconciled in the progressivist accommodation of Liberal Protestantism. By contrast, in the realm of *postmodernity*, prefigured in Hegel's parable and in the idea of the 'Unhappy Consciousness', this consciousness is in a state of dialectical irresolution. It is

> itself the gazing of one self-consciousness into another, and itself is both, and the unity of both is also its own essence; but objectively and consciously it is not yet this essence itself – it is not yet the unity of both.
>
> (Hegel, 1910, p. 251)

Yet this irresolution affords the *possibility* of a creative life lived in the midst of antitheses. It is in the residual eschatology, in the *necessity* of living proleptically, at the juncture where pre-modern theological tradition, critical modernity and the ethical and religious demands of postmodernity coincide, that the remit of 'Divinity' is now to be located. Once more we now live *between the times* (*zwischen den Zeiten*); it is in *difference* that new life will emerge.

The contemporary task of 'Divinity' is both religious and theological. It is *religious* in the very traditional sense of *religio*, that is in a concern with the binding together of humankind on the level of the claim that ultimate cultural *universals* manifest themselves, paradoxically, in the *particularities* of the extraordinary diversity of socially-embedded cultural practices of religion. It is *theological* in that this ultimacy has frequently presupposed a transcendent reference point in relation to which *all* human activity is experienced as *relative*. 'Divinity' is also rhetorically committed to *Christian* theology as the distinctive tradition and a central metanarrative source of European, and indeed Scottish culture.

As William Storrar (1990) has shown in his study of Scottish Christian identity we might well reconstruct an argument parallel with that pursued in this essay for the metanarratives of contemporary Scotland.[40] In the latter, the suffering pathos and Europeanism of an Edwin Muir might be set over against the chthonic urges and Lenin-hymning modernism and 'greater Christ' of Hugh MacDiarmid, in a newly contextualised juxtaposition of Christ and Prometheus. Now, however, each culture must write the narrative of its own identity within the ambience of postmodernity. The theologian stands at the confluence of these streams, where he or she must strive to enunciate, symbolize and enact principles of human cohabitation in a pluralist and particularist environment.

Theology, understood as the uncritical advocacy and proclamation of a logocentric 'God' conceived apart from such a critical framework as we have outlined, might well involve what Ernst Bloch once called with regard to Karl Barth a *Herrschaftstheologie*, a theology of Lordship. Theology is difficult; it implies engagement with a purpose largely obscured in contemporary culture. It would be easy – indeed painless – to relinquish the task and substitute for it a variety of *technai*, technical skills and competences. Alternatively, overt postmodern theological strategies can look little different from regression and sophisticated fundamentalism.

In what the sociologist Stewart Clegg has called the 'multi-dimensional pleasure dome of postmodern society', the assumption of tradition as *privilege* by any denomination or religious grouping is to infringe the 'postmodern democratic freedom of the market' and to make a compact with obsolescence (1989, p. 275). This may be the militant obsolescence of fundamentalism or the planned obsolescence of a fatalistic adjustment, made without adequate self-interrogation to demographic decline of church membership. Either way, this involves a failure of active intergenerational transmission that paradoxically takes place in an era in which religions and religiosities are thriving.

Until, and unless, the increasingly marginal vested interests represented by the Christian Churches are prepared to enter, albeit self-critically, into the dialectics of the human community as we have presented them, then this decline may well prove terminal. There is, of course, always the possibility of that special form of continued existence as commodified 'heritage'. Even prison camps may survive in this form – or even be re-created – as theme parks. As in the former Eastern Europe, where obsolete industries face extinction, so, the dying spiritual monopolies of the West should hope for a planned transition, rather than a slow or rapid death. Yet, and this is crucial, in abandoning blatant hegemonies and in going through an experience analogous to 'market-testing', the Christian Church must re-learn – even re-create – whatever it might be that it has to offer.

This act of self-exposure is a learning process to be conducted in a spirit inspired by the President of my fatherland, Vaclav Havel, who wrote in 'The Power of the Powerless',

> The profound crisis of human identity brought on by living within a lie, a crisis which in turn makes such a life possible, certainly possesses a moral dimension as well; it appears, among other things, as a deep moral crisis in society. A person who has been seduced by the consumer value system, whose identity is dissolved in an amalgam of the accoutrements of mass civilization, and who has no roots in the order of being, no sense of responsibility for anything higher than his or her own personal survival, is a *demoralized* person. The system depends on this demoralization, depends it, is in fact a projection of it into society. (1987, p. 62)

It is not possible intelligently or authentically to distinguish oneself from something of which one has no knowledge. *Regaining roots in the order of being* is a moral task, yet it is also religious and theological. As the poet Friedrich Hölderlin put it: '*Wo die Gefahr ist, wächst das Rettende auch*' – Where danger is, there lies salvation.

Far from being an option for refugees fleeing from the core of life, the remit and task of *Divinity* involves a degree of self and contextual interrogation few can perhaps consistently sustain. Yet without risking – even on occasion passing through – death, full life is unattainable. The specific Christian hope in the resurrection of life should strengthen the resolve of those prepared, as Havel would have it, to exhibit a sense of responsibility for something higher than an individual's personal survival. It is at this very basic level that religion and theology should operate. It is here that the critical and facilitative remit and task of Divinity should be dedicated to the creation of the responsible autonomy of the theologian. We may also add that the training of so-called religious professionals entails immersion in the problematic depicted above.

Such relative autonomy may now be regarded by some as incompatible with the all-pervasive commodification of knowledge, and with the invasive power and the false ultimacy of an inadequately relativized and triumphalist capitalism, the veritable 'jealous God' of our age. But there can, in the final analysis, be no compromise. Anyone active in 'divinity' must daily face the following dilemma: in the light of the conflict at the core of my own personal and my own disciplinary existence do I choose to retreat into premodern tradition, or do I escape into the textual technology of a philological or historicist modernity? Or, alternatively, do I grasp the ethical and theological dialectics of the postmodern condition, and seek, as Vaclav Havel wrote from the prison cell, to *live in truth*?

Acknowledgement

I owe much to William Storrar and Jock Stein, who invited me to take part in a series of Carberry Conversations after the 1991 General Election, organized by the Mair Institute.

Notes

1 See R. H. Roberts (1995).

2 The logic of isolation confronted the present writer in the conclusion of his doctoral thesis on the theology of Karl Barth (R. H. Roberts, 1975). The subsequent collection of essays (R. H. Roberts, 1992b) summarizes these conclusions and juxtaposes them with a comprehensive study of the reception of Barth's thought in the Anglo-Saxon world together with a contextualization in the 'first postmodernity' of Weimar culture. The present chapter is thus part of an attempt to articulate and enact in outline form a positive theological methodology which is both theoretically informed and culturally entrenched.

3 From a Reformed theological standpoint, the German theologian Jürgen Moltmann provided an effective if now somewhat dated exposition of this dilemma. See Moltmann (1976), Introduction and ch. 1.

4 For an introduction to the growing literature, see Marty and Appleby (1991) and Riesebrodt (1990).

5 Thus, in purely hypothetical terms, if present demographic trends were to continue unchanged, the last members of the Church of Scotland would die out towards the end of the first quartile of the twenty-first century. The fate of Welsh chapel culture should not encourage complaceny. See Northcott (1992).

6 In this book and other works Dawkins proposes a consistent theory of culture in terms of genetic survival. This approach is strongly reminiscent of Ernst Haeckel's *Der Welträtsel*. Dawkins has recently staged a series of attacks upon the continued teaching of 'theology' in British universities.

7 See, for recent examples, Pam Lunn (1993) and the Neo-Pagan Monica Sjöö (1992).

8 The topical importance of Scotland in Europe consists not least in the continued, though much threatened, existence of wilderness, the close proximity of widely differing local cultures, an astonishing layering of languages, and a distinctive constitutional tradition. Scotland is a societal retort in which the assertion and transformations of cultural identity can be studied at first hand, thankfully without, as yet, the violent and disastrous characteristics manifested elsewhere in the United Kingdom. Scotland is thus exemplary in the European context: premodernity, modernity and postmodernity closely co-exist – and the sociopolitical dialectics of Lordship and Bondage are alive in the consciousness of the nation. There is a pervasive concern with cultural identity on the part of many Scottish intellectuals; this contrasts markedly with contemporary England where one might think that: *identity is to have no identity.* See McCrone (1992) and McCrone et al. (1989).

9   The most recent survey of the ground is to be found in Beyer (1993).

10 The contrasting receptions and resolutions of the Hegelian dialectic allow us primary insight into a profound problematic that has worked itself out in later nineteenth- and twentieth-century events. See R. H. Roberts (1988).

11 K. Hübner provides a wide-ranging account of theories of myth in Hübner (1985). See ch. 3, 'Zur Geschichte der Mythos-Deutung'.

12 The maiden Europa sleeps in her father's palace, dreams that two women are struggling over her, and awakes in great fear as the dream seems real. She plays with her friends in a meadow (and the poet recounts the story of the three golden baskets and the history of Zeus). Zeus sees the playing girls, transforms himself into a stag, and crosses the meadow, where the girls pass the time with him. Europa trustingly rides on Zeus's back, who rides away with her and swims over the sea to Crete. Europa laments and prays to Poseidon, 'Oh woe is me the deeply unhappy one, who has left the house of my father'; Zeus reveals who he is and prophecies her wedding. The poem concludes with the fulfilment of the words of the father of the gods: 'So he spoke, and what he spake, was fulfilled.' See *Literatur Lexikon* (1964), vol. II, columns 2513–14.

13 See Denys Hays (1968) and Steinbuchel (*c*.1953).

14 Ernst Troeltsch tackles this problematic comparatively in Troeltsch (1992a, b), where he reviews the periodizations offered by Hegel, Ranke, Guizot, Harnack, Weber and Sombart, amongst others.

15 For further reading relating to historical schematization, see Ozment (1990), Arend (1964), Wallace-Hadrill (1962) and Weidenfeld and Wessels (1981).

16 Here we follow the inspiration of Hayden White (1973) and his analysis of the rhetorical constitution of historical periodization as the commonplaces or *topoi* in a comprehensive analysis of nineteenth-century strategies of historical representation.

17 Pope John-Paul (1981), Apostolic letter 'Egregiae Virtutis', proclaiming the Apostles to the Slavs, SS Cyril and Methodius, co-patrons of Europe along with St Benedict; and Pope John-Paul II, Cyril and Methodius, 31 December 1980; 'Europe and the Faith', 11 October 1985.

18 This is an extremely complex set of events, with many disputed. See Dvornik (1948).

19 It is remarkable that given John-Paul II's expert acquaintance with phenomenology he rejects the construal of the European condition as 'crisis'. Thus Husserl (Karol Woytla's intellectual mentor) lectured in 7 and 10 May 1935 in Vienna under the original title of 'Philosophy in the Crisis of European Mankind'. Pope John-Paul's Letter of 1985 might perhaps be understood as a deliberate repudiation of Husserl's representation of the idea of Europe. See Husserl (1970, pp. 269–99).

20 See Mehl (1959), Pfeffer (1957), Roser (1979), Rendtorf (1977; 1980) and Walz (1955).

21 The pathos of the Reformation was well expressed in the words put into Cajetan's mouth by John Osborne in his play *Luther* (1961, p. 74): 'You know, a time will come when a man will no longer be able to say, "I speak

Latin and am a Christian" and go his way in peace. There will come frontiers, frontiers of all kinds – between men – and there'll be no end to them.'

22 See Troeltsch's celebrated article 'Historicism' in James Hastings (ed.) (1926).
23 Spengler extended his ideas in a second book, *Der Mensch und die Technik*. See Spengler (1931).
24 For general background see: Ansprenger (1989), Beacher et al. (1988), Beloff (1957), Jaspers (1947), Kennedy (1989), J. M. Roberts (1985), Rosenstock-Huessy (1931/1951) and Steiner (1971).
25 This distinction is developed in R. H. Roberts (1992b).
26 For a brief sociological account of this emergence in Britain, see R. H. Roberts (1992a).
27 The comment dates from December 1917.
28 Karl Löwith (1946) addresses related problems.
29 The allusion to the 'logic of space' interestingly prefigures a pervasive concern within current sociological theory with the figuration, control and allocation of space. See Harvey (1989).
30 Said's arguments have a particular relevance here. Spengler stresses the historical construction of identities and deconstructs local pretensions.
31 The quasi-theological undertones of Spengler's argument is apparent in his citation of Goethe's correspondence with Eckermann in footnote 1 of p. 49 of the English text of *The Decline of the West* (Spengler, 1926): 'I would not have one word changed in this: "The Godhead is effective in the living and not in the dead, in the becoming and the changing, not in the become and the set-fast; and therefore, similarly, the reason (*Vernunft*) is concerned only to strive towards the divine through the becoming and the living, and the understanding (*Verstand*) only to make us of the become and the set-fast".'
32 For background information, see Castles et al. (1984), Cecchini et al. (1988), Edwards (1988), Herrin (1987), Lehmann (1984), Watt (1972) and Wright (1982).
33 The literature is vast. See, for an introduction, Rubenstein and Roth (1987).
34 See Bauman (1989). The problematic consequences of the Enlightenment and its core role in Western thought is confronted in Horkheimer and Adorno (1972).
35 See Foucault (1970), ch. 3, 'Representing', and Foucault (1972), part IV, ch. I, 'Archeology and the History of Ideas'. Maxime Rodinson (1988) provides a complementary account of Western misconceptions of Islam.
36 It is significant that Francis Fukuyama entitles ch. 18 of *The End of History and the Last Man* (1992) 'Lordship and Bondage'.
37 It is important to recognize that 'secularization' is not to be understood solely as a loss of the religious and the sacred but as its complex transmigration and reconstitution.
38 See the anguished journalism of Tom Nairn (1992). For informed background information see Gallagher (1991), Harvie (1992), McCrone et al. (1989) and Northcott (1992).
39 See Aganbegyan (1988), Ash (1989; 1990), Dahrendorf (1990), Dawisha (1988), Gorbachev (1987), Lane (1990) and Ramet (1989).

References

Aganbegyan, Abel 1988: *The Challenge: The Economics of Perestroika*. London: Hutchinson.

Ansprenger, Franz 1989: *The Dissolution of the Colonial Empires*. London: Routledge.

Arend, Theodor 1964: *Christianity and World History*. London: Edinburgh House Press.

Ash, Timothy Garton 1989: *The Uses of Adversity*. Cambridge: Granta Books.

—— 1990: *We the People: The Revolution of 89*. Cambridge: Granta Books.

Bartlett, Robert 1993: *The Making of Europe: Conquest, Colonization and Cultural Change*. London: Penguin.

Bauman, Zygmunt 1989: *Modernity and the Holocaust*. Cambridge: Polity Press.

—— 1991: *Modernity and Ambivalence*. Cambridge: Polity Press.

Beacher, Jean, Hall, John and Mann, Michael 1988: *Europe and the Rise of Capitalism*. Oxford: Blackwell.

Beck, Ulrich 1992: *Risk Society: Towards a New Modernity*. London: Sage.

Beloff, Max 1957: *Europe and the Empires*. London: Chatto and Windus.

Bernal, Martin 1987 (1991): *Black Athena: The Afroasiatic Roots of Classical Civilization*, 2 vols. London: Free Association Press.

Beveridge, Craig and Turnbull, Ronald 1989: Scottish thought in the twentieth century. In Craig Beveridge and Ronald Turnbull (eds), *The Eclipse of Scottish Culture: Inferiorism and the Intellectuals*, Edinburgh: Polygon, pp. 91–111.

Beyer, Peter 1993: *Religion and Globalization*. London: Sage.

Castles, Stephen, Booth, Heather and Wallace, Tina 1984: *Here for Good: Western Europe's New Ethnic Minorities*. London: Pluto Press.

Cecchini, Paulo, et al. 1988: *The European Challenge*. New York: Wildwood House.

Chadwick, Owen 1975/1990: *The Secularization of the European Mind in the Nineteenth Century*. Cambridge: Cambridge University Press.

Clegg, Stewart 1989: *Frameworks of Power*. London: Sage.

Dahrendorf, Ralf 1990: *Reflections on the Revolution in Europe*. London: Chatto and Windus.

Dawisha, Karen 1988: *Eastern Europe, Gorbachev and Reform*. Cambridge: Cambridge University Press.

Dawkins, Richard 1989: *The Selfish Gene*. Oxford: Oxford University Press.

Dawson, Christopher 1932: *The Making of Europe: An Introduction to the History of European Unity*. London: Sheed and Ward.

—— 1948: *Religion and Culture*, Gifford Lectures. London: Sheed and Ward.

—— 1952: *Understanding Europe*. London: Sheed and Ward.

Dray, W. 1980: *Perspectives on History*. London: Routledge & Kegan Paul.

Dvornik, F. 1948: *The Photian Schism: History and Legends*. Cambridge: Cambridge University Press.

Edwards, John 1988: *The Jews in Christian Europe*. London: Longmans.

European Identity, The 1973: *Bulletin of the European Communities* 12 (14) (December): 118–22.

Foucault, Michel 1970: *The Order of Things: An Archeology of the Human Sciences*. London: Tavistock.

—— 1972: *The Archeology of Knowledge.* London: Tavistock.

Fukuyama, Francis 1992: *The End of History and the Last Man.* London: Heinemann.

Gallagher, Tom (ed.) 1991: *Nationalism in the Nineties.* Edinburgh: Polygon.

Giddens, Anthony 1991: *Modernity and Self-Identity: Self and Society in the Late Modern World.* Cambridge: Polity.

Gorbachev, Mikhail 1987: *Perestroika: New Thinking for Our Country and the World.* London: Collins.

Gramsci, Antonio 1971: *Selections from the Prison Notebooks of Antonio Gramsci,* ed. Quintin Howe and Geoffrey Nowell Smith. London: Lawrence and Wishart.

Harvey, David 1989: *The Condition of Postmodernity: An Inquiry into Cultural Change.* Oxford: Blackwell.

Harvie, Christopher 1992: *Cultural Weapons: Scotland and Survival in a New Europe.* Edinburgh: Polygon.

Hastings, James (ed.) 1926: *The Encyclopaedia of Religion and Ethics.* Edinburgh: T. & T. Clark.

Havel, Vaclav 1987: The power of the powerless. In Jan Vladislav (ed.), *Living in Truth,* London: Faber and Faber.

Hays, Denys 1968: *Europe: The Emergence of an Idea in History.* Edinburgh: Edinburgh University Press.

Hegel, G. W. F. 1910 (orig. 1807): *The Phenomenology of Mind,* trans. J. Baillie. London: Allen and Unwin.

Helps, A. (ed.) 1966: *Spengler Letters 1913–1936.* London: George Allen and Unwin.

Herrin, Judith 1987: *The Formation of Christendom.* Oxford: Basil Blackwell.

Horkheimer, Max and Adorno, T. W. 1972: The concept of Enlightenment. In *Dialectic of Enlightenment,* London, Allen Lane, pp. 3–80.

Hübner, K. 1985: *Die Wahrheit des Mythos.* Munich: C. H. Beck.

Hughes, H. S. 1952: *Oswald Spengler: A Critical Estimate.* New York: Schribner.

Husserl, Edmund 1970: *The Crisis of the European Sciences and Transcendental Phenomenology: An Introduction to Phenomenological Philosophy.* Evanston: Northwestern University Press.

Jaspers, Karl 1947: *Vom Europäischen Geist: Votrag gehalten bei den Rencontres Internationales de Genève, September 1946.* Munich: Piper Verlag.

John-Paul II, Pope 1981: Cyril and Methodius. In *The Pope Teaches,* London: CTS, vol. IV, nos. 1–3 (January–March), pp. 15–18.

—— 1985: Europe and the Faith, Address to the European Council of Bishops' Conferences, 11 October 1985. London: CTS.

Kees, Irmgard 1960: *Die europäische Christenheit in der heutigen säkularisierten Welt.* Nyborg: Knospel Verlag.

Kennedy, Paul 1989: *The Rise and Fall of the Great Powers.* London: Collins.

Lane, David 1990: *Soviet Society Under Perestroika.* London: Unwin Hyman.

Lehmann, A. G. 1984: *The European Heritage: An Outline of Western Culture.* London: Phaidon.

Literatur Lexikon 1964: Zurich: Kindler Verlag.

Lortz, Joseph (ed.) 1959: *Europa und das Christentum.* Wiesbaden: Steiner.

Lowith, Karl 1946: *Meaning in History.* Chicago: Chicago University Press.

Lunn, Pam 1993: Do women need the GODDESS? Some phenomenological and sociological reflections. *Journal of Feminist Theology,* 4 September: 17–38.

Lyotard, Jean-François 1979: *The Postmodern Condition: A Report on Knowledge*. Manchester: Manchester University Press.

McCrone, David 1992: *Understanding Scotland: The Sociology of a Stateless Nation*. London: Routledge.

McCrone, David, Kendrick, Stephen and Straw, Pat (eds) 1989: *The Making of Scotland: Nation, Culture and Social Change*. Edinburgh: Edinburgh University Press/British Sociological Association.

Marty, Martin E. and Appleby, R. Scott 1991: *Fundamentalism Observed*. Chicago: Chicago University Press.

Mehl, Roger 1959: *Das protestantische Europa*. Stuttgart: Fischer.

Moltmann, Jürgen 1976: *The Crucified God: The Cross of Christ as the Foundation and Criticism of Christian Theology*. London: SCM.

Nairn, Tom 1992: *Auld Enemies: Essays from the Nairn on Monday column in 'The Scotsman'*. Glasgow: Common Cause Declarations.

Nicoll, William and Salmon, Trevor 1990: *Understanding the European Communities*. London: Harvester Wheatsheaf.

Northcott, Michael 1992: *Identity and Decline in the Kirk*. Edinburgh: Centre for Theology and Public Issues.

Osborne, John 1974: *Luther*. London: Faber and Faber.

Ozment, Steven (ed.) 1990: *Culture and Belief in Europe, 1460–1600: An Anthology of Sources*. The Hague: Van Leeuwen.

Pfeffer, Karl-Heinz 1957: Der Protestantismus in Europa; Dokumente. *Zeitschrift für internationale Zusammenarbeit* 13: 171–4, 183–278.

Pirenne, Henri 1939: *Mohammed and Charlemagne*, trans. Bernard Miall. New York: W. W. Norton.

Ramet, Pedro (ed.) 1989: *Religion and Nationalism in Soviet and East European Politics*. Charleston, N.C.: Duke University Press.

Rendtorff, Trutz 1977: Universalität oder Kontextualität der Theologie. Eine 'europäische' Stellungnahme. *Zeitschrift für Theologie und Kirche*, vol. 74: 238–54.

—— (ed.) 1980: *Europa. Theologische Versuche einer Ortsbestimmung*. Gutersloh.

Riesebrodt, Martin 1990: *Fundamentalismus als patriarchalische Protestbewegung: Amerikanische Protestanten (1910–28) und iranische Schiiten (1961–79) im Vergleich*. Tübingen: J. C. B. Mohr.

Roberts, J. M. 1985: *The Triumph of the West*. London: BBC.

Roberts, Richard H. 1975: Eternity and time in the theology of Karl Barth: an essay in dogmatic and philosophical theology. PhD, Edinburgh.

—— 1988: The reception of Hegel's parable of Lord and Bondsman. *New Comparison: A Journal of Comparative and General Literary Studies*, vol. 5: 23–9.

—— 1992a: Religion and the 'Enterprise Culture': the British experience in the Thatcher Era (1979–1990). *Social Compass* 39 (1): 15–33.

—— 1992b: *A Theology on Its Way: Essays on Karl Barth*. Edinburgh: T. & T. Clark.

—— 1995: 'Globalized Religion? The Parliament of the World's Religions' (Chicago 1993) in theoretical perspective. *Journal of Contemporary Religion*, vol. 10: 121–37.

Rodinson, Maxime 1988: *Europe and the Mystique of Islam*. London: I. B. Taurus.

Rosenstock-Huessy, Eugen 1931/1951: *Die europäischen Revolutionen und der Charakter der Nationen.* Stuttgart: W. Kohlhammer Verlag.

Roser, Hans 1979: *Protestanten und Europa.* Munich: Claudius Verlag.

Rubenstein, Richard L. and Roth, John K. 1987: The silence of God: philosophical and religious reflection on the Holocaust. In Richard L. Rubenstein and John K. Roth (eds), *Approaches to Auschwitz: The Legacy of the Holocaust,* London, SPCK, pp. 290–336.

Ruether, Rosemary Radford 1974: *Faith and Fratricide: The Theological Roots of Anti-Semitism.* New York: Seabury Press.

Said, Edward 1978/1991: *Orientalism: Western Conceptions of the Orient.* Harmondsworth: Penguin.

Schwarz, Jürgen (ed.): *Katholische Kirche und Europa. Dokumente 1945–79.* Munich/Mainz: Kaiser Verlag.

Sjöö, Monica 1992: *New Age and Armageddon: The Goddess or the Gurus? Towards a Feminist Vision of the Future.* London: The Women's Press.

Spengler, Oswald 1926: *The Decline of the West: Form and Actuality,* trans. Charles Francis Atkinson. London: George Allen and Unwin.

—— 1931: *Man and Technics.* London: Murray.

Steinbuchel, Theodor *c.*1953: *Europa als Idee und geistige Verwirklichung.* Cologne: Unbekannt.

Steiner, George 1971: *In Bluebeard's Castle.* London: Faber and Faber.

Storrar, William 1990: *Scottish Identity: A Christian Vision.* Edinburgh: The Handsel Press.

Taylor, Ronald 1970: *The Romantic Tradition in Germany: An Anthology.* London: Methuen.

Troeltsch, Ernst 1912: *Protestantism and Progress: A Historical Study of the Relation of Protestantism to the Modern World.* London: Williams and Norgate.

—— 1922a: Das Problem einer objektiven Periodisierung. Part 3 of Über den Aufbau der europäischen Kulturgeschichte, ch. IV of *Historismus und seine Probleme,* vol. I, Tübingen: J. C. B. Mohr.

—— 1922b: Der Europäismus. Part 2 of Über den Aufbau der europäischen Kulturgeschichte, ch. IV of *Historismus und seine Probleme,* vol. I, Tübingen: J. C. B. Mohr.

—— 1926: History. In James Hastings (ed.), *Encyclopaedia of Religion and Ethics,* Edinburgh: T. & T. Clark.

Wallace-Hadrill, J. M. 1962: *Bede's Europe.* Jarrow: St Paul's Rectory.

Walz, Hans Hermann 1955: *Der politische Auftrag des Protestantismus in Europa.* Tübingen: J. C. B. Mohr.

Watt, W. Montgomery 1972: *The Influence of Islam on Medieval Europe.* Edinburgh: Edinburgh University Press.

Weidenfeld, Werner and Wessels, Wolfgang (eds) 1981f: *Die Identität Europas.* Bonn: Goldmann.

White, Hayden 1973: *Metahistory: The Historical Imagination in the Nineteenth Century.* Baltimore: Johns Hopkins University Press.

Wright, A. D. (ed.) 1982: *The Counter-Reformation: Catholic Europe and the Non-Christian World.* London: Weidenfeld and Nicolson.

CHAPTER ELEVEN

post-Christianity

Don Cupitt

Why are we beginning to use the term 'post-Christianity'? Because we are now settling down into our new postmodern condition, even taking it for granted as normality, and we are becoming aware that a rupture has occurred. History has 'ended', in the sense that we suddenly find that we no longer have any form of the old belief in progress or in linear eschatological time. That is, we are no longer gripped by any of the old stories about a better hereafter. Such stories used to fill us with hope. They justified present faith, present action, present disciplinary authority, and they helped to make tolerable, present hardships and incompletenesses. But now the stories – whether Catholic, Marxist or liberal – seem all to have lost their strength. They have evaporated, leaving the institutions that depended upon them in crisis.

Why? Because the sudden collapse of the idea of a better future has meant also the breakdown of the idea of a legitimating past. Tradition is dying, the past has lost its old authority, and the whole idea that some great social institution is divinely authorized to set up and maintain over us a coercive regime of dogmatic Truth for the sake of a promised Good Time coming seems absurd. Ten years ago people in the Vatican were saying that while Western Europe was indeed probably a write-off, there was every reason to hope that poverty, hardship and oppression would long continue to keep faith alive in the East and the South. Today that judgement seems to have been much too optimistic. In the shanty towns of Latin America they are simply not impressed by the claim that God has authorized the Pope to tell them they cannot use condoms to limit the spread of AIDS. One begins to see that the hierarchy, the power-structure, of historic ecclesiastical Christianity could decay almost as quickly as the Communist Party has done already, and considering the mood in which the last three incumbents seem to have ended, one begins to understand that the Pope himself, as a human being, is probably the chief victim of the deeply unhappy system over which he presides. It is not surprising that in all the Western Episcopal churches neo-Congregationalist mutterings are beginning to be heard: the age of Authority, of grand institutions, of legitimating myths and capital-T Truth, is over.

The common cliché is to say that in our highly reflective and communicative age we have demythologized ourselves into nihilism; but the world 'nihilism' has been overworked for a century and we should not feel the need to use it any longer. It would be better to say simply that we find ourselves no longer experiencing life in the present as suspended between Memory and Hope, between a founding past and a vindicating future. Our sense of history used to depend upon the tension – but not any more. We are no longer 'expectant', or ardently hopeful, in quite that way. There isn't going to be any face-to-face vision of the Truth: it is going to be only shadows in a glass darkly, for ever. There will never be a state of arrival, or rest; we shall be forever on the way, militant. The human condition will always be pretty much as it is now. We will never know anything much different from all this.

What has happened, then, is that certain deep old assumptions about historically-maintained identity, continuity and objective Truth have disappeared, and as a result our whole experience of temporality has completely changed. The present is now best pictured as what I have elsewhere called 'the fountain', an outpouring flux of energies-read-as-signs. It's going, but it's not going anywhere; it is going everywhere, and carrying us away with it. Everything scatters at the speed of light, at the speed of thought, so fast it can seem still. It is an outsideless and 'Empty' world of transient feelings and fashions, images and lifestyles. Everything, everything dances away into the void and is lost. It is a highly aestheticized designer-world, with its own brief intense pleasures, and many people can and do live contentedly within it the sort of life that Kierkegaard has described as 'aesthetic'. But it is a radically post-Christian world, and one in which philosophy, religion and ethics need all to be drastically rethought.

People are most reluctant to recognize how rapidly the culture is changing, but here is a simple example. Amongst Cambridge undergraduates in the mid-1950s well over 90 per cent professed belief in God and 55 per cent claimed to practise religion. The decline of these figures was slow at first, but now is proceeding very rapidly. In 1994 a poll reported that 34 per cent professed belief in God, and only 10 per cent claimed to practise religion.

Such figures are by no means untypical. Dozens of parallel examples could be quoted. They suggest that whereas until 30-odd years ago large numbers of people still felt they needed to pay at least lip-service to traditional institutions and their associated beliefs, the mood has since then changed very sharply. We used to be historicists who believed in continuous progress by the reform and rationalization of our received ideas and institutions, but now many or most of those same ideas and institutions have come to look cruel, unhappy and stupid. They don't merit saving. Until very recently it was a matter of great grief to me that the Church seemed unwilling and even unable to reform itself: but now

it seems that people in general have decided that there is not enough left
to salvage. Reform isn't worth trying for: let the dead bury their dead.
It wasn't I who decided that it is now too late, but the general public.

In which case it is time to describe something new, and I shall describe
a version of post-Christianity. Because orthodoxy, essences and authority are dead, it is irrelevant to suggest that what I will propose represents
too big a departure from tradition, or is somehow blameworthy because
it contravenes the *'regula fidei'* (the law of faith) that the hierarchy
defined long, long ago. It is precisely because all such objections have
become utterly meaningless that we now find ourselves impelled to
make a fresh start.

In brief summary, we here sketch a philosophy that may be called
energetic Spinozism, together with a *poetical theology* and a *solar ethics.*

The main theme of what follows will be that we need to reverse
our received worldview and assumptions. Since the time of Parmenides
and Plato, Western philosophy, ethics and religion have been dominated
by what Heidegger and Derrida have led us to call 'ontotheology' and
'the metaphysics of presence'. At the summit of the whole scheme of
things was put absolute Being, eternally self-subsistent, self-possessed, self-
present. In it were grounded the timeless standards of rationality and
moral value by which we should live, and it was the origin and end of
everything. Furthermore, it was thought that we may be able to attain
– perhaps at the end of time, or at the end of our own lives – a final
intellectual vision of this superior Reality, which would resolve all doubts.

This system of thought has been under attack for a little over three
centuries. Cudworth's *True Intellectual System of the Universe* (1678) was
perhaps the last full-scale attempted defence of an orthodox Christian–
Platonic metaphysics. G. W. Leibniz and the Wolffians were the last substantial school of old-style dogmatic metaphysicians. After the impact
of Kant and Hegel, Feuerbach proposed to demythologize philosophy.
In their different ways, both Nietzsche and Heidegger thought after the
end of the old order. But it was only in the 1960s that the young Derrida
finally dissolved away, undermined, deconstructed the whole project of
Western metaphysics more subtly and more thoroughly than any of
his predecessors: and in the same decade 'Big Bang' or Standard Model
cosmology became established in physics.

Here in the early 1960s images of scattering, broadcasting or dissemination are found linking together a variety of interesting cultural movements. Everything is depicted as diverging, rather than converging. The
cosmos comes to be seen as a slow-motion explosion of minute dancing
physical energies. The cultural world is seen analogously, as a dance of
signs, Derrida's 'dissémination' of linguistic meanings, flickering, revers-
ing and scattering. In the economy generally, the leadership shifts from

producers to consumers, and so to packaging, advertising, communication and mass media. The background against which everyone thinks ceases to be Tradition and becomes instead 'the Mediascape'.

Such is the context for our 'energetic Spinozism': it is a pyrotechnic worldview, a world of broadcast physical energies and cultural signs, pouring out. Spinoza's version of religious naturalism was organized around ideas of substance, rational necessity and eternity. For us, all that is gone. Our philosophy cannot claim to be any more than what the world itself is – a dance of metaphors, pouring out and passing away. We aim only to supply unifying metaphors that can help people to see what we are, what our life is, how we should live, and how we can be completely happy with things as they are.

The metaphors that currently stir us up and make us burn most ardently are those of the sun, fire, the fountain, the firework display and the slow-motion explosion. They work in something like Spinoza's fashion, by making us joyfully aware of our utter immersion in and unity with the whole flux of existence. We are cured of realism or, as the Buddhists call it, 'craving', by which I mean the desire for some fixed objective Reality to hold on to. We find ourselves able to disappear happily into the End-less process of the world. 'Solar' love is love that *gives out* – a very good phrase, that – without attachment. It lets go: it is easy going. It skips away into the void.

One other theme needs to be signalled in advance. In philosophy just now the text needs to be composed in such a way as to keep the right balance between the sense in which we make the world and the sense in which the world makes us. Actually, I need to affirm both, because there is a neat trade-off. Through us, the world is able to get itself fixed into symbolic representation; and by describing and familiarizing the world, we in turn are able to find in it our own objective redemption. As will be seen.

Energetic Spinozism

Anyone who thinks of trying to restart the project of systematic philosophy today faces doubts much more severe than those that troubled Descartes. There are grave doubts about language itself, doubts bad enough to give a philosopher writer's block. Worse than that, there is the way in which almost every large philosophical statement we may currently want to make seems to produce an effect of absurdity when applied to itself. Statements about universal transience, relativity, secondariness and so forth seem to be trying to claim *for themselves* some exemption from the general weakness that they attribute to everything else. In addition, of any systematic statement one always wants to ask, 'Does the system as we state it include itself within itself, so that it demonstrates within itself the fulfilment of the possibility-conditions for its own present statement of itself?' The fear is that we have all become so self-conscious about this question that systematic completeness and 'closure' are now unreachable.

To solve this sort of difficulty and get going, I have elsewhere suggested that we should copy the old judo trick of turning the opponent's own strength against him. We should use reflexivity to conquer reflexivity, making the very utterance aloud of our doctrine reflexively self-confirming. Being itself only a stream of language-formed events that pours out, scatters and passes away, a statement to the effect that that's all there is is self-confirming, and evades crippling doubts about the relation of language to reality by being itself an entirely typical sample of just what it says there is. With apologies for repeating myself, I quote the opening sections of a recent summary statement, with some revisions (1995a, pp. 117–20):

What is there?

1 (to be read aloud) There is at least *language*. Here we are in it; and in any case, the existence of language cannot coherently be denied, denial being itself a linguistic act. For there to be language, moving as these sentences now are in being produced and received, there must also be temporality and a discharge and scattering of energies.

2 There must be *temporality*, in the sense of unidirectional succession in the production, presentation and scanning of a chain of signs. (There need not necessarily be 'linear time' in any stronger sense, for time that just goes by without going anywhere may also be unidirectional.)

3 There must be *scattering energies*, because uttered language needs a material 'body' to ride upon or to modulate. Language is *broadcast*, or *published*.

4 There is at least, then, an outpouring and scattering stream of language-formed events. And we do best to picture the world at large as a *beginningless, endless and outsideless stream of language-formed events* that continually pours forth and passes away. The stream of events becomes real and determinate, or 'formed', in being read as language by us.

5 By being read, in one vocabulary or another (natural, mathematical, etc.), the elements of the world become experience, by being described they become public, or 'real'. Thus the real world is the public world, which is the-world-in-language, *our* world.

6 Our worst mistake is that of supposing the world of consciousness to be a private subworld within each person. No: the world of consciousness is simply the public world, the world that our language has fixed,

objectified, illuminated and made public. Our consciousness is simply our participation in this common world.

7   A chain of signs like this one can claim to be an epitome of everything in so far as (a) it states that the world itself consists of lots and lots more stuff like this; and (b) the signs it contains resonate with and evoke many, many other strands in the flux of world-events.

8   Thus philosophy must (a) represent the world as a many-stranded stream of events-read-as-signs; and (b) must work somewhat as poetry does, by employing highly condensed and evocative metaphors.

By getting ourselves into philosophy this way, we avoid another reflexive difficulty that has plagued the tradition. The texts of Augustine, and many others between Descartes and Edmund Husserl, set up the philosopher as a solitary subject, thinking alone. But as texts, written by one person and then published and subsequently read by many others, they are, of course, public objects. They fiction their own privacy, and in many cases make a *public* problem of it!

Happily, we can avoid such difficulties by precipitating philosophy immediately into the public world, which is the world of language, the illuminated world of our common life of symbolic exchange, and the only 'real' world. We are happy, I say, because suddenly we realize that we are liberated from the old mind–body problem. It does not arise. Our 'consciousness' is *out in front*, it's our field of view, it is simply our angle upon and our participation in the common life of this always-already-language-formed public world. Look at your present visual field (as I look out now over Parker's Piece) and say to yourself: 'There's nothing inside your head, stupid! It's all out in front! *All this* is what fills your thoughts: your "consciousness" equals simply the brightness of the public scene before you!'

The old notion that one is somehow more real when solitary should be abandoned. As a character in a play is realized just by, and during, a performance of the play, so we are realized as our selves just in playing our part in the life of the public world. Each of us who has an angle on the world appropriates a bit of the world, so that selves come to overlap. But this overlapping is not a threat or a bad thing: it is what makes the public world so clear and bright. I quote, again with apologies, a little more:

16 Everything is made of only one sort of stuff, namely the stream of language-formed events, and the very same bits of world-stuff may be taken up into various constructions – for example, into both your subjectivity and mine. Selfhoods overlap, it may be very considerably.

17   The happiness that comes when one realizes that one is completely immersed in and interwoven with the whole endless flux of things is *ecstatic immanence*.

18   As a living being, one is an organism composed of various organs or subsystems which have slightly different aims. (There is, for example, a potential discordance between the need to preserve one's own life and the need, at whatever cost, to pass on one's genes.) Thus there is – it seems, irremediably – some conflict of forces within the self, which shows up in every first-person account of things as the distinction between text and subtext, conscious and subconscious etc. This conflict is *ambivalence*. 'Mixed feelings'.

19   Ambivalence within the self is at least partly resolved and relieved by talking, by artistic expression and by theorizing the world.

20   The sign as such is a compromise-formation, and all our symbolic expressions are more unified and beautiful than we who have originated them.

21   As our productive and expressive life-activity is a continual *creation* of the world of experience, so too the happiness that comes when we see our conflicting aims and feelings resolved in the beauty of the world is *our objective redemption*, that is, our redemption achieved in and through our expression. Hence 'expressionism'.

22   When we see in the public world our own objective redemption, we see the world as being *ours* in the strongest sense; that is, we see in it the concrete universal human, reconciled and perfected. (This 'cosmic humanism' is possible because (a) it is we who make the world look the way it does to us; and (b) the world is made of just the same stuff as the self is made of.)

In German Idealism, Process philosophy, and similar movements, the Whole of which we are part and into which our life is taken up is often equated with God. Here, and on the contrary, it is seen as being symbolically Anthropos, the Cosmic Man, whether Buddha or Christ. If I can learn to see in the world about me 'the concrete universal human, reconciled and perfected', then I can learn to forget self and subjectivity, and instead through world-love find objective immortality and objective redemption.

Notice a further point: language may differentiate the world, but metaphor crosslinks the world's many strands, tying them together again. In the present thumbnail sketch, we began with a single brief burst of sound: 'There is at least language . . .'; and we ended with images of solar love and cosmic redemption. How? Metaphors cause resonance, activating and invoking more and more other strands in the flux, and metaphors also provide crosslinks and maintain harmony.

A metaphor of metaphor: rather as a sheaf of corn-stalks are woven into a corn-dolly, so metaphor gathers together strands from the out-pouring flux of the world and binds them into a human likeness.

Poetical Theology

In antiquity the earliest philosophers were highly critical of what they regarded as the irrationality and even the immorality of popular religion, myth and epic poetry. Did not Homer and Hesiod portray the gods as subject to base human passions and as getting up to all sorts of immoralities, thereby setting a very bad example to us human beings? Plato, as is well known, vehemently disapproved of such unedifying material (1961, *Republic*, Book II, 376–end, pp. 622–30) and thought the young should be protected from it. By contrast, Aristotle (1941, *Poetics*, Book IX, pp. 1463–5) is a little kinder to the poets, saying that whereas history deals with what has actually happened in all its contingency and unsatisfactoriness, poetry is more universal and therefore more philosophical than history. It depicts ideal persons and deeds (or at least, we gather, it can and should do so).

Plato's suspicions are nevertheless shared by many other Greek and Latin writers. Augustine (1972, Book VI, pp. 234–6) preserves a lengthy quotation from the lateish Roman writer M. Terentius Varro, in which Varro distinguishes three kinds of theology, or 'discourses about gods'. They are, first, *the poetical theology*, also called fabulous or mythical, which consists of the myths retold by the poets; the place where this theology is enacted is typically the theatre, and Varro censures it firmly. Secondly there is *the civil theology*, which is the official State cult established by the legislator and celebrated in the temples according to the Calendar of feasts. And thirdly, there is *the natural or philosophic theology*, which is the doctrine about divine things, taught by the philosophers in the schools.

The founder of natural or philosophical theology had been Plato, who of course had also maintained that the philosophers should be kings. In a well-run state, then, the elite would be taught the natural or philosophical theology which is the Truth, while the people would assist in the temples at the rites of the civil religion, prescribed for them by the legislator. As for the poetical theology, it would exist only on sufferance and under strict control.

This dim view of the poetical theology was maintained by most of the leading thinkers throughout antiquity. Augustine's main purpose is to argue that the civil theology is no better than the poetical: both of them need to be abolished, and replaced by the revealed theology of Christianity.

The modern rehabilitation of the poetical theology is a complex story, as yet largely untold. One would have to mention the names of Vico,

Hume, Eichhorn, Hamann and many others before seeing, in the staging of Richard Wagner's *Ring* at Bayreuth, the first really large-scale and ambitious modern attempt to re-establish the old poetical theology in its original institutional setting, the theatre. Nietzsche is perhaps the philosopher who more than any other has attempted to incorporate into his own literary style and philosophical thinking the qualities we call 'epic' and 'heroic'.

As for theology, there has recently been a certain return of the poetical theology in the thoroughgoing theological constructivism of Gordon Kaufman (1993), and in the writing of such scholars as the late Hans Frei (1974) and Robert Alter (1981) in praise of narrative theology. When we no longer take fright at the use of the word 'myth', why shouldn't we see the Bible, and indeed the whole system of Christian doctrine, as epic narrative poetry? Indeed, why shouldn't we see the theologian as a poet who retells our traditional sacred stories, very much as other writers such as T. H. White (1970) or Robert Nye (1978) retell the Arthuriad?

I suggest, then, that a switch from the dogmatic to the poetical theology is now going on, and for various reasons. One of them is the marked shortage of true dogmas. If we ask which of the whole range of religious doctrines are philosophically just *true*, the answer is that there are perhaps only two. One is the Buddhist 'no-self' doctrine, (*anatta*), according to which there is no core-self or spiritual substance in us, because the self is only a collection of natural capacities and phenomena. The other is the traditional Abrahamic monotheist's attack on idolatry, which says that human beings become enslaved if they pay divine honours to anything empirical. Yes, that really is correct.

It seems, then, that the only religious dogmas that are philosophically just true are ones that deny the truth of some other religious dogma or practice.

It seems an oddly low score: but perhaps the point is that the function of the dogmas of a religion is to be its *law*. The set of dogmas you accept shows which group you belong to: if you deny the crucifixion and resurrection of Jesus you are a Muslim (for example), and if you accept them you are a Christian. (This, by the way, is only a partial exception to the claim made in the previous paragraph.) To say that the Pope is infallible is not to make any metaphysical claim, but merely to point out that in the Roman Catholic system the Pope is the last court of appeal. What is at issue here is not philosophical truth but group loyalty, and the ways in which different groups have come to define themselves over against each other.

To see dogma as law in this way is, then, to see why so few religious dogmas are actually philosophically true. They don't need to be true. If your real purpose is to create badges of membership that will differentiate

your community from every other community, straightforward philosophical truth is quite useless, because it is too easy. Most of it is staring
every single human being in the face already. It is blindingly simple and
obvious. But what the religious group needs is esoteric truth hidden from
the rest of humankind and revealed to the chosen few only. So it must
deny the obvious, and instead postulate a state of affairs in which all of
humanity are stuck in sin and darkness, unable to save themselves. To
us, to us alone there has been granted a special revelation of saving
truth. It is colourful, paradoxical stuff, but in joining us and accepting
our discipline you'll come to believe it, and by that you'll prove that you
really are one of us.

And so on, and so on. To understand all this is to understand why
today there is such an upsurge of fundamentalist religion, often in alliance with enthno-nationalism. But it is also to see why dogmatic belief
is non-rational, why it is in rapid decline, and why we must urgently
remake our philosophical and religious thinking.

Dogmatic religion works by the 'logic of difference': it includes by
excluding, encourages hostility and (to an astonishing degree) inhibits
thought. It makes people unable any longer to see the obvious. It puts
a brake on thinking, Wittgenstein used to say. In any case, the power of
historic institutions to create and police dogmatic belief is happily now
in very steep decline (except, perhaps, in Islam). By contrast, consider
the great founding epics of the Hindus, of Greece, of the Jewish people,
of the Scandinavian peoples, of the Irish: a religion based on the telling and retelling of such stories can achieve an intellectual and moral
'magnificence' or spaciousness far beyond the reach of dogmatic religion.
The cheerful acknowledgement that our religion is only a human fiction
exalts human beings, by suggesting that we too might be able to tell
such stories, and live lives like *that*. Dogmatic religion seeks closure and
enclosure, whereas the poetical theology is wide open to endlessly-varied
reinterpretation and re-enactment.

Philosophically speaking, only negative dogmas are true. Philosophically, there is only the firework-display – the flux, and the metaphors by
which human beings through their 'cultures' have fictioned themselves,
their gods and their world out of the flux. But the sheer variety and
exoticism of the faiths we have invented so far might encourage us to
think that we may be able to do better in the future.

Too much of our philosophy has in the past exploited the idea that the
Truth is accessible only to a small elite of exceptionally gifted persons
(who speak and write, of course, in an obscure code); and too much of
our theology has exploited the idea that ordinary humans are benighted
sinners who need to be rescued from their plight by an elect group of
supernaturally-accredited religious professionals. It is time to leave all

such notions behind, and to accept the simple truths that Wittgenstein used to put so clearly: we find the answer to the supposed riddle of human existence when the question has evaporated. There is only the stream of language-formed events. It is outsideless. Nothing is hidden. Everything can be put into words. When everything lies open to view, there is nothing left to be explained.

Nietzsche, romantically nihilist, says that the last truth is that there is no truth. Wittgenstein goes one better and says that the last truth is that we don't need Truth, and should forget about it. All this is all there is, and there is no basis for complaint. We can be entirely uncomplaining about things just as they are.

So the function of the poetical theology is not to give us any esoteric information or to save us from anything, but simply to ennoble our life. We may therefore reinterpret Christian doctrine as being a sacred poetry of divine love, love that takes human form in Christ, love that is entirely content to burn, burn out and pass away. When we really have come to understand that this life and this world are co-extensive and completely outsideless – when we see that this world is wholly *our* world – then we may become capable of what I have called 'ecstatic immanence', and 'glory' (of which more soon).

We may also rewrite the Christian epic narrative. Hegel says that in the modern world the Christian God has descended from the Catholic heaven to enter a Protestant heart on earth. Like Kant before him, Hegel is beginning the move towards a kingdom-theology. Perhaps the modern secular world, increasingly emancipated from the constraints of religious law, represents not an abandonment but a fulfilment of religious faith? At any rate, I suggest that perhaps a story along those lines can be told and made convincing.

Solar Ethics

Solar ethics represents a sharp reaction against the longtermism that in one form or another has dominated our moral tradition. The chief source of our longtermism is no doubt Plato, who located the supreme Good in the world above, beyond time and the passions. Platonism's natural successors included the monasticism that was oriented towards the heavenly world beyond death, and the moral theology that judged all acts in terms of their effect upon one's prospects of gaining final salvation. As for the realization of the good within history, Christianity even more than the other Abrahamic traditions originally looked forward ardently to an imminent arrival of the Kingdom of God on earth, but then found that the End was being postponed further and further into the future. Eventually it was admitted by Kant to be infinitely far away, being an ideal limit of ethical striving and 'not immanently realizable'.

Dissatisfied with this, Karl Marx insisted that on the contrary, the highest good, the communist society, certainly *was* 'immanently realizable'. Laws of historical development guaranteed its coming. But when the Communist Party came at last to power it soon found itself caught up in the same old business of deferral, postponing the historical realization of its hopes until, sadly, it lost faith in itself.

In retrospect, these cosmic and historicist forms of longtermism seem all to have made the same disastrous error. Starting from an assumption of our present profound alienation from the good, they made the Good World too 'other', and too remote. We end up too helpless, too dependent upon various promises to the effect that sundry unseen powers and forces are working in a hidden way to bring the Good World closer to us. Longtermism leads in the end to reliance upon authority, and to pessimism.

Today, we are all of us no doubt more directly influenced by secularized forms of longtermism: I mean the 'instrumental rationality' of the planner, the investor and the technologist who calculate carefully the long-term benefits and costs of different courses of action. They compete directly and explicitly with the other religious and philosophical ways of taking thought for the future.

For example: according to the Sanskrit biographies, the Buddha, when a young man out driving his chariot, was awakened to serious thought by seeing successively a very old man, a very sick man, and a corpse being carried to the funeral pyre. The Buddha decided upon reflection that our problem is that the self feels itself dreadfully threatened by 'ageing, sickness, death, and sorrow', and he changed his life – not, be it noted, in order to escape these things, but rather to escape from the self that fears them.

Today, our reaction is quite different. We all of us have insurance cover to protect ourselves against the threat of being caught unprepared by illness, old age and death. 'Peace of mind', say the advertisements. 'But surely I will nevertheless still grow old, grow sick and die; so where's the protection?' 'Well, your dependants will be protected.' 'But surely they too face exactly the same prospects? Won't they also succumb to illness, old age and death?' 'Ah, yes: you remind me that they need cover, too. I must sell it to them.' So our modern instrumental rationality sets out to make philosophy and religion redundant, deflecting our existential fears sideways into a network of financial provisions that are claimed to assuage our 'sorrow' at the brevity and uncertainty of life.

Fine: we are 'covered' in one sense, but in another sense we remain perfectly well aware that no genuine protection has been given. Indeed, the insurance industry can only work by setting out to exacerbate the very time-dread that it also promises to allay. The result, inevitably, is the extreme anxiety about the passage of time and the loss of youth that marks the most admired and privileged people in the most advanced societies. Film actors, for example.

Solar ethics seeks a radical cure, bringing death forward into life, and thereby making the Good immediately accessible. The sun symbolizes the religious ideal of a full synthesis of death and life, because the thermonuclear burning which is the sun's living is also and identically its dying. The sun's very existence is a unity of vitality and mortality. It burns and burns out; it expends itself gloriously; it lives not by thriftily saving itself but by recklessly giving itself away.

Those who thus die all the time have no fear of death. But it must be emphasized here that solar ethics is not existentialism. Both the Christian Kierkegaard and the atheist Sartre were ethical individualists, for whom the self affirmed and realized itself in its moment-by-moment ethical choice of itself, whether 'before God', or not. Solar, or 'expressionist' ethics is almost the opposite of that: it is that we so relate ourselves to life that we forget and lose ourselves. We find happiness by plunging ourselves into and identifying ourselves with the outpouring flux of existence – of which we are indeed just parts – so that we are lost in life, burning, rapt. Such is 'ecstatic immanence', a joyful dying into life.

We see here that people are quite right to appreciate watching performers perform as circus artists, as musicians, as dancers and so on. To see someone unselfconsciously engrossed in doing something difficult very well is to see a kind of acted parable of how we should live; and if the performer is also a highwire walker, climber, racing driver or bullfighter dicing with death, then so much the better. Again, here is something that can only be done really well if one is so engrossed in doing it that selfconsciousness, anxiety, pain, death and the future have all disappeared. I use the term 'glory' for this state of absorption, in which one is so given to life and in such perfect co-incidence with the 'hour' that evil has disappeared.

The comparison between a particular technical skill and the skill of living is familiar in Plato: but somehow he does not develop it along the lines one might wish for. Instead he becomes preoccupied with the longtermist ideas of living an examined life, and of philosophy as a preparation for death. We have argued, against this, that ethical longtermism leads in the end to scepticism, pessimism and high anxiety.

A better guide than Plato is Nietzsche, who in *The Anti-Christ* (1986, §§ 33–5, 39ff, pp. 145–8, 151ff.) sees Jesus as the teacher of a solar ethic, and his death as a solar death. 'A new way of living, *not* a new belief ... *evangelic practice alone* leads to God, it *is* God!' (1968, § 33, p. 146). That is correct, and if one sets aside the unfortunate influence of Dostoyevsky's *The Idiot* (1955) then Nietzsche's account of Jesus's message is close to what we call 'ecstatic immanence'. A noteworthy corollary of it is that we solar believers venerate a Jesus who went freely into death and stays dead, and *not* a Jesus who came back from the dead and now underwrites a self-serving, self-saving piety.

We now come to the perennial question, 'Why should I be moral? How are moral obligation and moral values to be explained and justified?' I have argued that the world is an outsideless and continuously outpouring stream of language-formed events. We can no longer look for moral justification either to a legitimating past, or to a perfect world Above, or to a promised vindication in the future. Everything therefore returns into the outpouring present.

But, you may say, in the present we can no more find a basis for morality than we can find a basis for the flux of existence. So how *is* morality to be justified?

I answer that the best way to 'justify morality' is to give up the whole way of thinking that needs to look for some extrinsic justification of morality. We cannot any longer look back, look up, or look forward. Instead, we learn solar living, affirming life's value just by the way we plunge into it.

There is, one might say, a starting point for moral discourse in the pleasure we take just in experience – still more, in experience *articulated, and so shared*. Experience gives us a world already language-formed, and therefore already valued, bright, *common*. We are always world-building, always (at least implicitly) with others, and always valuing. We are always already conscious, already ethically-productive, and already with others, and in the public realm. It is simply a mistake to imagine oneself sitting mournfully alone in a world without value, and wondering how the absent good is to be found and brought into this world. From a solar point of view, there is and can be nowhere else for the good to be but already here and waiting to be affirmed.

Have I made clear why it is that we are always already with others? Remember, the world is an outpouring stream of language-formed events. That is, it is never *the* world, in a realistic or mind-independent sense, because it is always already and only *our* world, that is, a world already formed by our language; and that is, again and in turn, a world that is already the product of human con-sent, co-feeling, and con-spiring, co-knowing. Look around the room, look out of the window: you may just at present be alone in the room, but the world you see is nevertheless already a public world, made conscious and bright by language. So I still insist that though I am alone as I write this, and you perhaps are alone as you read it, we both of us are already in the common world and with others.

So much for the sketch of a 'post-Christianity' that I undertook to give. Much, or most of it, is spelt out in more detail in other places, such as the recent books *After All* (1994), *The Last Philosophy* (1995a) and *Solar Ethics* (1995b). It should be clear that, on my own premises, it does not matter in the least whether in the end it is described as a mutation of Christianity, or as a new religion that may succeed Christianity. The political battle for the high ground, for the right to trade under a certain name, for legitimacy – all that should mean nothing to us any longer. But we ought to be very concerned about how human beings are going to make themselves and their world in the future.

References

Alter, R. 1981: *The Art of the Biblical Narrative*. New York: Basic Books.

Aristotle, 1941: *The Basic Works of Aristotle*, ed. R. McKeon. New York: Random House.

Augustine, 1972: *The City of God*, ed. H. Bettenson. Harmondsworth: Penguin.

Cudworth, R. 1678: *True Intellectual System of the Universe*. London: R. Royston.

Cupitt, D. 1994: *After All: Religion without Alienation*. London: SCM.

—— 1995a: *The Last Philosophy*. London: SCM.

—— 1995b: *Solar Ethics*. London: SCM.

Dostoyevsky, F. 1955: *The Idiot*, trans. D. Magarshack. Harmondsworth: Penguin.

Frei, H. 1974: *The Eclipse of the Biblical Narrative*. New Haven: Yale University Press.

Kaufman, G. 1993: *In the Face of Mystery: A Constructive Theology*. Cambridge, Mass.: Harvard University Press.

Nietzsche, F. 1968: *Twilight of the Idols and The Anti-Christ*, trans. R. J. Hollingdale. Harmondsworth: Penguin.

Nye, R. 1978: *Merlin*. London: Hamilton.

Plato, 1961: *The Collected Dialogues of Plato*, ed. E. Hamilton and H. Cairns. Princeton: Princeton University Press.

White, T. H. 1970: *The Once and Future King*. London: Collins.

CHAPTER TWELVE

kenosis and naming: beyond analogy and towards *allegoria amoris*

Graham Ward

At the end of modernity the doctrine of kenosis is having a revival both theologically and philosophically. Theologically, it is at the centre of two rather different forms of postmodern theology. For a number of American theologians developing their a/theologies out of the death-of-God school and in the wake of certain postmodern nihilistic philosophies, kenosis is a radical reading of Hegel's notion of negativity. The figure of Christ being poured out even onto death, rather than the myth of the sent-one who returns to the Father, is used as a metaphor for the absence of God in the contemporary world. Through the historical development of Christianity as a religion, Christ has increasingly come to be identified with the world to the point where the transcendent God is eclipsed and the particularism of Christianity also. Only the processes of the immanent remain. For Thomas J. J. Altizer (1967, pp. 55–75) these processes are identified with the movement of history, for Mark C. Taylor (1984, pp. 19–33, 97–120) they are identified with the endless circulations of significance and desire in intratextual reality.

Distinct from these discussions and uses of kenosis teaching, distinct also from the theological liberalism which although radicalized still pertains to the projects of these American postmodern theologians, is the work of a number of French, conservative Catholic theologians. For Jean-Luc Marion (1991), returning to the work of the early Church Fathers and developing the thinking of Hans Urs von Balthasar (1993), kenosis is linked to the Word becoming flesh, the gift of God's presence, in Jesus Christ and in the eucharist. The kenotic economy is inseparable from a trinitarian 'philanthropy' as it operates for the salvation of the world

and is evidenced in the incarnation, cross and resurrection (Marion, 1991, p. 178). Jean-Yves Lacoste relates kenosis to his thesis concerning *anthropologia crucis*, that is, an experience of dispossession (and transcendence) fundamental to the condition of being human which liturgy expresses, performs and orientates towards the divine. Kenosis is, then, an ecclesial concern, since *'Il est les liturgies habilité dans le monde à faire face à Dieu'* (Lacoste, 1994, p. 223). It has a Christological focus in the Passion, which is an image of the humiliated humanity of God Himself, but the experiential roots of kenosis lie in the human beings having been made in the image of God Himself. *'Le désir de l'eschaton (l"inquiétude")*
est inscrit en l'homme . . . et ce désir peut être apaisé par anticipation dans les
limites de l'être-dans-le-monde' (Lacoste, p. 231). Lacoste concludes his thesis by emphasizing that human beings will only come into the true sense of who they are when they accept existing in the image of God, that is, when they accept existing kenotically (p. 233).

Distinct from and yet nevertheless appertaining to these theological rereadings of kenosis is the philosophical use of the metaphor of 'pouring oneself out' towards the other, which is evident in the work of Emmanuel Levinas (1981), the later work of Jacques Derrida (1992; 1995) and the work of three French feminists, Luce Irigaray (1993), Julia Kristeva (1989) and Hélène Cixous (1991). For these poststructural thinkers, kenosis issues form an ethics and metaphysics of difference traced in writing itself. In 'Sauf le nom (post scriptum)', a recent essay by Derrida on writing, deconstruction and the negative theology of Angelus Silesius, negative theology itself is described as the *'Kenosis* of discourse' (1995, p. 50). He speaks of the passion in negative theology to locate a place, 'Over there, toward the name, toward the beyond of the name *in* the name' (1995, p. 59). In so far as negative theology comments constantly on its impossibility, performing endlessly a desertification of 'God' and 'being', acting as a critique of its own reference and plenitude of meaning, it is a wounded writing. Kenosis *is* language in crisis. Language which performs this crisis opens a space, a crack, an aporia within which a love can circulate which maintains the alterity of the other because it installs 'a movement or moment of deprivation, an asceticism or provisional kenosis' (Derrida, 1995, p. 74).

For Hélène Cixous this kenosis is not simply in and of language, it is in and of the reception of language (it pertains, that is, to the operation of reading as well as the operation of writing). For Cixous, kenosis describes the ex-propriation of the reading subject in relation to the text. Reading is an act of submission. She herself reflects upon the ethical and metaphysical implications of reading whilst examining her responses to the Brazilian writer Clarice Lispector. Through reading and writing there is a transfiguration of the self as a proper distance emerges in which the other voice, the other imaginary is confronted and respected. The discipline and ascesis of moving towards this proper distance is 'a relentless process of de-selfing, de-egoization' which acknowledges and respects the 'enigma', the 'mystery', the 'inexplicable' and the 'unavowable' (Cixous, 1991, p. 156). 'It's at the end, at the moment one has attained the period of relinquishing, of adoration . . . that miracles happen' (Cixous, 1991, p. 117).[1] We will come to the work of Levinas and Kristeva later.

In the wake of this current interest in the doctrine of kenosis a question emerges concerning the relationship between the kenotic economy (as described by the theologians) and the process of naming and reading (as set out by these benign poststructural philosophers).[2] The question, it seems to me, is pivotal for understanding the nature and operation of theological discourse itself, or the theology of doing theology, if you like. For theology is a form of discourse. That is, a specific use of language concerned with a specific field of inquiry composed of acknowledged criteria. With regard to the discourse of theology this essay wishes to raise three questions. What is theological discourse about? Whose discourse is it? And, where does it take place? To each of these questions anyone might simply reply: theology is about God, it is our discourse and it takes place in university faculties, seminaries or church-based activities such as sermons and bible-studies. Any deeper examination would subsequently have to investigate: first, a doctrine of God to probe what theology is about; secondly, a doctrine of revelation and analogy to probe the relationship between our words and the nature of the Godhead; and finally, a sociology of religion to evaluate the political and economic contexts within which this discourse is pursued, legitimated and given its particular colouring. But on the basis of the recent theological and philosophical treatments of kenosis, this essay will suggest a different approach to answering those questions, a theological approach which announces a *theological realism*. To date, the realism of theological discourse (in what manner and to what extent our words give us true knowledge of God) has issued from and referred to doctrines of analogy or, more recently, the nature of metaphor. This essay will conclude by arguing for a realism of theological discourse founded upon the notion of *allegoria amoris* – a kenotic discourse of love whose *dunamis* is the co-operation of an intra-Trinitarian and an anthropological eros, and whose domain is creation itself.

From an Exegesis of the Word

According to the *carmen Christi* of Philippians 2:5–11, the *locus classicus* for Christian teaching on kenosis, it is the incarnation, the Word becoming flesh, which allows us to trace the association between kenosis and naming, the event of God's love and the taking of form:

Have this mind among yourselves, which is yours in Christ Jesus, who, though he was in the form of God, did not count equality with God a thing to be grasped, but emptied himself, taking the form of a servant, being born like other human beings. And being recognised as a man, he humbled himself and became obedient to the point of death, even death on a cross. Therefore God has highly exalted him and graciously bestowed on him the name which is above every name, that at the name of Jesus every knee should bow, in heaven and on earth and under the earth, and every tongue confess that Jesus Christ is Lord, to the glory of God the Father.

In the mid-nineteenth century it was upon the basis of this song that Gottfried Thomasius constructed his kenotic Christology, in which he rendered a theological account of the descent of Christ from the Father.[3] In the descent, Christ empties Himself, makes Himself void. The verb *'kenóo'* is related to the noun *'kenos'* meaning 'vain', 'devoid of truth' or 'without a gift'. The central question of the doctrine for Thomasius (like Luther before him) concerned what exactly it was that Christ emptied Himself of; what gifts or charisms were left behind? Theologians from Thomasius to Barth to von Balthasar have offered answers to the question. For Thomasius (as for Luther) what was abandoned was Christ's divine attributes of omniscience and omnipotence. His incarnate life as the Divine Person is thus revealed, and solely revealed, through a human consciousness. With the doctrine of kenosis, then, we investigate exactly what it is to be incarnate. Put systematically, Christology grounds a theological anthropology, and a theological account of what we know of God and how we know it. As John Macquarrie has recently observed, the importance of the teaching lies in its insistence upon the material, the historical and the embodied. It offers a 'safeguard against those docetic tendencies which seem to have dogged the classical christology through the centuries' (Macquarrie, 1990, p. 245). With this teaching we are concerned with the relationship between the Logos and its mediation.

Kenosis is, then, a doctrine of divine representation. But as the account of the act of divine representation it calls into question the nature and status (ontological and epistemological) of human representations before and following the incarnation. Furthermore, if Christology grounds a theological anthropology, the God who becomes form grounds the human capacity to make forms. Being *Homo symbolicus* is integral to being made 'in the image of God'. It is therefore significant that the *carmen Christi* of Paul's letter reveals a concern with representations and consciousness, human and divine. 'Be mindful', verse 5 exhorts, and *'phroneo'* is intellectual understanding and the ability to think. The verse enjoins that we have the same consciousness as Christ. Verses 6 and 7 delineate that consciousness in terms of a certain morphology and a certain action. He existed in the form of God (*en morphé theou*) but in the emptying Christ became the form of a slave (*morphén doulou*). I will return to these phrases shortly. In this morphology, though he was equal to God he did not reckon (*hégésato*), think or consider that as something to be used for his advantage.[4] In this morphology he took on the likeness (*homoiómati*) of human beings and was found in human form (*schémati*). In verse 7, the 'taking form' and the 'becoming like' are both modalities of the main verb *kenóo*. Christ's kenosis is his incarnation (and death)[5] – that is the point. Christ's kenosis is not the abandonment of his divine attributes (as those nineteenth-century kenoticists would have it). We will return to this later. The result of kenosis is that God gives him 'the name above all names (*to onoma to uper pan onoma*)'; a name before which all others will bow and each tongue confess (*exomologésétai* – speak out publicly) the Lordship of Christ. Again, humiliation or submission (not Christ's this time, but ours) leads directly to acts of representation, to speaking out publicly.

One of the main shifts within the hymn is from the language of form (*morphé and schéma*) to the act of naming. The act of naming is a form of revelation – for the name revealed is God's own name, Lord. Furthermore, its concern with representation and human consciousness is worked out in terms of a poetic performance. Since Ernst Lohmeyer's study of the hymn in the 1920s, these lines have been understood to constitute a poetic unit composed with ellipsis, 'rhythm, parallelism, and strophic arrangement' (O'Brien, 1991, p. 198).[6] In other words, it is representation, a poetic enactment reflecting upon three forms of representation – the divine representation of God in Christ, the exemplary nature of Christ's self-giving for the Philippians (see 2:1–4), and the act of naming. The hymn is characterized by a self-reflexive meditation upon theological, ethical and linguistic imitation – salvation, the appropriate behaviour of those being saved, and language.

Morphé is an unusual word in the New Testament – it appears only once more in the longer ending of Mark's Gospel (16:12). According to Lightfoot it 'implies not the external accidents but the essential attributes' (Lightfoot, 1894, p. 108). Much has been written concerning the dative *en* and several commentators have stressed its importance for the interpretation of the whole passage (Martin, 1967, p. 99; O'Brien, 1991, p. 206). *En morphé theou* – the Godhead as a sphere within which Christ dwells – would then be the equivalent of the Johannine 'that glory I had with you before the world began' (17:5). The *en* as such would then suggest Trinitarian participation by the Son in the Father. Following Lightfoot, a host of more recent scholars have confirmed this reading by pointing out the affinity between *morphé* and *eikon*, where *eikon* suggests not a distinction between form and substance, but a participation of one in the other. Furthermore, *eikon* is associated both in the Septuagint and elsewhere in the New Testament with the glory of God, His *doxa*.[7] In the kenosis this participation is poured out and Christ clothes himself (*lambano*) in the essential attributes, *morphé*, of slavery.

Note the connection here between slavery and glory in the Godhead – both are icons of Trinitarian procession. As F. F. Bruce put it, challenging nineteenth-century kenotic Christologies which saw in Christ as servant the abandonment of his divine properties in the form of God: 'The implication is not that Christ, by becoming incarnate, *exchanged* the form of God for the form of a slave, but that he *manifested* the form of God in the form of a slave' (Bruce, 1980–1, p. 270). As this icon of slavery he was born in the likeness (*homoiómati*) of humankind. *Homoiómati* is an ambivalent word in the New Testament (and in the history of Christology). Battles have been fought over how to translate it. Lightfoot again points the way: 'Thus *homoióma* stands midway between *morphé* and *schéma*' (Lightfoot, 1894, p. 110). *Schéma* denotes the outward appearance, the accidents, in the Aristotelean sense, of human nature. But these appearances are not manifestations of the substance, they are more signifiers distinct from but detailing the signified substance. *Homoióma* operates at the threshold between the essential manifestation of the form, the icon, and the external appearances. The first, *morphé* is identical with the original, its ontological extension. The second, *schéma*, is an image or resemblance which is emphasized by the comparative *hos* – he was found *hos anthropos*, bearing all the hallmarks of a human being. A note of separation from the essence, the original, is evident.

But *homoiómata* can suggest both full identity with and difference from. R. P. Martin, in his extended analysis of the *carmen Christi* in Paul's letter, concludes: 'The sharp alternatives are: its meaning as "identity" or "equivalence" and its meaning as "similarity" or "resemblance"' (Martin, 1967, p. 200). The dative here, *en homoiómati*, is a dative of both respect ('with respect to being human') and participation ('entering into the condition of being human'). The move from *morphé*, through *homoióma* to *schémati* expresses a deepening progression towards externality, secondariness and appearance – towards a human externality which manifests the essential nature of being a slave. There is a descent from a logic of identity into a world of shifting appearances, and, with verse 9 of Paul's letter, there is a return to the logic of identity. The Father crowns the Son with His name; a name they share, Lord, Yahweh. In this presentation of kenosis, then, an economy of representation is outlined – form, analogy and figuration give way to the stability of denomination and identity, the name above all names. The return to the Father is a return to the 'form of God' from which he descended – the glory of self-identification within Trinitarian difference. This economy of representation is framed within a rhythm of exchange – acts of giving and receiving by both God and Christ. We will return to this later.

There remain, though, two important aporia in this process. The first, we have drawn attention to – the ambivalent and yet pivotal word *homoiómata*, where presence becomes representation for what is absent. For at what point in the word 'likeness' does identity shift towards resemblance? The second aporia also involves an absenting, a cancelling of presence. For the doctrine of kenosis makes inseparable from the incarnation the descent into death. The ultimate descent into non-being is part of, though not the end of, the kenotic trajectory. Dispossession lies at the centre of incarnation. This is important for understanding the nature of *Homo symbolicus*, the one 'made in the image of' who subsequently makes images or resemblances. It is important because in so far as Christ's humanity is true humanity, the kenosis of incarnation defines the human condition as crucified, as constantly abiding in a state of dispossession and resemblances. We descend, in the hymn, from true presence in God, into the symbolics of being human, into textuality. From textuality we move out again into the silent margin of death, which erases both our humanity and our representations. Crucifixion presents a moment when the sacramental is eclipsed.

Not that crucifixion, absence and autism is the end of the kenotic story. There is resurrection, a renaming and a re-empowerment to speak. We pass, with Christ, through the textuality of the cosmos from one margin of transcendence to another; we move towards and then beyond death. In the middle, in the textuality of the cosmos, is the incarnation–crucifixion–resurrection of the form. Of course, the other way of seeing this would be to say that the textuality of the cosmos is the single aporia transgressed by the Trinity which frames it. We exist, then, in the aporia created by God in the initial *diastasis* that opens with creation itself (von Balthasar, 1993, pp. 156, 173–5). Only *post-mortem* are we re-empowered to speak. Only *post-mortem* is identification possible (von Balthasar, 1989, p. 84). We find the same sentiment expressed in the Book of Revelation, in the letter to the angel of the church at Pergamum: 'To him who conquers . . . I will give a white stone, with a new name written on the stone which no one knows except him who receives it' (Rev. 2:17). *Post-mortem* one is given the personhood one always knows is possible; *ante-mortem* is a process of becoming through obedience, humility and descent. *Ante-mortem* is time for realizing our dispossession, our secondariness; realizing what Emmanuel Levinas describes as our position as accusative in a transcendental grammar. The dispossession is integral to the fact we are 'in the image of' and image makers. It is an expression of that initial *diastasis* separating the uncreated creator from the created creation. The *ante-mortem* realization of our 'dependence though', and the secondariness of our representations, is lived within the horizon of *postem-mortem* hopes. The economy of our representations and self-representation is, theologically, inseparable from our eschatological participation in the Godhead. In the words of von Balthasar: 'Only in death, through divine judgement, does a man receive his definitive orientation' (von Balthasar, 1990, p. 13).

Towards a Theological Account

As suggested, this account of the doctrine of kenosis goes against those nineteenth-century theologians like Thomasius (1845; 1853) and Gore (1890). For Thomasius, what Christ 'poured out' was certain properties of His divine nature, two in particular: omnipotence and omniscience. Thomasius was influenced here by Protestant neo-scholastic discussions of the *communicatio idiomatum* and, ultimately, an Aristotelean approach to theological analysis. God is an object and every object has certain specifying properties.[8] He was influenced too by the idea of God as absolute subject, and a theology of consciousness that arose with Schleiermacher and Hegel as part of a Romantic and Cartesian concept of personhood. Such an account can be found in that *locus classicus* of British kenoticism, Gore's *Lux Mundi* contribution, 'The Holy Spirit and Inspiration'. There, in the context of developing the thesis that no 'spiritual illumination, even in the highest degree, has any tendency to lift men out of the natural conditions of knowledge that belong to their time' (Gore, 1890, p. 354), Gore emphasizes that even Christ experienced historical contingency and possessed an historically governed consciousness. 'When he speaks of the "sun rising" He is using ordinary human knowledge. He willed so to restrain the beams of Deity as to observe the limits of the science of His age, and He puts Himself in the same relation to its historical knowledge' (Gore, 1890, p. 360). In Christ's consciousness the historically contingent part is placed in its final context, the eternal whole. He embodies the ultimate sublation and object of the historical movement of the Spirit. More than His omnipotence, it is Christ's omniscience which is sacrificed in the kenotic act.

One can see that in such an account, focusing upon Christ's consciousness, there is no connection between the incarnation and the passion. The obliteration of the consciousness and the limitation of knowledge by death is not the final outworking of the incarnation, merely its cancellation. And yet, on the basis of Paul's *carmen Christi*, we have seen the logic relating incarnation, crucifixion and resurrection. In the theological work of the twentieth century death-of-God school, Christ's kenosis is emphatically related back to the cross. But here no account is taken of the resurrection, and the emphasis again is upon certain properties of the divine nature – omniscience, omnipotence, the God's-eye-view – which are terminated. These are working out of the same model of Cartesian personhood as Thomasius and Gore. Their project is the continuation of modernity's concern with the apotheosis of liberal humanism. But we have seen that it is a Trinitarian disposition in Christ (of love humble and obedient) not a mental attribute (omniscience) which is at the heart of Paul's understanding of kenosis. Hence O'Brien (with the work of Gore, Forsyth and Mackintosh in mind) writes: 'There is no basis for such speculations in the text of the hymn' (O'Brien, 1991, p. 218).

If we return to the doctrine of kenosis as it was expounded in pre-modernity, by the early Church, in the work of Origen, Athanasius and Cyril among the Alexandrians, Gregory of Nyssa among the Cappadocians, and Hilary of Poitiers, a rather different picture emerges that makes these more modern views of kenosis seem Pelagian. Beset as it was by the dangers of subordinationism, modalism and theopaschitism, the kenosis of Christ was depicted in terms of a Trinitarian procession (Origen, 1966, *De Princip.*, 1, ii, 8; and Nestorius, 1925, *Liber Heraclitus*, I, i, 61); what Maximus the Confessor called 'an eternal movement of love' (Lossky, 1957, p. 60).[9] A distinction was drawn between God in Himself – who was unknowable and inaccessibly concealed in mystery – and those divine energies or operations whereby he is manifested and gives Himself to us. Thus St Gregory Palamas wishes to speak of a 'divine power and energy common to the nature in three' (Lossky, 1957, p. 70). A force or energy whereby there is communication, the gift of God being understood as the operation of love within the Trinity, the abandoning of one to the other; and salvation issued from a participation within this intra-Trinitarian procession. It is a participation made possible through the incarnation of Christ, the revelation of the true image of God possessed by all. We are saved and deified through the economy of love. The distinctive nature of love is to give, a continual act of self-abandonment; and it is this abandonment in love which characterizes kenosis. To paraphrase Karl Barth's understanding of kenosis, God's freedom to love is a self-giving not a giving up (Barth, 1956, p. 184).

The doctrine of kenosis outlines, then, the giving of the gift. But what is given is God in a form, the Word enfleshed. Most recently, it is the Swiss theologian von Balthasar, building upon the work of de Lubac and Danielou on the patristic fathers and his own work on Origen, Gregory of Nyssa and Maximus the Confessor, who has outlined the kenotic economy of the Son.

In *Mysterium Paschale*, like the early Fathers he quotes (Cyril, Hilary, Chrysostom), kenosis is a Trinitarian event. Laconically, von Balthasar writes that Christ's *'missio* by the Father is a modality of his *processio* from the Father' (von Balthasar, 1982, p. 134). We can elucidate this with reference to a prayer he composed which describes the self-emptying love within the Trinity from which creation and incarnation proceed. 'You, Father, give your entire being as God to the Son; you are Father only inasmuch as you give yourself; you, Son, receive everything from the Father and before Him you want nothing other than one receiving and giving back, the one representing, glorifying the Father in loving obedience; you, Spirit, are the unity of these two mutually meeting, self-givings, their We as a new I that royally, divinely rules them both' (von Balthasar, 1982, pp. 428–9).

Kenosis, then, is not the act of the Son, it is the disposition of love within the Trinitarian community. It is a community constituted by differences which desire the other. This circulation of amatory desire is the *processio*. Obedience to that desire to abandon oneself is the nature of one's calling or *missio* – for the going out or the *missio* is always the act of love towards the other. Both *processio* and *missio* exemplify kenosis, and this kenosis is the operation which enjoins the immanent Trinity to the incarnation. Thus there arises an analogy of natures between the form of God and the form of a servant. All incarnation is kenotic; all Word becoming flesh, all acts of representation, are kenotic. We will return to this when we examine Kristeva's metaphysics of desire. For the moment it is important to grasp that kenosis always made possible the sacrifice of Jesus Christ on the cross; for Christ was sacrificed before the foundations of the world in his utter givenness to the Father. He is the Son because he is sent. In his being sent God becomes form and he, the Son, becomes the transcendental signifier, the name above all names.

For von Balthasar, it is this kenotic presentation of the Trinity – Christ's *missio* issuing from *processio* – which is the basis for his own theological aesthetics, concerned as it is with 'seeing the form': the form of God, the form of revelation, the form of faith and the mediation of those forms. Kenosis is a theological economy of representation. Christ the Word descends into all the eloquence, rhetoric, mimesis and endless deferral of meaning in human signs. He is erased by them and through them on Good Friday before sinking down into the silence and the absence of Holy Saturday. But for von Balthasar it is in this descent into Hell, 'this dying away into silence, that we have to understand precisely his non-speaking as his final revelation, his utmost word' (von Balthasar, 1990, p. 79). Through the Cross, judgement falls on all eloquence, rhetoric, mimesis and the endless deferral of meaning in signs. Representation experiences its crisis. And a new word appears, 'his utmost word', on the far side of death's profound *passio*. Only in and through the Cross, the death of God, is there redemption and an ability to 'see the Form'.

'Seeing the Form' is the subtitle to Volume One of von Balthasar's *The Glory of the Lord* (1993). In that volume he begins to describe the relationship which exists between *pistis* and *gnosis*, faith and knowledge. Faith cannot operate without love (or hope) for von Balthasar. Faith, understood as trustful self-abandonment in obedience, is intrinsic to the kenotic economy of desire in the Trinity. He writes: 'the Spirit is not so much a divine object of faith as the divine medium of the gift of faith made to the Father in the Son' (1993, p. 118). Our faith is the human response to God's faith, a response of obedience which enables our participation in God's triunal and kenotic love.[10] Through and with and in this faith the 'light of grace comes to the aid of natural ability: it strengthens and deepens the power of sight' (von Balthasar, 1989, p. 175). We see and know differently because the realm of signs surrounding us is read through the hermeneutic of God's poured out love: 'a synthesizing power to penetrate phenomena, a power that derives from God and is capable of interpreting phenomena so that they disclose what God wishes to reveal of his own depths in them' (von Balthasar, 1993, p. 42).

In this epistemology of faith, opinion or view [*Ansicht*] is transformed into true sight [*Sicht*]; the images [*Abbilden*] of the world become true pictures [*Urbilden*] of God. Von Balthasar is not appealing, then, to an *analogia entis* as Barth understood it; but to an analogy rooted in faith (von Balthasar, 1992, Part I, chapters 3, 4). God's Word is Christ's form as archetype [*UrgeStalt*] (von Balthasar, 1989, p. 212). This 'primal form can never be adequately and exhaustively reproduced by any rational construction [*Gebilde*]' (von Balthasar, 1989, p. 212). And hence without that faith as kenotic, self-abandoning love we are simply left in the strident darkness of clashing empty symbols. 'In this amorphous condition, sin forms what one can call the second "chaos" (generated by human liberty)' (von Balthasar, 1990, p. 173). Von Balthasar writes that: 'This is the Hell Christ descended into on Holy Saturday and from which the redemption of form and representation will issue on Easter Sunday. Christ descends into the hiatus, the aporia, the margins. It is precisely here that non-speaking becomes "his final revelation"' (1990, p. 79). In the margins, a new discourse announces itself which is theological: 'in the presence of the hiatus, the "logic" of theology can in no way rest on the (unbroken) continuity of human (and scientific) logic, but only on that theo-"logic" established by God himself in the hiatus of the "death of God"' (von Balthasar, 1990, p. 79). This is the death of the sign – its silencing, its judgement – which only faith in the transcendent meaning of a love which frames the text can read aright.

Language too must experience its passion – that is the central intuition of the economy of representation, the movement towards naming,
which the doctrine of kenosis expresses. Or, in the words of Emmanuel
Levinas, language 'expresses the gratuity of sacrifice' (1981, p. 120). In
experiencing its passion, it experiences its redemption. As von Balthasar
puts it 'Hell is a *product* of the Redemption' (1990, p. 174). Passion is
understood here as being ambivalent – the word ties together the twin
themes of love and suffering. We must always recall that what is poured
out is love, a love that in giving itself suffers and through that suffering
is able to name. What persists when the continuity of human discourse
and reasoning comes to its end or reaches its edge, is the economy of
love: 'the continuity is the absolute love of God of man, manifesting
itself actively on both sides of the hiatus (and so in the hiatus itself), and
His triune Love in its own intrinsic reality as the condition of possibility
for such a love for man' (von Balthasar, 1990, p. 79). Von Balthasar concludes: 'Everything turns on his inner-Trinitarian Love' (1990, p. 81).

Towards a Theological Anthropology

The theology here can seem speculative and abstract. It finds its roots in
this world in a theological account of what it is to be human. That is,
in reading, on the basis of faith, the watermark of God's glory in the
experience of being 'made in the image of'. Theology therefore precedes and makes possible anthropology. This is how Augustine comes to
relate the Trinity to his concept of personhood, theology to psychology, in
De Trinitate (Augustine, 1970). We are going to make a similar move, for
what is at stake in the ineradicable correlation between *Homo symbolicus*,
kenosis and an anthropology grounded upon the mission of Christ can be
seen more clearly by developing von Balthasar's understanding of God's
kenotic love through an examination of Kristeva's phenomenology of
desire. Most particularly, we need to examine her work on the relationship
of love to language, the order of the symbolic to the abject.

We can legitimately develop von Balthasar's work through Kristeva's
because they share so much. Let me briefly point to the main parallels.
(a) An appeal to the primacy of love as an anthropological root. Von
Balthasar develops this through his notion of the *imago dei* and divine
eros, based upon his work on Gregory of Nyssa. Kristeva develops this
from the attention given by psychoanalysis to sexual desire and, more
specifically, Freud's discussion of narcissism and the Oedipal triangle. (b)
A shared notion of selfhood as caught up in and constituted by wider economies of desire than simply the intentions of an I. For von Balthasar, the
significance of human eros (man/woman, mother/child, self/neighbour)
is located in the larger economy of divine eros, and so self-autonomy is

always fissured: one moves towards a realization of personhood in following Christ and obeying the call to intra-Trinitarian participation. Here an *anthropologia crucis* is sketched, which can only enter the condition of an *anthropologia resurrectionis* through entering the divine performance of redemption. Nevertheless the condition of *anthropologia crucis* is the existential condition for the possibility of entering this economy-of-resurrection life. For Kristeva, the ability to love oneself aright is dependent upon loving others. The ego is not the *ego cogito* of Enlightenment reasoning, but the *ego affectus est* of Bernard of Clairvaux. The self is always in process, always part of an ongoing performance, always being displaced, because it is always only constituted in relation to being affected by that which is other. Finally, (c) Kristeva herself recognizes the connections between her own semanalysis of amatory discourse, kenotic abandonment, and Christ's passion. In her short book *In the Beginning Was Love* (1988a), she writes:

> Christ's Passion brings into play even more primitive layers of the psyche; it thus reveals a fundamental depression (a narcissistic wound or reversed hatred) that conditions access to human language. The sadness of young children just prior to their acquisition of language has often been observed; this is when they must renounce forever the maternal paradise in which every demand is immediately gratified. The child must abandon its mother and be abandoned by her in order to be accepted by the father and begin talking.... [L]anguage begins in mourning.... The 'scandal of the cross', the *logos tou stavron* or language of the cross ... is embodied, I think not only in the psychic and physical suffering which irrigates our lives ... but even more profoundly in the essential alienation that conditions our access to language, in the mourning that accompanies the dawn of psychic life.

She goes on to conclude in a way that returns us from Lacanian psychology to von Balthasar:

> Christ abandoned, Christ in hell, is of course the sign that God shares the condition of the sinner. But He also tells the story of that necessary melancholy beyond which we humans may just possibly discover the other, now in the symbolic interlocutor rather than nutritive breast. (Kristeva, 1988a, pp. 40–1)

In what follows, the theological implications of this astonishing passage will be drawn out in relation to von Balthasar's depiction of Christ's kenotic love and the aphasia of Holy Saturday, and the descent towards the name and beyond the figurative in Paul's letter to the Philippians. For what Kristeva presents us with is an account of the inseparability of a morphology of selfhood from a theory of representation on the basis of kenosis. We recall that there is a concern with the morphology of selfhood in Paul's *carmen Christi* – with the move towards one's true identity *post-mortem*. For Kristeva, our initial entrance and any subsequent entrance into language is an experience of kenosis. It is an experience correlative with our self-constitution as persons through the mirror-stage and our entry into the symbolic order.

The mirror-stage is associated now with the work of Jacques Lacan, though Lacan developed the notion from Henri Wallon, who probably was developing Freud's meditation on primary narcissism. The stage describes the effects of that scene when the child confronts its image in a mirror. Before this stage, the child occupies an imaginary phase in which it experiences, produces and stores up various images of itself and its body. In the mirror-stage the child comes upon a unified conception of itself, which, at first, it takes as being itself – later realizing it is separate from itself. This realization that the unified 'I' is not the real I develops into the realization that it needs the images, the substituting representations of itself, if it is to be, and to have any conception of, itself as a subject. With the mirror-stage, then, the child enters into the symbolic order. It recognizes both its own need for symbols and yet also its own separation from full identity: all because of the uncrossable bar between the symbolic and the real. It is at this stage that Kristeva places the child's descent into depression. The realization of separation is a profound realization of loss – a loss which is continually sublimated by the employment of symbols or language. Semanalysis is, for Kristeva, the inquiry into the relationship between that which is sublimated – which she terms the semiotic – and that which is being symbolized. This fundamental sense of loss, which Kristeva associates with the passion of Christ and which I am describing as a kenotic economy, Kristeva terms abjection. 'Abjection', she writes, 'is the journey to the end of the night' (Kristeva, 1988b, p. 58).

The economy of abjection outlines the logic of separation, which begins earlier in life and then informs the mirror-stage. *Anthropologia crucis* is a condition established primordially in the individual's life with separation from the body of the mother, the abjection of the mother, and the move towards the law of the father. For the father governs the creation of firm identities in the realm of the symbolic. This separation from the body of the mother, Kristeva views as a separation from the semiotic *chora*. This has to occur prior to the move through the thetic or image stage and the arrival at the semantic concern with the proper name. Abjection institutes an exclusion which marks a beginning and a boundary. On one level, abjection marks the beginning of the social order by defining that which is forever external, distinct and threatening its domain. On another level, abjection marks the initiation into subjectivity as the I discovers what is not-I, that which is other (both the semiotic body of the mother and the imaginary father). On a final level, abjection marks entrance into the symbolic order – what we necessarily leave out and remain silent in order to construct. In all these cases, abjection both constitutes the possibility for the autonomy of the order – social, subjective, symbolic – while haunting such an order by identifying its frailty, its instability, its ephemerality. As such, abjection constitutes what Kristeva calls 'the margin of a floating structure' (Kristeva, 1988a, p. 69).

Kristeva discerns the effect of this separation in the melancholia which affects children just prior to entrance into language, prior that is to entering the realm of the symbolic. The separation which institutes primary narcissism also creates a space. The child as presubject, enters an emptiness which will lead to the entry into the symbolic order at the mirror-stage. Kristeva locates, in this emptiness and the separation which precedes it, a primary identification with what she terms the 'imaginary father' – that is, the loving father/husband of the mother. These are troubled waters in studies of Kristeva for the 'imaginary', loving father prepares the subject for desiring the Phallus in which is the dynamic for entry into the symbolic order and the Oedipus complex. For our purposes, this haunting by the 'imaginary' father – whatever the coherence of the idea in Kristeva's work and her dialogue with Freud and Lacan – is another example of how Kristeva's morphology of the self parallels the doctrine of kenosis in the *carmen Christi*. As Kelly Oliver remarks in her commentary upon Kristeva's work: 'The irrepresentable that makes representation possible is represented . . . by the imaginary father. . . . It is only in the context of "his" love that the Symbolic can become meaningful' (Oliver, 1993, pp. 83–4).

The melancholy moment before entering language is a moment where meaning is lost. It is not only in children learning to speak that this occurs, and so Kristeva's work is not limited to the psychology of child development. This loss, this use of symbolic substitutions, and the dialectic of demand and desire that all representations participate in, place the self always in process, always searching for a place to belong to, always experiencing a certain dispossession. What is important, in terms of Kristeva's semanalysis, is that representation remains infected by that which is abjected.[11] The semiotic drives operate dialectically within and upon the symbolic, so that 'writing causes the subject who ventures into it to confront an archaic authority' (Kristeva, 1988b, p. 75). What this means is that the melancholy moment, where meaning is lost, is rediscovered and performed in every act of representing.

Some acts of representation appeal to the suppressed melancholy more than others. Hence, when discussing Holbein's 'Dead Christ' in *Black Sun*, Kristeva writes: 'very much like personal behaviour, artistic *style* imposes itself as a means of countervailing the loss of other and of meaning' (Kristeva, 1989, p. 129). The death of Christ becomes a portrayal of a paradox – representing the erasure of beauty, transcendence and form; presenting ironically an icon being iconoclastic. The experience of depression, of descent into emptiness, is endemic to the economy of representation as it is also to the self-in-process – both of which are constantly searching for, but can never attain, stable identity. Such stability, the stability of a proper Name not infected by the body of the mother, the semiotic *chora*, remains forever futural, and eschatological, and yet constitutive of the present as hope and promise. Holbein's presentation of Christ in the tomb, then, leads us 'to the ultimate edge of belief, to the threshold of non-meaning' (Kristeva, 1989, p. 135).

For Kristeva, the logic of separation, of *diastasis* as the plural and heterogeneous site for the origin and endless constitution of language and selfhood, is part of a more general economy of love. This she depicts in terms of the love of the mother for and by the father. Participation in and desire for complete reconciliation with this love functions as the utopian horizon which makes psychological healing possible. Without this love there is only objection and melancholy; the material world is without meaning for it cannot signify at all. The concern to re-establish the primacy of a transcendental love is yet another reason why Christianity haunts her own analyses and why her work can be paralleled with von Balthasar's. She asks what psychoanalysis is, 'if not an infinite quest for rebirths through the experience of love' (Kristeva, 1987, p. 1). Psychoanalysis probes never the genesis (for we are born into a love always already in operation), but the *dunamis* of love. This is the economy of desire which, for Kristeva, we enter with that primordial separation from the mother. We are born to love because we are born divided. As Kristeva writes, elliptically: 'Love is a death sentence which causes me to be' (Kristeva, 1987, p. 36). The ego issues then from an economy of love and death (as separation) already in operation. Since this issuing is inseparable from entering the symbolic order then it is the economy of love which infects the symbolic order with its desire for identification with the Other.

All discourse, then, is amatory discourse: 'The speaking subject is a loving subject', she writes (Kristeva, 1987, p. 170). All representation is a kenotic act of love towards the other; all representation involves transference – being caught up in the economy of giving signs. Kristeva, taking up Lacan's structuralist understanding of language, views metaphor as the condensation of this love present in discourse, and seeks desire for the other as the operation of displacement or metonymy. As she herself concludes, in a way which returns us to theology: 'the literary experience stands revealed as an essentially amorous experience, unstabilizing the same through its identification with the other. In this it emulates theology, which, in the same field, has strengthened love into faith' (Kristeva, 1987, p. 279).

These two elements of Kristeva's semanalysis – the relation between objection, the symbolic, and descent into non-meaning (the logic of separation), on the one hand, and the relation between representation and the transcendental economy of love (the logic of identification), on the other – not only parallel the doctrine of kenosis in Paul's *carmen Christi* and von Balthasar's analysis of Holy Saturday. Kristeva's work, to my mind, roots a theological examination of the doctrine in an anthropology which relates the fundamental experience of human existence as one of dispossession (or in Schleiermacher's term 'absolute dependence') to our nature as the creators of signs and symbols. We are makers of images because we are 'made in the image of'.

The kenotic economy becomes the very root of the sign production, and therefore of theological discourse. Of course, it could be argued that what Kristeva presents us with is a demythologized, psychoanalytic reading of the Christian faith. And there are emphases in her work which support the view that psychoanalysis 'explains' the religious phenomena – codes of practice, liturgies, symbols, narratives – which make up Christianity. Without making psychoanalysis into a metanarrative, I am unsure how we could ever decide which discourse is explaining the nature of the other – especially since both discourses are discourses upon and within the economy of love. Kristeva's own theory of the dialectical relationship between the semiotic and the symbolic would, in fact, militate against placing one discourse above another; giving symbolic priority to one form of language. To make such a claim 'creates the danger of transforming psychoanalysis not only into an ideology but also into a religion' (Kristeva, 1988a, p. xi). Certainly, Kristeva's reflections upon her Catholicism have caused embarrassment among several of her admirers and critics.[12] But if Kristeva is right, then on the basis of the theological account of kenosis, we can understand each act of signification (speaking or writing) and each act of performing that act (reading, liturgical practice) as a move in love, a kenotic giving towards an ineffable Word, a name above all names, a name which gathers up all our naming and within which we too are named (*en to onomati Jesou*). If she is also right that this descent to the marginalized is a movement towards the recovery of the lost semiotic body of the mother, then Christianity must possibly refigure its doctrine of the Trinity in terms of sexual difference. But that is another essay.

Homo Symbolicus: Made and Making in the Image of God

We return to the three questions set out at the beginning – answering them on the basis of a theological and philosophical analysis of the relationship between kenosis and naming. It has been an analysis in which the poststructural concern with *difference* has been read in terms of a theological understanding of *diastasis*. First, then, what is the subject of Christian theology? Well it is only about God in so far as it is about God incarnate, Jesus of Nazareth. For theological discourse can only inform us about what is human, about ourselves, our social and political priorities in relation to the incarnation of Christ. Theological discourse can *never* make any truth claims about the Godhead in and of itself. The Godhead lies outside the margins of human representation. It instigates the crisis of our representations; our language has to experience its passion, its descent into the silent hiatus. In the words of von Balthasar (so reminiscent of Barth's): 'God "judges" all human thoughts that strive upwards of themselves to attain the utmost, and requires of them something that they can accomplish only in self-denial' (von Balthasar, 1989, pp. 15–16). This is Derrida's '*Kenosis* of discourse', but now as a description of theological discourse *tout court*, not just the discourse of negative theology. The discourse of negative theology articulates a particular theological self-consciousness about its own discourse. It constitutes one of those small convex mirrors in the background of Dutch realist paintings.

The subject of theology, on the basis of the relationship between kenotic Christology and representation, is the economy of the gift, or more accurately, the economy of giving, receiving and responding. This economy of the gift, which is inseparable from the exchange and economy of the sign, is the very crux of the incarnational problematic, the crux of the question concerning mediation. Theological discourse is always a meditation upon, as it is also an operation within, the divine–human exchange. As Derrida has recently observed, a gift is never pure (Derrida, 1992, pp. 34–70). There is no pure giving of the gift: its recognition and reception as gift involves it within an exchange and economy. Nevertheless there is what he here explores as 'continuity with respect to [the] difference' between giver–gift–and receiver.

What is Christian theology about? It is about the play, the irresolvable dialectical play between presentation and representation, between divine disclosure and reception. It is about the economy of grace; an economy inseparable from our own attempts to grapple with and grasp the meaning of that grace. It is not only a meditation upon grace (for then it would place itself above grace); rather it is also a meditation from grace and within grace. True theological discourse is a means of grace; of incorporation into that which is given. If Derrida is correct and the gift cannot be given without obligation, then our human condition before the Godhead (as conscious recipients of grace, made conscious, that is, by faith) is one of being under obligation (there are echoes here of Levinas's recent exploration of ethics and Derrida's recent exploration of negotiation as it issues in and through intertextuality[13]). And God's grace cannot operate without prior and eternal covenant. The question then emerges as to who or what maintains the continuity in difference, the *sine qua non* of any exchange, in a theological investigation of divine and human kenosis. If the incarnation provides the primary example, then God becoming form in Christ provides the ontological possibility for such a continuity. The continuing noetic possibility is the work of the Spirit of Christ.

This leads into our second question: Whose discourse is theological discourse? It is not simply mine. The inquiry is not being governed, then, by authorial intention or authorial desire as the animator of intention – not if the inquiry is proceeding by faith. The human eros is made part of a wider economy of desire – the desires of other people which propels my desire and the divine eros drawing me out in love, worship and obedience, pouring me into a Trinitarian kenosis. Kristeva demonstrates how language is motivated by and abides within desire. Theological discourse, then, is always an amatory discourse proceeding through a never to be entangled interplay of human and divine desire. It is a desire which both affirms and requires representation and yet denies and puts representation into crisis. Its enfleshment, its incarnation, is both its prison and its possibility of freedom.[14] To employ one of Kristeva's definitions of psychoanalytic discourse, theology is a 'discourse[s] of love directed to an impossible other' (Kristeva, 1988a, p. 7). It is both a meditation and a mediation; a coming to understanding and a participation; knowledge as love. We gain access to God and God to us through a transferential discourse.

It has been recognized by many theologians (Karl Barth, George Lindbeck, and Nicholas Lash most recently) that theology is a second-order reflection and redescription upon the faithful practice of the Church. Hans Frei sums up this observation: theology 'is an enquiry into the logic of the Christian community's language – the rules, largely implicit rather than explicit, that are exhibited in its use of worship and Christian life, as well as in the confessions of Christian beliefs' (Frei, 1992, p. 20). These rules constitute the cultural linguistics of the Christian religion. What this chapter outlines is an expansion of, by detailing the economy of, that 'logic of the Christian community's language', placing it within what von Balthasar would call the theo-logic of Trinitarian love.

Finally, this leads to our last question, which is where this discourse takes place. For it is not simply within our textbooks, our teaching and writing of such textbooks, our seminars, conferences and conventicals. And it only takes place here if these textbooks and these teachings are meditations upon their own impossibility. Where this discourse takes place between the margins of our textuality, it is infiltrated and constantly moves towards the theological space which frames our texts and silences

them. We noted, when discussing Paul's *carmen Christi*, that we can
either view the images, forms and deferrals of meanings, the textuality
of this world, as caught between two aporia – incarnation and death. Or
we can view the textuality of this world as a hiatus within the economy
of love within the Trinity. The textuality of this world is a product of the
diastasis stamped upon the human creator in terms of being made 'in the
image of'. As the creature is made, so the creature makes. Theological
discourse issues from this *diastasis*, for this is the space created by the
love that gives and the love that responds; where giving and responding
are two sides of the same act of abandonment. The space emerges in our
abandonment to *another*; a womb from which the Word of God and the
word of being human both are birthed; a name in which I too am
named. Theological discourse as such is constitutive of personhood *en to
onomati Christo*. Here 'I am' is named; and the *I am* is God in me, and me
(I in the accusative) in God. Practising theology, engaging in theological
discourse as writer and reader (and any reader re-writes just as any
writer reads), becomes an act of faith (and faithfulness). It is an ongoing
liturgical act, a sacramental and soteriological process, in which knowledge of God is inhabited rather than possessed. Put briefly, what is
suggested here is that *en Christo* it is by our sign-giving and receiving, by
our wording and reading, that we are redeemed.

Allegoria Amoris

On the basis of this relationship between kenosis and naming, then,
there is a shift of emphasis away from doctrines of analogy which suggest that certain words present us with a true knowledge of God. With
these words, even though (as in Aquinas) they are restricted to certain
limit concepts (like 'good' or 'pure' or 'wise' or 'love'), there is a semantic
concentration on the fixity of the abstract adjective, the stability of identi-
fiable predicates. These adjectives and adjectival nouns name and establish both human and divine properties (although in relation to the divine
they are made perfect, whereas with humans they are imperfectly and
inappropriately understood). Names here designate. These words are sites
upon which the divine–human correspondence is neither univocal nor
equivocal, but identical within differences proportionate to that which is
human and that which is divine.

But our investigation into the theology of representation, the Christology of representation, that is both a Biblical and traditional Church teaching on kenosis, suggests that our knowledge of God does not focus upon
certain semantic concentrations. Rather it involves us in a narrative
process in which there is always a semantic dissemination. Meaning is
never fixed. It is always being supplemented and deferred. Names do not

designate, rather they perform. Read through the Christ story – incarnation, crucifixion, resurrection – which is a Trinitarian story. The human experience of the temporal and spatial is here both historically specific and allegorical. That is not to deny the concrete nature of events, objects and processes, but to view this concrete nature itself as also signifying; as also signs bearing the watermark of God's glory. The particular participates in the universal because it participates in the eschatological reordering of creation through Christ. As Christians, then, we are caught up not in a knowledge but a knowing of God, a revelation of God about God, that issues from the movement of His intra-Trinitarian love. Epistemology and ontology, the philosophical roots for doctrines of analogy, fall as metaphysical idols before the economy of God's love. We are not brought to know without also being brought to understand that we are known. We do not grasp the truth without being grasped by what is true. Our knowledge of God is, then, both active and passive, a knowing as a being known; a form of incorporation coupled with the realization that we are incorporated.

Analogy as a category for thinking through the nature of, and theological possibility for, knowledge of God, is concerned with the properties of objects and proportionality. Analogy is concerned with spatiality, hierarchical relationships, and universality. We need then a category that is concerned with the problematic of mediating identity in difference, univocity in equivocity, but also with temporality, the transiency of circumstances and historical embeddedness. We need such a category because the significance of signs is not fixed, ever, but changes constantly. This category has to inscribe a narrative of love – divine and human – and an economy of desire, divine and human – in which the one and the Other each seek out that which relates and separates them. Such a narrative will plot a progressive incarnation, crucifixion and resurrection. It will plot a movement from communication (within and across the *diastasis*) to communion (not endlessly deferred but endlessly deepened). The transcendental significance, the theological truth, of this narrative will not be (as in doctrines of analogy) constituted along a vertical, synchronic axis: without, at the same time, being constituted along a horizontal, diachronic axis.

The kenotic economy provides such a narrative. It narrates a story of coming to know through coming to love – love given, love endured. Hence, the category employed as a vehicle for this dwelling within and performance of the knowledge of God as it emerges through the doctrine of kenosis, is an allegory (rather than an analogy). It is an allegory of love empowered by God-inspired desire. Only *allegoria amoris* can theologically account for the operation of the Trinity in the constitution of our knowledge of God and the human experience of being makers who are 'made in the image of'. Viewed as allegory, as Walter Benjamin understood, the material is no longer soulless and Satanic (Benjamin, 1977, p. 230).

Notes

1 See Ward (1996).

2 I am not the first to make a distinction between postmodern thinkers of a radical nihilism (see Roland Barthes, Gilles Deleuze, Jean Baudrillard, Jacques Lacan) and postmodern thinkers of difference (Emmanuel Levinas, Jacques Derrida, Luce Irigaray, Julia Kristeva and Hélène Cixous). The distinction is made by Wyschogrod (1990). Milbank (1990) also makes a distinction between nihilistic postmodernism and 'benign' postmodernism. Who would be deemed nihilistic and who benign is contestable. Lyotard and Foucault, though undoubtedly neo-Nietzschean, deemed their work political and ethical.

3 Thomasius's concern to elaborate a doctrine of kenosis was first expressed in Thomasius (1845) and subsequently expanded and revised in Thomasius (1853). For a translated selection from Thomasius (1853), see Thomasius (1965).

4 See O'Brien (1991, pp. 211–16) on interpretations of this phrase *'ouk harpagmon hègésato'*.

5 Jeremias (1963), on the basis of a comparison between this action and the pouring out of the Suffering Servant's soul in Isaiah 53, argues that the kenosis is not the incarnation, but only the death. But central to my thesis is that an act of incarnation is also an entry into death. Incarnation initiates separation, that is, death. The two events share a single economy.

6 Though it still remains contentious as to how many strophes there are – two (Martin, 1967) or three (Dibelius) (see Martin, 1967).

7 See Martin (1967, pp. 99–119) for a detailed discussion of this association. See also 2 Cor. 4:4 and Col. 1:15 for Christ as the *eikon tou theou*, developing a second Adam Christology.

8 The German discussion of kenosis in the mid-nineteenth century, by Thomasius, Dorner and Biedermann, developed the seventeenth-century Lutheran appreciation of the incarnate Christ and his humiliation in terms of the emphasis upon consciousness and historical development current in Romantic philosophies of *Bildung*. Thomasius, while understanding the relationship between kenosis and the operation of the Trinity (where the 'being-man becomes a moment of the inner-divine relationship' (1965, p. 83), modifying that relation while also always being presupposed by it, still wishes to understand the mechanics of kenosis as concerning the impartation or limitation of certain properties of God's being. He distinguishes between essential attributes of God – freedom, holiness, absolute truth, and absolute love – and relative attributes of omniscience, omnipotence and omnipresence. The relative attributes appear only in relation to the world, and it is these which are relinquished in the incarnation of Christ (1965,

pp. 67–72). As Alois Emmanuel Biedermann comments on Thomasius's doctrine, 'the relative attributes . . . [God] can surrender, because the world and thus the relation to it is not necessary for him. In giving them up he gives up nothing which makes him to be God, his essence suffers no diminution thereby' (Thomasius, 1965, p. 303). Biedermann criticizes these distinctions in Thomasius as a Gnostic–Docetic split.

9 Forsyth's analysis of kenosis (which he understands as part of a dialectic that embraces the plerosis or self-fulfilment of Christ) does draw upon the notion that divine love is the dynamic for the action. 'Love alone has any key to those renunciations which do not mean the suicide but the find-ing of the Soul' (Forsyth, 1909, p. 320). This analysis did not fully explore a Trinitarian basis for the operation of this love, while observing that the kenotic act 'was the most condensed expression of holy love' (1909, p. 316). Nevertheless, Forsyth's main focus remains a psychological account of the reduction in divine qualities – the effects, that is, of Christ's eternal know-ledge becoming 'discursive, successive, and progressive' (1909, pp. 310–11).

10 See Kristeva's definition of faith (1988a, p. 24): 'faith could be described, perhaps rather simplistically, as what can only be called a primary identi-fication with a loving and protective agency'.

11 Semanalysis treats three interrelated forms of representation: 'representa-tions of words (close to the linguistic signifier), representations of things (close to the linguistic signified) and representations of affects (labile psychic traces subject to the primary processes of displacement and condensation)' (Kristeva, 1988a, p. 4).

12 Kelly Oliver has spoken of Kristeva's 'nostalgic relation to Christianity' and of how her work 'privileges and recreates the Christian imaginary' (Oliver, 1993, p. 128).

13 For Levinas's understanding of the ethics of being under obligation, see Levinas (1981, pp. 9–11). For 'negotiation' in Derrida, see 1987, pp. 159–202.

14 This follows a line of thought in the work of Bernard Silvestris on the importance of the flesh, as translated in Waddell (1933, p. 119).

References

Altizer, Thomas J. J. 1967: *The Gospel of Christian Atheism*. London: Collins.

Augustine, 1970: *The Trinity*, trans. S. Mckenna. Washington, DC: Catholic Uni-versity of America Press.

Barth, Karl 1956: *Church Dogmatics*, IV. 1, trans. G. W. Bromiley. Edinburgh: T. & T. Clark.

Benjamin, Walter 1977: *The Origin of German Tragic Drama*, trans. John Osborne. London: New Left Books.

Bruce, F. F. 1980–1: St Paul in Macedonia, 3, The Philippian Correspondence. *Bulletin of the John Rylands Library* 63: 270.

Cixous, Hélène 1991: *Coming to Writing and Other Essays*, ed. Deborah Jenson, trans. Sarach Cornell et al. Cambridge, Mass.: Harvard University Press.

Derrida, Jacques 1987: En ce moment même dans cet ouvrage me voici. *Psyche*, Paris: Galilee, pp. 159–202.

—— 1992: *Given Time: I Counterfeit Money*, trans. Peggy Kamuf. Chicago: Chicago University Press.

—— 1995: *On the Name*, ed. Thomas Dutoit, trans. David Wood et al. Stanford: Stanford University Press.

Forsyth, P. T. 1909: *The Person and Place of Jesus Christ*. London: Congregational Union of England and Wales.

Frei, Hans 1992: *Types of Christian Theology*. New Haven: Yale University Press.

Gore, Charles 1890: *Lux Mundi*, 8th edn. London: John Murray.

Irigaray, Luce 1993: *An Ethics of Sexual Difference*, trans. C. Burke and G. Gill. Ithaca, N.Y.: Cornell University Press.

Jeremias, J. 1963: 'Zu Phil 2, 7. EAUTON EKENOSEN, *Novum Testamentum* 6.

Kristeva, Julia 1987: *Tales of Love*, trans. Leon Roudiez. New York: Columbia University Press.

—— 1988a: *In the Beginning Was Love: Psychoanalysis and Faith*, trans. Arthur Goldhammer. New York: Columbia University Press.

—— 1988b: *Powers of Horror*, trans. Leon Roudiez. New York: Columbia University Press.

—— 1989: *Black Sun*, trans. Leon Roudiez. New York: Columbia University Press.

Lacoste, Jean-Yves 1994: *Expérience et Absolu*. Paris: Presses Universitaires de France.

Levinas, E. 1981: *Otherwise than Being or Beyond Essence*, trans. Alphonso Lingis. The Hague: Martinus Nijhoff.

Lightfoot, J. B. 1894: *St Paul's Epistle to the Philippians*. London: Macmillan.

Lossky, Vladimir 1957: *Mystical Theology in the Eastern Church*. London: James Clarke.

Macquarrie, John 1990: *Jesus Christ in Modern Thought*. London: S.C.M.

Marion, Jean-Luc 1991: *God Without Being*, trans. Thomas A. Carlson. Chicago: University of Chicago Press.

Martin, R. P. 1967: *Carmen Christi: Philippians 2. 5–11 in Recent Interpretation and in the Setting of Early Christian Worship*. Cambridge: Cambridge University Press.

Milbank, John 1990: *Theology and Social Theory*. Oxford: Basil Blackwell.

Nestorius, 1925: *The Bazaar of Heracleides*, trans. G. R. Driver and L. Hodgson. Oxford: Clarendon Press (*Liber Heraclitus, I, i, 61*).

O'Brien, P. T. 1991: *The Epistle to the Philippians*. Michigan: Eerdman.

Oliver, Kelly 1993: *Reading Kristeva: Unravelling the Double-Bind*. Bloomington: Indiana University Press.

Origen, 1966: *On First Principles*, trans. P. Koetschau. New York: Harper & Row.

Taylor, Mark C. 1984: *Erring: A Postmodern A/theology*. Chicago: University of Chicago Press.

Thomasius, G. 1845: *Beitrage zur kirchlichen Christologie*. Erlangen: Theodore Bläsing.

—— 1853: *Christi Person und Werk*. Erlangen: Theodore Bläsing.

—— 1965: Christ's person and work. In Claude Welche (ed. and tr.), *God and Incarnation: In Mid-Century German Theology*, New York: Oxford University Press, pp. 23–101.

von Balthasar, Hans Urs 1982: *The Von Balthasar Reader*, ed. Medard Kehl and Werner Loser, trans. Robert J. Daly and Fred Lawrence. Edinburgh: T. & T. Clark.

—— 1989: *The Glory of the Lord VII: Theology – The New Covenant*. Edinburgh: T. & T. Clark.

—— 1990: *Mysterium Paschale*, trans. Aidan Nichols. Edinburgh: T. & T. Clark.

—— 1992: *The Theology of Karl Barth*, trans. Edward T. Oakes. San Francisco: Ignatius Press.

—— 1993: *Explorations in Theology III: Creator Spirit*, trans. Brian McNeil. San Francisco: Ignatius Press.

Waddell, Helen 1933: *Peter Abelard*. London: Constable.

Ward, Graham 1996: Words of Life: Postmodern plenitude and the work of Hélène Cixous. *The Way*, July 1996.

Wyschogrod, Edith 1990: *Saints and Postmodernism*. Chicago: University of Chicago Press.

CHAPTER THIRTEEN

sublimity: the modern transcendent

John Milbank

I

'And God said, Let there be light and there was light' (Genesis 1:3). In the history of modern attempts to relate the Bible to the inheritance of classical rhetoric, this sentence has been accorded a status equivalent to the 'I am who I am' of Exodus for earlier attempts to co-ordinate the language of revelation with ontological speculation. It was cited, as a supreme example of sublime or elevated utterance, by Pseudo-Longinus, an unknown pagan author who probably wrote towards the end of the first century AD. His treatise *Peri Hypsous* was first translated into a vulgar tongue by Nicolas Boileau in the late seventeenth century, after which the concept of the sublime came to dominate modern aesthetic theory (Longinus, 1965, pp. 97–158; Boileau, 1712).

The enthusiasm for Longinus amongst Boileau and other French theorists of a 'classicist' aesthetic was contemporary with the first influence of Cartesian philosophy in France, a philosophy which completes metaphysics as epistemology and therefore achieves a so-called 'turn to the subject'. The treatise *On the Sublime* in its own way also foregrounds the subjective. However, it does so in a fashion that can involve the interest, today, of so-called 'postmodern' thinkers preoccupied with a dislocated and unstable subjectivity. For already, with Longinus, the discourse on the sublime was concerned not only with the manifestation of the singular individual, but with the elevation of this individual above himself, often in circumstances which pose a threat to his own survival. Thus the sublime experience characteristically mediates between an indeterminate interiority and an equally indeterminate object which threatens to overwhelm the subject and indeed provokes and reveals his subjective depths. Because it still concerns at the limit a subject representing an object, the sublime can best be defined as that *within* representation which none the less *exceeds* the possibility of representation. And since thereby it invokes at once the subjective as such, as the unrepresentable ground of representation, and yet also the subject as on the brink of collapsing its distinction from the represented object, it can be said that 'the sublime experience' is at once modern and postmodern in a way which problematizes this very divide. It is notable, in this regard, that a 'poststructuralist' concern with the sublime is correlated with a stress that we cannot consistently maintain a step outside the *illusion* of a secure identity, a secure subjectivity, but have always to return to this apparently stable ground – just as the sublime gesture is necessarily on the *brink* of the abyss without completely succumbing to it. Equally, however, the poststructuralist reading of the sublime – especially with Locoue-Labarthe – insists that the indeterminate abyss not only *undoes* the subjective, but also gives rise to it, since a constitutive openness is precisely what renders it not an object (Lyotard, 1989a, pp. 196–212; 1989b, pp. 7–10, 19–26; 1994; Lacoue-Labarthe, 1989b, pp. 139–208; 1989a, pp. 11–14).

The discourse on sublimity, therefore, tends to open up a necessary continuity between the turn to the subject and the dissolution of the subject. But it has a third characteristic, and this is its continued echo of the idea that the transcendent, or the unrepresentable creator God, is the paradigmatic instance of the sublime. However, where once the sublime God was *also* beautiful, also regarded as the eminent infinite reality of every mode of harmonious proportion and value, modernity and postmodernity tend strictly to *substitute* sublimity for transcendence. This means that all that persists of transcendence is sheer unknowability or its quality of non-representability and non-depictability. Hence Kierkegaard, in his journals, defined the sublime as merely an 'aesthetic accounting' for transcendence (Kierkegaard, 1938, p. 346).

Now what must be asked at this point, is whether the modern and postmodern sundering of the sublime from the beautiful and consequent substitution of sublimity for transcendence is an authentic critical gesture. *Is* it truly reason that grounds the representation of the unrepresentable as the void, as the univocal, as the indifferent? Or is this elevation of the sublime without beauty *itself* merely a contingent gesture towards the unknown, a gesture which absolutizes the unknown simply *as* the emptiness of that gesture? This is all the more a crucial question because it would then be that same mere gesture which ensures that the subject remains opposed to and indifferent to the object, whether, as for modernity, because it is over against the object, or else, as for postmodernity, the subject is nothing other than the inevitable substitution of one indifferent object for another.

To substantiate this notion that the substitution of the sublime for transcendence is but an arbitrary gesture, rendering the subject unnecessarily empty and unmediated by objectivity, I want, in what follows, to trace a genealogy of the sundering of the sublime from the beautiful, and to show how this development was not genuinely critical, but determined both by an impoverished theology and by political economic theory. In particular I shall show how this sundering follows from a *de-eroticizing* of the beautiful.

II

In the Patristic and mediaeval eras, 'the beautiful' was not an autonomous subject of discussion, since the infinite truth was deemed to shine forth in due proportion in every aspect of the created world and so to attract those of good disposition towards it. Beauty was so implicitly omnipresent in knowledge and practice that, to echo Eric Gill, she 'took care of herself' (Gill, 1947). If 'sublimity' was herself adverted to, then this concerned the 'elevation' of the soul through a certain sequence of ordered form towards that which is unlimited, and exceeds our sense of order.

There was certainly a wounding, a shock and a rupture involved here, and yet not a total rupture, since the unlimited was held to be, in its simplicity, an unimaginable infinite fullness of beautiful form, not its negation (von Balthasar, 1989, pp. 317–413).

Now when one turns to consider the French classicist interpretens of Longinus, who mostly moved in an Augustinian theological *milieu*, it is clear that in many respects they retain this medieval perspective. In so far as they diverge from it, then this is because they inherit the general Baroque concern not just with *finding* analogies for God, but rather with *performing* them, either in the guise of 'spiritual exercises' or else in theatrical works of art. In fact Baroque aesthetics had become so concerned with originality of performance as denoting openness to the divine, that it tended to identify the beautiful as such with the ingenious and surprising (Ong, 1958; Tagliabue, 1955). Boileau, despite his classicism, embraced Longinus essentially under this Baroque *aegis*; hence for him the sublime discloses the beautiful as the *je ne sais quoi*, such that it is impossible to have a *theory* of the sublime, and the only way to explain it is to exemplify it (Boileau, 1713, x, p. 52).

However, Boileau deploys Longinus to veer away from the Baroque in two significant respects. First of all, the more elaborate Baroque conceits are seen as collapsing under the weight of their own artifice – sublime figures of speech, by contrast, are not usually elaborate. On the contrary they are ideally such as not to appear figurative at all, though precisely for this reason, says Boileau, they are all the more *successfully* figurative – just as nature only appears to us 'natural' because she is supremely good at concealing her own artifice. Examples of sublime figures include, for Longinus and Boileau, repetition, inversion of word order and abrupt switch of addressees (Boileau, 1713, Preface, p. 7; x, pp. 56, 58ff; xi, pp. 71–5; xii, p. 76; Longinus, 1965, chapters 16–28, pp. 125–38). Compared with Baroque conceits therefore, they are less to do with content and more with *force of expression* (repetition, word order) or else they depend entirely upon *circumstance*: as when an orator makes what he is saying about a third party suddenly redound upon his immediate audience.

If sublime figures are more simple, then, it is this concern with *context* which marks their second divergence from Baroque rhetoric and poetics. The latter, in its sole concern with elocution, had tended to lose all contact with the two prior rhetorical moments of determination and disposition of a subject matter, thereby reducing its political relevance to that of propagandist mass manipulation, first perfected within the Baroque era (Maravall, 1986, pp. 207–67). By contrast, the sublime helps Boileau to reintroduce an ethical and 'civic humanist' political context for poetics, since he regards an ingenious and surprising utterance as only truly *sublime* in relation to its attendant circumstances: *non quid sit, sed quo loco sit* (Boileau, 1713, x, p. 61). Sometimes this concerns the invocation of the strength and nobility of the speaking subject which can be suggested but not represented. To cite Boileau's example, Parmenio says: 'were I Alexander, I would accept the offer from Darius King of Persia of one half of my kingdom in return for marriage to his daughter', to which Alexander replies: 'So would I, were I Parmenio' (Boileau, 1713, x, p. 56). Or, again, context may assume that a sheerly verbal performance can negate objective disaster. To cite an example of Longinus: when Demosthenes mentions to the Athenians in the same breath, 'those who fought in the forefront of the battle at Marathon'; and 'those who fought on board ship at Salamis', this is sublimely figurative, not literal utterance, since the Athenians won at Salamis but lost at Marathon, and therefore the implication is that by fighting at all they achieved the *same* victory on behalf of political freedom (Longinus, 1965, chapter 16, p. 126).

The invocation of Longinus, therefore, served to re-ethicize the political context for the consideration of ingenious utterance. And just because of this embedding in an interpersonal context, sublime suggestions of the inconceivable and excessive were not yet divorced from specific beautiful form. Rather they were only effective if they were somehow conjoined to such form, a conjunction often achieved by a reduction to simplicity. But use of 'complex metaphors' could *also* be an instance of the sublime, since the sublime unites an invocation of the unknown with the utterance of the completely unexpected and yet superlatively apt phrase. Were it not for this metaphorical effect, 'the sublime' would no longer remain a figure of rhetoric, even though, according to Longinus and Boileau, it exceeds the rhetorical by 'transporting' rather than merely 'persuading'.

If one were to ask here, just what is it that mediates the obscure hinter-land of that which is merely conjured up, with the clear foreground or utterance, then the answer is precisely verbal *performance*. That is to say, words which *do* something and therefore suggest a surprisingly indeterm-inable – even indeterminate – force in the speaker. For Boileau as for Longinus this is supremely the case with God: here the Mosaic oracular repetition concerning the existence of light corresponds to a divine trans-ition from word to deed, such that we know that God's will is (incom-prehensibly) identical with his power or capacity (Boileau, 1713, x, pp. 59–62; Longinus, 1965, chapter 9, p. 111). However, the sublime does not reside in the obscure divine background alone: it is *also* the manifest, sudden and unbearable light. This light, although intolerable and excessive, is none the less visible and clarifying. Hence in Boileau it remains the case that, as for Longinus, the sublime concerns non-representability in a double sense: first, in an 'aesthetic' register it is the non-representability of that which cannot be made to appear; secondly, in a 'rhetorical' register it is the non-representability of that which arises as a unique moment through speech, and cannot be identically repeated. The performed event is itself sublime: here, as Lyotard implies, Boileau anticipates a non-mimetic and *avant-garde* view of art as event, which the spectators must judge acceptable or otherwise, yet without being able to subordinate it to pre-established criteria of what is acceptable (Lyotard, 1989a).

However, Lyotard suppresses the fact that for Boileau this sublime event has not ceased to belong to the realm of the beautiful, precisely because of its ethico-political connotations: that is to say, to be sublime it must be universally and 'politically' acceptable and therefore must succeed in blending with other established instances of social beauty.

III

During the course of the eighteenth century, by contrast and emphatically with the work of Edmund Burke, the beautiful and the sublime – or, one might say, the relatively determinate and the relatively indeterminate – became dualistically separated from each other. And it may be contended that both German Romanticism *and* recent 'poststructuralism' remain con-fined in this dualism, despite its questionability. I would now like to insinu-ate precisely wherein this questionability might lie, by suggesting that, despite the fact that the sublime/beautiful dichotomy can be read as one way of constructing the secular, it none the less has paradoxically a twofold *theological* genealogy. This genealogy is to be located, first of all, in Protestant attitudes to the language of the Bible and to the imagistic in general; secondly, in mystical traditions regarding a recommended 'indifference' with respect to the love of God.

First of all, the question of Biblical language. By the time one gets to Burke and Rousseau, the context of discourse about the sublime has mainly shifted from rhetoric to aesthetics. No longer is sublimity construed as something to which one gives voice: instead it is something which one regards, or rather (for both subjective and objective reasons) endeavours to regard but cannot regard. What caused this shift? At least in part the answer would appear to lie in the realm of attitudes to the language of the Bible. Boileau engaged in a polemic with the Protestant Jean le clerc and the Catholic Bishop Daniel Huet, concerning Longinus's attribution of sublimity to the Biblical text. Le Clerc and Huet argued that Longinus, knowing nothing of Hebrew, simply mistook ordinary Hebrew usage of parallelism for a figure of speech (Le Clerc, 1708, x, pp. 154–70; Huet and Le Clerc, 1708, x, pp. 21–50). Furthermore, they claimed that eloquence was inappropriately attributed to the Bible when it is describing plain 'fact', albeit theological fact, and that while one might find rhetorical sublimity in the Psalms, it was not to be located in the book of Genesis (Le Clerc, 1708, p. 162). To the first objection, Boileau replied that Le Clerc and Huet had missed the point: for he had not been talking about a definable 'sublime style', but a sublimity whose figurative character depended on *occasion*, such that parallelism, for example, could still be used to remarkable effect, however banal custom might have rendered it (Boileau, 1713, x, pp. 59–62). To the second point, which argued that the purportedly 'plain speech' of Genesis was more appropriate to the solemn proclamation of a theological fact, Boileau replied that remote, lofty, sublime matters required all the more to be spoken of in a sublime fashion.[1] This amounts to the claim that something inherently inconceivable is not 'a fact' which can be represented in language, but rather can only be gestured towards, or in some fashion *performed* by language that in a small way repeats and echoes the passage from creator to creation. There can be no 'plain' discourse about the creator in his infinity, but there can be a certain sort of figured language which invokes his bringing about of the finite, through which alone the infinite comes to be known by us at all.

As a counterpart of their subordination of sublimity *within* language, Le Clerc and Huet also insisted that one could speak of sublimity *outside* of language, or apart from rhetorical performance. First of all, they argued, it was God himself, the act of creation and the sight of creation by us that were sublime, rather than the textual citations of these things.[2] This essentially Protestant insistence then becomes one source of the view expressed by, amongst others, the British writer on the sublime, John

Baillie, that there is no need to say much concerning the sublime in words, as such words merely *represent* the sublime in nature (Baillie, 1747, pp. 15–16; de Bolla, 1989, pp. 40–2). Such a point of view should, however, by no means be taken as entirely dominant within British aesthetics of the eighteenth century: for example, early in the century the aesthetician John Dennis, and later the highly influential Anglican Bishop Robert Lowth, perpetuated and extended in a proto-romantic direction the French classicist interest in uncovering a *rhetoric* of sublimity within the Bible and especially in poetic parallelism. For Lowth the sublimity of nature is not so much *represented* in language, but rather is something which irrupts *through* language as an expressive event: a figurative expression which is also in itself sublime (Dennis, 1701; 1704; Lowth, 1787).[3] Here also, a contrast of the sublime with the beautiful does not seem to be relevant: sublimity is rather construed as the highest intensity of rhetorical expression and of figurative beauty, an intensity that is 'Hebrew' rather than 'classical'. (Just the same new respect for a 'Hebrew aesthetic' forms part of the background to Handel's Biblical oratorios (Smith, 1995, pp. 108–27).)

While much Anglican thought therefore by no means succumbed to the 'Protestant' removal of sublimity from language, the position exemplified by Baillie was widespread in Britain, and blended seamlessly with a Lockean empiricist attitude to language which regards words as standing for signs which 'represent' external facts. Within the perspective of Boileau or Lowth, the sublime as rhetorical event is at once 'external' and 'inward' and indeed is the emotive as well as intellectual event of the manifestation of the first in the second, such that the distance between them is none the less preserved. By contrast, for an empiricist outlook there arose a *problem* as to how an external massiveness and indeterminacy, registered as mere objective fact, nevertheless gives rise to feelings of awe and fear within. As Peter de Bolla intimates, this was a pseudo-problem, for empiricism overlooks the truth that the externally mighty and indeterminate is only so for a subjective apprehension – which from the outset is as much emotive as intellectual – in the first place (de Bolla, 1989, pp. 40ff).

Now although Kant and the later German idealists clearly were apprised of this ineliminability of the subjective and feeling-imbued moment in the apprehension of the sublime, they none the less remained still somewhat captivated by the primacy of *representation*, and therefore the idea that the sublime resides at the extreme paradoxical limits of conceptual capacity: it is a nowhere–somewhere to be (not) represented. Within their fuller carrying out of an epistemological realization of the ambition of ontology to represent, they did *not* recover the sense that the unknown is not simply that which cannot be represented, but is *also* that which arrives, which ceaselessly but imperfectly makes itself known again in every new event. Thus for Kant what is sublime in subjectivity is not the actual performed deeds of each individual (as it might well be for Boileau), but rather the abstract fact of his possession of an indeterminate freedom. The consequences of this failure within idealism to recover the rhetorical perspective on sublimity will be returned to presently.

The second element of theological genealogy for the eventual separation of the sublime from the beautiful concerns the idea of the 'disinterested' love of God. As Hans Urs von Balthasar and others have shown, in the early-modern period spiritual writers became more and more obsessed with the idea of loving God for himself alone, quite apart from any questions of one's own salvific destiny and the regard of God towards oneself (von Balthasar, 1991, pp. 124ff, 496–531). Although much in this attitude is in keeping with Christian tradition, there are perhaps two main reasons why the tradition had, on the whole, earlier drawn back from such an extreme conclusion. First of all, as von Balthasar remarks, if our relation to God has ceased to be in any sense a matter of hope – since of course God himself is not in need of hope – then has not this relationship become strikingly depersonalized? For to claim to acknowledge God in abstraction from our own hopes and fears may indicate a self-obliteration in the face of otherness, but it *also* – and paradoxically – indicates a hubristic identification with this otherness, and an impossible crossing of the creator–created divide. The second reason concerns the problem of exactly what constitutes God's lovability, if we love him for his own sake alone? For every charm, every attractive feature of anything radiates outwards, rendering things apprehensible and thereby specifically lovable only in the measure that they affect the state of the observer in a positive fashion. By a second paradox it therefore follows that to love anything *purely* for itself, in abstraction from the quality of its influence upon oneself, is not at all to love that thing in its specificity, but rather to love it for that mere abstract quality of 'being' that it shares with anything else whatsoever. In the case of persons, the qualifier 'free' may be adjoined to the ontic term, but the same abstractness, non-specificity and generality remain. In the case of God, it follows that 'to love him purely for his own sake' turns out to mean, not only to over-identify with him, but also to over-identify with a mere cipher, or at best a hovering will.

Hence the mystical discourse on indifference tended to determine the essence of the unknown as empty freedom or even, incipiently, the void. In this respect it appears to have something in common with the aesthetic discourse on sublimity. Did the two discourses ever, historically, converge? There is evidence that they did, and particularly in the person of Fénélon, who was concerned with both poetics and spiritual mediation (von Balthasar, 1991, pp. 124ff, 496–531). However, by the time we reach

Kant, such convergence is quite manifest: the aesthetic sublime is now a mere pointer to the true *ethical* sublime whose essence is freedom, and which we are to love *utterly* for its own sake (Kant, 1987, Part I, 29, pp. 124–43; 1993. pp. 212, 226). For us this true sublime is wholly without attraction, without reward, without any link to our own happiness. The influence of the spiritual discourse on disinterestedness, in this case mediated by pietism, is here quite undeniable. And it therefore follows that it is an association of 'the sublime' with the quality of disinterested love for the good or for duty which in Kant's case has helped to wrench the sublime away from the emanating attractiveness of the beautiful, and to ensure it exclusive association with painful shock and rupture: that is to say, a break with our natural pursuit of happiness and tranquillity. For Kant, the element of displeasure within the sublime experience is a sign of the necessary *sacrifice* of the pleasurable, which is the only possible mode of access to the purely moral domain.

However, this was only one relevant effect of the tradition concerning 'disinterested love' within aesthetics. For not only did it help to prise apart the sublime and the beautiful, it also helped to *sublimate* the beautiful itself. Platonic and neoplatonic discussions of the beautiful, as inherited by the whole Western tradition, had linked it closely with *eros*: creaturely and especially human beauty was deemed to lead one to a higher *eros* for the true intellectual beauty. And the later irruption of subjectivity and 'personality' into this ultimate principle through Biblical influence means that within certain Jewish, Islamic and Christian writers a passionate component in our relationship to a God who himself draws us by the force of his own desire, acquires a yet more leading and ultimate importance. At the same time, the Christian insistence on the persistence of a horizontal society into the most ineffable depths – love of God as always manifest in love of neighbour – allowed Dante to conceive of an erotic love for one woman as persisting in a transfigured mode into the heart of the beatific vision, whereas for Platonism on the whole the initial love for an individual is something later to be 'left behind' (Osborne, 1994; von Balthasar, 1991, pp. 265–7) – though this is not true in Plato's *Phaedrus* (Pickstock, pp. 272–3).

In the case of Christianity, it is only relatively modern writers, in the wake of the Reformation, who have argued, in contrast to the Church Fathers, for an exclusion of all *eros* from *agape*, regarded as a purely other-regarding and self-giving love (Nygren, 1937–9). And this supposed rigour, far from preserving Christianity from Greek metaphysical contamination, has had precisely the opposite effect, in a fashion analogous to the paradoxes of indifference as outlined above. For a person, or even a God who exercises a merely agapeic love towards others is locked within a needless self-sufficiency which renders him simply uncharacterizable.

This position cannot therefore even allow that God desires without lack in ceaselessly attaining to his own beatitude. Hence it makes subjectivity collapse back into substance, ignoring specifically Biblical erotic metaphors for God's relationship to us and to his own inner emanations (of Son and Spirit). A God who offers only a 'cold love' is thereby 'objectified', just as, if he is the object only of *our* 'cold love', he is rendered abstract and empty.

In semi-blindness to such consequences, modern spiritual discourse has tended to distance *eros* from the absolute, both in the sense that it denies it to the absolute itself, and in the sense that it denies it to our attainment of the absolute, and even to our aspiration towards it. But since, traditionally, beauty is associated with the absolute, and with consummation, it is not surprising that this same attitude should encourage a sundering of *eros* from the beautiful. By whatever precise historical routes this occurred, the transfer is evident in the case of Kant: now the beautiful can only be a sign of the moral if it is purged of contamination by desire. Hence even though, for Kant, the beautiful is a sign of the moral *blending* of material happiness with spiritual freedom,[4] whereas the sublime is a sign of the latter alone, none the less, all the more social and rhetorical aspects of 'beauty' are relegated beneath the level of the genuinely aesthetic. Hence the observer's delight in fine painting is taken as paradigmatic of the aesthetic experience, whereas 'the use' of beauty in rhetorical persuasion, sexual seduction, bodily adornment, cuisine and architecture is systematically disparaged. Tellingly, he declares that the tattooing of the body as practised by the benighted Caribs and Iroquois is a 'misuse of the decorative'. This is because true beauty is held *not* to incite desire, and to be quite above the merely 'charming'. It is, rather, a matter of a disinterested delight in form for its own sake (Kant, 1987, Part I, 16, pp. 76–8; 29, p. 130; 41, p. 164; 42, pp. 166–8). Now by making 'art' instead of 'God' the object of a disinterested contemplation, Kant has placed himself at a double remove from previous Christian tradition: first of all art has become a secular end in itself, no longer an erotic incitement to our higher desire for God. Secondly, *as* an end in itself, it nevertheless appropriates the new de-eroticized mystical conception of our relationship to God. Hence not only does Kant's category of the sublime echo a previous disassociation of God from *eros*, his category of the beautiful does so also.

What does this double circumstance really betoken? It shows that, just as a reduction of language to representation helps to sunder the sublime from the beautiful, so, likewise, does a refusal of an erotic path of access to transcendence. This follows, because if a God loved purely for himself is a sublime void voiding our desires, and if our desire in consequence no longer leads through and beyond immanence, then it becomes natural to conceive of this world also, in its formed beauty, as a *terminus* for desire, and as something for which we must acquire a 'disinterested' feeling. For if desire is not regarded as a cognitive probe that is revelatory of the other, it will tend to be defined as a mere lack, which is therefore effaced by arrival at a goal whose inherent order and harmony is most adequately disclosed as a passionless gaze. Hence a refusal of the mediation of finite with infinite through *eros*, ensures that we are suspended between a disinterestedness as regards indeterminate freedom, *and* a secondary disinterestedness as regards the sensible *phenomena* which for Kant constitute finitude.

However, there is one further element to be noted: in Kant (and perhaps necessarily) the gulf between the sublime and the beautiful is only constituted in terms of the hierarchical superiority of the former. Were this not the case, then the beautiful, as that which synthesizes happiness with freedom, would so permeate freedom with happiness, that freedom would be accessible only in a specific harmonious arrangement. But conversely such synthesis would also suggest a 'depth' to immanence, a transcendent background which would be the manifestation of the sublime in, through and as the beautiful itself. Therefore, the phenomenon 'beauty' would itself always involve a manifestation of 'more' than what is given *in* what is given, an excess coincident with a registration of desire. Again the latter element correlates with the sublime, since a beauty only registered with desire *is* also terrible, is also painful and piercing, drawing us towards an unknown background which is given precisely *in* the mysterious perspective which confronts us. Against Kant one should therefore argue that there *is no* beautiful which is not also sublime, whereas his distinction of the sublime from the beautiful leaves us with the residue of the 'merely' beautiful, without terror.

But in denying that there exists any such extra-erotic, disinterested beauty, one can *also* see that there is no sublime terminus except that which is opened up by a beautiful approach. What mountain is sublime merely because of its size? Surely its grandeur is rather a matter of the way its specific form suggests the uniquely overwhelming, and the way it both is and is not in continuity with a harmonious, beautiful approach towards it, or the *picturesqueness* of a vista (to avert to another eighteenth-century aesthetic category). Or again, in Bach's St John's Passion, sudden switches to chromatic atonality are only 'sublime' as temporary suspensions of tonal intervals, which they both interrupt and *yet* somehow mediate. In fact one can say that Kant's own recognition that the occurrence of beautiful proportion always coincides with an absolutely unique judgement not subordinate to any already constructed categories or criteria (Kant, 1987, Part I, 15, pp. 73–5), itself shows that the acuteness and surprise of specifically aesthetic harmony (as opposed, say, to geometric tedium) depends upon the risk of a sublime interruption of our expectations, which none the less our judgements can accept. Thus, it can be contended, the sublime is only sublime as a rupture in *this* or *that* context, or this or that beautiful proportion, but this is precisely because the beautiful is itself only a continuity sustained *despite* sublime discontinuity. It is true that certain experiences are relatively more beautiful and others relatively more sublime, yet neither can be entirely the one without something of the other.

It follows that, were Kant to have made the beautiful as significant as the sublime, he would have had to construe the beautiful as the mediation of beauty with sublimity, and in consequence both the hierarchy and the distinction would have been abolished. Likewise, as we shall shortly see, the distinction and hierarchy between happiness and freedom: with the supremacy of the mediation of beauty through desire would follow also the co-supremacy of the pursuit of happiness along with freedom, and the idea that we are only truly free when we attain a genuine social beatitude. But since, to the contrary, it is the sublime, not the beautiful, which for Kant leads from the aesthetic to the superior ethical realm – the latter hierarchization being but one aspect of the same dubious complex of ideas I am criticizing – it is unsurprising that the beautiful should be seen as possessing the same essential characteristic as the sublime, namely disinterestedness, but in an inferior degree. Inferior, because one more fully sustains disinterest when nothing meets the sight to please, just as it is the case that while the beautiful represents the instantiation of the moral virtues and the ethical harmony which results, only the sublime discloses their principle and ground, namely the upholding of the autonomous freedom of 'self-possession' which exceeds specific form.

Nevertheless, the hierarchical sundering of the sublime from the beautiful did not, in the eighteenth century, always take the de-eroticized form exemplified by Kant. The latter inherits the distinction from Edmund Burke, and yet in Burke it is established in a distinctively different fashion, which rather than placing the sublime over the beautiful by removing the role of *eros*, instead achieves the same thing by *dividing the erotic itself* (Burke, 1990). In this scheme the beautiful is by no means sublimated, but rather arises as an emotive effect of whatever happens to please the physical senses. It is to be explained at once in theological and functionalist terms: God has placed this response within us in order to promote erotic union and social cohesion. However, the mere charm of the beautiful is, for Burke (in this respect like Kant), less poetically compelling than the awe of the sublime, which arises not from any attraction, but rather from pain, or the threat of death either temporarally postponed or held at a spatial distance. The true opposite of the beautiful, which is a static, empirical registration of pleasure, is *not* in fact the sublime, but rather, equally static pain: sublimity concerns a dynamic invocation and yet retreat from pain, and so its opposite is mourning or *melancholy*, the equally dynamic loss of beauty or the pleasurable (Burke, 1990, Part I, section X, pp. 39–40; Part II, section V, pp. 59–65; Part IV, section XIX, pp. 131–6). But where melancholy is actively relation-seeking, since it concerns the loss of something or someone desired, sublimity concerns simply self-preservation in the face of a threatened dissolution of self. Yet it is the latter, for Burke's male, martial tastes, which is the more overwhelming and influential. The explicit articulation of this preference again involves a fusion of theology with a utilitarian functionalism. God, as most clearly portrayed in the Old Testament, is seen by Burke to be most fundamentally invoked by human beings as an object of fear, and concomitantly Burke conceives God as ensuring social order *primarily* through the drive to self-preservation and the fear of the other, rather than through the drives of sympathy and shared pleasure. As with Kant, the hierarchical elevation and distinction of the sublime undergirds the primacy of individual self-autonomy over social bonding in the constitution of the social order. What is truly *exchangeable*, what truly constitutes a public currency, is the universally substitutive value of fear-for-self-warded-off. By contrast the explicit *investment* of this value in that which diverts and delights within the bounds of safety, is a strictly private matter.

One should note here that the main thing differentiating Burke from Kant and other Germans, as Howard Caygill has explained, is that whereas providence in his case and that of other British writers as a matter of empirical fact co-ordinates diverse freedoms through the marketplace (like Adam Smith's hidden hand), for the Germans such divine co-ordinating is mediated by the *a priori* of human reason, which is also the centralized 'police' procedure of the state (Caygill, 1989, pp. 38–188). (Although Kant's *Third Critique*, as Caygill contends, is precisely an attempt to surpass these two epistemological–political alternatives.)

In the Burkean scheme it would seem that the erotic is not banished twice, as with Kant, but only once, in relation to transcendence, since it is allowed to flourish in the immanent realm of the beautiful as the motor of our blind strivings, which God must co-ordinate 'behind our backs' through the empirical miracle of the marketplace. However, at a deeper level, the erotic is surely accepted twice, since the *frisson* of delight in pain and death withheld is not ethicized by Burke, as by Kant, into a solemn cold acknowledgement of the unknown as freedom. The uncontaminated *frisson* can only be erotic, and therefore it follows that Burke has split the erotic between the *lesser* heterosexual play of quiet charms furthering procreation, and a higher homoerotic thrill of male combat and male confrontation of danger deemed to 'frame' society more fundamentally than the business of heterosexual eroticized beauty (Burke, 1990, Part I, section X, pp. 39–40; Part II, section V, pp. 59–65; Part IV, section XIX, pp. 131–6). But of course it goes without saying that this construction is entirely questionable: the 'heterosexual', 'beautiful' aspect could be held equally to 'frame', and its division from sublime, relatively sado-masochistic elements is also unsustainable. Yet what is to be noticed here is that the whole framework is upheld by a certain deviant theology: a theology which construes God as abstract will without transcendental goodness, truth and beauty, and which regards him, not fundamentally as the author of being, but rather, idolatrously, as an actor in our plot, manipulating fear to produce order.

The same loss of erotic mediation of the finite with the infinite as observed in Kant follows from this starting point: but whereas Kant abandons erotics, Burke produces a pseudoerotics in which *on the one hand* a man desires not the *other* (female) body but rather death, which is also the (male) same (since what is most proper to oneself is that one is to die and hence necrophilia is the most perfect autoeroticism); while *on the other hand* a man desires the female other without reference to his or her death, so without reference to the loss, sacrifice, self-giving and thrill of fear of the other which traverses any possible erotic relationship. Eventually I shall suggest that in this questionable dualism one has *in nuce* the structure of that Bataillean erotics which undergirds the whole of 'poststructuralism' and 'postmodernism' and for which love of death stands above love of the living other, which is subordinated as an illusory and yet necessary moment.

However, today we see that alongside an eroticizing of the sublime void, also stands – less as an alternative and more as another aspect of the same thought-complex – an *ethicizing* of the void – Levinas, Marion, Derrida (Milbank, 1995, pp. 119–61). And where the former has an anticipation in Burke, the later has an anticipation in Kant. Implausibly, the German philosopher sought to spiritualize Burke's divine utilitarian regulation of a primordial violence into mutual recognition of freedom by noumenal selves. Implausibly, since freedom is only more than a fictional supposition when it is enacted, and as soon as it is enacted must impose upon the other as violence, unless there are norms for legitimate giving and receiving over and above those for the preservation of freedom.

Such norms over and above freedom would *either* have to impose the rigid stratifications of a traditional society, or *else* would belong to an emergent social harmony arising from a shared but constantly re-expressed sense of the beautiful, or of legitimate give-and-take. The latter would represent a radical rather than reactionary alternative to a formal liberalism that is merely a mask for the violence of state and marketplace. Now what is extraordinary and truly striking is that in a sense *the entire effort* of German philosophy, from the Kant of the *Third Critique* through the idealists, concerns the search for just such an alternative, and that this search is always, and with necessity, construed as an attempt to resurrect the role of the beautiful and of *eros* in the face of the dominance of the sublime (1987). Therefore, it can be said to be characterized by a yearning for the genuinely theological and for transcendence *rather than* sublimity, since the former construes the beautiful as itself sublime through the mediation of finite and infinite by an *agape* that is itself *eros* (Lacoue-Labarthe, 1989b, pp. 208–48, 267–300; 1988, pp. 97–149).

And yet, as I shall now show, this attempt failed, and the hierarchical differentiation of the sublime was always reinstated. Since the so-called 'postmodern' version of the sublime repeats this same construction, it will also be suggested that the gap between poststructuralism and idealism is exaggerated, and the incipient nihilism of the latter overlooked.

IV

In the case of Kant himself, first of all, the supremacy of the sublime is not unambiguous. In the most fundamental principle of his philosophy, namely the supremacy of practical (not theoretical, nor aesthetic) reason, it does, indeed, appear to be affirmed. For the ascent from the beautiful to the sublime is but an interlude mediating a more fundamental ascent from that 'purposiveness-without-purpose' which characterizes the aesthetic as such, to the pure capacity of freedom as the *source* of all purpose. Yet the judgement of beauty involves, for Kant, a harmonious blending without prior rules of reason and intuition, according to a 'free play' of the faculties in which one can no longer, as in theoretical reason, assign the relative contributions of schematizing concepts and schematized sensory input (Kant, 1987, Part I, 16–17, pp. 76–84; 22, pp. 91–5, 131). *This* construal of aesthetic feeling depends upon the *abolition* of the hierarchy of the noumenal activity of reason over sensible receptivity of the phenomenal. And yet, as Caygill and Jean-Luc Nancy in different fashions have indicated (Caygill, 1988; 1989, pp. 284–393; Nancy, 1988), if the supremacy of the sublime leads one back to the priority of the noumenal, then this must *secretly* be already at work in the judgement of the beautiful, such that the apparently harmonious coincidence of reason and intuition – which is like an event of 'grace'[5] – is in fact an arbitrary construct, and the violent, arbitrary imposition of a certain freely-chosen form by noumenal reason acting with priority. Therefore it follows that a supremacy of duty over a virtue integrating duty with happiness deconstructs the integrity of virtue. (This is what needs to be said regarding Onora O'Neill's attempted defence of Kantian virtue against Alasdair MacIntyre (O'Neill, 1989).)

The only way to save Kant from such an immanent deconstruction would be to develop hints in his work towards an overthrow of hierarchy, and a reverse prioritization of the beautiful which would draw back the sublime within its sway; hints most apparent whenever he invokes the theological. Thus, in *Religion within the Limits of Reason Alone*, Kant transgresses the purity of the categorical imperative which concerns only duty, by adding that there is *also* an imperative to add happiness to freedom (Kant, 1960, Preface, pp. 1–13). And for Kant every *actual* moral act always involves such addition, and can therefore never be purely situated in the noumenal kingdom of ends. Thus he consistently links the possibility of a genuine social harmony with the idea of that imprescribable aesthetic judgement of the beautiful which exceeds the theoretical bringing of intuitions under an *a priori* categorical organization (Kant, 1987, Part I, 20–7, pp. 87–91; 59, pp. 225–30). That such harmony is possible, and that we should believe it to be possible, Kant further links to divine grace and faith in God respectively.[6] I do not at all mean by this that Kant encourages a certain secularizing substitution of 'artistic grace' for 'religious grace'. On the contrary, it is rather that the admission by Kant that one cannot bring the aesthetic under the determinate judgement of either reason or the senses ensures that it retains the character of an event disclosing a transcendent depth which had been lost both to principles of reason and to sensory existence since at least the time of Descartes. The aesthetic is here no 'modern equivalent for the religious', but rather, in its integrity, bears the theological ineliminably within its heart, remembering that the aesthetic is only *judged* with a kind of faith, and unpredictably *arrives* through a kind of grace.

However, despite these hints, which would point to a reversal of his whole philosophy, and a prioritization of feeling over theory and practice which would subsume them both (as the beautiful would subsume the sublime), Kant does not consistently develop them. Instead, he holds that aesthetic feeling concerns only a kind of surplus expressive enjoyment of the adaptation of rational category to sensory intuition, and points to no real theoretical truth.[7] This precisely corresponds to a reduction of the divine blending of freedom and happiness – and of nature and subject, phenomena and noumena, 'regulatory' invocation of God with actual 'postulation' of God[8] – to a mere extrinsic rewarding of genuine freedom with an empirical experience of happiness, within time or at the 'last judgement' (Kant, 1987, Part II, 87, p. 339). Here happiness does not require to be judged, and does not admit of degrees of authenticity which would disclose the authenticity of the freedom in question. Just as the aesthetic reveals no truth, but is only a surplus pleasurable adjunct, so also happiness does not truly guide us to the good. And since both the true and the good are deemed to exceed the pleasurable, Kant cannot finally allow that an interpersonal search for consensus and

'mutual placement' might define ethical endeavour, but instead retreats
to a modern reworking of the antique (pre-Christian) concentration on
a private war of reason with the passions, in which sacrificial pain is
the mark of authenticity. He never dared fully to entertain an alternative
autonomy-within-heteronomy of a reason which is *throughout* an aesthetic as well as a theoretical and practical reason, and which therefore
operates *only* on the ground of intersubjective acceptance of judgement
of harmony without reasons other than those of its own subjective
occurrence.

But after Kant, Schiller moved somewhat in this direction, which, for
Hegel in his *Aesthetics* (1975a), defines precisely what he means by the
Absolute Idea (Schiller, 1971, pp. 69–171). Here *all* truth has become
'aesthetic' in the sense that truth unfolds or performs itself, such that
freedom and necessity perfectly coincide: freedom chooses what it should
choose, yet this compulsion is apparent *only* for freedom. However, the
Absolute Idea did not succeed in remaining within the bounds of the aesthetic judgement of the beautiful, and this *precisely* because of the continuing hierarchized duality between the beautiful and the sublime. Even for
Schiller, the categorical imperative based solely on freedom remains the
highest quality: this is 'dignity' (*Würde*) or Venus in her naked beauty
without her girdle of aesthetic charm (*Anmut*), even if Juno's stealing of
the girdle in order to seduce Jupiter indicates the need to complete dignity with grace (Schiller, 1971, pp. 69ff). But there is a twofold problem
with Schiller's categorization. First of all, his graceful beauty is not really
a gift of *divine* grace, but a feature of a purely immanent reality; in consequence it tends to be downgraded to an instance of a fateful necessity
(von Balthasar, 1991, pp. 513–46). Secondly, the dignity of freedom still
retains its superiority, and that hierarchy leaves one only two ways to
construe the charm of beauty which is the concretized social harmony
of established custom (*Sittlichkeit*). Either, as with the deconstruction of
Kant, charm is secretly an arbitrary and violent ruse, or else one must seek
to derive charm from grace, or beauty from freedom, as a logical requirement of the outworking of freedom itself. And this is the course taken
by Hegel.

While it would seem, on the face of it, that Hegel's entire endeavour is an effort to reconcile the sublime with the beautiful, or freedom
with *Sittlichkeit*, all he in fact *succeeds* in doing, as Slavoj Zizek (1989) has
demonstrated, is to establish a more radical philosophy of sublimity.[9]
For while it is true that, in Hegel, the Absolute Idea includes a moment
in which the divine Notion expresses itself in the finite created order
– such that the sublimely indeterminate is in itself self-determining
as beauty – this negation of the infinite is itself negated. Again, while
it is true that the Absolute certainly involves *both* moments, such that

it affirms *both* the identity of identity and non-identity, *and* the non-identity of identity and non-identity, this by no means allows the resumption of the concrete contents of finite order into divinity.[10] There is no analogical 'eminence' in Hegel, as with Aquinas, since in the moment of identity particularity is simply sublated as freedom, while in the moment of non-identity (admittedly retained within the absolute), these concrete contents remain alien to infinite freedom in terms of their finite freedom, accidentality and contingency.

The problem with Hegel, from a theological point of view, is in part the opposite from what one usually takes it to be: instead of a genuine providence he offers not *just* a fateful necessity but *also* too much sheer surd autonomous chance and freedom in the finite realm. Thus in the moment of sublated freedom, finite 'beautiful' contexts are left behind in their sheer accidentality: all that is resumed is the need for spirit to express itself in *some* such contingent fashion for it to establish itself as freedom at all, and for it to become a more than quasi-finite individual freedom. In like manner, state and corporation reinterpret the self-interested economic motivations of the marketplace as a necessary concretization of freedom, which alone ensures that many freedoms will harmoniously blend: yet they are also thereby resigned to the *sheer* self-interested pleasure-seeking and fear-avoiding character of this moment.

This ontology and this politics both correlate with – and perhaps are reducible to – Hegel's notion of a 'Christian' or 'romantic' aesthetic. For Hegel, it is antique classical art which represents 'the beautiful', or a perfect, indivisible union of free form with essential content. This is contrasted with a sublime, 'symbolic' art of more primitive eras, concerned not with the embodying of human grace, but with the invocation of something superhuman and monstrous. However, 'romantic' art, which arises in the Christian era, revives, in a higher mode, a sublime and symbolic art (Hegel, 1975a, pp. 75–100, 313, 435–6, 517ff). This new sublimity on the one hand permits a greater artistic realism in the depiction of the purely secular and contingent, and yet on the other hand negates *all* form – in which spirit cannot truly fulfil itself – in order to point back towards a purely noetic spiritual fulfilment.[11] In this economy, and *not* in bodily incorporation, lies for Hegel the truth of the Incarnation, such that for him the crucifixion represents a kind of necessary completion of incarnation in disincarnation, rather than a moment independent of incarnation, which reveals the essence of sin to be the impulse to destroy God as the gift of Being itself (Hegel, 1975a, pp. 534ff). In a similar fashion, for Hegel the eating of the eucharistic elements betokens a sacrificial *cancelling* of their materiality, and not, as for Catholic tradition, the paradoxical transformation of us *into* the divine body which we are consuming (Hegel, 1975a, p. 104). In all these three instances

– romantic art in general, the Incarnation, the eucharist – the sublime and the beautiful are only conjoined in the sense that first, the sublime is only real in its self-negation as the beautiful, and yet secondly, the *truth* of the beautiful resides only in its negation of the negation to establish a sublimity which, as noetic, will be 'in and for itself'.

Hence Zizek is right: Hegel's philosophy is a more exclusive 'sublimatics' as opposed to 'aesthetics' when compared with that of Kant, and Zizek is further right to say that this is precisely because Hegel does *not* hypostasize the sublime abyss by gesturing towards it as a kind of hidden noumenal 'something'. Let us see how this is the case. There is, for Hegel, no real, inert abyss of freedom 'to begin with', lying beyond the margins of formed, beautiful finality. Instead, the noumenal, the freely indeterminate, only first exists in the moment where it *exercises* its freedom and thereby negates its indeterminate essence in determining it as something or other. Sublimity is for this reason first manifest along with the beautiful, or rather it only resides in the *sign* of the beautiful that none the less symbolizes something overwhelmingly more than itself. However, in a second instance one eliminates, or rather leaves to its pure residue of contingency, the specific form of the beautiful to grasp it *only* as symbol, and in this moment one grasps that while freedom must express itself to be, such particular enactment never corresponds to the indeterminate essence of freedom. Consequently, only the sublime remains: it is no longer that real beyond to which we gesture, but rather, the ultimate emptiness of all our gestures, reducing their 'beautiful' content to an empirical residue. Hegel *effaces* the beautiful in favour of the sublime.

It follows that the Kojèvian construal of Hegel as an incipient nihilist is essentially right, and that the mode of his 'theology' confirms rather than negates this. And Kojève's successors, from Bataille and Lacan through to other poststructuralists, especially Derrida, can indeed be read as expounding an extension of Hegelian logic, when they take the absolute to be a sublime void present only when a-voided in difference, and re-voided only in re-differentiation, in ceaseless oscillation. The true alternative to nihilism cannot be the Hegelian sublimation of the aesthetic, but only a subverted Kantianism which extends aesthetic judgement to the whole field of knowledge and holds the sublime and the beautiful together in harmonious suspense, allowing merely a relative distinction between the two. Only such a conception of the aesthetic as the unpredictable advent of grace saves it, along with knowledge and practice, from the imputation of either violent arbitrariness or logical necessity (or both inseparably).

And yet, despite this 'Kantian' preference, there remains something distinctive to be learnt from Hegel. Like Schiller, Hegel rejected the possibility of a return to classical beauty, or to the 'aesthetic state' of the Athenian *polis*, on the grounds that this imposed from the centre a single fixed order, and took too little account of human freedom (Hegel, 1975a, pp. 96ff). Judgement of the beautiful without a sublime moment too much suggests the autonomous unfolding of a single organism through time. It does not allow sufficiently for the spatial confrontation of different individuals who do not truly compose one single subjectivity. Unfortunately, as we have seen, Schiller's and Hegel's proposals at this point do not transcend the bounds of political economy: only a formal mediation of freedom is entertained, such that actual human choices in their content seem so much dross, contributing nothing to an unfolding idea of the human. Thus Hegel finally abandoned classical political hope of aesthetic consensus, in favour of a logic of sublimity.

Nevertheless, if one is to avoid organicist illusions it would appear to be true that the beautiful must be construed as also sublime, or that aesthetic judgement demands of itself to be constantly *suspended* in order to allow for the non-representable perspective of the other – 'object' or 'subject' – for its, his or her regard of *us*, and for its inherent non-completion or promise. And yet since the beautiful, as I have argued, is itself the arrival of surprising harmony, even 'our own' art is only the impinging upon our own perspective of the perspective of the other also. Hence beyond the Kantian construal of the beautiful as the free determination of the object by the subject – which is also the manifestation of the object to the subject – must be added the notion of an ineliminable co-determination by the freedom of 'the other'. This is most crucial of course in the collective art of a human society, but one can allow that even non-conscious things manifest a certain 'subjective' spontaneity. Hence not only does the aesthetic blend person with person, it only does so in a mode which retains the otherness of the other, and *through* form manifests an ecstatic reaching towards the other in excess of form (though never without form). In this case the other does not reside at Burke's *melancholic* distance, since it is not a distance of loss, but of presence: a disclosing and therefore sublime distance which reveals through withholding and suspension. But neither is a sublime which discloses the beautiful a withholding of pain; instead terror is here converted by trust into the thrill of promise.

And such a view blends well with a refusal of the aesthetic as pure disinterested contemplation, and a re-instatement of its link with desire. This does not, of course, mean that the beautiful can be possessed, but that by opening a hidden depth it exposes also sublime or *ethical* dimensions of both gift and promise. The beautiful opens as a distance in which it in part consists, and consummation resides in the *remaining* of this distance, the persistence of a certain delightful longing, not in the cancellation of a lack. This implies that any aesthetic work is in a radical sense incomplete – not in the sense that it only exists in part, but in the sense that every element in its completion is also a concrete mode of incompletion: hence it is always a new, specific theme in music which calls out to be developed further; hence also it is the truly original individual work that tends to give rise to an entire new genre. For, as Jean-Luc Nancy (1988) points out, the firmer the boundary the more the suggestion of something beyond that boundary; yet I would add, not of a mere abyss, rather of something *in analogical continuity* with what lies within the boundary.

If every definite work of art or aesthetic experience is for just that reason indefinable and incomplete, then it also follows, on the subjective side, that every true judgement is a *suspended* judgement: not a refusal to judge, nor a judgement taking no form, but a judgement which takes the only possible form of giving to the other – 'object' or 'subject' – its due, of allowing that it possesses its own standards, its own inner principles, whose future development one cannot altogether anticipate. These alien standards of formation we can *recognize* and can continuously *blend* with our own, yet the moment of recognition includes a dimension of non-control which renders an aesthetic judgement not *just* an occurrence of reason without criteria, and not *just* a surrender to the other (though it is both those things), but also a gift towards the other of our own mode of being, which we request that she complete in her own particular way. An expression, then, is also a gift, but a gift is also a request: a 'prayer'.

In this mode therefore, one could seek to restore the sublime to the beautiful and close the duality. And the mode discloses that the key to such restoration is once more to construe the beautiful as part of a movement towards desire of the other. Where this is denied, and the sublime is sundered from the beautiful – eventually, as in postmodern nihilism, to the point of obliterating the latter – then the passage to the beautiful leads not to union with a living other, but to a dispassionate freedom which beckons us beyond encounter, to total fusion. And then *either* this lure of the sublime is the command of absolutely self-sacrificial duty, ethics as our commitment to a future we shall not live to see, or *else* this is a delirious necrophiliac narcissism, in which we are beckoned by that of which we cannot be robbed, our own death, which is yet absolutely other, but only as the *nihil* (Pickstock, 1997, pp. 101–18). In the first case, no-one lives to see a salvation in time which is always postponed; in the second case also, salvation is an exit from time and being, and not in any sense participated in by them. In the first case, politics (the social body to which the individual surrenders himself) obliterates the individual; in the second case there is no political hope, only a hysterical interruption of the political sphere.

Hence in either case, the distinction and hierarchical elevation of the sublime discloses its secret truth to be *absolute self-sacrifice without return* (Milbank, 1996). By contrast, the re-integration of the sublime with the beautiful does not locate supreme value at this point. In this re-integration the beautiful leads desire back to an Other only partially disclosed in finite others, to a distance disclosed but always also withheld, but a distance which we trust – have 'faith in' – as an always ever greater depth of harmony, and do not rationalistically construe simply as a shuddering abyss, since this is to render the unknowability of the unknown its ontological essence (in a fashion natural to conceptual reason, yet without adequate conceptual warrants). This re-integration returns us from the sublime to a genuine transcendent, and then, in consequence, allows us to rethink the sacrificial. For where there is a genuine transcendent, where the finitely beautiful *participates* in an absolute unknown beauty, this absolute *gives* the finite without fall, without rupture, without dissimulation. And then in turn our giving back to the absolute, by which we respire or exist at all, is not a sacrificial self-cancelling, but an equally total giving in order to receive back a being always different, which is only participated by us. But more fundamentally, both our receiving and our counter-giving are but one single movement, namely the passage through us in time of the desired other (which is quite different from Lyotard's account of art as the temporal event of sublime rupture).[12] Through this movement we are completed in our very incompletion, beautiful in our very sublimity. For no longer is this incompletion a source of anxiety, nor of a black eroticism that is but the inverse face of lack of bodily emotional warmth, but rather it is a source of erotic delight, both in human others and in the divine Other.

Thus, we can conclude: the dualism of sublime and beautiful is the inner secret of modern 'critical' philosophy, both 'modern' and 'postmodern'. And yet it turns out to be no transcendental truth whatsoever, but a mere subjective gesture, derived from a 'Protestant' genealogy, together with an unacknowledged resignation to a capitalist duality of public indifferent value mediating private and meaningless preference. To this I have opposed a different phenomenology of the beautiful, and appealed to a different mode of experience. Yet it is possible to refuse, deny or reduce this experience, if one insists on making the gesture of *mere* (objectifying) reason, which is ultimately a nihilistic gesture. All that I can insist upon is that there remains *another* critical possibility, another possible gesture, a gesture which does not situate indifference over against formed differentiation as that which both governs and subverts it. Rather, this other gesture incorporates both the sublimely indeterminate and the beautifully determinate within a single manifestation: that of *Kabod*, glory, as the Old Testament describes it. If one asks, what is the (ungroundable) transcendental presupposition of the gesture towards such manifestation, then the answer can only be, a genuine transcendent, or power which is both infinitely free and infinitely formed, both differentiating and unifying, and both in virtue of the other aspect. In consequence this power is deemed to give at once both freedom and formation. Here is no moral nor perverse rupture, but only expectancy to increase delight.

Notes

1 Boileau: '[one needs words] whose elegant and majestic obscurity makes us conceive a great many things beyond what they seem to express' (Boileau, 1713, 'Reflections' x, pp. 59–60). See also pp. 60–5, especially 64: 65: 'Moses himself did not himself think of graces and niceties of art but the Divine spirit who inspir'd him, thought of it for him, and made use of 'em accordingly, with so much the more Art, in that no Art at all is perceived.'

2 Le Clerc (1708, 'Remarks' p. 164); Huet and Le Clerc, 'The sublime of Things is the true sublime, the sublime of Nature, the original sublime, the rest are only by Imitation and Art' (Le Clerc, 1708, 'An Examination', pp. 34, 41–3).

3 On the perpetuation of the 'aesthetic' approach to the Old Testament in Wilhelm de Wette, see Briggs (1993).

4 '. . . a lily's white colour seems to attune the mind to ideas of innocence and the seven colours [of the spectrum] from red to violet [similarly seen to attune it, respectively, to the ideas of] (1) sublimity, (2) courage, (3) candour, (4) friendliness, (5) modesty, (6) constancy and (7) tenderness. A bird's song proclaims his joyfulness and contentment with his existence' (Kant, 1987, Part I, 42, p. 169).

5 See note 6 below.

6 'In this ability [taste] Judgement does not find itself subjected to a heteronomy from empirical laws, as it does elsewhere in empirical judging – concerning objects of such a pure liking it legislates to itself, just as reason does regarding the power of desire. And because the subject has this possibility within him, while outside him there is also the possibility that nature will harmonize with it, judgement finds itself referred to *something that is neither nature nor freedom* and yet is linked with the basis of freedom, *the supersensible, with which the theoretical and the practicable are in an unknown manner combined and joined into a unity*' [my italics] (Kant, 1987, Part I, 59, p. 229). Since aesthetic judgement is here construed as participating in a divine coordination of nature and freedom which is *unknowable*, it is clearly like an event of grace. Likewise it tends to encourage in us a belief in an orderedness of nature that goes *beyond* mere means–end relations as a 'purposiveness without purpose', yet this is not apodictically provable and so requires *faith*. See, further, 'Appendix: Methodology of Teleological Judgement', 79–91, pp. 301–69. And see also Kant (1960), in which he finds room within a 'reasoned faith' for an eschatological dimension in terms of the hope for an arrival of a *supplement* of freedom by happiness in the last judgement, which however includes a restoration of happiness here on earth: 'The teacher of the Gospel revealed to his disciples the Kingdom of God on earth as in its

glorious, soul-elevating moral aspect, namely in terms of the value of citizenship in a divine state, and to this end he informed them what they had to do, not only to achieve it themselves, but to unite with all others of the same mind and, so far as possible, with the entire human race. Concerning happiness, however, which constitutes the other part of what man inevitably wishes, he told them in advance not to count on it in their life on earth . . . yet he added . . . Rejoice and be exceedingly glad, for great is your reward in heaven. The supplement, added to the history of the church, dealing with man's future and final destiny, pictures men as ultimately *triumphant*, i.e. as crowned with happiness while still here on earth' (1960, p. 125; see also, pp. 4–5, 48–9, 70–1, 179–80). This element of eschatological faith, in Kant, also takes the form of a belief in a providentially guided process towards a state in which the moral law will increasingly be socially and politically realized and co-ordinated with happiness (the 'supplement'), thanks to the *co-operation* of 'the great artist nature in whose mechanical course is clearly exhibited a predetermining design to make harmony spring from human discord, even against the will of man' (Kant, 1903, first supplement, p. 143).

7 Kant (1987, Part I, 15, pp. 73–5): 'Hence in thinking of beauty, a formal subjective purposiveness, we are not at all thinking of a perfection in the object' (p. 74).

8 See Kant (1993, pp. 200–57): 'both *technical practical* and *moral practical* reason *coincide* in the idea of God and the world, as *synthetic unity of transcendental philosophy*' (p. 225). In this work it is stressed that there is a 'technical practical' aspect to theoretical reason, and that our discovery of laws of nature presupposes the *free* operation of mind upon nature, and even a certain 'faith' that a rational treatment of nature will go on being possible in the future. Hence 'nature and freedom, both of which must be treated theoretically and practically' [my italics]. Theoretical reason seems to require a certain transcendental presupposition of freedom, and yet freedom is only *guaranteed* by moral duty in practical reason (p. 223).

9 'Not only as *substance*, but also as *subject*' (Zizek, 1989, pp. 201–31). Zizek is here criticizing Yovel (1982).

10 'The Idea is the dialectic which again makes this mass of understanding and diversity understand its finite nature and the pseudo-independence in its productions, and which brings the diversity back to unity. Since this double movement is not separate or distinct in time, nor indeed in any other way . . . *the Idea is the eternal vision of itself in the other, notion which in its objectivity has carried out itself, object which in inward design is essential subjectivity* [my italics] (Hegel, 1975b, 214, p. 278). Here the idea *only* is in its self-negation in objectivity, yet the 'alien' moment of objectivity (including such contingency) essentially remains, even though it is rooted back in subjectivity. (See also pp. 240–4.); 'The end . . . is consequently the unity in which both of these firsts, the immediate and the real first, are made constituent stages in thought, merged, and at the same time preserved in the unity' (242, p. 295). Hence the 'immediacy' of the 'natural', objective world, is for Hegel first shown up as illusion in relation to the real mediated work of 'spirit', yet finally reclaimed

as one essential moment of spirit, even as that through which it alone is *all*, that is as the very illusion which occludes it. The postmodern logic of 'double annihilation' is not very far away. . . . Finally, see Hegel's concluding sentences' (1975b, 244, p. 296), 'The idea does not merely pass over into life, or as finite cognition allow life to show in it: in its own absolute truth it resolves to let the "moment" of its particularity, or of the first characterization and other-being, the immediate idea, as its reflected image go forth freely as Nature (i.e. that Idea which is independent or "for itself", the objective, immediate, contingent, merely "given").' By a crucial paradox, *Nature*, not *Geist*, is literally Hegel's last word.

11 The sublime is that instant where 'the revelation of the content is at the same time the supersession of the revelation' (Hegel, 1975a, p. 363). The true content of Romantic Art is 'absolute inwardness, stripped of all external relations and processes of nature' (1975a, p. 519). The coincidence of 'realism' with 'symbolism' here – one could say, 'Balzac' with 'Mallarmé' – which exactly corresponds to the paradoxical finality of *Nature* in the Shorter Logic, is best expressed in the following passage: 'God is no bare ideal generated by imagination. . . . On the contrary, he puts himself into the very heart of the finitude and contingency of existence, and yet knows himself there as a divine subject who remains infinite in himself and makes this infinity explicit to himself.' In consequence art can now make 'the human form and mode of externality in general . . . an expression of the absolute' (p. 520).

12 See von Balthasar, *The Glory of the Lord* (1991). I am grateful to Alison Milbank for conversations concerning debates on the sublime in the eighteenth century.

References

Appignanesi, Lisa (ed.) 1989: *Postmodernism: ICA Documents*. London: Free Association.

Baillie, John 1747: *An Essay on the Sublime*. London: R. Dodsley.

Boileau, Nicolas 1712: *A Treatise of the Sublime, translated from the Greek of Longinus* (*Traité du sublime*). London: E. Curll.

—— 1713: 'Preface' to *A Treatise of the Sublime 2; Posthumous Works of M. Boileau*, vol. III, *Three New Reflections on Longinus*. London: E. Curll.

Briggs, Sheila 1993: The deceit of the Sublime. *Semeia* 59: 2–35.

Burke, Edmund 1990: *A Philosophical Enquiry into the Origin of our Ideas of the Sublime and the Beautiful*, ed. Adam Phillips. Oxford: Oxford University Press.

Caygill, Howard 1988: Post-modernism and judgment. *Economy and Society* 17, I: 1–20.

—— 1989: *Art of Judgment*. Oxford: Blackwell.

de Bolla, Peter 1989: *The Discourse of the Sublime: History, Aesthetics and the Subject*. Oxford: Basil Blackwell.

Dennis, John 1701: *The Advancement and Reformation of Modern Poetry*. London: R. Parker.

—— 1704: *The Ground of Criticism in Poetry*. London: G. Strahan and B. Linott.

Gill, Eric 1947: *Essays*. London: Jonathan Cape.

Hegel, G. W. F. 1975a: *Aesthetics*, trans. T. M. Knox. Oxford: Oxford University Press.

—— 1975b: *Hegel's Logic*, trans. W. Wallace. Oxford: Oxford University Press.

Huet, Daniel and Le Clerc, Jean 1708: An examination of the opinion of Longinus upon this passage in Genesis chap. I verse 3: 'And God said let the light be made and the light was made'. In Jean Le Clerc, *Bibliothèque Choisie*, Amsterdam: H. Schette, vol. x, pp. 2–50.

Kant, Immanuel 1903: *Perpetual Peace*, trans. M. Campbell Smith. London: Swan Sonnenschein.

—— 1960: *Religion within the Limits of Reason Alone*, trans. T. M. Greene and H. H. Hudson. New York: Harper.

—— 1987: *Critique of Judgment*, trans. Werner S. Pluhur. Indianapolis: Hackett.

—— 1993: *Opus Postumum*, trans. E. Foister and M. Rosen. Cambridge: Cambridge University Press.

Kierkegaard, S. 1938: *Journals*, trans. A. Dru. London: Oxford University Press.

Lacoue-Labarthe, Philippe 1988: La vérité sublime. In J-F. Courtine et al. (eds), *Du Sublime*, Paris: Belin, pp. 97–149.

—— 1989a: On the sublime. In Lisa Appignanesi (ed.), *Postmodernism: ICA Documents*, London: Free Association, pp. 11–14.

—— 1989b: *Typography*. Cambridge, Mass.: Harvard University Press.

Le Clerc, Jean 1708: Remarks upon Boileau's Tenth Reflection upon Longinus. In *Bibliothèque Choisie*, vol. x, pp. 154–70, Amsterdam: H. Schette.

Longinus 1965: On the Sublime. In Aristotle/Horace/Longinus: *Classical Literary Criticism*, trans. T. S. Dorsch, London: Penguin.

Lowth, Robert 1787: *Lectures on the Sacred Poetry of the Hebrews*. London: J. Johnson.

Lyotard, J-F. 1989a: The sublime and the avant-garde. In A. Benjamin (ed.), *The Lyotard Reader*, Oxford: Blackwell, pp. 196–212.

—— 1989b: Defining the postmodern. In Lisa Appignanesi (ed.), *Postmodernism: ICA Documents*, London: Free Association, pp. 7–10.

—— 1989c: Complexity and the sublime. In Lisa Appignanesi (ed.), *Postmodernism: ICA Documents*, London: Free Association, pp. 19–26.

—— 1994: *Lessons on the Analytic of the Sublime*, trans. E. Rottenberg. Stanford: Stanford University Press.

Maravall, José Luis 1986: *Culture of the Baroque*, trans. Terry Cochran. Minneapolis, University of Minnesota Press.

Milbank, John 1995: Can a gift be given? In L. G. Jones and S. E. Fowl (eds), *Rethinking Metaphysics*, Oxford: Blackwell, pp. 119–61.

—— 1996: Stories of Sacrifice. *Modern Theology*, 12 (1), pp. 27–56.

Nancy, Jean-Luc 1988: L'Offrande sublime. In J-F. Courtine et al. (eds), *Du Sublime*, Paris: Belin, pp. 37–77.

Nygren, Anders 1937–9: *Agape and Eros*, trans. P. S. Watson. London: SPCK.

O'Neill, Onora 1989: Kant After Virtue. In *Constructions of Reason*, Cambridge: Cambridge University Press, pp. 145–62.

Ong, Walter J. 1958: *Ramus: Method and the Decay of Dialogue*. Cambridge, Mass.: Harvard University Press.

Osborne, Catherine 1994: *Eros Unveiled*. New York: Oxford University Press.

Pickstock, Catherine 1997: *After Writing: On the Liturgical Consummation of Philosophy*. Oxford: Blackwell.

Schiller, Friedrich 1971: *Über Anmut und Würde*. Stuttgart: Philippe Reclam.

Smith, Ruth 1995: The Biblical Sublime. In *Handel's Oratorios in Eighteenth Century Thought*, Cambridge: Cambridge University Press, pp. 108–27.

Tagliabue, Guido Morpurgo 1955: in E. Castello (ed.), *Retorica barocco*. Rome: Bocca, pp. 119–95.

von Balthasar, Hans Urs 1989: *The Glory of the Lord: A Theological Aesthetics, IV: The Realm of Metaphysics in Antiquity*, trans. Brian McNeil et al. Edinburgh: T. and T. Clark.

—— 1991: *The Glory of the Lord, V: The Realm of Metaphysics in the Modern Age*, trans. Oliver Davies et al. Edinburgh: T. and T. Clark.

Yovel, Yirmiyahu 1982: *Hegel et la Religion*. Paris.

Zizek, Slavoj 1989: 'Not only as *substance*, but also as *subject*'. In *The Sublime Object of Ideology*, London: Verso, pp. 201–31.

CHAPTER FOURTEEN

the primacy of theology and the question of perception

Phillip Blond

Theology has lost its object. It can no longer point to anything with ostensive certainty and say the word 'God'. This loss of reality has prompted theology (a theology that seeks empirical consequences) to pursue correspondence with secular words and objects. Things that possess a bare existentiality are now made the measure by which religion must judge itself. Theology now finds itself identified with that cultural practice and with this form of behaviour. God has apparently lost any specificity appropriate to him. He has become pluralized into a general spirituality and identified with virtually anything whatsoever. Conceptual theology has long recognized this loss of reality, but equally it has long ceased to be troubled by it. God, such theologians feel, is not threatened by being denied any discernible presence in the world. For this type of theology any relationship between God and objectivity can of course only be conceptually secured. There can never be any question of understanding the relation between God and universality as involving anything empirical whatsoever, because no doubt such a position would call into question the very project of conceptually codifying theology in the first place. For is not the origin of a reductive conceptuality precisely this loss of faith in the external world? And, is not the contemporary polytheism of those who seek a God in the world one reason why?

Obviously and unfortunately this is the situation theology finds itself in today. Conceptually empty, theology no longer recognizes itself in its purity. Empirically blind, theology finds itself hopelessly abstract in its search for relevance. However, to hope to recover theology as a 'grammar of assent', requires that theology must ascertain what it is assenting to.[1] If theology is to recover itself and re-envisage its sensorium, it must as a first step abandon the contemporary concern for conceptual purity or secular legitimacy. If we are right, and this situation stems from theology's loss of its object, from its inability to achieve a *clara et distincta perceptio*, then the solution to the situation initially appears obvious. Theology only has to recover its fundamental 'data', and so prove once again the *veracitas dei*. If theology is now this positive project, then it ought, obviously, to begin with a restoration of what has been lost. And if theology has lost its object, then theology as the queen of the sciences should restore what science has always aimed at in respect of its objects – knowledge. Here then we have both our beginning and our solution, we must seek to restore God to human cognition.

However, to speak of restoring God to cognition is to speak of something that most would consider a fundamentally misguided orientation. To suggest that theological cognition is a goal that should be advocated, let alone achieved, is an end which most would find hard to accept. It would, perhaps, not be acceptable even to most of the leading minds in theology. Those thinking within the contemporary milieu would, one suspects, feel embarrassed at having to offer an account of God and how we might come to know Him. Unfortunately, this is hardly surprising as theology has, since the time of Kant, largely surrendered any non-conceptual means by which an account of God might be offered. And since we moderns operate largely within the parameters of this Kantian lexicon, my wish to restore a cognitive dimension to the experience of God sounds almost immediately as if it is a conservative project; an endeavour that would serve the interests of those who wish to make God a matter for ontic rule-giving and predication. For it sounds as though I plan to guarantee and found conceptual theology by providing the content for its claims and inferences about God.

None the less, nothing could be further from the truth. It would be utterly idolatrous to suggest that any content can be found for the concept of God, or indeed that there can be a concept of God in the first place. No, my wish is to lift the Kantian prohibitions on the sphere of sensibility and recover it as a genuine (*reell* in the Husserlian sense) source of theological cognition. Plainly though, any attempt to articulate a sphere of sensibility, one capable of being cognized outside the sway of the categories, is already ruled out of court by modern conceptuality. Modern conceptuality would view this 'cognition without categories' as unthinkable. But my concern is not to secure the conceptual framework of this era against scepticism, it is to recover the God lost to both conceptual theology and religious sensibility by this construction of modern rationality. I hope to do this by uncovering a cognitive relation between empirical sensibility and transcendence. Not only would this be a refusal of the Kantian dismissal of God from the empirical world, it would also be a denial of the Kantian account of knowledge. The moderns, by confining transcendence to the noumenal world of the in-itself, prohibited any perception that the transcendent could also be phenomenologically disclosed to us. Theology now needs to free transcendence from the realm of the noumenal and open it up to the possibility of perception. To do this, theology would have to reveal transcendence as already intruding upon the empirical world. A position that would allow theology to reclaim for itself and for God a certain reality.

The Flight of Faith from Cognition

Christianity is not a doctrine, not, I mean, a theory about what has happened and will happen to the human soul, but a description of something that actually takes place in human life.

(Wittgenstein, 1980, p. 28e)

Of course, Kant attempted to limit knowledge in order to make room for faith. However, the distinction between faith and knowledge, despite the intent of its author, seems to have fallen into an opposition whereby each side is denied to the other.[2] Furthermore, this antagonism redefined as the opposition between the infinite and the finite (to use the language of German idealism) is, it seems, so desperate to confer upon finitude absolute value that everywhere this distinction is argued for, it promotes nothing but the secular option. The Enlightenment having placed God so squarely outside and beyond human scope has condemned, as Hegel put it, the highest idea to having no reality (1977a, p. 56). The resulting opposition between the most high and the most real has bequeathed to contemporary human life a curious and dreadful situation. That which is the most high – the good, the beautiful and the true – is denied any existential purchase; whilst that which is the most real, is acquainted with the most depraved, the most ubiquitous and hence the most wicked.

In order to give an account of this phenomenon, we need to attend to the structure of modern conceptuality that perpetuates and maintains this situation. Consequently, it will be the Kant of the First *Critique* (1978) that will be the oblique subject of this engagement. However, for now let me simplify the modern, and suggest that the principle of modernity that lies at the heart of the secular is the principle of self-sufficient finitude. A principle that owes its existence not to any concern to save faith, but rather from a requirement to secure the possibility of knowledge. If indeed it is the idea of self-sufficient finitude (a materialist immanentism) that lies at the heart of the secular dismissal of the most high, then this principle has already by definition both cognized and proscribed the eternal. Whilst this immanentist principle produces a Feurbachian aware-ness in us that having re-spiritualized ourselves we are no longer domin-ated by that which is beyond our reach, at the same time this very consciousness recognizes, to quote Hegel again, 'something higher above itself from which it is self-excluded' (1977a, p. 61).

To deny that this idea of a cognizant self-exclusion from the most high is an outcome which is inevitable is to raise the possibility, a possibility not without scriptural precedent, that God might actually offer Himself to us through participation and inclusion as our highest possibility. From the Old Testament: 'I know that God is at my side' (Psalms 56:10), to the New: 'to have seen me is to have seen the Father' (John 14:9), it seems Biblical scripture would suggest that God would claim for Himself, and hence for us, nothing less than a decisive existential import, a mode by which He makes Himself manifest and offers Himself to be known. This in a sense constitutes the very promise of Christian theology: 'we shall see him as he really is' (1 John 3:2). But the promise of theology is not simply the abstract Kantian hope of possibility and duty, not least be-cause for Christianity this futural event has already occurred: 'we our-selves saw and we testify' (1 John 4:14). Furthermore, Christianity does not accept that the dialectic of recognition, self-exclusion and denial is one that takes place between God and man. To suggest that man and God stand apart from one another is to deny what Christianity has testified to for nearly two thousand years – that man already participates in God as God does in man: 'God lives in him and he in God' (1 John 4:15).

But believing this to be the case, and speaking subsequently of how the contemporary human subject should relate to such a situation, is already, of course, to enter the realm of faith. Yet in using this word we must immediately disengage ourselves from the consequences of the modern thinking of faith. For why is it that faith is now understood as a subjective act that concerns something wholly invisible, something so interiorized that it is no longer a matter for the senses? It is almost as if, when one speaks of faith in these times, one is speaking of a wholly privatized and solipsistic God. A God who has been so denuded by the flight from cognition that *any* subjective gesture can, it seems, be faithful to this absent deity.

Let us follow Hegel once more, and perhaps extend the scope of his claim. Hegel writes that the Enlightenment with its principle of subject-ivity expresses itself religiously in Protestantism (1977a, p. 57). Protest-antism concerns us because in its most pejorative form, this thinking drains the external world of any relation to the most high. As such this departure of the most high from the most real appears to be the ground for the modern situation. For Luther any understanding of the external world as being in the image of Christ was an idolatrous imposition by human beings on a wholly free and sovereign God – a God who owes nothing to us. This theological absolutism withdraws God from the world and hence from the realm of human cognition. Even though Protestant thinking does this in an attempt to avoid the mind reducing God to the objects it contemplates, and even though Protestant thinking then focuses on the interior event of revelation between the sinner and God (*Simul justus et peccator*), I would suggest that the price of this theological evacuation of the external world is the rise of immanentist subjectivity and its denial of any external relation whatsoever with the most high.

For me, however, this situation is avoided by refusing to drain the external world of theological import. Whilst I would accept the injunction of Romans 1:23, the condemnation of those who 'exchanged the glory of the immortal God . . .' for 'the image of mortal man'; and whilst I understand the terrible risk of worshipping 'creatures instead of the creator' (Romans 1:25), and although I would wholly endorse Luther's refusal to allow secular reason to harmonize the relation between God and man, by the same token, we would need to insist that creatures are not wholly sundered from God, and God does not have to be wholly sundered from them in order to avoid idolatry. Indeed the drive to conceal and veil God from human appropriation only bespeaks an earlier failure to understand that 'ever since God created the world his everlasting power and deity – however invisible – have been there for the mind to see in the things he has made' (Romans 1:20). For once faith 'flees from the objectivity of cognition', and embraces methodological negation as the only path to a non-idolatrous conception of God (Hegel, 1977a, p. 57), then the original intuition of Luther, the attempt to preserve God's mystery, will be lost, as this mystery is not allowed to show itself except via denials that human beings can approach it.

Against this interiorization of faith (which makes God a noumenal in-itself which transcends human knowledge), we would need to suggest that faith has an exterior correlate. And if my interpretation of Hegel is right and it is the interiorization of faith that has denuded the external world, culminating in the abstract and unknowable deity of Kant, then the contemporary understanding of faith, the interior Kantian demand for moral duty where 'nothing remains for the creature but endless progress', is no longer one which we should support (Kant, 1956, p. 135). For Kant faith has no stronger ground other than as a necessary fiction (on the part of pure reason) to maintain a harmony between nature and a moral disposition. Faith conceived in this way has no legitimacy other than as an adjunct to human will or volition. However, since I would claim that faith is as present in nature as it is in us, then faith is not so much a subjective act as it is a mode of cognitive recognition – a perception that is already a response to God's prior revelation in the world. The world by this reading is a world of an already given gift, and faith cannot be the author of this manifold. For faith is not a necessary nor sufficient condition for God's self-disclosure in the world. God after all reveals himself to those who do not believe as well as to those who do. No, faith is an act of positioning, recognition and response, or as von Balthasar puts it 'the act of faith is dependent on God's antecedent revelation' (1982, p. 131).

Cognition as a Denial of Faith

Un idéalisme transcendental conséquent dépouille le monde de son opacité et de sa transcendance.

(Merleau-Ponty, 1945, p. vi)[3]

If we have, then, brought faith towards cognition, have we brought cognition to faith? Obviously not – whilst I have perhaps indicated the price paid by faith when it abandons knowledge, I have not shown how knowledge fails when it is unable to perceive and give an account of God. Or to put this another way, one can readily understand why theology requires the objectivity it has lost, but why does objectivity require theology? It is here that theologians must exercise extreme care. If we simply argue that theology must meet a standard of objectivity, an independent objective standard, one that is shared in by all other discourses that seek to have the status of knowledge, then we will have failed to articulate the unique status of theology. Theological knowledge cannot be conceived within the same ontological rubric as secular knowledge. If I feel that in my pursuit of reality I have succeeded by arguing that theology can meet the requirements of a secular realism, then I will have done nothing but make theology subordinate to a secular understanding of reality. To do this would be but to parallel the Scotist attempt to achieve theological knowledge by reducing God to a secular object. Duns Scotus did this by elevating a secular understanding of being over God, so that God could be known by secular conceptuality (Duns Scotus, 1966). Theology must not repeat this error, elevating a secular understanding of reality over God, and thereby reducing Him to the level of an ontic entity, in order to facilitate His acknowledgement by an atheist form of conceptuality.

Theology can have no standard of objectivity other than God. This is a point that the most advanced theologians of the twentieth century have rediscovered and insisted upon. For Karl Barth this is because

'God's revelation is a ground which has no higher or deeper ground above or below it but [it] is an absolute ground in itself, and therefore for man a court from which there can be no possible appeal to a higher court. Its reality and truth do not rest on a superior reality and truth' (1975, vol. 1, i, p. 305). For this reason theological cognition is quite different from those cognitions associated with secular knowledge, not least because theological truth often stands at odds with other claims to veracity: a point again made by Barth in his *Church Dogmatics* when he quotes Thurneysen, ' "The Old and New Testaments are fully at one in the view that the divine oracles as they went forth to men according to their witness constitute a self-contained *novum* over against everything men can say to themselves or to one another" ' (1975, vol. 1, i, p. 305). What though is the relation between secular and theological cognition? If theology must understand itself as 'a self-contained *novum*', then what relation, if any, does this have with what men can say about themselves, each other and the world?

Here then we confront another danger. If theology is to avoid the solipsism and performative self-contradiction that arises from denying the possibility of other knowledge claims whilst advancing its own, then the relationship of theological to secular cognition cannot simply be one of negation. This would have the effect of relativizing truth while claiming to pursue its unity. How, though, could the relationship between secular and religious cognition be thought, if not in terms of each negating the other? We could be Platonic here and suggest that theological cognition relates to secular cognition in much the same way that a form relates to what it informs. Figured in this manner we would be able to imply that the theological universal could be approached by secular thought, but not fully actualized nor exhausted. We could further refine this, via a neo-Platonic introduction of a hypostasized theory of divine emanation. If we proceed in this way we could open up a distinction between theological and secular cognition, and by positing a spectrum of increasing and decreasing perfection (with religious cognition placed at the most elevated pole, and secular at the most diminished), we could argue that secular cognition was merely cognition at a lower level than theological knowledge. Roughly conceived, this schema would avoid simply negating secular knowledge by suggesting that the secular could gradually ascend to theological insight through its ever closer approximation to the theological universal. In this way we could maintain a distinction between the two forms of cognition without denying that both were indeed forms of knowledge.

This schema would provide an answer, but it would not be a Christian one. God thought in this way would fall under the most debased accounts of metaphysics. This God would be figured as a supreme object, one whose true essence would ground other essences, and one who would maintain Himself as the most perfect entity in this order. Not only would this model fulfil the Heideggerian account of onto-theo-logy, but the twofold unity of being in general and beings configured according to the most high would be guaranteed through the perfected use of an epistemological method (Heidegger, 1957, p. 50). This method would obviously have to utilize metaphors of failing sight versus correct perception. And whilst I will indeed go on to advocate the use of these terms, their use within this schema would make God an ontic object without us realizing that this is what has taken place. For we would be unable to wrench apart a description of this onto-theological God from a description of any other entity; for God and that which was existent would have become too closely bound in their mutual identification. A God who was configured in this way would pay the price of seeking a common foundation with its creations, He would become indistinguishable from them, and the secular project of founding knowledge would have once again levelled the qualitative distinction between the Creator and his creatures.

A Christian account of the situation that pertains between secular and theological cognition would then require both an absolute distinction between the two and an account of their relation. Moreover this relation would have to be thought in such a way that the distinction between the two forms of cognition would not be placed under threat. Perhaps the most successful way to fulfil these requirements is to suggest that since God must lie at the source of all existents, then any cognition of these existents relies upon them having been created and actualized in the first place. But if the relation of theological to secular cognition is that the former makes possible the latter, then will this not simply be another transcendental assumption? An assumption that will tend to push us towards a reductive conceptual theology? No, if this order of succession is thought through an account of God's love and solicitude. For transcendental thinking gains all of its force from its deemed necessity. The *a priori* is only inferred because we are told that if this were not the case then knowledge would not be possible. Yet there is nothing necessary about the gratuity of God's acts of creation. Indeed most theological thinking recognizes God's freedom and absolute sovereignty, and hence His ability to undo all that He has made possible. But equally theology has always stressed that as the created order does exist, it springs forth from nothing *but the solicitude of God*, 'for this he created all' (Wisdom 1:14), and 'it was for no reason except his own compassion' (Titus 3.3). Given that all which is existent springs forth from nothing but God's love and solicitude, then it appears that necessity no longer has any necessary place in theological thinking; not least because love cannot be love unless it is wholly unconditional. Transcendental thinking cannot think this gift because it cannot, as Kant repeatedly stated, think the unconditioned. Critical philosophy claims to have dispensed with this naive faith in the simple givenness of things. However, this position precludes for transcendental reflection any recognition that this pre-critical naïveté might be an acknowledgement that consciousness does not wholly determine what is possible for experience. As such transcendental thinking cannot accept what is given because it has no faith in it. For transcendental thought the true nature of things is forever precluded from consciousness.

But for theology, because God gives everything without remainder, there can be no noumenal thing in-itself (*Ding an sich*), hidden for all time from human possibility. In truth the highest possibility of everything is there for human life. Because God loves what he has created – 'you love all that exists' (Wisdom 11:24) – nothing of this can be held back. Indeed for the very highest all is given 'without reserve' (John 3:33), and nothing is lost: 'now the will of him who sent me is that I should lose nothing of all that he has given me' (John 6:39). For theology then all is given and nothing is lost. Do we have then, suddenly, the common ground between the secular and the religious that we have been seeking – the very plenitude of the given? And is the distinction, and the relation, between theology and secular thinking to be found in their differing accounts of the given, of what is cognitively available for human understanding?

However, before I enter any description of this theological givenness we must ensure that in our quest for a positive account of theology we do not become positivists. We must not seek out a given event in the empirical sphere and repeat the structures of onto-theological thinking that we believed had been left behind with our now discarded conceptuality. To do this would be to make theology into the ontic science that Heidegger once claimed it was.[4] No, to understand theology as an account of this givenness without necessity, is already to have broken with the onto-theology that would make God the necessary guarantor of all the goodness, beauty and truth of the world. And even though God is undoubtedly the source of such qualities, to orientate ourselves towards the perceptual awareness of the incessant presence of these 'goods' is not necessarily to repeat onto-theological thinking. We can avoid this positioning by refusing all the attempts of modern metaphysics to make God a necessary being. In the realm of the given and its perception, this would be akin to refusing to see beyond what is seen. It would be to say that necessity was not a perceptual given but a conceptual imposition. To say this is to claim that God announces Himself not as the necessary guarantor of the world but rather as its loving creator. And whilst I would deny perceptual import to the former, there appears in the case of the latter, every reason not to do so.

This break with necessity initiates a break (or epochē) with all the assumptions that govern our account of the given. For even though we suddenly discerned the common ground between secular and theological knowledge to be the given, I have almost immediately claimed for theology an understanding of the given that is unrecognizable by secular thought. Secular thinking (and here I will once again simplify for the sake of clarity), whatever position it takes with respect to the given, will not be able to perceive the presence of transcendence within it. If it does so it will only recognize transcendence through the figure of the sublime, and think of it as some sort of irreducible excess that conceptuality cannot account for. Perhaps not surprisingly, a theological approach to the given would need to be quite different. Pregnant within the given would be all the forms and grammar necessary for our acknowledgement, reception and participation in transcendence. Given this dispute about the status of the given, about what it is possible for the given to give, and if we are not to retreat to mutually indifferent positions, then we must return to this givenness to ascertain which of the two descriptions pertains.

If suddenly we have found the given to be the measure by which the competing descriptions of theological and secular cognition can be adjudicated, then we must be concerned that we have equally suddenly decided that this dispute is of such a nature that it can only be resolved by means of an epochē (a bracketing out of all our conceptual assumptions and subsequent standpoints on the world), because to return to the given whilst disputing its nature would seem to leave us with little option except to abstain from all of our assumptions about its character. The hope of this procedure remains that we might re-envisage the object of our analysis and as a consequence decide which of the competing depictions appears to pertain most closely. But the overwhelming problem concerning this method is one that Husserl himself acknowledged. In *Ideas* he asks 'for what can remain over when the whole world is bracketed, including ourselves and all our thinking?' (1962, p. 101). And in many ways phenomenology, as the study of what is essential in phenomena, has failed to recognize the extent and legitimacy of this concern, as it is precisely ourselves and our ways of thinking that help to make up, if not constitute, the very world we experience. However, the epochē or reduction is not a way to revisit the potency of the human mind over and against the world, it is not a way to smuggle in conceptuality through the back door by revealing the attempt to think a world without us as unthinkable. Rather the reduction puts out of play our intentional relation to the world so that the very nature of the world and our intrinsic involvement with it can be revealed anew. As Merleau-Ponty said, the suspension of conceptuality that is the epochē, allows us to step back from the world 'to watch the transcendencies spring forth' (1945, p. viii).[5]

Thought in this way the epochē is not a path to incoherence, but a means whereby theology can overturn the secular account of the given. For once theology recognizes that it must proceed without the safety of legitimating concepts, then theology is offered the opportunity to be come truly faithful. Faithful that is, not to secular priorities and concerns, but rather faithful to what presents itself to human consciousness as theological. And if I am correct and it is presentation itself that is theological, and all secular thinking is an illegitimate departure from this given, then a concern with the transcendent status of this givenness could mark the point at which the solipsism and self-contradiction of holding to the superiority of theological cognition over and against secular knowledge could be avoided. Perhaps this could be because theological cognition would no longer be the private exclusive domain of those who chose to inhabit its conceptual architectonic, so it would be there, as a communal possibility, for all those who are capable of experience. This would be to say that the given might reveal (for all those who would care to look), intertwined within itself, possibilities other than ontic description.[6] For theology some sort of epochē appears necessary because without such a procedure it would seem as though the theological aspect of experience could not reveal itself, for the secular model of the given appears to do nothing but assert itself at every turn.

As secular thinking has absorbed so much of the world, it is at first hard not to see the world primarily as a secular phenomenon. But as I have said, theology cannot concede to this secular understanding of reality. For theology must always maintain the distinction between the created and the uncreated order. If the created order is allowed to maintain that it, and it alone, is the arbiter of what is, then no account of that which transcends, and yet informs, the natural order will be possible. To contend that the secular picture of the world does not have a necessary ascendancy is to postulate that the given is interpenetrated with both the created and the non-created order, with each sensible being bearing the mark of one order whilst being intertwined and shot through by the other.

Although this characterization of the situation would allow us to ascertain why both forms of cognition are both possible and yet different it does carry some theological risks. Perhaps the most obvious is that of pantheism. Conceptual theology understands any theological focus on sensibility as a collapse of God into his creatures and hence a form of pantheism. But the situation I am beginning to describe could not be a pantheism because though both orders can indeed be perceived, they cannot be subsumed into one another. To argue from perception is not necessarily to endorse the classic account of the sensible world as an inchoate sphere of ever-changing and indistinct flux, where nothing is able to discriminate itself, and all is absorbed by the all. Moreover, as Merleau-Ponty pointed out, it is a characteristic of conceptual thinking to perceive any philosophical accentuation of sensibility as courting pantheism (1968b, p. 11).[7] At the other extreme the concern would be that of endorsing a two-order dualism. But we have already said that God gives everything and nothing is held in reserve. Which would be to say that if the uncreated and the created orders are distinguishable, they are not separable since God is wholly for his creatures and so not thinkable apart from them.

Now the same is not true of the created order: whilst God is for his creatures, his creatures are not necessarily for him. The created appears to be free to ignore and turn away from God and their own highest possibilities: 'They knew God and yet refused to honour him as God or to thank him' (Romans 1:21). None the less God does not abandon us, for though we are free to turn away from God, if he turned away from us we would fall into nothingness. God overcomes our turning away and assumes our sin 'through the free gift of grace', so that we are not irretrievably damaged by our own activities (Romans 3:24). So it appears that whilst theology must understand the secular world as having existent validity and independence only by virtue of the free gift of God's grace, the secular world owes God no such debt of recognition.

And it is exactly this lack of recognition that necessitates for theology the epochē. Because whilst theological cognition attempts to account for secular knowledge, secular thinking feels it owes no such debt to theology. For although we have been pursuing a certain rapprochement between theology and secular thinking, we have overlooked something rather crucial. Whilst theological thinking cannot negate secular thought, secular thinking negates God. Secular thought does not even accept that there can be a common ground between faith and knowledge. Modern conceptuality only allows an institutional space for theology because it believes that all religious claims have been neutralized. In my attempt to discern a cognitive sphere for theology I have accepted that this project requires a return to what is original in experience. I have done this in the belief that God, who stands at the source of all that is and might be, has been denuded by the separation of faith from knowledge, and denied the purchase on reality that is proper to Him and utterly necessary for us. Yet secular thinking does not see what theology claims it is possible to perceive. To quote Husserl again, 'from the natural standpoint nothing can be seen except the natural world' (1962, p. 103). To those who are committed to the primacy of the natural standpoint, theology contends 'that they may see and see again, but not perceive; may hear and hear again, but not understand' (Mark 4:12). I will now examine the form that this blindness takes in the modern world, in order to propose its abandonment 'so that those without sight may see' (John 9:39).

Cognition and its Other Possibilities

What is real in intuitions cannot be invented a priori
(Kant, 1978, § A375, p. 349)

. . . et la qualité n'est pas un élément de la conscience, c'est une propriété de l *'object'*
(Merleau-Ponty, 1989, p. 10)[8]

But what do I mean by conceptuality and what do I think is left over after the field is levelled and all that is not original to what is given has been discarded? Earlier I had claimed that my hope was to uncover a cognitive relation between sensibility and transcendence. To do this, I suggested, would require a refiguring of the role of sensibility vis-à-vis conceptuality. For conceptuality has always functioned to deny cognitive weight to empirical transcendence. For Kant, not only is transcendence defined as that which oversteps 'the limits of all experience', but the experience of the empirical is itself limited in terms of what it can deliver (1978, § A327, § B384, p. 319). Kant repeatedly tells us that though the 'thing itself is indeed given . . . we can have no insight into its nature' (1978, § A614, § B642, p. 514).

However, if theology can indeed be knowledge, and if we have already refused the consolations of conceptual theology and its onto-theological claim to have an *a priori* account of God, then we are forced to agree with Kant's opening to the B edition of *The Critique of Pure Reason* that '[T]here can be no doubt that all our knowledge begins with experience' (1978, § B1, p. 41). Having said this, the less than equivalent opening of the earlier 'A Introduction' to the first *Critique* reads as follows: '[E]xperience is, beyond all doubt, the first product to which our understanding gives rise, in working up the raw material of sensible impressions (*sinnliche Empfindungen*)' (1978, § A1, p. 41).

Experience, then, occupies a curious position: it is both a primary phenomenon and yet a secondary product. For Kant this interesting discrepancy is due in no small part to his belief that both experience and its raw material of sensible impressions remain inadequate to the task of knowledge. For by themselves experience and sensibility cannot give a demonstration of inner necessity, that is they cannot exhibit a 'true universality' (1978, § A1, p. 42). Thus *The Critique of Pure Reason* opens with a denial that the universal might be available from mere experience, and it is this denial that turns Kant inward to 'a knowledge that is thus independent of experience and even of all impressions of the senses'. 'Such knowledge', he continues, 'is entitled *a priori*, and distinguished from the *empirical*, which has its sources *a posteriori*, that is, in experience' (1978, § B2, p. 42).

The *a priori* itself is, however, hidden. From the perspective of the *a posteriori* the *a priori* can only be inferred rather than encountered. It is, of course, Kant's innovation to underpin the realist world with a transcendental reality, a move that enables him to claim to be both a realist and an idealist. For by his own terms his inquiry is not a transcendent enterprise for it does not depart from experience; rather it is a transcendental inquiry for it underpins experience with its own possibility. As one interpreter puts it: 'Kant thrust the ideality behind the real quite literally *beyond* the threshold of perception. . . . Ideality never peeks out at us through the curtain of experience; it has no empirical manifestation whatsoever, and so – like the thing in itself – plays no role whatever in empirical explanation' (Waxman, 1991, p. 66).

To thrust the origin of the world beyond the threshold of perception is of course, for me, to repeat the attempts to conceptually secure reality (whilst in fact abandoning it altogether) for the sake of some fictive unity. Moreover, to sunder the ideal from the real is not only to condemn the highest ideal to having no reality, it is to preclude the possibility of its perception by human beings. It is for this reason that a theology which would align itself with the real must consider the question of perception as having a certain primacy. If I, broadly speaking, understand perception to refer to that first cognitive zone of interaction between the human mind and the world, then one can see how debates about what is given, and what is original to this givenness, must centre around the question of perception. For what is it possible for us to perceive? Conceptuality, especially in its most critical variant, claims to perform the function of making possible perception in the first place, and it consequently views the contribution from the external world as being one of bare and undifferentiated existentiality only. To suggest the contrary, to suggest that sensibility possesses its own uniqueness and contributes its own form to cognition – this would be to take a different stance towards the possibilities of perception, a stance that would necessitate both a critique of the conceptual account of what is perceived, and an elucidation of a different understanding of phenomenal appearance.

Unfortunately, owing to the exigencies of space, I cannot attempt here a full description and critique of the conceptual account of perception. None the less, I hope to fulfil something of this requirement through a brief examination of the oblique exemplar that we have used for conceptuality – the work of Immanuel Kant. Moreover, I would like to use Kant's account of perception and sensibility taken from the transcendental deduction found in the first *Critique*. This transcendental deduction is perhaps the most persuasive and powerful account by conceptuality of its decisive role in perception. For even though Kant wrote, 'What is first given to us is appearance. When combined with consciousness, it is called perception' (1978, § A120, p. 143), he went even further and gave the synthetic activity of the mind a role in constituting the very appearances that were subsequently combined with consciousness to form perception. For example, Kant goes on to say, 'since every appearance contains a manifold and since different perceptions therefore occur in the mind separately and singly, a combination of them, such as they cannot have in sense itself, is demanded' (1978, § A120, p. 144). And leaving aside whether this power of combination, given by Kant a few lines later to the imagination, places or finds raw instances of sensation in relations of time and space before they are synthesized into a manifold suitable for perception, we can already begin to ascertain that the senses, prior to the supervening of the *a priori* forms of both intuition and the understanding, are restricted merely to being conduits of passage for brute sensible impression: a type of datum that apparently has no inherent integrity or form itself – such that any form sensibility might have 'exists only in being known' (1978, § A120ff, p. 143ff).

And we might throw the terrain into a sharper relief by opposing the conceptual absorption of the empirical sphere to a methodology that has increasingly found itself defending the integrity and uniqueness of appearance itself – phenomenology. Indeed Husserl, who can be rightly credited with 'discovering' this new method, announced that if phenomenology was the study of appearances in their own right, that is if the very appearance of appearance was to be a source of authority for phenomenology, then the principle of principles for phenomenology, its governing mode, was to be 'that whatever presents itself in intuition in primordial form . . . is simply to be accepted as it gives itself out to be . . .' (1962, p. 83). Whatever the intention of its author, this legitimization of intuition has had the consequence of preserving for phenomenology a certain regard for the foundational and unique status of intuition vis-à-vis the derived and derivative nature of the understanding.

Now, it remains a defining mark of conceptuality that it will always construe the interests of sensibility as lying with subordination to the demands of the understanding. For conceptuality will maintain that cognition, or rather knowledge, would simply not be possible if sensibility were not to fulfil all of conceptuality's requirements. For instance, though Kant wrote the following in § A90 of the transcendental deduction: 'The categories of understanding, on the other hand, do not represent the conditions under which objects are given in intuition. Objects may, therefore, appear to us without their being under the necessity of being related to the functions of understanding; and understanding need not,

therefore, contain their a priori conditions' (1978, § A90, p. 124); if in
fact he held otherwise, the very distinction between sensibility and the
understanding would be at risk. None the less, Kant resolved this possibility – at least in the A deduction – through negating it. For instance
he writes that intuitions 'are nothing to us, and do not in the least concern us if they cannot be taken up into consciousness' (1978, § A116,
pp. 141–2).

For even if 'appearances might very well be so constituted that the
understanding should not find them to be in accordance with the conditions of its unity' (1978, § A90, B123, p. 124), Kant's claim is that appearances cannot be like this. Appearances cannot be thought to operate against
the concerns of the understanding, since if they did there would be no
such thing as appearance at all. Thus Kant sought to show how the *a
priori* concepts of the understanding 'also serve as antecedent conditions'
without which appearances would not be possible (as objects of thought)
either (1978 § A93, B125, p. 126).[9] Hence Kant insists that these concepts claim the loyalty of intuition because only by 'presupposing them
is anything possible as an *object of experience*' (1978, § A93, B126, pp.
125–6). Indeed Kant seeks to demonstrate that *a priori* concepts of thought
must also serve, along with the *a priori* forms of intuition, as antecedent
conditions of appearances *in so far as experience can be brought to thought
at all*. Whilst this is not to confuse intuition with understanding, it does
suggest that if intuition wishes to become cognition, then intuition must
(we are told) accept that conforming with the form of the understanding
is a necessary, if not a sufficient, condition for knowledge.

Kant thus declares that 'all appearances, as possible experiences, thus
lie *a priori* in the understanding, and receive from it their formal possibility, just as in so far as they are mere intuitions, they lie in the
sensibility, and are, as regards their form, only possible through it' (1978,
§ A127, p. 148). So from the point of view of both understanding and
intuition, sensation is considered to be a formless existential affectation
that is only rendered as an appropriate unit for apprehension and cognitive
synthesis by being thought through the *a priori* structures of the Kantian
schema. Indeed from the perspective of the sensations themselves Kant
tells us exactly this:

> That in the appearance which corresponds to sensation I term its *matter*;
> but that which so determines the manifold of appearance that it allows of
> being ordered in certain representations, I term the *form* of appearance.
> That in which alone the sensations can be posited and ordered in a certain
> form cannot itself be sensation; and therefore, while the matter of all appear-
> ance is given to us *a posteriori* only, its form must lie ready for the sensations
> *a priori* in the mind, and so must allow of being considered apart from all
> sensation.   (1978, § A20, B34, p. 66)

Now whilst Kant gave both intuition and the understanding their own formal dimension, I am interested in disengaging sensibility not only from the understanding but also from the formal *a priori* structures that conceptuality deems to constitute intuition. For if it becomes possible to think that intuition could operate against the formal *a priori* categories of the understanding, then why should such a sensation be required to stand under the formal *a priori* conditions of intuition (space and time)? Whilst Kant claims that these *a priori* forms of intuition make possible perception, since it is they that enable the raw units of sense to be placed in relations of succession and juxtaposition, making them suitable for uptake by the understanding, if we take the Husserlian principle of principles seriously, then these *a priori* forms which claim to anticipate perception by dwelling 'in us as forms of our sensible intuition, before any real object' should also be disregarded in any attempt to explain the perceived and what is original to it (Kant, 1978, § A373, p. 348).

Accepting whatever might present itself in intuition as whatever it gives itself out to be, would, it seems, require also that we purge intuition of that which is foreign to it. And it is this that might well mark the point at which it becomes possible to think that appearances could operate contrary to the interests of *a priori* form. Intuition could then be truly aligned with the possibilities of what might be presented to it. For if (with reference to the long quotation from Kant above), as Merleau-Ponty suggests, 'matter is "pregnant" with its form' (1964a, p. 12), then to recast this point in terms of my earlier vocabulary, this would be to say that sensibility already has a cognitive form, one that does not require the intervention of conceptuality to render it thinkable. To say this is to say that that which is sensible already displays itself as cognizable. This is to contend that sensibles already present themselves with forms and qualities, attributes which they have for themselves and ones which do not derive or descend from any *a priori* form.

To render this thinkable, and hence perhaps also possible, is to attempt a description of a world that is not all covered over in human projections, whether these projections be unconscious or not. Whilst phenomenology is indeed many things, it should be at least the attempt to offer forth something like this. For the phenomenological claim is that appearance does indeed contain within itself both universality and reality. By way of an example, for Max Scheler, one of the early German phenomenologists, the world is a realm of eidetic essences that the mind participates and shares in. For Scheler it is this realm that is occluded by Kant when he (illegitimately) posits beneath such a reality the transcendental and constitutive acts of the mind, 'of which the empirical is a mere consequence' (Kant, 1978, § A114, p. 140). Cognition does not for Scheler 'produce objects', rather, cognition is 'consciousness-of-something'

– phenomenology would in this sense be for Scheler more of a passive acknowledgement. For him 'cognition has nothing to do with any production, formation or construction of the given' (Scheler, 1973, pp. 159ff). Perhaps the crucial difference for Scheler, between phenomenology and Kantian thought is that the former wishes to speak of 'the self-givenness of the object', whilst the latter manages and indeed denies this actuality through an evasion of experience and a retreat into subjective formalism (1973, pp. 140ff).

To argue phenomenologically and theologically against the Kantian notion of the *'a priori'* is to be paradoxically more Kantian than Kant. It is to argue that any philosophy of reflection, any turning away from objects to a consciousness of objects, presupposes a pre-reflective or pre-predicative world. This world is already there prior to the transcendental assumptions of *a priori* thought. Merleau-Ponty, by seeking to distinguish the phenomenological relationship with the object from Kant's understanding, makes just this point: 'What distinguishes intentionality from the Kantian relation to a possible object is that the unity of the world, before being posited by knowledge in a specific act of identification, is lived as ready-made (*déjà faite*) or already there (*déjà là*)' (Merleau-Ponty, 1945, p. xii). It is this sense of a turning of consciousness to the 'already there' that best illustrates the phenomenological approach to the question of human cognition and the appearances which are possible for it. Whilst it is true that for Husserlian phenomenology, the object is also (as with Kant) a result of synthetic operations, in Husserl's case this synthesis is achieved via a constitution of perspectival adumbrations (*Abschattungen*), achieved through a multiplicity of recession-phases (*Ablaufsphasen*) in internal time-consciousness. But even Husserl, according to Merleau-Ponty, distinguished between the intentionality of the act 'which is that of our judgments and of those occasions when we voluntarily take up a position' (a mode which Merleau-Ponty claims is the 'only intentionality discussed in *The Critique of Pure Reason*'), and operative intentionality (*fungierende Intentionalität*), or that 'which produces the natural and antepredicative unity of the world and of our life' (Merleau-Ponty, 1945, p. xiii).

For Merleau-Ponty, '[T]hrough this broadened notion of intentionality, phenomenological "comprehension" is distinguished from traditional "intellection" – and so phenomenology can become a phenomenology of origins' (*phénoménologie de la genèse*) (1945, p. xiii). All of which suggests that for phenomenology, transcendental knowledge is no longer the primary issue, for transcendental knowledge has been revealed as a derived phenomenon. The investigation of the nature of that from which the transcendental is derived, the pre-divided world, is complex. For the Heidegger of *Sein und Zeit* it is here, at this juncture, that phenomenology becomes the *Sehenlassen* (letting be seen) of that which shows itself from itself (*von ihm selbst her*). For Heidegger, in this way, and in this way only, can phenomenology obey the maxim of return – 'to the things themselves' (*zu den Sachen selbst*)' (1962, § II, p. 58; 1977, p. 46). Indeed he gives the formal meaning of phenomenology as 'to let that which shows itself be seen from itself in the very way in which it shows itself from itself' (1962, § II, p. 58; 1977, p. 46). Phenomenology so understood attempts to separate the whatness of a thing, its thinghood (*Sachheit*), from the howness of how that thing is exhibited and understood. Moreover, we should recall what was written by Hegel in *The Phenomenology* as the *first injunction* against consciousness in respect of its primary encounter with the world – 'Our approach to the object must also be *immediate* or *receptive*; we must alter nothing in the object as it presents itself. In *ap*prehending it, we must refrain from trying to *com*prehend it' (1977b, p. 58).

To refrain from comprehension, in order to enable perception, that is a phrase which Kant would regard as both misconstrued and ridiculous. For Kant perception was already comprehension, part of consciousness. However, for me perception can be disengaged from the formal dimension of comprehension (that is from its *a priori* element), and so offer us something new, an experience which we had not previously recognized or prepared for. Conceptuality cannot think the new; it has already by definition prepared for it *a priori*. For conceptual thought the new can only occur on the side of rationality, in the pulse of the imagination and its flights of fancy. That experience could offer us this futurity is something that, apparently, cannot be thought. As I have indicated, in conceptual thinking formalism is claimed to permeate even the intuitions, such that cognition is thought not to touch any form that does not originate from itself or from its own preparations.

At best I have perhaps shown that this assumption derives from the interests of conceptuality and not from what is found in the world. For as soon as we ask whether sensations can be considered apart from concepts, we think of sensation as distinct from conceptuality and hence we almost immediately break with the immanentist circle that argues they can only be thought of together or not at all. And leaving aside whatever concordat might be established between these two realms for the sake of knowledge, be it Leibniz's harmonious pre-formationism or indeed Kant's account of mutually purposive epigenesis, the point remains that at the very least it must be considered unproven that that which I perceive derives its possibility from me: in which case perception might mark a contact with reality. A contact that is, it seems, not licensed by any prior order, cause or concern. It quite simply befalls us.

Theology and the Passage from Secular to Religious Perception

How hard I find it to see what is right in front of my eyes!
(Wittgenstein, 1980, p. 39)

Believe that you have it already and it will be yours.
(Mark 11:25)

Earlier I contended that theology's task lay in overturning the secular account of the given. I had even come close to asserting that a perception of the given that was freed of its conceptual en-framing could not avoid being theological. By asserting this sort of direct theological realism, accessed via an epochē of conceptuality, I had hoped to distinguish a theological account of perception from a secular one. I had perhaps also hoped to suggest that perception itself was theological, since reality must in some sense be spiritual as 'all things were created through him' (Colossians 1:17). By claiming that this situation was disguised and hidden by conceptuality, I avoided the oppositional negation of secular knowledge by theological truth and eschewed theological solipsism by opening up the possibility of perceiving theologically to all. To suggest this, I argued, was to contend that cognition and reality are not necessarily aligned to an atheist orbit. It was a consequent hope of mine that cognition could be opened up to reality, such that an account of the real need not culminate in secular descriptions of a world already totalized by human projection. For I had not broken from conceptuality to endorse an atheistic account of sensibility. A theology that left a secular concept for a Godless world would be at one with the nihilism that originally denied God to experience. For my hope has been rather that an empiricism freed from the categorizations of finite understanding would now look radically different – different from all the secular realisms and their descriptions of what reality amounts too. However, and unfortunately, even if one accepts that the rule of conceptuality can be expunged from the cognitive process, and that the real (whatever it might be) can emerge from the noumenal into the phenomenal, thereby granting to perception possibilities previously denied, it is still by no means certain that the reality encountered by perception will be a theological one!

The given can look *both* theological and secular because there is a paradox of immanence and transcendence in perception. Immanence, because the perceived object cannot be foreign to him who perceives it; transcendence because perception always contains more than is actually presented in it.[10] It is at this point that theology confronts both the possibility of idolatry and also the hope of 'seeing face to face' (1 Corinthians 13:12). For whilst I may have argued for the possibility of theological perception, I cannot guarantee its practice by perceivers, not least because I have dispensed with all arguments regarding necessity in theology. It is the nature of this world that perceivers are free to acknowledge God or not (Romans 1:21). Though I have perhaps indicated that its secular limitations are no longer necessary, the immanentist standpoint cannot free itself from these assumptions. These assumptions are built into the cognitive structures of a perception that wills itself to see only its immanent dimension. The secular perceiver cannot embrace the transcendence at the heart of immanence because he lacks the requisite faith.

As has been suggested, this denial of the transcendent dimension in perception has its origin not in sensibility itself but elsewhere. It lies in some sort of *failure* of the secular gaze. The refusal to see transcendence, to see what 'has been made visible' (1 John 1:2), produces the point at which perception turns away from the possibilities of experience and retreats into immanence. Because turning away from transcendence is a turning away from a higher possibility, this act must be disguised from the actor that performs it. It is here that a retreat into an immanentist perception produces its idols. The idol takes the possibility of the most high and inverts it into what is no longer possible. This is how God becomes a Kantian idea that 'cannot be paralleled in any experience' (Kant, 1978, § A638, B666, p. 529). In this way idols ensure that what is not immanent is maintained as cognitively inaccessible rather than actually possible. To speak very simply, immanence produces idols that stand in front of transcendence and conceal a higher phenomenology.

In *Dieu sans l' être*, Jean-Luc Marion describes this structure as being akin to the function of an invisible mirror (1991). For Marion the idol constitutes itself through fulfilling the function of an invisible mirror. The secular gaze approaches the mirror, and the mirror (as an idol) reflects back the look so that this gaze never transcends itself. Yet the idol never announces itself as an idol; as its reflective function wholly conceals its form, the mirror never reveals itself as a mirror. Moreover, Marion goes on to suggest that this idolatrous structure is itself a product of the thought which unknowingly venerates the idol as something glorious and external. The idol, he suggests, owes its origin to the fatigue of the immanentist gaze, *'il révèle une manière de fatigue essentielle'*; it is as far as the secular can go and consequently the idol represents the highest possibilities and furthest limits of idolatrous immanence (Marion, 1991, p. 22). To go beyond this point would necessitate dispensing with the secular gaze altogether, and for secular thought this is the very possibility that must be discounted. As a consequence idols do not allow the transcendent dimension of perception, the invisible, to become visible. Idols thus block the fullest possibility of perception. As Marion writes *'L'idole n'admet aucun invisible'*, the invisible is prohibited by the idol, and the divine, in consequence, is only allowed to occur by human measure (1991, p. 23).

In which case, we are perhaps in a position to offer a tentative, and all too brief, account of what the passage from a secular to a theological perception might be. If a perception, or description, is immanentist, then it is in some sense closed. By this I mean that most secular positions claim to pursue knowledge, and secular thought tells us that knowledge is not possible of infinite things. For if things are not limited and bound then it is thought that we can never claim to know them in their fullness and finality. Leaving aside whether these immanentist positions are idealist or realist, that is, whether they close on the side of a self-identical subject or on the surface of a fully exhausted and known object, let us take a position on secular knowledge. Though I suggested at the outset that as the queen of the sciences theology should seek knowledge, we have perhaps come to understand that theological cognition is *quite different* from any other form of knowledge. Secular knowledge understands itself as a self-sufficient project. This form of knowledge is not countenanced by theology because the task of theology is to maintain and show that nothing in the created order is self-sufficient.

Secular knowledge believes that it can constitute a finite world out of an infinite one without accounting for the origin of this possibility. And it is not that the knowledge that is derived from this activity is wrong, or false; the world is indeed for us, objects do give themselves over to us so that we might know them. It is just that as an account of reality, of what is possible, the secular is insufficient. This insufficiency is marked and revealed by the inability of secular knowledge to provide its own foundations. It can *never* secure itself against scepticism. The secular can never, despite its best intents, level the world into an immanentism that is not fractured by transcendence. For immanentism is also of course an insufficient account – a fact which is also revealed and marked by the inability of immanentism to collapse all the disjunctures and discrepancies of phenomenal life into its uniform ontology. For instance, and by way of example, immanentist thought still cannot adequately account for the distinction between the subject and the object. Between the mind and the world there seems to exist a gulf that forbids knowledge from claiming a universal status for itself. A true knowledge would not or could not endorse an immanentist account of the world. As I have been suggesting, any reflection upon our own experience of experience would suggest that transcendence fractures every cognition we have. Even if this fracture, or aporia, is read as a secular phenomenon, it is not. The disjunctures that have obsessed epistemology, whilst they do indeed testify to the insufficiency of finite life, can if looked at anew provoke a recognition and acknowledgement of transcendence and a passage to a new cognition.

To chart this passage I will follow, up to a point, the work of Maurice Merleau-Ponty. For his work leads us into an account of the real that I (speaking theologically) have been arguing for all along. Here, though, I must be very clear. I do not wish to, nor can I, co-opt Merleau-Ponty's *oeuvre* into a religious metaphysic.[11] For he was not unopposed to theology. However, it could be said that Merleau-Ponty's main opposition to theology came from a (mistaken) belief that theology was opposed to the world.[12] Now if we have dispensed with the abstract conceptual theology of a necessary being (because we found it an unnecessary concept for theology), then it is perhaps not surprising that one can find common cause with a phenomenology that uncovers, when looking at creation, transcendence.

Merleau-Ponty was always concerned with the paradox of immanence and transcendence in perception. In *Le Visible et l'Invisible*, Mereau-Ponty testified to this when he described the relation between the seer and the visible as a world of immanence crossed with something else. For him, human access to this world is achieved by the body. The body, though it is born through segregation from the world, is alone in being that which can bring us to the things themselves (*mener aux choses mêmes*) (1964b, p. 179). For the body is of this world and though separated from this milieu it is inseparable from it. The body, as a being of two leaves (*feuillets*), reflects and indeed constitutes the objective and subjective side of the world, the side of the world that is thought and the side which thinks. But since, for Merleau-Ponty, the world is the infinite totality of what is sensed, then even this understanding reveals itself as too derived and oppositional. The seer becomes wholly intertwined with the visible. They become inseparable moments of each other. But when Merleau-Ponty asks 'what we have found with this strange adherence of the seer (*voyant*) and the visible' (1964b, p. 183), he discerns that there pertains a form of visibility which belongs to neither him who sees, nor to that which is seen. Like a reflection between two mirrors, this element or flesh (*chair*) provokes out of nothing a plenitude of visibility. This infinite visibility or *chair* announces itself as both present and prior to its participating elements; it conducts itself as the most universal through producing the most singular and represents, as Merleau-Ponty says, a domain which is unlimited (1964b, p. 185). He continues, 'If we can show that the flesh is an ultimate notion (*une notion dernière*), that it is not the union or compound of two substances, but thinkable by itself, if there is a relation of the visible with itself that traverses me and constitutes me as a seer, this circle which I do not form, which forms me, this coiling over (*enroulement*) of the visible upon the visible can traverse, animate other bodies as well as my own' (1964b, p. 185). The visible as flesh then becomes a kind of condition of both individuation and communication. It is as if the empirical possesses all the qualities and distinctions it requires and its being consists in distributing them to all the existent and singularized beings that participate in it.

This visibility then is in one sense the phenomenological world that I maintained was concealed by conceptuality. It is a world where everything derives or arises from a more primordial and anterior empirical element. Obviously though, this does not sound like a theological universe. Not only does it approach a description of an immanent universe extending itself beyond finitude to infinity, there is also no crossing or presence within this created order of a non-created element. All transcendence here seems to pass from the sentient being back to the flesh of the world.

However, let us put aside for now questions as to the nature and status of *chair*. For ultimately this is not our final destination, nor indeed is it Merleau-Ponty's final recognition. Let us go to what Merleau-Ponty suggests some lines later is the most difficult point. He detects in amid this visibility in general, a disjuncture between the subject and the object, between what he previously described as the two leaves of the body. In the heart of immanence, between a hand touching a hand which touches the world, Merleau-Ponty now senses a porosity or pregnancy in the previously unbreachable flesh, clear zones (*zones claires*) of the invisible (1964b, p. 195). For the hand touching the hand which touches the world testifies to a disjuncture in immanence that cannot be argued away. The sensate being sensing itself sensing cannot be explained by the sheer voluptuosity of the visible. The fracture between this world and the thought of it requires a fracturing of the immanent world of the visible. Consequently Merleau-Ponty discerns the presence of something invisible residing in this internal visibility. Merleau-Ponty calls this invisibility the idea, and the realm of ideas cannot, according to him, stand over against the flesh, rather the idea is an invisible attached to the visible. 'This invisible . . . cannot be detached (*se laissent*) from the sensible appearances and be erected into a second positivity.'[13] These ideas are now apparently thoroughly carnal and cannot stand apart from the flesh of the world. Indeed 'they could not be given to us as ideas except in a carnal experience' (Merleau-Ponty, 1964b, p. 197).

This invisibility does not simply take its place alongside and within the visible, nor does it stand apart from and above the folds of immanence that constitute the world. For Merleau-Ponty that which is absent from all flesh opens a dimension that can never again be closed. The invisible establishes 'a level in terms of which all experiences will henceforth be situated'. It is now the invisible that inhabits and makes visible this world, *l'invisible de ce monde* (1964b, p. 198). It is this ideality that sustains and gives to flesh all its interior dimensions and possibilities. Moreover Merleau-Ponty speaks of the visible as having an invisible reserve (*une réserve invisible*), a possibility that grants to flesh all of its singularities and landscapes. In short, philosophy has found here in the heart of the world a transcendence that does not, indeed cannot, stand apart from that which it informs. Merleau-Ponty impugns the opposition between this transcendence and this immanence and yet he does not collapse them together. He finds the ideal already streaming (*fuse déjà*) along the contours and articulations of sensible things (1964b, p. 200).

Merleau-Ponty concludes by postulating that this invisibility can account for thought: that the interior mental life of the body has a perception, that for the inner leaf of the body there corresponds a second visibility for the mind. This, however, is where he and I will part company. For where Merleau-Ponty claimed this invisibility for thought I will claim it for God. Indeed, I will claim, albeit in passing, that here Merleau-Ponty held back from transcendence. That here he found immanence to be so profoundly crossed with a more original solicitude; that he retreated, almost without knowing it, into a projection of human thought and structure on that which he could not understand. For by claiming that the presence of thought accounts for this invisibility, Merleau-Ponty reads back the structure of the subject and object onto the invisible, and so fails to take account of the invisible itself. He views the fracturing of the immanent universe as a transcendent event but he reads this event as an immanent phenomenon rather than as the passage to the theological that it really is.

For it is with Christianity, with the permeation of creation by the logos and supremely with the incarnation of the word into flesh, that perception is granted its fullest range. For Christ incarnates what was invisible into the visible. Whilst 'no one has ever seen God' (John 1:18), 'whom no man has seen and no man is able to see' (1 Timothy 6:16), Christ is the son 'who has made him known' (John 1:18). Christ announces himself through this communion of invisibility with the visible. 'To have seen me is to have seen the Father' (John 14:9) and 'whoever sees me sees the one who sent me' (John 12:45). If my inquiry is orientated by what Merleau-Ponty has termed perceptual faith (*la foi perceptive*) then this is precisely what theology must maintain that it is possible to see.[14] Earlier, if not initially, I had asked what a theological perception might be. We have now perhaps come close to describing the world it might deliver. Like Merleau-Ponty's *chair* it is an 'empirical' world that will not be closed over or exhausted; its perspectival possibilities and adumbrations forbid a final synthesis by any viewer. Yet, as we have shown, this is not the undifferentiated, aimless and merely immanent world that the empirical is commonly taken to be. As an unlimited world of possibilities, possibilities high and low, each element wears its own form as a future to be realized. As a differentiated, singular and yet communal sphere, this 'empirical' universe is held together, not by the human mind, but by an ideal that does indeed traverse and mark out all its contours. This ideal does not stand over and against the world as a concept would do to a content. It bonds to the real, it is the real, and it facilitates all showing as such. It runs over all beings, adhering to them, bequeathing to them all their qualities, possibilities and structures. Breathing into them their form. Marking them out from nothingness as light brings objects out of darkness. But this ideal does not derive from thought, does not come or derive from the synthetic or analytic power of the human mind. It is 'light from light'. And this light is the invisibility I have been speaking of. The invisible which runs along all reality as a penumbra which holds creatures to their visible form is a transcendent gratuity granted to all creation. It is this invisibility which hollows out creatures and grants them their being.

This is why it is a final false cognition to look into the invisible and see analogies of mental life. The world we are now describing, if there was no God, would be a purely immanent void of total presences. It would be ontologically flat but replete and pregnant with similarity. The world of human aspiration and projection would construct within such a world various internal geometries, and claim priority for this image and that horizon. Theology, however, displays all these hierarchies as false, unmasks them as idolatrous. For the immanent world of the empirical materialist is crossed by something far more real. Invisibility brings a vertical plane to the sensible, a plane of glory, that cuts across and indeed shapes all visibles, so as to give to them a possibility higher than mere presence. All visibles rest on this invisibility. Indeed, in one of the working notes to *Le Visible et l'Invisible* (1964b), Merleau-Ponty approaches a similar conclusion. He writes 'the invisible is there without being an object, it is pure transcendence, without an ontic mask. And the visibles themselves, in the last analysis, they also are only centered on a nucleus of absence (*noyau d'absence*) . . .' (1964b, p. 283).[15] This transcendence lies in the heart of all phenomena as a visibility too bright to be seen by a secular eye. Yet the visible itself, through the dimensions of its beauty, through the harmony of its surface with its vibrating and sustaining form, marks out positively the dimensions of the invisible. For the invisible as a formless donator of forms does not stand apart from that which it informs, it clings to the visible as an embodied incarnation of another possibility, a possibility that asks to be made real.

Obviously, though my descriptions are taking us beyond a secular

account of transcendence, the nature of the visible phenomena themselves requests that our phenomenology become instead a theology. For
we have been led by the phenomena to a reality which does not stand
apart from the highest idea. And, moreover, we have been led away
from the secular world where transcendence always stands as an ineffable
unknown against an immanent universe. For we have pursued the
possibilities of perception, down through all the conceptual architectonics,
all the transcendental conditioning, to the origin of our cognitions – our
contact with the external world. And here we did not remain within the
ontic universe of secular description. We discerned instead, in amidst the
fractures and disjunctures of a secular world struggling to father itself, a
truer origin. The presence 'of his inexpressible gift' (2 Corinthians 9:15).
For though we found transcendence and invisibility at the heart of all
things, we do not remain there dazzled by the wonder at the heart of
creation.

Because 'the Word was made flesh' (John 1:14), we are not blinded
by this invisibility, it is for us and we are for it. The secular eye will
always be dazzled and ravished by invisibility. The secular cannot escape
its own idolatrous miscognition of the invisible. For the immanent, the
transcendent will always be an exterior oppressive sublimity. But for us,
our phenomenology becomes theology because 'the reality is Christ'
(Colossians 2:18). We are led from a generalized wonder into the heart
of the Word, because 'He is the image of the unseen God' (Colossians
1:15). It is He that theological perception approaches in invisibility: 'the
mystery is Christ among you, your hope of glory' (Colossians 1:27).
Theology discerns in the heart of this invisibility the glory and dimensions of the most high. Christian perception does not remain within the
created order; rather it is granted to it to describe the passage into
Trinitarian participation and salvation. For theology has offered an entirely
new account of seeing. 'Happy the eyes that see what you see, for I tell
you that many prophets and kings wanted to see what you see and
never saw it' (Luke 10:24). The theological task now becomes one of
describing an entirely new account of human possibility – following the
path that takes the human body through the Son to its origin in the
Father. This is what constitutes the fulfilment of the highest human
possibility, a possibility that is there for all to see. For 'the glory on the
face of Christ' (2 Corinthians 4:6) supervenes upon the world and us,
calling upon us to fulfil nothing but our own form.

Notes

1   I take the phrase 'grammar of assent' from John Henry Newman (Newman,
1985).

2 'I have therefore found it necessary to deny *knowledge*, in order to make room for *faith*' (Kant, 1978, § B, p. 29).

3 'A (logically) consistent transcendental idealism strips the world of its opacity and transcendence.'

4 Heidegger's famous remarks concerning the similarity between the ontic sciences and theology were made at Tübingen in 1927, the same year as the publication of *Sein und Zeit*, in a lecture entitled 'Phänomenologie und Theologie' (Heidegger, 1976). In this lecture we can read remarks such as the following: 'Our thesis, then, is that *theology is a positive science, and as such, therefore, is absolutely different from philosophy*,' and, 'It is immediately clear from the thesis that theology, as a positive science, is closer to chemistry and mathematics than to philosophy.'

5 '*La réflexion ne se retire pas du monde vers l'unité de la conscience comme fondement du monde, elle prend recul pour voir jaillir les transcendances . . .*' (Merleau-Ponty, 1945, p. viii).

6 See, for example, Marion, 1989.

7 '*Toute tentative pour faire entrer en compte la finitude de la conscience sensible est récusée comme un retour au naturalisme ou même au panthéisme*' (Merleau-Ponty, 1968b, p. 11).

8 '. . . and quality is not an element of consciousness, (but) a property of the object' (Merleau-Ponty, 1989, p. 10).

9 Though I have made an affirmation out of what Kant poses as a question, further reading of this section of the Critique will, I trust, indicate that Kant did indeed resolve the matter in this way.

10 I take this remark from Merleau-Ponty (1964a, p. 16). But the realization that perception has a transcendent element, that is that it leads beyond itself, is not confined to the continental style of thinking. For instance, as Strawson comments for A. J. Ayer, 'our normal perceptual judgments always "go beyond" the sensible experience which gives rise to them, for those judgments carry implications which would not be carried by any "strict account" of the experience' (Strawson, 1988, p. 92).

11 It is interesting to note that in the manuscript notes, made apparently in May 1960, for the possible arrangement of the publication, Merleau-Ponty considered devoting a chapter of *Le Visible et l'Invisible* (1964b) to God.

12 See, for example, Merleau-Ponty's remarks concerning Maritain's inability to see bowing to the world as anything but idolatry (1953).

13 Here I give the English translation by Lingis (Merleau-Ponty, 1968a, p. 149) although I would formulate this as 'This invisible cannot detach itself from sensible appearances'.

14 The phrase is taken from the subtitles to the first two chapters of this posthumous publication (Merleau-Ponty, 1964b, pp. 17, 75).

15 The note is dated January 1960.

References

Barth, K. 1975: *Church Dogmatics: The Doctrine of the Word of God*, trans. G. W. Bromiley. Edinburgh: T. & T. Clark.

Scotus, Duns 1966: *A Treatise on God as First Principle*, trans. A. B. Wolter. Chicago: Forum Books.

Hegel, G. W. F. 1977a: *Faith and Knowledge*, trans. W. Cerf and H. S. Harris. Albany: State University New York Press.

—— 1977b: *Phenomenology of Spirit*, trans. A. V. Miller, ed. J. N. Findlay. Oxford: Oxford University Press.

Heidegger, M. 1957: *Identität und Differenz*. Pfullingen: Günther Neske Verlag.

—— 1962: *Being and Time*, trans. John Macquarrie and Edward Robinson. Oxford: Blackwell.

—— 1976: Phenomenology and theology. In J. G. Hart and J. C. Maraldo, trans. *The Piety of Thinking*, Bloomington: Indiana University Press.

—— 1977 *Sein und Zeit*: Frankfurt: Klostermann, Gesamtausgabe, bundz.

Husserl, E. 1962: *Ideas*, trans. W. R. Boyce Gibson. London: Collier Macmillan.

Kant, I. 1956: *Critique of Practical Reason*, trans. L. W. Beck, 3rd edn. New York: Macmillan.

—— 1978: *Critique of Pure Reason*, trans. Norman Kemp Smith. London: Macmillan.

Marion, J-L. 1989: *Réduction et donation*. Paris: Presses Universitaires de France.

—— 1991: *Dieu sans l'être*. Paris: Quadrige Presses Universitaires de France.

Merleau-Ponty, M. 1945: *Phénoménologie de la perception*. Paris: Librairie Gallimard.

—— 1953: *Éloge de la philosophie*. Paris: Librairie Gallimard.

—— 1964a: *The Primacy of Perception and Its Philosophical Consequences*, ed. and trans. J. Edie. Evanston: Northwestern University Press.

—— 1964b: *Le Visible et l'invisible*. Paris: Nouvelle Revue Française, Gallimard.

—— 1968a: *The Invisible and the Invisible*, trans. A. Lingis. Evanston: Northwestern University Press.

—— 1968b: *Résumés de cours: Collège de France 1952–1960*. Paris: Gallimard.

—— 1989: *Le Primat de la perception et ses conséquences philosophiques*. Grenoble: Cynara.

Newman, J. H. 1985: *An Essay in aid of A Grammar of Assent*. Oxford: Clarendon Press.

Scheler, M. 1973: Phenomenology and the theory of cognition. *Selected Philosophical Essays*, trans. David R. Lachterman. Evanston: Northwestern University Press.

Strawson, P. F. 1988: Perception and its objects. In Jonathan Dancy (ed.), *Perceptual Knowledge*, Oxford: Oxford University Press.

von Balthasar, H. U. 1982: *The Glory of the Lord*, vol. 1, trans. E. Leiva-Merikakis, eds S. J. Fessio and J. Riches. Edinburgh: T. & T. Clark.

Waxman, W. 1991: *Kant's Model of the Mind*. Oxford: Oxford University Press.

Wittgenstein, L. 1980: *Culture and Value*, trans. Peter Winch, ed. G. H. von Wright, 2nd edn. Oxford: Basil Blackwell.

CHAPTER FIFTEEN

the impossible

Kevin Hart

I

We recollect the scene: a book is published, a review appears, and both are elevated by the reviewer's authoritative judgement, 'We thus find ourselves once again at the heart of the most serious debate, where perhaps our destiny is at stake' (Blanchot, 1993, p. 37).[1] It is a debate over poetry and the sacred, an ordinary enough topic as these things go, although this one will prove to be extraordinary in both complexity and scope. We are used to discussions where art and religion engage one another, where the aim is to show that the one grounds, illuminates, re-figures or supersedes the other, or that, taken together, they generate something new, like philosophy or romanticism. So this particular debate begins on recognizable territory with the first speaker condemning a divine poetry that detaches itself from the material world and endorsing a mortal poetry that is earthed in the here and now, a poetry that none the less affirms the sacred nature of what is. Once the second speaker begins, though, we are quietly led in another direction. For he asks us to consider that those eminent human possibilities, art and religion, both respond to an obscure dimension that tolerates no God or gods, is impossible to name since it is neither phenomenon nor noumenon, and is therefore to be called 'the impossible'.

Who are the speakers in this debate? The first is Yves Bonnefoy. In 1959, when this exchange takes place, he is the author of two powerful collections of poems and, more recently, a volume of essays, *L'Improbable* (1992a), that has prompted the review already mentioned, a commentary over two numbers of *La Nouvelle Revue Française* (Blanchot, 1993). This brings us to the second participant. Speaking for the negative is Maurice Blanchot, the brilliant author of several enigmatic novels, *récits* and critical studies, and an admirer of Bonnefoy's poetry. Over the 1940s and 1950s he has become an important if somewhat mysterious figure in French literature, something that Bonnefoy had been trying to explain to English readers no more than a year before. And to that end he paraphrased the argument of Maurice Blanchot's most recent critical volume, *L'Espace littéraire* (1982):

The essence of literature is not to be found in what it explicitly asserts but in its continual annihilation of the meanings which language forces it to compound with, in its flight toward its goal of silence. The poem exists in an 'essential solitude', an eternal separation ... something which tends to break down any kind of structure, because it is man's relation with nothingness and death'. (Bonnefoy, 1958, p. 44)

As he wrote these words, Bonnefoy could not have been in complete accord with them, or at least could not have regarded them as telling the full story about poetry. Blanchot and Bonnefoy often speak from contrary, though seldom from contradictory, quarters.[2] At a distance they might seem akin, as 'philosophical' or even 'existential' writers, but on closer inspection those descriptions seem too loose to wear. Besides, there are clear divergences of stance and style. Over surrealism, for one thing: where Bonnefoy was attracted to surrealism for its affirmation of the underlying unity of the world, Blanchot values the same movement for its rigorous dissociation of language and the human subject (Bonnefoy, 1964, p. 135; Blanchot, 1949, p. 94). Over philosophy, for another thing: where Bonnefoy regards the elevation of the intelligible over the sensible with dismay, and draws only occasionally from Hegel and Heidegger, Blanchot reflects perpetually on the interlacing of philosophy and literature, and testifies to the importance of his early encounter with *Being and Time* (Blanchot, 1988, p. 45). And finally, once they pass beyond a general conception of poetry as struggle, the two writers differ over the proper valencies of poetry: while Mallarmé is an exemplary poet for Blanchot, the one who saw through the writing of verse that God is dead, for Bonnefoy Mallarmé marks a dangerous temptation. He is an inescapably modern poet who seeks 'la notion pure', not by dismissing this world in search of another but more subtly by following a tradition of rhetoric to the point of identifying reality and language. Mallarmé denies poetry's essential finitude and erases the speaking subject, Bonnefoy tells us, and adds, with feeling, that the poet who envisioned *Le Livre*, the man who was fascinated by the abyss and believed that absence is creative, remained blind to the truth that God is still to be born.

II

As he crosses the vestibule of hell, Dante recognizes 'The coward spirit of the man who made / The great refusal' (Dante, 1949, pp. 60–1). It is most likely Celestine V, the hermit who was elected Pope in 1294 at eighty years of age and who resigned after just five months. No believer in heaven or hell, Bonnefoy also speaks of a *'great refusal'*: a denial of death, implicitly made by poetry like Dante's , Racine's and Mallarme's, that is in its own way an abdication of the poet's responsibility to speak truly of life and death. 'One kind of poetry will always seek to detach itself from the world, the better to grasp what it loves'; it may be called 'divine' but it is 'chimerical and untrue and fatal'. It requires a separation of 'a concept [*idée*] of itself that it thus knows or feels to be its essence, its divine part, from the degradations of lived experience' (Bonnefoy, 1989, pp. 101–2). The fault does not originate in poetry, however, but in a trust as old as Greece that the concept is neatly fitted to reality. 'Doubtless the concept [*concept*], this almost unique instrument of our philosophy, is a profound refusal of death everywhere it bestows itself' (Bonnefoy, 1992a, pp. 13–14). And so it is possible, at least in principle, for there to be another kind of poetry, one that freely acknowledges finitude and therefore frustrates the rule of the concept.

We have already heard Bonnefoy use the word 'divine' and I have said that he speaks of a God to come. These are not isolated quotations. A theological vocabulary can be found everywhere in Bonnefoy's writing, sometimes overtly and sometimes covertly, although the pressure of particular poems or essays will frequently change or even reverse the received meaning of a word. For instance, where mortality is traditionally regarded as a direct consequence of the Fall, Bonnefoy understands a fall to have occurred whenever death is denied; and far from being a *felix culpa*, this refusal thwarts salvation. Poetry suffers when it yields to the blandishments of the concept: it may transcend the here and now and eloquently testify to a universal order but only at the cost of losing touch with particulars. This is the movement of 'excarnation', as Bonnefoy calls it, an inevitable process whenever there is writing and one that can easily go unchecked by dint of its strong, if aberrant, religious appeal. To explain that, we are referred to the gnostic syndrome, that fuzzy set of beliefs in absolute dualism that places a transcendent deity beyond the reach of any positive theology, and that regards the earth with suspicion if not contempt.

For the gnostic there is a sharp difference between God, who remains distant and veiled, and the Creator, who has fabricated the universe through evil. In order not to remain immured in the lower orders of existence, the gnostic adept must see through the illusions of creation, including the *psyche*, and attain a saving knowledge of the *pneuma*, the uncreated spark hidden in each one of us. Since gnostic dualism is not only irreducible but also conflictual, only the most rigorous negative theologies can help in uncovering that divine spark in ourselves. The adept must vigilantly strip away all the predicates conventionally attached to the divinity, for if taken literally or even figurally they will fatally mislead.

One need not examine the traces of Basilides or Valentinus to find a gnostic attitude to life; it is vibrant in the twentieth century. In the *Second manifeste* (1930/1969), André Breton memorably describes surrealism as a quest for 'a certain point of the mind at which life and death, the real and the imagined, past and future, the communicable and the incommunicable, high and low, cease to be perceived as contradictions' (1969, p. 123). How to interpret this? One can say, as the young Bonnefoy did, that the romance of surrealism lies in its affirmation of the fundamental unity of the world, that when Paul Éluard writes of 'aigles d'eau pure' the image spans the gulf between appearance and reality (in Bonnefoy, 1964, p. 135). Or one can say, as Bonnefoy came to think, that idealism was tacitly assumed in this vision and that the 'certain point' became the haunt of gnostic fantasies that seduce one away from the body and the material world. It is a view that Breton was to confirm in 1953, after Bonnefoy had left this circle. Surrealism has finally identified the essence of poetic intuition, the master says, and now it seeks,

> not only to assimilate all known forms but also boldly to create new forms
> – that is to say, to be in a position to embrace all the structures of the
> world, manifested or not. It alone provides the thread that can put us
> back on the road of Gnosis as knowledge of suprasensible Reality, 'invisibly
> visible in an eternal mystery'. (Breton, 1969, pp. 258–9)

Breton had sharply attacked Georges Bataille in the *Second manifeste* as a defector from the camp of truth. And yet the Bataille of *L'Expérience intérieure* (1943; 1988b) and *Le Coupable* (1944; 1988a) was important for Bonnefoy, who found there a passionate critique of the Western presumption that systems of representation are capable of recovering presence. Once again, though, this critique can be variously understood. One can see Bataille attempting, through a paroxysm of ecstasy, to transgress received limits in order to touch the unknown original plenitude. Like Rimbaud, Bataille would be attempting to expose a pact between language and reason, a complicity to value convention over essence, appearance over reality (Bonnefoy, 1973, pp. 448–9). It is a vision that could not fail to attract Bonnefoy. However, one can read Bataille another way, as trying to communicate through death with a frightening 'indefinite reality' that cannot be reduced to the self or the world (Bataille, 1988a, p. 139). And this is indeed how Bataille interprets his raptures. Inner experience turns out to be a quest for gnostic illumination, though one that eschews any deep interiority, any *pneuma*, in favour of a glimpse of the wholly unconditioned, that inhuman and godless continuum from which we are exiled by life itself.

What alerted Bonnefoy to this propensity to excarnation in Bataille and Breton was, rather surprisingly, the discovery in one of the stalls along the Seine of a second-hand copy of an unconventional theological work, Lev Shestov's *Potestas Clavium* (1923) (see Bonnefoy 1990, p. 77). That was in 1944, several years before his break with the surrealists over the occultist tendencies of *Rupture inaugurale* (1947), though the Russian's affirmation of presence over essence, his dismissal of universal norms and his prizing of the individual, began to work on the young poet in their own ways. Doubtless too, Shestov helped Bonnefoy to diagnose a gnostic longing in himself, a feeling that had found form by reading an early essay by Bataille on materialism and gnosticism.[3] But this longing was different from that of the ancient gnostics, and it outlasted any enthusiasm for Bataillian ecstasy. It is an ache for another country, a feeling that true life can be lived only elsewhere. Bonnefoy will use Virgil's eclogues or Poussin's landscapes to evoke that *arrière-pays*, as he calls it, though it must be stressed that the longed-for country is a place where one lives, grows old and dies. 'Yes indeed our country is beautiful, I cannot imagine anything else,' he writes, 'all the same, if the true life is over there, in a placeless elsewhere, that alone is enough for this place to seem like a desert.' Living here, in the keen awareness of another place, is a lack 'whose grandeur is desire and whose frequentation is an exile'. And so this ache is, in its way, a 'gnostic refusal' (Bonnefoy, 1982, pp. 19–20). The recognition that living in a 'placeless elsewhere' can be dreamed, not lived, is the painful burden of many of Bonnefoy's poems and essays, and it forces him to seek the plenitude of being in the here and now. Like concepts, dreams reveal only by concealing, and the task is to overcome both dreams and concepts in a quest for what is already here, if only we would see it. 'The incarnation, that outside of the dream, is a nearby good,' we are told, and poetry will be the means to achieve that end (Bonnefoy, 1977, p. 279).

Poetry is *ancilla theologiae*, then, though of course we are dealing with a 'theology of the earth' (Bonnefoy, 1990, p. 47). Reading and writing poetry will lead to the One, the plenum of being at the heart of the material world: such is Bonnefoy's confession of faith. And yet there must be further clauses in his *credo*, since language, even poetic language, is incapable of simply expressing that sacred presence. The situation is dialectical, and thus a counter-thesis appears: 'To write, yes, – who has ever not done so? But to *unwrite* as well, by way of an experience complementary to the poem.' Art brings experience into the light, though never completely; and the poem must be tested against experience: not so much to revise it (although that happens) but to offer what has thus far remained in shadow as the material for another poem. Without this interplay one would produce books that merely confirm one another, but with it one can slowly make a life that bespeaks 'a presence, a destiny: the finitude that clarifies and watches over meaning' (Bonnefoy, 1977, p. 76). And if we ask why no poem is fully adequate to experience, we will get a response at odds with an influential contemporary view of language that draws from nineteenth-century philosophy and twentieth-century linguistics. On this understanding, the structures of language promote a fiction of presence. Thus for Nietzsche God is an effect of grammar, while for Saussure meaning is formed in a linguistic system composed of negative differences. Coming from the opposite direction, Bonnéfoy teasingly suggests in a prose poem that one day in the eternal world of essences 'words were invented, and through them absence' (1992b, p. 147).

In the world, however, the situation is quite different. Here the concept obscures death, while language makes mortality a notional truth at best. How then can one hope by reading and writing poetry to discover the true place, the gleaming presence of the here and now, that depends on a full and unconditional acceptance of finitude? Bonnefoy sketches an answer:

> Nothing exists except through death. And nothing is true that does not prove itself through death.
>
> If there is no poetry without language [*discours*] – and Mallarmé himself said just that – how, therefore, can the truth and the grandeur of poetry be preserved, except by appealing to death? By the stubborn exigency that death be said – or, better, that it speak? (1992a, p. 34)

An appeal to death may help to bring presence into view but it cannot guarantee it can be grasped in language, even when language is charged with metaphor. Another assurance is needed. Or perhaps I should say that the act of faith that presence is sacred calls forth another act of faith, that in mortal poetry the concept can be suspended or denied:

> this poetry which cannot grasp presence, dispossessed of all other good, will be in anguished proximity to the great accomplished act, as its *negative theology* . . . in authentic poetry nothing remains but those wanderers of the real, those categories of possibility, those elements without past or future, never entirely involved in the existing situation . . . They appear on the confines of the negativity of language, like angels telling of a still unknown god. A negative 'theology'. (Bonnefoy, 1989, p. 114)[4]

Let us pause before these remarks. We know that for Bonnefoy the word 'theology' must be carefully guarded by quotation marks in case it suddenly files to a transcendent God, but we need to consider what assumptions might be assigned night duty behind the words 'death' and 'negative'.

Blanchot responds to Bonnefoy in two phases: 'Le grand refus' examines the assumptions of *L'Improbable* and opens them onto a more fundamental level of analysis where they uneasily re-situate themselves, while 'Comment découvrir l'obscur?' seeks to rework the themes by way of a discussion of possibility and impossibility. 'I have always found concepts less important than obsessions': Bonnefoy quotes Jean-Pierre Richard's apothegm immediately after introducing Blanchot to English readers in 1958, and he may well have recalled the sentiment in September and October of the following year when reading Blanchot's critique of his book in *La Nouvelle Revue Française* (Bonnefoy, 1958, p. 45). For in that double review *L'Improbable* is absorbed into an intense meditation that had begun before the war and that would continue until Blanchot's final writings. One important aspect of that meditation is a deepening reflection on Bataille's work, not least of all on the notion to which he lent the title of a late book, *L'Impossible* (1962/1991), formerly called *Haine de la poésie*.

Hatred of poetry? Bonnefoy will suggest that Bataille indicts the poets 'because he is unwilling to follow their lesson and subordinate subjectivity to a higher reality, the one that in fact we can encounter in the slightest thing in the world, pebbles along a path or a gleam in the water' (Bonnefoy, 1991, p. 176). Yet Bataille tells another story when explaining why he changed the title of his book. 'It seemed to me that true poetry was reached only by hatred. Poetry had no powerful meaning except in the violence of revolt. But poetry attains this violence only by evoking the *impossible*' (Bataille, 1991, p. 10). We have already brushed up against this notion in pondering inner experience. Bataille expands on it when distinguishing two kinds of communication. The first is familiar: it connects two beings, 'laughter of a child to its mother, tickling, etc.'; the second, however, is altogether strange:

> Communication, through death, with our beyond (essentially in sacrifice) – not with nothingness, still less with a supernatural being, but with an indefinite reality (which I sometimes call *the impossible*, that is: what can't be grasped (*begreift*) in any way, what we can't reach without dissolving ourselves, what's slavishly called God). If we need to we can define this reality (provisionally associating it with a finite element) at a higher (higher than the individual on the scale of composition of beings) social level as the sacred, God or created reality. Or else it can remain in an undefined state (in ordinary laughter, infinite laughter, or ecstasy in which the divine form melts like sugar in water). (Bataille, 1988a, p. 139)

One ground against which this passage cuts its figure is Hegel, for whom the negativity of action is exhausted in realizing the realm of the possible;

and it is a difference over Hegel that marks Blanchot's divergence from Bonnefoy.

Hegel had been variously significant for both writers. At the threshold of *De mouvement et de l'immobilité de Douve* (1953), the poetry of his first maturity, Bonnefoy had placed an epigraph from the *Phenomenology of Mind*, a passage that speaks of how 'the life of the mind is not one that shuns death and keeps clear of destruction; it endures death and in death maintains its being [*das ihn erträgt und in ihm sich erhält*]' (Hegel, 1967, p. 93). And in the late 1940s Blanchot had counterpointed Jean Hyppolite's and Alexandre Kojève's readings of Hegel in a major speculative essay, 'La Littérature et le droit à la mort', in which those same words ring out several times.[5] So while one can easily imagine the debate involving other philosophical figures – and I will introduce another before very long – there are particular reasons why it turns on Hegel. Certainly it is no surprise to open *L'Improbable* (1992a) and find Bonnefoy, an ardent advocate of the here and now, alluding to Hegel's discussion of sense-certainty at the beginning of the *Phenomenology*. For there the philosopher shows that, far from presenting particulars, any uttering of a 'here' or 'now' will necessarily involve universals, that is, concepts. Now Bonnefoy is mistaken, Blanchot suggests, to imply that Hegel simply contributes to the great refusal of death. The philosopher's account of the concept does not show that language is divine by dint of a purported ability to freeze a word and consequently form an eternal concept. Rather, the concept's force resides in an eerie ability to introduce the negativity of death into language, so that speech has, in Hegel's words, 'the divine nature of directly turning the mere "meaning" right round about, making it into something else' (1967, p. 160).

On Blanchot's understanding then, Hegel alerts us to two rival tendencies in literature, a regard for the concept and a fascination with language. It is a claim whose broad features had been sketched years before in 'Comment la littéture est-elle possible?' (1943), Blanchot's first conversation with Jean Paulhan, and which had later been explored with Hegel in mind in 'La Littérature et le droit à la mort'. Since that latter essay tracks the different motifs of death and dying, let us turn to it for clarification.[6] I interrupt the meditation half-way through, just after Blancot has quoted for the first time Hegel's evocation of the moment when life 'endures death and in death maintains its being'. In the first place, modern literature – roughly, since the French Revolution – is an affair of the concept; it 'contemplates itself in revolution', conceives itself as a quest for what precedes its inevitable recourse to language, and assumes a tie between the concept and death. To name something is to annihilate its unique existence and make it into an idea as well. Literature, here, idealizes death by making it into a dialectical power:

the negativity of death is not given in senseless dissolution of life but in its purported ability to shape 'the life of the mind'. In the second place, however, literature is linked to language; it is not concerned with the eternity of the idea but with retracing the passage from nothingness to speech. A word is not the representation of something that pre-exists it. Not at all: it is a sensible presentation, 'a nonexistence made *word*', a matter of *Darstellung* more than of *Repräsentation* or *Vorstellung* (Blanchot, 1981, p. 44). Viewed in this way literature is no longer in the realm of possibility and power but rather attends to the materiality of words: 'and thus it is meaning detached from its conditions, separated from its moments, wandering like an empty power, a power no one can do anything with, a power without power' (Blanchot, 1981, p. 50). Released from the concept's grip, literature shakes itself free of death as a shaping force and in that movement renders negativity unemployed. Literature will have no work to do – or, if you prefer, literature's work will *be* this nothing. At any rate, the very inability of literature to invest dying in meaningful action consigns it to speak endlessly of the 'impossibility of dying', an anguished suspension of both life and death.

At the beginning of this chapter, when I was introducing Blanchot's role in the discussion with Bonnefoy, I said that he was 'speaking for the negative'. Protocols of debating aside, it turns out that Blanchot is speaking both for and against negativity, *Negativität*. 'Common language' is animated by negativity, he says, while 'literary language' reveals the weakness of the negative, its incapacity to impose the categories of being and nothingness (1949, p. 314). The one works with the realm of the possible, progressively determining that which is: it is the space of 'meaningful prose', and Blanchot associates it with Mallarmé (1949, p. 321). The other unworks possibility – it is the realm of the impossible – and it is here the poets may be found, and certainly Mallarmé, perhaps for Blanchot the only poet to follow both tendencies of literature in an exemplary fashion. Neither the one nor the other, literature is the doubling of common and literary language; it generates aporias of negativity and neutrality, death and dying, success and failure, power and weakness. In no way then is this a criticism that calls for 'the death of the Author', as Roland Barthes (1977, p. 148) once put it, for Blanchot would have us ponder the author's perpetual resurrection into a state of interminable dying. Nor is it an appeal to let death speak in poetry, such as Bonnefoy makes, since Blanchot insists that death cannot speak in poetry because it is forever interrupted by the murmuring of an endless dying. The concept is not an enemy of poetry, that which prevents it from recognizing finitude; it is what introduces mortality into poetry but, in doing so, compels poetry to speak of both death as possibility and dying as impossibility.

IV

The sacred is immediate presence, Bonnefoy tells us, while adding the rider that 'The immediate does not give itself; one cannot reach presence through images' (1977, p. 62). If poetry is a theology of earth it also calls for a supplement of negative theology to ensure it remains before the sacred radiance. For there is always a danger that the poetic image can be regarded as absolute and so become an idol. No poetry can grasp the immediate; the here and now can never fully present themselves to consciousness, and therefore we must accept that the sacred reveals itself only in withdrawal. The most that we may legitimately hope for is a poetry that constitutes a negative theology of the unpresentable.

In clarifying this formulation it is tempting to begin by excluding the Kantian notion of the sublime, where the imagination sacrifices itself in an attempt to present what is strictly speaking unpresentable. After all, Bonnefoy is not concerned with a sensible presentation of the ideas of reason, and he certainly has no wish to disclose a supersensible destination of humankind. It is equally tempting to say that, in terms of Kantian aesthetics, Bonnefoy is more attracted to the beautiful than to the sublime, as his favourite emblems suggest – a torn ivy leaf, the dark panes of an orangery, a window gleaming in the evening sun – and this is reinforced by recalling that for Kant aesthetic experience does not require the particular to be subsumed by a concept. Quoting Bonnefoy's conviction that 'L'imperfection est la cime' scarcely counters this view (Bonnefoy, 1978, p. 117). There is no logical difficulty in loving natural beauty while rejecting the alexandrine, say. Accordingly one could argue that for Bonnefoy the beautiful resists presentation. And yet he is in no way an apologist for the 'merely beautiful', for beauty drained of the sublime. We must therefore distinguish two claims. First, immediate presence is always cast adrift in space and time, and poetry is an attempt to present it. Like the early German Romantics, Bonnefoy knows that no *Darstellung*, no sensible presentation, can wholly capture what is absent; unlike them, though, he eschews romantic irony in favour of honouring the referent. So much for the first claim. The second is that, following Jean-Luc Nancy's reading of the *Critique of Judgement* (Kant, 1987), the sublime and the beautiful occur together. Sublimity is not raised above beauty but is a flaring of beauty at the limit, an effulgence that can be simple and serene rather than magnificent and violent, and beyond which there is nothing (Nancy, 1993). It is the sensing of the unconditioned beyond presentation, *das Unbedingte*, which constitutes the feeling of the sublime. While Bonnefoy offers no comment on it, Blanchot, as we shall see, almost never ceases to write of it, albeit in his own terms.

These various considerations, both 'aesthetic' and 'theological', can be brought into focus by turning to one of Bonnefoy's most haunting lyrics, 'La Lumière, Changée':

> Nous ne nous voyons plus dans la même lumière,
> Nous n'avons plus les mêmes yeux, les mêmes mains.
> L'arbre est plus proche et la voix des sources plus vive,
> Nos pas sont plus profonds, parmi les morts.
>
> Dieu qui n'es pas, pose ta main sur notre épaule,
> Ébauche notre corps du poids de ton retour,
> Achève de mêler à nos âmes ces astres,
> Ces bois, ces cris d'oiseaux, ces ombres et ces jours.
>
> Renonce-toi en nous comme un fruit se déchire,
> Efface-nous en toi. Découvre-nous
> Le sens mystérieux de ce qui n'est que simple
> Et fû tombé sans feu dans des mots sans amour.
>
> (Bonnefoy, 1978, p. 211)

Having achieved a mortal vision, like the older Wordsworth, the speaker has experienced a deepening of relations with nature and humans. Interpretation becomes more complex, however, at the beginning of the second stanza with the sublime prayer to the divinity 'qui n'es pas'. For 'Dieu' has itself changed. The God whom Nietzsche's madman declared dead can return only as a fully incarnate divinity, a god of earth. No longer separable from the world, our souls are to be mixed with nature; while the notion of a divine spark in humankind is to be renounced as firmly as the human longing to return to God. That achieved, we do not thereby eliminate mystery. On the contrary, we finally realize that transcendence is all about us, in simple things and ordinary acts. It is a truth which had long been in us, hidden by our longings for excarnation, which are at odds with human love and complicit with writing.

The sensible presentation that is poetic speech therefore acknowledges an inability to present the immediate. Let us listen to Bonnefoy: 'in authentic poetry nothing remains but those wanderers of the real, those categories of possibility . . . which are the wind, fire, earth, the waters'. He goes on to speculate that 'they *are* words, being no other than a promise' and that they form, as we have seen, 'A negative "theology"' (Bonnefoy, 1988, p. 114). Now when Blanchot reads Bonnefoy he does so with Heidegger's illumination of Hölderlin, and when concluding *L'Espace littéraire*: 'The immediate is in a strict sense impossible [*unmöglich*] for mortals and for the immortals' (1982, p. 273). It is not a matter, Blanchot thinks, of being unable to grasp immediate presence because it is fleeting, and poetry therefore having to establish itself as a negative theology. The point is that there never has been immediate presence. Or, more accurately, it is impossible for such a presence to present itself: if it imposes itself immediately it is not experienced, since subject and object will have been fused, while if it offers itself in a mediation it cannot be experienced as immediate.

This allusion to Hölderlin opens an abyss between the two writers just as surely as did the earlier reference to Hegel. Where Bonnefoy speaks of poetry and the sacred by way of 'categories of possibility', Blanchot approaches the same concerns by evoking a relation of impossibility: 'if the immediate is infinitely absent, exceeding and excluding any present, the only relation with the immediate would be a relation reserving in itself an infinite absence' (1993, p. 38).[7] Blanchot does not deny that this relation can rightly be considered sacred, only that it can have any redemptive value. Indeed, in earlier meditations on Hölderlin he preserves the word. For Hölderlin, the poet speaks in a space between two spheres, the withdrawal of the gods and the turning of mortals from the gods, and, like Heidegger, Blanchot does not hesitate to take the great rhapsodist at his word and call 'this empty and pure place . . . *the sacred*' (Blanchot, 1982, p. 274).

V

The import of the transcendental argument of the *Critique of Pure Reason* (Kant, 1978) is to yield two realms: a theoretically stable world of possible experience, where ethics and even religion can found themselves, and a deceptive and dangerous world of impossible experience, a place that Kant believes to be almost wholly a dangerous illusion. Mystical experience is consigned there; it is impossible in theory and an affront to morality. Now when Blanchot writes of 'critique' he does so partly in the Kantian sense of the word. What intrigues him is uncovering 'the possibility of literary experience', and yet he realizes that he cannot develop a theoretical inquiry since literature constitutes itself by contesting its condition of possibility (1963, p. 13). Like Kant and like Hölderlin, Blanchot rejects mystical experience: there can be no immediate apprehension of the immediate. And yet writing, especially poetry, can open onto an ecstatic state that escapes all dialectics and that dissolves the subject.

That Blanchot has an intense interest in mysticism is plain from his earliest writings, where it is also evident that he is intrigued by parallels between medieval mysticism and contemporary though, especially poetry and philosophy. Not all mysticism falls into this category. That of Nicolas of Cusa, for instance, remains stubbornly dialectical; it is 'a double movement by which the spirit posits and maintains the contrary of what it posits'. The cardinal never attains 'inner experience', and the non-knowledge he advocates is merely a term in a dialectic whose end is the Unknowable. Meister Eckhart has a truer sense of non-knowledge – that which is irreducible to knowledge rather than that which is not yet known – and it is under that sign that he calls for the 'renunciation of everything, including God' (Blanchot, 1943c). And he knows too that 'the ground of the human soul is absolutely unfathomable, that there is in it a spark where it merges with the primordial unit', which sanctions his tireless recourse to paradox.

It is their use of paradox and their avoidance of dialectic that Blanchot values in the Rhineland mystics, and he is less interested in their successes than in their failures. 'Angelus Silesius thus appears as a mystic without profound and binding mystical experiences, like William Blake, asking of speculation and poetry the movement towards the heights which his faith, afterwards, would not know how to confirm' (Blanchot, 1943b). Indeed, faith is precisely what obscures the truth of ecstasy. In another early review he ventures that the 'true mystical poems of our language, those born of an inner discovery, of a ravishing, of a revelatory anxiety, have been construed outside the religious traditions' (1943d). And he praises Bataille for making that truth evident: his friend's raptures appear no different from mystical ecstasy except that they are free from 'all religious presuppositions which frequently alter it and, in giving it a meaning, determine it' (Blanchot, 1943a, pp. 49–50).

For Blanchot it is Hölderlin rather than Bonnefoy who best exposes the relation between poetry and the sacred. Both poets are right to regard the immediate as sacred, he thinks, though Hölderlin better understands that the immediate is forbidden to both mortals and gods. As we have seen, 'Das Höchste' is used as a lens for reading 'Wie wenn am Feiertage . . .', especially the opening lines of the third stanza;

> Jetz aber tagts! Ich harrt und sah es kommen,
> Und was ich sah, das Heilige sei mein Wort.
>
> (Hölderlin, 1966, p. 372)[8]

Blanchot observes that the speaker does not claim to have seen the sacred, *das Heilige*, only 'a coming, being what dispenses everything that can come to pass' (1993, p. 39). And here he is perfectly in tune with Heidegger, who regards the sacred as a mode of Being. 'The sacred is the essence of nature,' he tells us, though 'nature' is to be grasped in the original sense of *fusis*: that which enables beings to come into presence rather than that which is opposed to spirit or even, in the thinker's earlier terms, that which is present-to-hand (Heidegger, 1971, p. 59). No pure and simple revealing, being preserves itself in concealment in the very movement by which it allows beings to enter into presence. The sacred cannot present itself, still less can it be presented poetically; not because it belongs to an eternal order, which mortals are forbidden to represent, but because there is nothing to represent. One can talk about prohibiting all representations of God or the gods but the sacred is absolutely untransgressable, being prior to both immortals and mortals. As a mode of Being, the sacred is a perpetual coming into presence; it is older than human attempts to measure time yet, since Being and time are to be thought together, it is not older than time.

So although the speaker in Hölderlin's hymn says 'das Heilige sei mein Wort' the poem is not sacred speech; rather, it is a witness that the sacred precedes all possible experience, and a desire that this witness be legible. The sacred does not communicate, it is what enables communication to take place. In saying that, however, it becomes evident that the status of poetry needs to be investigated a little more closely. I have said that a poem bears witness to the anteriority of the sacred, and in general it is true that a poem gains authority by referring to its origin in experience. At the same time, however, a poem – in order to be a poem – must renounce that authority and affirm its radical independence: its total resistance to lexical change makes it absolute. Poetry abides in a fraught space, both searching for and contesting the original experience to which it answers. Blanchot's evocation of Orpheus comes to mind here. Orpheus turns to gaze at the dead Eurydice, the inspiration of this poem, and in doing so consigns her to a second death: the origin of the poem withdraws in granting the poem. The poem is granted to the poet but the event is a disaster, for the poet is destined to be scattered by the poem. And here we see a certain gnosticism in Blanchot. It is not a longing for a transcendent reality but a consequence of regarding artistic creation as a fall. Orpheus's error, without which he could not be a poet, is to think that Eurydice is transcendent, a subject whose experience is irreducible to his own, when, constituted as inspiration, she is transcendental, both the condition of possibility for him writing the poem and the condition of impossibility that its origin be presentable.

More generally, Blanchot distinguishes himself from religious belief and most critiques of religious belief by conceiving the sacred as transcendental rather than transcendent; and once more I underline that 'transcendental' includes conditions of possibility and impossibility. Anguished or calm, our relation with divine immediacy assumes the form of impossibility; it escapes all attempts to master it by presentation or representation, whether they be positive or negative, and that is one reason why Blanchot also calls this dimension the *neutre*. One would be mistaken then to conceive the sacred as an object of possible experience, yet every experience answers to it and is divided by it. What is personal in experience can imperceptibly give away to something impersonal; and 'I am', with its assertion of presence, its will to act and drive meaning, yields to an anonymous and passive 'There is', at which point one has passed from perception to fascination. What Bataille called 'inner experience' could perhaps be characterized as the dilation of a moment as a subject glides from the personal to the anonymous and thus places subjectivity in question. A gnostic of a very different kind from Blanchot, Bataille believed that sliding into this ungraspable state was a communication with our beyond, a sublime event that could not be confirmed by memory but whose non-knowledge was none the less to be affirmed.

Bataille did not hesitate to regard *Inner Experience* (1943, 1988b) as raising the questions of 'the new theology (which has only the unknown as object)', and although he set himself in sharp rhetorical opposition to the Judaic–Christian God his attention to the unknown generates effects of negative theology. In the same breath he claimed Blanchot for the same project, and cited his friend's protocols for founding 'all "spiritual" life' (Bataille, 1988b, p. 102).[9] I would suggest that, for all their deep accord, Blanchot differs from Bataille in eschewing any assimilation of the sacred and the transcendent. There is no plenitude for Blanchot, no lost continuum to be regained by sacrifice. What we call the sacred, remains anterior to experience, unable to be put to work and least of all for that grandest work, the salvation of the soul. Blanchot is not concerned to link the impossible with quasi-mystical experiences. Rather, his focus is inspired writing, of which poetry is both an emblem and a noble instance, since, whatever else it does, such writing is always an oblique response to the impossible. And it does do something else, for as we have seen, writing is always double, proceeding dialectically and making death into a power, and escaping the rule of the dialectic, being otherwise, caught in the fascination of time's absence.

The debate between Bonnefoy and Blanchot does not turn on whether there is or is not a realm of the sacred. The two participants differ over the status of the sacred; for the one it is transcendent (though certainly not removed from the earth) while for the other it is transcendental. Blanchot advocates a thoroughgoing atheism, to be sure, yet he recognizes the intimate connection between art and the sacred, even when the category of the sacred has been radically put into question by the death of God. He concludes *The Space of Literature* (1982) talking of the plight of the poet in the age of God's default, an age contemporary with every period:

> 'At every time he lives the time of distress, and his time is always the empty time when what he must live is the double infidelity: that of men, that of the gods – and also the double absence of the gods who are no

longer *and* who are not yet. The poem's space is entirely represented by this *and*, which indicates the double absence, the separation at its most tragic instant. But as for whether it is the *and* that unites and binds together, the pure word in which the void of the past and the void of the future become true presence, the "now" of dawn – this question is reserved in the work' (1982, p. 247).

Impossible and sacred, impossible in its sacredness, the poem is 'prophetic isolation which, before time, ever announces the beginning' (Blanchot, 1982, p. 247).

Notes

1 Blanchot (1969) makes a number of changes from the journal publication of his review 'Le grand refus' and 'Comment découvrir l'obscur?' For example, in its first publication the sentence I have quoted reads, 'Nous nous retrouvons, aussi, au coeur du débat le plus grave, où il y va peut-être de notre sort, et d'abord du sens de toute poésie'.
2 For another example of Blanchot's and Bonnefoy's contrary responses to a particular writer, see their discussions of Louis René des Forêts's *Le Bavard* (Blanchot, 1971; Bonnefoy, 1988).
3 Bonnefoy (1989, pp. 145–6) mentions Bataille's essay (Bataille, 1985).
4 In an essay in the same collection, 'Baudelaire Speaks to Mallarmé', however, Bonnefoy modifies his view: 'I used to think that words, desiccated by their conceptual use, failed to convey presence, were forever limited to a "negative theology". Now I sense that some sort of archeology is possible, which would reveal, piece by piece, the essential elements of our form' (Bonnefoy, 1989, p. 63).
5 Blanchot published the essay over two numbers of *Critique* in 1947 and 1948. It was later reprinted as the final piece of *La Part du feu* (1949).
6 Although both essays stress the word 'Terror', the word functions differently in each one. In 'Comment la littérature est-elle possible?' Blanchot uses 'terror' in Paulhan's sense of the word: a prizing of concept over word. In 'La Littérature et le droit à la mort', however, he speaks of the 'Terror' that followed the French Revolution and values it precisely for its suspension of the concept.
7 The discussion of Hölderlin's 'Das Höchste', broached in the concluding essay on *L'Espace littéraire*, is found in Blanchot (1969) but not in the original journal article. In the years separating the two versions of 'Le grand refus' Blanchot would appear to have been influenced by Derrida's deconstruction of the metaphysics of presence, especially by those essays collected in Derrida (1967).
8 In Blanchot (1993) the translation runs, 'But now day breaks! I waited and saw it come. And what I saw, the holy be my word' (p. 39).
9 For an analysis of Blanchot's "spiritual" life see my forthcoming essay 'Blanchot's Primal Scene'.

References

Bataille, Georges 1985: Base Materialism and Gnosticism. In A. Stoekl (tr.), *Visions of Excess: Selected Writings, 1927–1939*, Minneapolis: University of Minnesota Press, pp. 45–52.

—— 1944/1988a: *Guilty*, trans. B. Boone. Venice, Cal.: The Lapis Press.

—— 1943/1988b: *Inner Experience*, trans. L. A. Boldt. Albany: State University of New York Press.

—— 1962/1991: *The Impossible*, trans. R. Hurley. San Francisco: City Lights Books.

Barthes, Roland 1977: *Image, Music, Text*. New York: Hill and Wang.

Blanchot, Maurice 1943a: *Faux pas*. Paris: Gallimard.

—— 1943b: La Mystique d'Angelus Silesius. *Journal des Débats*, 6 October.

—— 1943c: Nicolas de Cues. *Journal des Débats*, 6 January.

—— 1943d: La Poésie religieuse. *Journal des Débats*, 9 June.

—— 1949: *La Part du feu*. Paris: Gallimard.

—— 1963: *Lautréamont et Sade*. Paris: Éditions de Minuit.

—— 1969: *L'Entretien infini*. Paris: Gallimard.

—— 1971: *La Parole vaine*. In *L'Amitié*, Paris: Gallimard, pp. 137–49.

—— 1981: *The Gaze of Orpheus*, trans. L. Davies. Barrytown, New York: Station Hill Press.

—— 1982: *The Space of Literature*, trans. A. Smock. Lincoln: University of Nebraska Press.

—— 1988: Penser l'apocalypse. *Le Nouvel Observateur*, 22–8 Jan. 43–5.

—— 1993: The Great Refusal. In *The Infinite Conversation*, trans. S. Hanson, Minneapolis: University of Minnesota Press, pp. 33–48.

Bonnefoy, Yves 1958: Critics – English and French, and the distance between them. *Encounter* 58: 39–45.

—— 1964: The feeling of transcendency. *Yale French Studies* 31: 135–7.

—— 1973: *Rimbaud*, trans. P. Schmidt. New York: Harper and Row.

—— 1977: *Le Nuage rouge*. Paris: Mercure de France.

—— 1978: L'Imperfection est la cime. *Poèmes*, Paris: Mercure de France.

—— 1982: *L'Arrière-pays*. Paris: Flammarion (first published by Éditions d'Art, Albert Skira, 1972).

—— 1988: Une écriture de notre temps. *La Vérité de parole*, Paris: Mercure de France.

—— 1989: *The Act and the Place of Poetry: Selected Essays*, ed. J. T. Naughton. Chicago: University of Chicago Press.

—— 1990: *Entretiens sur la poésie: 1971–1990*. Paris: Mercure de France.

—— 1991: *Alberto Giacometti: A Biography of His Work*, trans. J. Stewart. Paris: Flammarion.

—— 1992a: *L'Improbable et autre essais suivi de Un Rêve à Mantoue Notes*, nouvelle édition. Paris: Gallimard.

—— 1992b: L'Origine de la parole. In *Rue Traversière et autre récits en rêve*, Paris: Gallimard.

Breton, André 1930/1969: *Manifestos of Surrealism*, trans. R. Seaver and H. R. Lane. Ann Arbor: University of Michigan Press.

Dante 1949: *The Divine Comedy*, vol. 1: *Hell*, trans. D. L. Sayers. Harmondsworth: Penguin.

Derrida, Jacques 1967: *L'Écriture et la différence*. Paris: Seuil.

Hegel, G. W. F. 1967: *The Phenomenology of Mind*, trans. J. B. Baillie. New York: Harper and Row.

Heidegger, Martin 1971: *Erläuterungen zu Hölderlins Dichtung*, fourth edn. Frankfurt: Vittorio Klostermann.

Hölderlin, Friedrich 1966: *Poems and Fragments*, trans. M. Hamburger. London: Routledge and Kegan Paul.

Kant, Immanuel 1978: *Critique of Pure Reason*, trans. N. Kemp Smith. London: Macmillan.

—— 1987: *Critique of Judgement*, trans. Werner S. Pluhur. Indianapolis: Hackett.

Nancy, Jean-Luc 1993: The sublime offering. In J-F. Courtine et al., *Of the Sublime: Presence in Question*, trans. J. S. Librett. Albany: State University of New York Press, pp. 25–53.

index

Abrams, M. H., 3
aesthetics, 258–82 *passim*
Aganbegyan, Abel, 213
Ahmed, Akbar, 16–17
alchemy, 10, 39–43, 52
Alexander, Jeffrey, 56, 77
allegory, 14, 233–55 *passim*
Alter, Robert, 226
Altizer, Thomas, 233
Amir, Yigal, 93
Ammerman, Nancy, 89
analogy, 14, 233–55 *passim*
Anderson, Benedict, 153
Andreas, Carol, 121
Ansprenger, Franz, 213
AOKI Tamotsu, 184
Appleby, Scott, 100
Arend, Theodor, 212
Aristotle, 225
Asad, Talal, 100
ASADA Akira, 181–2, 184
Ash, Timothy, 213
Augustine of Hippo, 19, 21, 223, 225, 244

Baader, 43
Baillie, John, 263–4
Barber, Bernard, 56
Barlow, John Perry, 46
Barshay, Andrew, 184
Barth, Karl, 200, 209, 211, 241, 250–1, 290–1
Barthes, Roland, 181, 254, 322
Bartlett, Robert, 192
Barton, Greg, 148
Bataille, Georges, 276, 317, 320, 326, 328
Baudelaire, Charles, 43, 254
Baudrillard, Jean, 46, 103–4, 139, 141

Bauman, Zygmunt, 5, 10–11, 12, 17, 77, 107, 127, 130, 190, 213
Beacher, Jean, 213
beauty, 14–15, 258–82 *passim*
Beck, Ulrich, 105, 116, 190
Becker, Howard, 21
Beckford, James, 4–5, 150
BEFU Harumi, 170
Bell, Daniel, 2, 141, 183
Bellah, Robert, 151, 175–6, 183
Beloff, Max, 213
Belsey, Catherine, 104
Benedict, Ruth, 174, 182
Benhabib, Seyla, 6
Benjamin, Walter, 254
Berger, Peter, 23, 33, 34, 106–7, 142, 148, 150–1
Bernal, Martin, 192
Berry, Philippa, 17
Beyer, Peter, 212
Blanchot, Maurice, 15–16, 314–29 *passim*
Bloch, Ernst, 209
Blond, Phillip, 15
Boddy, Janice, 165
Bohme, Jacob, 53
Boileau, Nicolas, 258, 260–5, 280
Boland, B. J., 157–8
de Bolla, Peter, 264
Bonnefoy, Yves, 15, 314–29 *passim*
Boone, Kathleen, 90
Bowen, Kurt, 122, 125
Braisted, William, 172
Brand, John, 46
Breton, André, 55, 317–18
Briggs, Sheila, 280
Bruce, F. F., 238
Bruce, Steve, 10–11, 19, 25, 33
Brunner, Emil, 200
Brusco, Elizabeth, 133–4

Brydon, Lynne, 115
Bull, Malcolm, 26
Bultmann, Rudolf, 200
Burdick, John, 125, 129
Burke, Edmund, 262–3, 269–71, 277

Calvin, 30
capitalism, 98–9, 102–42 *passim*,
    179–81, 186–210 *passim*
Cardoso, Eliana, 117
Carroll, John, 61, 77
Casanova, Jose, 151, 157, 164
Castles, Stephen, 213
Cattaneo, Carlo, 205–6
Caufield, Catherine, 142
Caygill, Howard, 270, 272
Cecchini, Paulo, 213
Chadwick, Owen, 204
Chant, Sylvia, 115
Charles, Prince of Wales, 3, 5
Chesnut, Andrew, 125
church, 10, 19–34 *passim*, 71,
    219–20
civil religion, 150–1
Cixous, Hélène, 234–5, 254
Clegg, Stewart, 209
Cobb, Jonathan, 73
Coleridge, Samuel, 43
conceptual thinking about God,
    285–312 *passim*
Connor, Steven, 6–7, 17
consumer culture, 5–6, 11, 16, 29,
    68–74, 85, 103, 209, 229
Cox, Harvey, 151
Cribb, Robert, 158
Crook, Stephen, 7
Cucchiari, Salvatore, 129, 131–2,
    134–6
Cudworth, R., 220
Cupitt, Don, 9, 13–14, 222–4

Dahrendorf, Ralf, 213
Dale, Peter, 169–71, 182
Dante, 315–16
Davis, Winston, 12–13, 165
Dawisha, Karen, 213
Dawkins, Richard, 188, 211
Dawson, Christopher, 193–5

death, 64–6, 315–16
DeBord, Guy, 48
dedifferentiation, 1–17 *passim*, 20–1,
    36–53 *passim*, 57, 103, 218–32
    passim, 186–210 *passim*
Dekmejian, Richard, 91–2
Delaunay, Robert, 38
Deleuze, Gilles, 181, 254
Delumeau, Jean, 63–4
Dennis, Norman, 120, 264
denomination, 10, 19–34 *passim*
Derrida, Jacques, 14, 51, 181, 220,
    234, 250, 254–5, 271, 276, 329
desacralization, 12, 147–65 *passim*
Descartes, René, 221, 223, 273
De Soto, H., 115
detraditionalization, 4, 8–9, 11, 16,
    27, 79–87 *passim*, 218–32 *passim*,
    249, 186–210 *passim*
Dhofier, Zamakhsyari, 163
differentiation, 1–17 *passim*, 74–5,
    88–100 *passim*, 103, 150, 169–84
    passim, 226–7
Dimenstein, Gilberto, 116
divinity, 186–213 *passim*
DOI Takeo, 181
Dray, W., 199
DuMoncel, Theodore, 51
Durkheim, Emile, 1, 9, 24, 106, 116,
    150–1
Dvornik, F., 212

Edwards, John, 213
Effendy, Bahtiar, 148
egalitarianism, 10, 24–5, 31
electricity, 44–5
Eliade, Mircea, 36, 39–42, 51, 53, 75
Ellen, Roy, 163
Erasmus, 23
Erdos, George, 120
Erickson, Eric, 182
essentialism, 13, 60, 169–84 *passim*

Falwell, Jerry, 90
Featherstone, Mike, 5–6, 17, 105
Feillard, Andrée, 160
feminization, 133–6
Fenn, R. K., 151

Flanagan, Kieran, 17
Flint, R. W., 37–8
Forster, E. M., 84
Forsyth, P. T., 255
Foucault, Michel, 17, 57, 59, 95, 103, 181, 187–9, 190, 213, 254
Frei, Hans, 226, 251
Freud, Sigmund, 27, 41, 49–53, 244, 247
Fukuyama, Francis, 199–201, 206, 213
FUKUZAWA Yukichi, 177
fundamentalism, 11, 26–7, 72–5, 83, 88–100, 104, 107–8, 127, 141, 187, 209, 227

Gablik, Susan, 75
Gallagher, Tom, 213
Gandhi, 81
Garvey, John, 26
du Gay, Paul, 17
Geertz, Clifford, 100, 151, 154–5
Gehlen, Arnold, 67–8
Gellner, Ernest, 5, 24–5, 34, 149, 152–4, 158
Gibson, William, 36, 47–8
Giddens, Anthony, 58, 76, 105, 116, 147, 190
gift, the, 233–55 *passim*, 293, 296
Gilbert, Alan, 113–14, 120, 143
Gill, Eric, 260
Gillespie, Charles, 114
gnosticism, 314–29 *passim*
Goethe, Johann Wolfgang von, 200–1, 213
Gogarten, Friedrich, 200
Gorbachev, Mikhail, 206, 213
Gore, Charles, 240–1
Gorer, Geoffrey, 65
Goudsblom, Johan, 76
grammer of assent, 285–312 *passim*
Gramsci, Antonio, 203
Granato, James, 107, 142
Gray, Robert, 41–2, 53
Greer, Paul, 21
Griffin, David, 16
Gugler, Josef, 114
Guillermoprieto, Alma, 143

Habermas, Jürgen, 183
Hackett, Rosalind, 134
Hadden, Jeffrey, 26
Haeckel, Ernst, 211
HAMAGUCHI Eshun, 170, 177, 184
Hammond, Phillip, 151
Harris, Nigel, 111
Hart, Kevin, 15–16
Harvey, David, 16, 105, 213
Harvie, Christopher, 213
Hassan, Muhammad Kamal, 159
Havel, Vaclav, 210
Hays, Denys, 192, 212
Heelas, Paul, 6, 9, 17
Hefner, Robert, 12, 148, 155–6, 158, 160, 164
Hegel, 43–5, 53, 82, 176, 190–1, 197, 203, 205, 208, 212, 228, 233, 240, 274–7, 281–2, 287–9, 303, 315, 320–1, 325–7
Heidegger, Martin, 66, 220, 292, 293, 303, 312, 315, 324
Heine, Heinrich, 205
Helps, A., 202
Helwege, Ann, 117
Herrin, Judith, 192, 213
Heuberger, Frank, 105
Hewitt, William, 126
HIRATA Atsutane, 171–2
Hobsbawm, E. J., 99
Hodgson, Marshall, 89, 95, 100, 154
Hoffman, Daniel, 116, 119
Hölderlin, Friedrich, 43, 210, 325–7, 329
Horkheimer, Max, 213
Howald, Ernst, 68
Hubner, K., 212
Huet, Daniel, 263, 280
Hughes, H. S., 199
Huidobro, Vincente, 38
humanity, 3, 13, 14, 61–2, 147–65 *passim*, 188, 208, 224, 299
von Humboldt, Alexander, 43
Humphrey, John, 115
Husserl, Edmund, 59, 76, 190, 212, 223, 294, 296, 302
Huxley, Aldous, 66

identity, 10–11, 68–75, 169–84
  passim, 186–210 *passim*, 233–55
  passim, 258–9
IENAGA Saburō, 182
immanentist subjectivity, 285–311
  passim
individualism, 2, 4–5, 11, 27–32,
  73–4, 83, 87, 103, 107–42 *passim*,
  148–9, 168–9 *passim*
Inglehart, Ronald, 107, 142
intuition, 285–99 *passim*
Ireland, Rowan, 108, 125, 136
Irigaray, Luce, 234, 254
ISHIDA Takeshi, 182
ISHII Takemochi, 170
ITAMI Hiroyuki, 170
Ivy, Marilyn, 184

Jaspers, Karl, 213
Jefferson, Thomas, 95
Jelin, Elizabeth, 110
Jencks, Charles, 17
Jeremias, J., 254
Johnson, Benton, 21
Juergensmeyer, Mark, 151
Jung, C. G., 27
Jupp, Peter, 17

Kamen, Henry, 19, 20, 30–1
KAMISHIMA Jirō, 170, 184
Kant, Immanuel, 228, 264–74, 276,
  280–1, 286, 287, 289, 293,
  297–305, 312, 323, 325
KARATANI Kōjin, 184
KARATSU Hajime, 178
KATŌ Shuichi, 177
Katsman, Rubem, 120–1
Kaufman, Gordon, 226
Keen, Donald, 172
Kellner, Hansfried, 105
Kennedy, Barbara, 142
Kennedy, Paul, 213
kenosis, 14, 233–55 *passim*
Kepel, Gilles, 72, 75, 77
Kesey, Ken, 46
Kierkegaard, Soren, 174, 219, 230,
  259
Kim, Hyung-Jun, 155–6

KIMURA Bin, 177
Kolakowski, Leszek, 58, 60
KOMORI Yoshihisa, 178
Kristeva, Julia, 14, 234–5, 242,
  244–9, 251, 254–5
Kumar, Krishan, 105
KUMON Shumpei, 180

Lacan, Jacques, 246–8, 254, 276
Lacoste, Jean-Yves, 234
Lacoue-Labarthe, Philippe, 259
Lancaster, Roger, 124, 143
Lane, David, 213
Larin, Menjivar, 115
Lash, Nicholas, 251
Lash, Scott, 1, 17, 105–6, 111, 113,
  117–18
Lawrence, Bruce, 11–12, 99–100
Leary, Timothy, 47
Le Clerc, Jean, 263, 280
Lehman, David, 130–1
Lehmann, A. G., 213
Levinas, Emmauel, 234–5, 239, 244,
  254–5, 271
liberalism, 6, 12, 14, 83–4, 147–65
  passim, 176–7, 197–9, 208, 233
liberation theology, 102–42 *passim*
Lifton, Robert, 182
Lightfoot, J. B., 237–8
Lindbeck, George, 251
Linde, Armando, 142
Locke, John, 83
Lockhart, Keith, 26
Loeffler, Reinhold, 92–3, 100
Longinus, Pseudo, 258, 260–3
Lossky, Vladimir, 241
Lowith, Karl, 213
Lowth, Robert, 264
Luckmann, Thomas, 57, 77, 151
Lunn, Pam, 211
Lustick, Ian, 93–4
Luther, Martin, 20, 30, 199, 236,
  288–9
Lyon, David, 9
Lyon, Margaret, 164
Lyotard, Jean-François, 6–7, 102,
  186, 189, 193, 254, 259, 262,
  279

MacIntyre, Alasdair, 272
Macquarrie, John, 236
Madeira, Felicia, 114
Madjid, Nurcholish, 148–9, 158–9
Mallarmé, 315–16, 322
MANABE Kazufumi, 170
Maravall, Jose Luis, 261
Marinetti, Filippo, 37–9
Marion, Jean-Luc, 233–4, 271,
   305–6, 312
Marshall, Ruth, 134
Martin, Bernice, 11–12, 17, 129, 136
Martin, David, 30, 107–8, 122,
   125–6, 128, 136, 142, 151, 156,
   161, 164–5
Martin, R. P., 237–8, 254
Marty, Martin, 100, 211
MARUYAMA Masao, 13, 172, 176–8,
   183
Marx, Karl, 50, 61, 95, 187, 190,
   197, 199, 229
Maslow, Abraham, 69, 77
McCrone, David, 211, 213
McLuhan, Marshall, 39, 43, 45–6,
   141
McNeill, William, 99
Megill, Allan, 184
Mehl, Roger, 212
Merleau-Ponty, Maurice, 290, 294–5,
   297, 301–3, 307–10, 312
Milbank, Alison, 282
Milbank, John, 14–15, 254, 271,
   279
millenarianism, 36
Mirandola, Pico della, 61
Mitchell, Richard, 159
MIYOSHI, Masao, 184
Moltmann, Jurgen, 211
Mongardini, Carlo, 76
Morner, Magnus, 143
Morris, Paul, 17
MOTOORI Norinaga, 171
Moussalli, Ahmad, 159
Mu, Queen, 47, 53
Munson, Henry, 154
MURAKAMI Yasusuke, 184
Murray, Charles, 120
myth, 186–210 *passim*

Nairn, Tom, 213
NAKAMURA Masanao, 172
NAKANE Chie, 177–8
Nanak, Guru, 96
Nancy, Jean-Luc, 272, 278, 323
nationalism, 11–12, 79–87 *passim*,
   88–100 *passim*, 147–65 *passim*,
   169–84 *passim*
negative theology, 233–55 *passim*
Nestorius, 241
new age, 1–2, 9–10, 21, 27–8, 36–8,
   46, 49, 52–3, 83, 187
Newman, John Henry, 312
Nicoll, William, 205–6
Nietzsche, Friedrich, 14, 95, 150–1,
   174, 187, 190, 197, 199, 200–1,
   220, 226, 228, 230–1, 319, 324
NISHIDA Kitarō, 181, 184
Northcott, Michael, 211, 213
Novalis, 43, 205
Nye, Robert, 226
Nygren, Anders, 266

Oberoi, Harjot, 100
Obeyesekere, Gananath, 165
O'Brien, P. T., 237, 241, 254
Oliver, Kelly, 247, 255
O'Neill, Onora, 272
Ong, Walter, 260
ontological insecurity, 68
ontological security, 58
orientalism, 203–5
Origen, 241
Osborne, Catherine, 266
Osborne, John, 212–13
Otto, Rudolf, 56
Outram, Dorinda, 157
Ozment, Steven, 212

pantheism, 295–7
Paracelsus, 41
Paul, St., 236, 238, 240, 245–6, 249,
   252
perception, theological, 285–312
   passim
perennialism, 10, 20, 30
Pescatello, Ann, 115
Pfeffer, Karl-Heinz, 212

phenomenology, 285–312 *passim*
Pickering, W. S. F., 1
Pickstock, Catherine, 278
Piovesana, Gino, 184
Pirenne, Henri, 204
Piscatori, James, 99
Plato, 225, 228, 230
pluralism, 12, 19–43 *passim*, 108, 147–65 *passim*
poetry, 15, 225–8, 237, 314–29 *passim*
Pollack, David, 184
Pope, John-Paul II, 193, 195–7, 212
Pope, Paul VI, 195, 212
poverty, 72–3, 99, 110–42 *passim*, 218
Pranowo, Bambang, 155–6
Preston, David, 113
Protagoras, 61

de Quincey, 43

Rabin, Yitzak, 93
Radhakrishnan, 81
Ramet, Pedro, 213
relativism, 5, 20, 29–30, 33, 95, 102, 104, 141, 147–8, 210
religion, defining, 55–60
Renan, Ernest, 205
Rendtorf, Trutz, 212
retraditionalization, 11, 79–87 *passim*
Rheingold, Howard, 39, 48, 52–3
Rhodes, Cecil, 200–1
Riesebrodt, Martin, 211
Rifkin, Jeremy, 111, 117
Rimbaud, Arthur, 317
Roberts, J. M., 213
Roberts, Richard, 9, 13, 203, 211–13
Robertson, Pat, 90
Robertson, Roland, 21
Rodinson, Maxime, 213
Roff, W. R., 163
Ronnell, Avital, 49, 53
Rorty, Richard, 5
Rosenstock-Huessy, Eugen, 213
Roser, Hans, 212
Ross, Andrew, 53
Roszak, Theodore, 53

Rousseau, Jean Jacques, 263
Roy, Olivier, 160
Rubenstein, Richard, 213
Rudolf, Susanne, 99
Ruether, Rosemary Radford, 202
Ruini, Mariele, 76

sacralization, 147–65 *passim*
sacrifice, 15, 233–55
Said, Edward, 203–5, 213
Sainz, Perez, 115
Sartre, Jean-Paul, 85, 190, 230
Scheler, Max, 302
Schelling, F. W. J. von, 43–4, 49
Scheper-Hughes, Nancy, 116, 119–20
Schiller, J. C. F. von, 274, 276–7
Schleiermacher, Friedrich, 240, 249
Schneider, Gregory, 127
Schopenhauer, Arthur, 76
Schubert, Franz, 43
Scott, Alison, 114
Scotus, Duns, 290
Seabrook, Jeremy, 111
Seago, Alex, 17
sect, 10, 19–34 *passim*, 71
secular knowledge, 285–312 *passim*
secularization, 23–34, 60, 147–65 *passim*, 182, 186–210 *passim*, 219
Segal, Alan, 56–7
Sennett, Richard, 73
Shaiken, Harley, 113
Shestov, Lev, 318
Shils, Edward, 151
Silvestris, Bernard, 255
Singer, Paul, 114
Singh, Guru, 96
Sirius, R. U., 47, 53
Sivan, Emmanuel, 92, 93
Sjoo, Monica, 211
Smart, Ninian, 11–12
Smith, Houston, 16
Smith, Margo, 115
Smith, Ruth, 264
Snelders, H., 43
Sorokin, Pitirim, 55
speed, 37–53 *passim*, 219–32
Spengler, Oswald, 197, 199–203, 213
Spinoza, Baruch, 221

338 *Index*

Squires, Judith, 8
Stacey, Judith, 119
Stein, Jock, 211
Steinbuchel, Theodore, 212
Steiner, George, 187, 191, 213
Stolcke, Verena, 143
Storrar, William, 209, 211
Strange, Paul, 165
Strawson, P. F., 312
sublimation, 40–1
sublimity, 14–15, 258–82, 294
SUZUKI Shōsan, 179
Swaggart, Jimmy, 90

Tagliabue, Guido, 260
Tagore, Rabindranath, 99
Tatlow, Tissington, 20, 22
Taylor, Mark, 10–11, 14, 233
Taylor, Ronald, 205
technology, 50–3, 99–100, 137–42, 201–2, 229
Thomasius, Gottfried, 236, 240–1, 254–5
Thompson, Kenneth, 17
Tibi, Bassam, 152–3
Tillich, Paul, 200
Toulis, Nicole, 134
Toulmin, Stephen, 3
Touraine, Alain, 62–3
tradition, 1, 86–7, 169, 186–210 *passim*, 218–32 *passim*, 267; *see also* detraditionalization; retraditionalization; traditionalization
traditionalization, 79–87 *passim*
Trevelyan, George, 21
trinitarian theology, 233–55 *passim*
Troeltsch, Ernst, 21, 110, 197–9, 203, 212–13
TSUNODA Ryusaku, 171
Turner, Bryan, 17

UMESAO Tadao, 177
Urry, John, 105–6, 111, 113, 117–18

Vasquez, Manuel, 126
Vattimo, Gianni, 17

van der Veer, 151
Virilio, Paul, 38, 53
virtual reality, 48
Vivekananda, Swami, 81–2
von Balthasar, Hans Urs, 233, 236, 239, 240–2, 244–5, 248–51, 260, 265–6, 274, 282, 290

Wallace-Hadrill, J. M., 212
Wallis, Roy, 21–2, 33
Walz, Hans, 212
Ward, Graham, 14, 254
Warf, Barney, 111
WATSUJI Tetsurō, 173–8, 180, 184
Watt, W. Montgomery, 213
Waxman, W., 298
Weber, Max, 23, 33, 34, 70, 109–10, 128, 151, 178, 182, 212
Weidenfeld, Warner, 212
Welch, John, 117
von Welling, Georg, 42
Wernick, Andrew, 17
White, Hayden, 212
White, T. H., 226
Wilson, Bryan, 21, 26, 148, 150, 152
Wilson, John, 95
Wittgenstein, Ludwig, 102, 227–8, 287, 304
Woodhead, Linda, 16
Wordsworth, Wiliam, 324
Woytla, Karol, 212
Wright, A. D., 213
Wright, C., 25
Wuthnow, Robert, 152
Wyschogrod, Edith, 69, 99, 254

X file culture, 16

Yamaguchi, 48
YAMAMOTO Shichihei, 178–80
YAMAZAKI Masakuzu, 170
YOSHINO, Kosaku, 184
Yovel, Yirmiyahu, 281

Zizek, Slavoj, 274, 276, 281
Zwingli, Ulrich, 30–1